CDX Learning Systems™

FUNDAMENTALS OF
Automotive Technology
TASKSHEET MANUAL | 2017 NATEF EDITION

Kirk VanGelder

ASE Certified Master Automotive Technician & L1 & G1
Technology Educators of Oregon – President
Certified Automotive Service Instructor
Vancouver, Washington

JONES & BARTLETT
LEARNING

World Headquarters
Jones & Bartlett Learning
5 Wall Street
Burlington, MA 01803
978-443-5000
info@jblearning.com
www.jblearning.com

Jones & Bartlett Learning books and products are available through most bookstores and online booksellers. To contact Jones & Bartlett Learning directly, call 800-832-0034, fax 978-443-8000, or visit our website, www.jblearning.com.

Substantial discounts on bulk quantities of Jones & Bartlett Learning publications are available to corporations, professional associations, and other qualified organizations. For details and specific discount information, contact the special sales department at Jones & Bartlett Learning via the above contact information or send an email to specialsales@jblearning.com.

Production Credits
General Manager: Douglas Kaplan
Executive Publisher: Vernon Anthony
Content Services Manager: Kevin Murphy
Senior Vendor Manager: Sara Kelly
Marketing Manager: Amanda Banner
Manufacturing and Inventory Control Supervisor: Amy Bacus
Composition and Project Management: Integra Software Services Pvt. Ltd.
Cover Design: Scott Moden
Rights & Media Specialist: Robert Boder
Media Development Editor: Shannon Sheehan
Cover Image (Title Page): © Umberto Shtanzman/Shutterstock
Printing and Binding: Edwards Brothers Malloy
Cover Printing: Edwards Brothers Malloy

Library of Congress Cataloging-in-Publication Data

6048

Printed in the United States of America

21 20 19 18 17   10 9 8 7 6 5 4 3 2 1

Contents

Section AO: General Safety

CONTENTS

General Safety

Student/Intern information:

Name _____ Date _____ Class _____

Learning Objective/Task	CDX Tasksheet Number	2017 MAST NATEF Reference Number; Priority Level
• Identify general shop safety rules and procedures.	C451	OA1; RS
• Identify marked safety areas.	C456	OA6; RS
• Identify the location and the types of fire extinguishers and other fire safety equipment; demonstrate knowledge of the procedures for using fire extinguishers and other fire safety equipment.	C458	OA7; RS
• Identify the location and use of eye wash stations.	C459	OA8; RS
• Identify the location of the posted evacuation routes.	C460	OA9; RS
• Locate and demonstrate knowledge of safety data sheets (SDS).	C465	OA15; RS
• Draw a diagram of the shop and label all parts.	N/A	N/A

Materials Required

- Program's shop policy and other safety information
- SDS book
- Fire extinguisher(s) from the shop
- Safety Data Sheets for the products listed

Some Safety Issues to Consider

- Comply with personal and environmental safety practices associated with clothing; eye protection; hand tools; power equipment; proper ventilation; and the handling, storage, and disposal of chemicals/materials in accordance with local, state, and federal safety and environmental regulations.
- Shop rules and procedures are critical to your safety. Please give these your utmost attention.
- Marked safety areas play an important role in maintaining a safe work environment. Always understand and heed marked safety areas.
- Fire blankets are an important component of fire safety in the shop. Always know their location, purpose, and use.
- Fire extinguishers come in a variety of types and sizes. It pays to understand the differences before they are needed.
- Eye wash stations are an important component of shop safety. Always know their location, purpose, and use.
- Pre-planned evacuation routes are an important component of shop safety. Always know the location of all evacuation routes for your shop.
- Being able to locate information in an SDS is critical to your safety and health. Make sure you are familiar with their location and use.

Performance Standard

0–No exposure: No information or practice provided during the program; complete training required

1–Exposure only: General information provided with no practice time; close supervision needed; additional training required

2–Limited practice: Has practiced job during training program; additional training required to develop skill

3–Moderately skilled: Has performed job independently during training program; limited additional training may be required

4–Skilled: Can perform job independently with no additional training

Time off_____

Time on_____

Total time_____

CDX Tasksheet Number: C451

1. List the location(s) of the following items.

   a. Program's general shop rules and policies:

   b. Safety Data Sheets (SDS) book:

   c. Procedure for operation of a fire extinguisher:

   d. Procedure for operation of a vehicle hoist:

2. List the shop's policy for the wearing of safety glasses while in the shop:

3. List the shop's policy for driving vehicles:

4. **List the shop's policy for clothing in the shop:**

5. **List the shop's policy for jewelry in the shop:**

6. **Pass the shop's safety test and record your score here:** _____

7. **Have your supervisor/instructor verify satisfactory completion of this procedure, any observations found, and any necessary action(s) recommended.**

Performance Rating

CDX Tasksheet Number: C451

0	1	2	3	4

Supervisor/instructor signature _____ Date _____

MAST
OA6

Time off_____

Time on_____

CDX Tasksheet Number: C456

Total time_____

1. **Research the uniform color code system used to designate safety areas in a shop. List each color and its designation:**

   a. Color: _____ designates: _____

   b. Color: _____ designates: _____

   c. Color: _____ designates: _____

   d. Color: _____ designates: _____

2. **Label all of the marked safety areas on the diagram of the shop at the end of this section.**

3. **Have your supervisor/instructor verify satisfactory completion of this procedure, any observations found, and any necessary action(s) recommended.**

Performance Rating

CDX Tasksheet Number: C456

0	1	2	3	4

Supervisor/instructor signature _____ Date _____

Identify the location and the types of fire extinguishers and other fire safety equipment; demonstrate knowledge of the procedures for using fire extinguishers and other fire safety equipment.

MAST
OA7

Time off_____

Time on_____

Total time_____

CDX Tasksheet Number: C458

1. **Research the types, location, and use of fire extinguishers.**
   a. **List the different types of fire extinguishers (dry chemical, CO_2, etc.) available:**
      i. **Type: _____ ; for use on what class of fire: _____**
      ii. **Type: _____ ; for use on what class of fire: _____**
      iii.**Type: _____ ; for use on what class of fire: _____**
      iv. **Type: _____ ; for use on what class of fire: _____**

      In the above list, put a star next to the type(s) of fire extinguishers in this shop.

2. **List the steps for proper use of a fire extinguisher:**

3. **Research the location, purpose, and use of fire blankets in your shop.**
   a. **Describe the purpose of a fire blanket (under what circumstances should a fire blanket be used?):**

   b. **Describe how a fire blanket puts out a fire:**

4. **Label the location of all fire extinguishers on the diagram of the shop at the end of this section.**

5. **Label the location of the fire blanket(s) on the diagram of the shop at the end of this section.**

6. Have your supervisor/instructor verify satisfactory completion of this procedure, any observations found, and any necessary action(s) recommended.

Performance Rating

CDX Tasksheet Number: C458

0	1	2	3	4

Supervisor/instructor signature _____ Date _____

MAST
0A8

CDX Tasksheet Number: C459

1. Research the location, purpose, and use of eye wash stations in your shop.

   a. Describe the purpose of an eye wash station:

   b. Describe the proper use of an eye wash station (including time):

   c. What type of eye injury would use of an eye wash station NOT be appropriate for?

2. Label the location of the eye wash station(s) on the diagram of the shop at the end of this section.

3. Have your supervisor/instructor verify satisfactory completion of this procedure, any observations found, and any necessary action(s) recommended.

Performance Rating

CDX Tasksheet Number: C459

0	1	2	3	4

Supervisor/instructor signature _____ Date _____

Identify the location of the posted evacuation routes.

Time off_____

Time on_____

Total time_____

CDX Tasksheet Number: C460

1. **Research the location and purpose of evacuation routes.**

   a. **Describe the purpose of evacuation routes:**

2. **Label the evacuation route(s) on the diagram of the shop at the end of this section. Also label the location of the posted evacuation route diagram(s).**

3. **Have your supervisor/instructor verify satisfactory completion of this procedure, any observations found, and any necessary action(s) recommended.**

Performance Rating

CDX Tasksheet Number: C460

0	1	2	3	4

Supervisor/instructor signature _____ Date _____

Locate and demonstrate knowledge of
safety data sheets (SDS).

Time off_____

Time on_____

Total time_____

CDX Tasksheet Number: C465

1. **List the safety precautions when handling motor oil:**

2. **List the flash point of gasoline/petroleum:** _____ °F/°C

3. **List the firefighting equipment needed to put out a gasoline/petroleum fire:**

4. **List the first aid treatment for battery acid in the eyes:**

5. **List the first aid treatment for ingestion of antifreeze (ethylene glycol):**

6. **Label the location of the SDS books on the diagram of the shop at the end of this section.**

7. **Have your supervisor/instructor verify satisfactory completion of this procedure, any observations found, and any necessary action(s) recommended.**

Performance Rating

CDX Tasksheet Number: C465

0	1	2	3	4

Supervisor/instructor signature _____ Date _____

Additional Task

Time off_____

Time on_____

CDX Tasksheet Number: N/A

1. **On a full-sized piece of paper, draw a diagram of the shop and label each of the following:**

   a. **Marked safety areas (floor lines, etc.)** _____ **(X when finished)**

   Total time_____

   b. **Location of the fire blanket(s)** _____ **(X when finished)**
   c. **Location of all fire extinguishers** _____ **(X when finished)**
   d. **Location of the exhaust fan switch(es)** _____ **(X when finished)**
   e. **Location of the electrical disconnect switch(es)** _____ **(X when finished)**
   f. **Location of the eye wash station(s)** _____ **(X when finished)**
   g. **Location of the SDS books** _____ **(X when finished)**
   h. **Evacuation route(s)** _____ **(X when finished)**
   i. **Location of the master air shut-off valve** _____ **(X when finished)**
   j. **Location of the over-head door switch(es)** _____ **(X when finished)**

2. **Have your supervisor/instructor verify satisfactory completion of this task.**

Performance Rating

CDX Tasksheet Number: N/A

0	1	2	3	4

Supervisor/instructor signature _____ Date _____

Personal Safety

Student/Intern Information:

Name _____ Date _____ Class _____

Learning Objective/Task	CDX Tasksheet Number	2017 MAST NATEF Reference Number; Priority Level
• Comply with the required use of safety glasses, ear protection, gloves, and shoes during lab/shop activities.	C461	OA10; RS
• Identify and wear appropriate clothing for lab/shop activities.	C462	OA11; RS
• Secure hair and jewelry for lab/shop activities.	C463	OA12; RS

Time off_____

Time on_____

Total time_____

Materials Required

- Regular safety glasses
- Gloves
- Shoes

Some Safety Issues to Consider

- Comply with personal and environmental safety practices associated with clothing; eye protection; hand tools; power equipment; proper ventilation; and the handling, storage, and disposal of chemicals/materials in accordance with local, state, and federal safety and environmental regulations.
- Shop rules and procedures are critical to your safety. Please give these your utmost attention.

Performance Standard

0–No exposure: No information or practice provided during the program; complete training required

1–Exposure only: General information provided with no practice time; close supervision needed; additional training required

2–Limited practice: Has practiced job during training program; additional training required to develop skill

3–Moderately skilled: Has performed job independently during training program; limited additional training may be required

4–Skilled: Can perform job independently with no additional training

▶ **TASK** Comply with the required use of safety glasses, ear protection, gloves, and shoes during lab/shop activities.

MAST
OA10

Time off_____

Time on_____

Total time_____

CDX Tasksheet Number: C461

1. Describe the safety glasses policy for your shop (be specific):

2. Describe the policy related to ear protection in the shop (be specific):

3. Describe the policy related to gloves for your shop (be specific):

4. Describe the policy related to work shoes for your shop (be specific):

5. These tasks require observation of the student over a prolonged period. Ask your instructor to give you a date for your evaluation.

   a. Write that date here: _____

6. Continue with your projects, complying with the safe use of safety glasses, gloves, shoes, clothing, and hair containment during all lab/shop activities.

7. On or after that date, have your instructor verify satisfactory completion of these tasks.

Performance Rating

CDX Tasksheet Number: C461

0	1	2	3	4

Supervisor/instructor signature _____ Date _____

MAST
OA11

Time off_____

Time on_____

Total time_____

CDX Tasksheet Number: C462

1. Describe the clothing requirements for your shop (be specific):

2. These tasks require observation of the student over a prolonged period. Ask your instructor to give you a date for your evaluation.

   a. Write that date here: _____

3. Continue with your projects, complying with the safe use of safety glasses, gloves, shoes, clothing, and hair containment during all lab/shop activities.

4. On or after that date, have your instructor verify satisfactory completion of these tasks.

Performance Rating

CDX Tasksheet Number: C462

0	1	2	3	4

Supervisor/instructor signature _____ Date _____

▶ **TASK** Secure hair and jewelry for lab/shop activities.

MAST
OA12

Time off_____

Time on_____

Total time_____

CDX Tasksheet Number: C463

1. List your shop's policy concerning securing hair in the shop (be specific):

2. List your shop's policy concerning jewelry in the shop (be specific):

3. These tasks require observation of the student over a prolonged period. Ask your instructor to give you a date for your evaluation.

   a. Write that date here: _____

4. Continue with your projects, complying with the safe use of safety glasses, gloves, shoes, clothing, and hair containment during all lab/shop activities.

5. On or after that date, have your instructor verify satisfactory completion of these tasks.

Performance Rating

CDX Tasksheet Number: C463

0	1	2	3	4

Supervisor/instructor signature _____ Date _____

General Safety **25**

Tool Safety

Student/Intern information:

Name _____ Date _____ Class _____

Learning Objective/Task	CDX Tasksheet Number	2017 MAST NATEF Reference Number; Priority Level
• Identify tools and their usage in automotive applications.	C466	OB1; RS
• Identify standard and metric designation.	C467	OB2; RS
• Utilize safe procedures for handling of tools and equipment.	C452	OA2; RS
• Demonstrate safe handling and use of appropriate tools.	C468	OB3; RS
• Demonstrate proper cleaning, storage, and maintenance of tools and equipment.	C469	OB4; RS
• Demonstrate proper use of precision measuring tools (e.g., micrometer, dial-indicator, dial-caliper).	C896	OB5; RS

Time off_____

Time on_____

Total time_____

Materials Required

- Standard toolkit and other tools as required
- Precision measuring tools: micrometer, dial-indicator, dial-caliper, etc.

Some Safety Issues to Consider

- Comply with personal and environmental safety practices associated with clothing; eye protection; hand tools; power equipment; proper ventilation; and the handling, storage, and disposal of chemicals/materials in accordance with local, state, and federal safety and environmental regulations.
- Tools allow us to increase our productivity and effectiveness. However, they must be used according to the manufacturer's procedures. Failure to follow those procedures can result in serious injury or death.

Performance Standard

0—No exposure: No information or practice provided during the program; complete training required

1—Exposure only: General information provided with no practice time; close supervision needed; additional training required

2—Limited practice: Has practiced job during training program; additional training required to develop skill

3—Moderately skilled: Has performed job independently during training program; limited additional training may be required

4—Skilled: Can perform job independently with no additional training

Time off_____

Time on_____

Total time_____

CDX Tasksheet Number: C466

1. Using the following list, describe the specific function/purpose of each of the following tools and any disadvantages/problems with using the tool, if any:

   a. Open-end wrench:

   b. Box-end wrench:

   c. Socket:

   d. Ratchet:

   e. Torque wrench:

   f. Slotted screwdriver:

   g. Phillips screwdriver:

h. Tap:

i. Die:

j. Feeler blade:

k. Line wrench/flare-nut wrench:

l. Allen wrench:

m. Torx screwdriver or socket:

n. Hacksaw:

o. Oil filter wrench:

p. Compression gauge:

q. DVOM/DMM:

r. Test light:

s. Diagonal side cutters:

t. Locking pliers:

u. Needle-nose pliers:

v. Brake spoon:

w. Micrometer:

x. Dial indicator:

y. Antifreeze hydrometer:

z. Snap-ring pliers:

3. Have your supervisor/instructor verify satisfactory completion of this procedure, any observations found, and any necessary action(s) recommended.

Performance Rating

CDX Tasksheet Number: C466

0	1	2	3	4

Supervisor/instructor signature _____ Date _____

Time off_____

Time on_____

Total time_____

CDX Tasksheet Number: C467

1. **Complete the following conversions from metric to standard and vice versa using the conversion charts below.**

Volume

Volume is the amount of space occupied by a three-dimensional object. The metric system uses liters (l) or cubic centimeters (cc or cm^3). The Imperial system uses gallons (gal) and quarts (qt) for "wet" volume and cubic feet (ft^3) for "dry" volume. You'll need to determine volume any time you fill a vehicle's reservoir with liquid. This includes petrol/gasoline, coolant, oil, transmission fluid, or lubricant.

Volume Conversions	
Imperial-Imperial	4 US qt = 1 US gal 1 ft^3 = 7.48 US gal 1 ft^3 = 6.22 UK gal
Metric-Metric	1 L = 1000 cc 1 cc = 0.001 L
Imperial-Metric	1 in.^{3} = 16.387 cc 1 US gal = 3.78 L 1 UK gal = 4.54 L 1 US qt = 0.95 L
Metric-Imperial	1 L = 61.0237 in.^{3} 1 L = 0.035 ft^3 1 L = 0.26 US gal 1 L = 0.21 UK gal 1 L = 1.05 qt

2. **Knowledge Check: Convert the following:**
   a. 3.0 L = _____ in.^{3}
   b. 350 in.^{3} = _____ L
   c. 3.0 gal = _____ L
   d. 9 L = _____ gal

Mass

Mass is a unit or system of units by which a degree of heaviness is measured. The metric system uses grams (g), kilograms (kg), and tonnes (t). The Imperial system uses ounces (oz), pounds (lb), and tons (T). In the workshop, you will use these measurements to determine the lifting capacity of equipment like hydraulic and engine hoists and floor jacks.

Mass Conversions	
Imperial-Imperial	16 oz = 1 lb 2000 lb = 1 T
Metric-Metric	1000 g = 1 kg 1000 kg = 1 t
Imperial-Metric	1 oz = 28.3 g 1 lb = 453 g 2.2 lb = 1 kg 1 T = 0.907 t
Metric-Imperial	1 t = 1.10 T

3. **Knowledge Check: Convert the following:**
   a. **8 oz** = _____ **g**
   b. **475 g** = _____ **oz**
   c. **6.6 lb** = _____ **kg**
   d. **4500 kg** = _____ **lb**

Torque

Torque is the twisting force applied to a shaft. The metric system uses the Newton meter (Nm). The Imperial system uses the inch-pound (in-lb) and the foot-pound (ft-lb). Vehicle manufacturers specify torque settings for key fasteners on the engine and wheels. You will need to follow the specifications or you could strip threads or break bolts. Torque is also an important concept when discussing engine performance. A foot-pound (ft-lb) is the twisting force applied to a shaft by a lever 1 foot long with a 1-pound mass on the end. A Newton meter (Nm) is the twisting force applied to a shaft by a level 1 meter long with a force of 1 Newton applied to the end of the lever. (1N is equivalent to the force applied by a mass of 100.)

Torque Conversions	
Imperial-Imperial	12 in-lb = 1 ft-lb 1 in-lb = 0.08 ft-lb
Imperial-Metric	1 ft-lb = 1.34 N·m
Metric-Imperial	1 N·m = 0.74 ft-lb 1 N·m = 8.8 in-lb

4. **Knowledge Check: Convert the following:**
   a. **48 in-lb** = _____ **ft-lb**
   b. **15 ft-lb** = _____ **in-lb**
   c. **65 ft-lb** = _____ **N·m**
   d. **142 N·m** = _____ **ft-lb**

Pressure

Pressure is a measurement of force per unit area. The metric system uses kilopascals (kPa) and bar. The Imperial system uses pounds per square inch (psi) and atmospheres. *Vacuum* is a term given to a pressure that is less than atmospheric pressure. The Imperial system measures vacuum in inches of mercury (" Hg) or inches of water. The metric system measures vacuum in millimeters of mercury (mm Hg). You'll need to understand pressure conversions when filling tires and replacing air conditioning refrigerants or using a vacuum gauge.

Pressure Conversions	
Imperial-Imperial	14.7 psi = 1 atmosphere 1" Hg = 14" H$_2$0 0" Hg = 1 atmosphere
Metric-Metric	100 kPa = 1 bar
Imperial-Metric	1 psi = 6.89 kPa 1 atmosphere = 101.3 kPa 1" Hg = 25.4 mm Hg 1 atmosphere = 1.013 bar

5. **Knowledge Check: Convert the following:**
   a. **14.7 psi** = _____ **kPa**
   b. **650 kPa** = _____ **psi**
   c. **22 psi** = _____ **bar**
   d. **5.5 bar** = _____ **psi**

6. Have your supervisor/instructor verify satisfactory completion of this procedure, any observations found, and any necessary action(s) recommended.

Performance Rating

0	1	2	3	4

Supervisor/instructor signature _____ Date _____

MAST
OA2

CDX Tasksheet Number: C452

1. **These tasks will require observation of the student over a prolonged period after the initial check. Ask your instructor to give you a date for your evaluation.**

   a. **Write that date here:** _____

2. **Continue with your other projects, utilizing safe handling of tools and equipment including proper cleaning, maintenance, and storage of the tools and equipment until the date of your evaluation.**

3. **On or after that date, have your instructor verify satisfactory completion of each task.**

Performance Rating

CDX Tasksheet Number: C452

0	1	2	3	4

Supervisor/instructor signature _____ Date _____

Time off_____

Time on_____

Total time_____

CDX Tasksheet Number: C468

1. **These tasks will require observation of the student over a prolonged period after the initial check. Ask your instructor to give you a date for your evaluation.**

    a. **Write that date here:** _____

2. **Continue with your other projects, demonstrating safe handling, proper cleaning, maintenance, and storage of the tools until the date of your evaluation.**

3. **On or after that date, have your instructor verify satisfactory completion of each task.**

Performance Rating

CDX Tasksheet Number: C468

0	1	2	3	4

Supervisor/instructor signature _____ Date _____

Demonstrate proper cleaning, storage, and
maintenance of tools and equipment.

MAST
0B4

Time off_____

Time on_____

Total time_____

CDX Tasksheet Number: C469

1. **These tasks will require observation of the student over a prolonged period after the initial check. Ask your instructor to give you a date for your evaluation.**

   a. **Write that date here:** _____

2. **Continue with your other projects, demonstrating safe handling, proper cleaning, maintenance, and storage of the tools until the date of your evaluation.**

3. **On or after that date, have your instructor verify satisfactory completion of each task.**

Performance Rating

CDX Tasksheet Number: C469

0	1	2	3	4

Supervisor/instructor signature _____ Date _____

MAST
OB5

Time off_____

Time on_____

Total time_____

CDX Tasksheet Number: C896

1. **These tasks will require observation of the student over a prolonged period after the initial check. Ask your instructor to give you a date for your evaluation.**

    a. **Write that date here:** _____

2. **Continue with your other projects, demonstrating safe handling, proper cleaning, maintenance, and storage of the tools until the date of your evaluation.**

3. **On or after that date, have your instructor verify satisfactory completion of each task.**

Performance Rating

CDX Tasksheet Number: C896

0	1	2	3	4

Supervisor/instructor signature _____ Date _____

Vehicle Protection and Jack and Lift Safety

Student/Intern information:

Name _____ Date _____ Class _____

Vehicle used for this activity:

Year _____ Make _____ Model _____

Odometer _____ VIN _____

Learning Objective/Task	CDX Tasksheet Number	2017 MAST NATEF Reference Number; Priority Level
• Identify purpose and demonstrate proper use of fender covers, mats.	C473	OC2; RS
• Utilize proper ventilation procedures for working within the lab/shop area.	C455	OA5; RS
• Identify and use proper placement of floor jacks and jack stands.	C453	OA3; RS
• Identify and use proper procedures for safe lift operation.	C454	OA4; RS
• Ensure vehicle is prepared to return to customer per school/company policy (floor mats, steering wheel cover, etc.).	C476	OD1; RS

Time off_____

Time on_____

Total time_____

Materials Required

- Vehicle
- Fender, seat, steering wheel, and carpet covers
- Floor jack
- Jack stand(s)
- Wheel chocks
- Vehicle hoist
- Shop rag
- Possible cleaning supplies

Some Safety Issues to Consider

- Comply with personal and environmental safety practices associated with clothing; eye protection; hand tools; power equipment; proper ventilation; and the handling, storage, and disposal of chemicals/materials in accordance with local, state, and federal safety and environmental regulations.
- Floor jacks and jack stands must have a capacity rating higher than the load lifted.
- Floor jacks and jack stands must be used on a hard, level surface. Do not attempt to lift or support a vehicle under any other conditions.
- Jacks are designed to lift a vehicle, not to support it. Always use jack stands once the vehicle has been lifted.
- Have the jack stands ready, and at hand, prior to lifting the vehicle.

- Vehicle hoists are important tools that increase productivity and make the job easier. But they also can cause severe injury or death if used improperly. Make sure you follow the hoist's and vehicle manufacturers' operation procedures. Also, make sure you have your supervisor's/instructor's permission to use a vehicle hoist.
- It is critical that the vehicle be returned to the customer in proper working order. Double-check your work before releasing the vehicle to the customer.

Performance Standard

0—No exposure: No information or practice provided during the program; complete training required

1—Exposure only: General information provided with no practice time; close supervision needed; additional training required

2—Limited practice: Has practiced job during training program; additional training required to develop skill

3—Moderately skilled: Has performed job independently during training program; limited additional training may be required

4—Skilled: Can perform job independently with no additional training

Time off_____

Time on_____

Total time_____

CDX Tasksheet Number: C473

1. **Identify the purpose of the following items:**

   a. **Fender cover:**

   b. **Seat cover:**

   c. **Steering wheel cover:**

   d. **Carpet cover/floor mat:**

2. **Properly prepare a vehicle for service or repair, using the above covers.**

3. **Have your supervisor/instructor verify satisfactory completion of this procedure, any observations found, and any necessary action(s) recommended.**

Performance Rating

CDX Tasksheet Number: C473

0	1	2	3	4

Supervisor/instructor signature _____ Date _____

Utilize proper ventilation procedures for working within the lab/shop area.

MAST
OA5

CDX Tasksheet Number: C455

1. **List the OSHA personal exposure limit for carbon monoxide over an 8-hour work period: _____ ppm**

2. **Properly position a vehicle in a work stall.**

3. **Properly connect the exhaust extraction system to the vehicle exhaust.**

4. **Turn on, or verify that the extraction system is on.**

5. **With your instructor's permission, start the vehicle and verify the extraction equipment is secure and operating properly.**

6. **Have your instructor verify your previously given answer, and proper exhaust extraction usage. Supervisor/instructor's initials: _____**

7. **Turn off the vehicle, return the exhaust hoses to their proper storage places, and shut off the extraction system if it isn't being used anymore.**

8. **Have your supervisor/instructor verify satisfactory completion of this procedure, any observations found, and any necessary action(s) recommended.**

Performance Rating

CDX Tasksheet Number: C455

0	1	2	3	4

Supervisor/instructor signature _____ Date _____

Identify and use proper placement of floor jacks and
jack stands.

MAST
0A3

CDX Tasksheet Number: C453

1. **Research the jacking and lifting procedures for this vehicle in the appropriate service manual.**

    a. **Draw a diagram of the vehicle's lift points:**

2. **Check to make sure the vehicle is on a hard, level surface. If not, move it to a safe location.**

3. **Install wheel chocks. Prepare the floor jack and stands for use.**

4. **Lift and support one end of the vehicle on jack stands according to the manufacturer's procedure.**

    a. **Have your instructor initial to verify proper jack stand placement:**

    _____

5. **Lift the vehicle and remove the jack stands. Return the jack and stands to their proper storage places.**

6. **Return the vehicle to its beginning condition and return any tools you used to their proper locations.**

7. **Have your supervisor/instructor verify satisfactory completion of this procedure, any observations found, and any necessary action(s) recommended.**

Performance Rating

CDX Tasksheet Number: C453

0	1	2	3	4

Supervisor/instructor signature _____ Date _____

Identify and use proper procedures for safe lift operation.

MAST
0A4

Time off_____

Time on_____

Total time_____

CDX Tasksheet Number: C454

Vehicle, if different than above:

Year _____ Make _____ Model_____

Odometer_____ VIN_____

1. **Position the vehicle in proper relation to the lift, taking into consideration the center of gravity of the vehicle.**

   > **NOTE** Check the vehicle for unusual loading, such as heavy loads in the trunk or truck bed. If you find this situation, notify your instructor immediately.

2. **Position the lift arms in the proper location as specified by the manufacturer.**

3. **Raise the lift until one of the arms lightly contacts the lift point. Check the position of the lift arms to make sure they are in contact with (or just about to contact) the proper points.**

   > **NOTE** Make sure the lift arms are not touching or pinching anything they shouldn't be in contact with, including the rocker panel, running boards, and fuel or brake lines, etc.

4. **If the arms are in the proper position, raise the vehicle a few inches off the ground. Using a strong part of the vehicle, moderately shake the vehicle to make sure it is stable.**

   > **NOTE** If the vehicle shifts position at all or is out of balance, lower the vehicle and reset the lift arms or reposition the vehicle.

5. **If the vehicle is stable, lift the vehicle to the height indicated by your instructor and engage the locks or lower the lift onto the locks. Instructor/Supervisor Initial _____**

6. **Verify that there are no obstacles under the vehicle, and that all doors are closed. Lower the vehicle and move the lift arms out of the way of the vehicle.**

7. **Return the vehicle to its beginning condition and return any tools you used to their proper locations.**

8. Have your supervisor/instructor verify satisfactory completion of this
   procedure, any observations found, and any necessary action(s) recommended.

Performance Rating

CDX Tasksheet Number: C454

0	1	2	3	4

Supervisor/instructor signature _____ Date _____

Ensure vehicle is prepared to return to customer per school/company policy (floor mats, steering wheel cover, etc.).

Time off_____

Time on_____

Total time_____

CDX Tasksheet Number: C476

> **NOTE** A properly protected vehicle and good work habits will make this task much easier.

1. **Double check that all work has been completed. Nothing can be missing, loose, or leaking.**

   a. **Student initial when completed:** _____

2. **If your instructor deems it necessary, test-drive the vehicle to be sure of proper repair and operation of the vehicle.**

   a. **Have your instructor initial here:** _____

3. **Double check that all tools are put away and stored properly.**

   a. **Student initial when completed:** _____

4. **Remove all fender covers, seat covers, floor covers, and steering wheel covers. Return them to their storage place or dispose of them properly, depending on the type of cover.**

   a. **Student initial when completed:** _____

5. **Check the exterior of the vehicle for greasy fingerprints or grime. Clean with an appropriate cleaner. Follow your shop's policies on this procedure.**

   a. **Student initial when completed:** _____

6. **Check the following interior locations for dirt or greasy spots. Clean with an appropriate cleaner. Follow your shop's policies on this procedure:**

   a. **Carpet and floor mats. Student initial when completed:** _____
   b. **Seats. Student initial when completed:** _____
   c. **Steering wheel and parking brake handle. Student initial when completed:** _____
   d. **Door panel and handles. Student initial when completed:** _____

7. **If the vehicle is ready to return to the customer, the vehicle may need to be moved out of the shop. Get your instructor's permission to move the vehicle to the customer pick-up area.**

   a. **Have your instructor initial here:** _____

8. **Return to your work stall and clean up the floor, benches, and related area.**

   a. **Student initial when completed:** _____

9. Have your supervisor/instructor verify satisfactory completion of this procedure, any observations found, and any necessary action(s) recommended.

Performance Rating

CDX Tasksheet Number: C476

0	1	2	3	4

Supervisor/instructor signature _____ Date _____

Vehicle, Customer, and Service Information

Student/Intern information:

Name _____ Date _____ Class _____

Vehicle used for this activity:

Year _____ Make _____ Model _____

Odometer _____ VIN _____

Learning Objective/Task	CDX Tasksheet Number	2017 MAST NATEF Reference Number; Priority Level
• Proper vehicle identification information: Define the use and purpose of the VIN, engine numbers, and data code; locate the VIN, and apply knowledge of VIN information.	N/A	N/A
• Identify information needed and the service requested on a repair order.	C472	OC1; RS
• Demonstrate use of the three Cs (concern, cause, and correction).	C474	OC3; RS
• Review vehicle service history.	C475	OC4; RS
• Complete work order to include customer information, vehicle identifying information customer concern related service history, cause, and correction	C590	OC5; RS

Time off_____

Time on_____

Total time_____

Materials Required

- Vehicle
- Service information
- Completed repair order assigned by your instructor
- Several repair orders for the same vehicle from repairs/services performed over an extended period of time
- Scheduled maintenance chart for this vehicle
- Blank repair order

Some Safety Issues to Consider
- Comply with personal and environmental safety practices associated with clothing; eye protection; hand tools; power equipment; proper ventilation; and the handling, storage, and disposal of chemicals/materials in accordance with local, state, and federal safety and environmental regulations.

Performance Standard
0—No exposure: No information or practice provided during the program; complete training required
1—Exposure only: General information provided with no practice time; close supervision needed; additional training required

2–Limited practice: Has practiced job during training program; additional training required to develop skill

3–Moderately skilled: Has performed job independently during training program; limited additional training may be required

4–Skilled: Can perform job independently with no additional training

Proper vehicle identification information: Define the use and purpose of the VIN, engine numbers, and data code; locate the VIN, and apply knowledge of VIN information.

Additional Task

CDX Tasksheet Number: N/A

1. **Research the location and description of the VIN in an appropriate service manual.**

    a. **Location of VIN:** _____

    b. **VIN:** _____

2. **Using the VIN on the vehicle assigned to you, identify the following information. (Write both corresponding VIN code designation and what it represents.)**

    a. **Country of origin:** _____

    b. **Location of manufacturing plant:** _____

    c. **Passenger restraint system:** _____

    d. **Engine designation:** _____

    e. **Model year:** _____

3. **Which position in the VIN is the model year?** _____

4. **Which position in the VIN is the engine designation?** _____

5. **Have your supervisor/instructor verify satisfactory completion of this procedure, any observations found, and any necessary action(s) recommended.**

Performance Rating

CDX Tasksheet Number: N/A

0	1	2	3	4

Supervisor/instructor signature _____ Date _____

Identify information needed and the service
requested on a repair order.

Time off_____

Time on_____

Total time_____

CDX Tasksheet Number: C472

1. **Familiarize yourself with the assigned repair order. Locate and list the following information below.**

   a. **Date:** _____

   b. **Customer:** _____

   c. **Address:** _____

   d. **Daytime phone number:** _____

   e. **Year:** _____

   f. **Make:** _____

   g. **Model:** _____

   h. **Color:** _____

   i. **License and state:** _____

   j. **Odometer reading:** _____

   k. **VIN:** _____

   l. **Customer concern(s)/service requested:**

2. **Did the customer sign the repair order authorizing the repairs?**
   Yes: _____ **No:** _____

3. **Return the sample repair order to its proper storage place.**

4. **Have your supervisor/instructor verify satisfactory completion of this procedure, any observations found, and any necessary action(s) recommended.**

Performance Rating

CDX Tasksheet Number: C472

0	1	2	3	4

Supervisor/instructor signature _____ Date _____

Demonstrate use of the three Cs (concern, cause, and correction).

MAST
OC3

Time off_____

Time on_____

Total time_____

CDX Tasksheet Number: C474

1. **Using the following scenario, write up the three Cs as listed on most repair orders. Assume that the customer authorized the recommended repairs.**

   A customer complains that his vehicle is leaving what looks like oil spots on the landlord's driveway after he ran over something in the road a few days ago. You check the engine oil find that it is about 1/2 a quart low, but looks pretty clean, like it was changed recently. The engine oil life monitor indicates 92% oil life remaining. You safely raise and secure the vehicle on the hoist. While visually inspecting the underside of the vehicle, you notice oil dripping off of the engine oil drain plug. Checking the torque of the drain plug shows that the drain plug isn't loose. Closer inspection reveals a shiny spot on the aluminum oil pan near the drain plug. There is a small crack in the oil pan that is seeping oil and dripping slowly off of the drain plug.

2. **Concern/complaint:**

3. **Cause:**

4. **Correction:**

5. **Have your supervisor/instructor verify satisfactory completion of the previous answers, and any necessary action(s) recommended.**

Performance Rating

CDX Tasksheet Number: C474

0	1	2	3	4

Supervisor/instructor signature _____ Date _____

Time off_____

Time on_____

Total time_____

CDX Tasksheet Number: C475

1. **Familiarize yourself with the repair history as listed on the repair orders and answer the following questions.**

   a. **What was the first date this vehicle was serviced?** _____
   b. **What was the last date this vehicle was serviced?** _____
   c. **What was the most major repair performed?**

   d. **Was this vehicle ever returned for the same problem more than once?**
   Yes: _____ **No:** _____

   i. **If so, for what and how many times?** _____

   e. **Compare this list to the scheduled maintenance chart and list any missed maintenance tasks between the first service and the last service:**

2. **Have your supervisor/instructor verify satisfactory completion of this procedure, any observations found, and any necessary action(s) recommended.**

Performance Rating

CDX Tasksheet Number: C475

0	1	2	3	4

Supervisor/instructor signature _____ Date _____

MAST
OC5

Time off_____

Time on_____

Total time_____

CDX Tasksheet Number: C590

Vehicle used for this activity:

Year _____ Make _____ Model _____

Odometer _____ VIN _____

1. **Use your company's repair order to complete this task.**

   Fred Smith brings in a 2008 Hyundai Santa Fe AWD, with a 3.3 L engine, automatic transmission, 72,426 miles on the odometer, silver paint, VIN 5NMSH73E28H192794. It needs some work before going on a 3000-mile trip. He would like an estimate of repairs needed and has agreed to let your technician inspect the vehicle while you write up the repair order. He gives you the following information:

   a. Home address: 1234 NE Main Street, Anytown, CA 13579
   b. Cell phone: (111) 222-1234
   c. Work phone: (111) 333-4567
   d. Vehicle license number: CDX – 111

2. **The customer listed the following concern/complaints:**

   a. Small oil leak from under the engine
   b. Small coolant leak from under the engine
   c. Squealing noise coming from the front brakes

3. **The technician found the following conditions:**

   a. Both valve covers have leaking gaskets.
   b. The water pump is leaking from the shaft and the bearing is worn.
   c. The front brake pads are worn down to the wear indicators, the rotors are a bit under specifications, and the calipers are starting to seep brake fluid past the caliper piston seal and need to be replaced.

4. **Complete the repair order as if all tasks were completed including parts, their cost, and labor.**

5. **Have your supervisor/instructor verify satisfactory completion of this procedure, any observations found, and any necessary action(s) recommended.**

Performance Rating

CDX Tasksheet Number: C590

0	1	2	3	4
☐	☐	☐	☐	☐

Supervisor/instructor signature _____ Date _____

SRS and ABS Safety

Student/Intern information:

Name _____ Date _____ Class _____

Vehicle used for this activity:

Year _____ Make _____ Model _____

Odometer _____ VIN _____

Learning Objective/Task	CDX Tasksheet Number	2017 MAST NATEF Reference Number; Priority Level
• Demonstrate awareness of the safety aspects of supplemental restraint systems (SRS), electronic brake control systems, and hybrid vehicle high voltage circuits.	C464	OA13; RS
• Demonstrate awareness of the safety aspects of high voltage circuits (such as high-intensity discharge [HID] lamps, ignition systems, injection systems, etc.).	C895	OA14; RS

Time off_____

Time on_____

Total time_____

Materials Required

- Vehicle with SRS and anti-lock brake system (ABS)
- Special tools or equipment, if specified

Some Safety Issues to Consider

- Comply with personal and environmental safety practices associated with clothing; eye protection; hand tools; power equipment; proper ventilation; and the handling, storage, and disposal of chemicals/materials in accordance with local, state, and federal safety and environmental regulations.
- Deployment of the SRS system could cause serious injury or death. Follow all of the manufacturer's procedures before working on this system.
- The ABS system may hold brake fluid under extremely high pressure. Follow the manufacturer's procedures to relieve this pressure before working on this system.
- Hybrid and electric vehicles have batteries with VERY high voltage, which can kill you if handled improperly. Always get permission from your supervisor/instructor before working on, or near, the system. Also, ALWAYS follow the manufacturer's procedure when servicing a hybrid or electric vehicle.

Performance Standard

0–No exposure: No information or practice provided during the program; complete training required

1–Exposure only: General information provided with no practice time; close supervision needed; additional training required

2–Limited practice: Has practiced job during training program; additional training required to develop skill

3–Moderately skilled: Has performed job independently during training program; limited additional training may be required

4–Skilled: Can perform job independently with no additional training

Demonstrate awareness of the safety aspects of
supplemental restraint systems (SRS), electronic
brake control systems, and hybrid vehicle
high voltage circuits.

MAST
OA13

CDX Tasksheet Number: C464

1. **Research the following procedures for a hybrid vehicle in the appropriate service information.**

   a. **List the precautions when working around or on the SRS system on this vehicle:**

   b. **List the steps to disable the SRS system on this vehicle:**

   c. **List the steps to enable the SRS system on this vehicle:**

   d. **List the precautions when working on or around the electronic brake control system on this vehicle:**

e. Identify the high-voltage circuit wiring on this vehicle. What color is the wire conduit?

f. List or print out the high-voltage disable procedure for this vehicle.

2. Have your supervisor/instructor verify satisfactory completion of this task.

Demonstrate awareness of the safety aspects of high voltage circuits (such as high-intensity discharge [HID] lamps, ignition systems, injection systems, etc.)

MAST
0A14

Time off_____

Time on_____

Total time _____

CDX Tasksheet Number: C895

Vehicle used for this activity:

Year _____ Make _____ Model _____

Odometer _____ VIN _____

1. **Using appropriate service information, identify system voltage and safety precautions associated with high-intensity discharge headlights, ignition systems, and injection systems.**

   a. **HID lamp voltage:** _____ **volts**
   b. **List the safety precautions required when working on HID system:**

   c. **Maximum secondary ignition system voltage:** _____ **volts**
   d. **List the safety precautions required when working around ignition systems:**

   e. **Injection system voltage (on a vehicle with a high-voltage injection system):** _____ **volts**
   f. **List the safety precautions required when working around high-voltage injection systems:**

2. **Have your supervisor/instructor verify satisfactory completion of this task.**

Performance Rating

CDX Tasksheet Number: C895

0	1	2	3	4

Supervisor/instructor signature _____ Date _____

Section A1:
Engine Repair

CONTENTS

Vehicle, Customer, and Service Information

Student/Intern information:

Name_____ Date_____ Class_____

Vehicle used for this activity:

Year_____ Make_____ Model_____

Odometer_____VIN_____

Learning Objective/Task	CDX Tasksheet Number	2017 MAST NATEF Reference Number; Priority Level
• Complete work order to include customer information, vehicle identifying information, customer concern, related service history, cause, and correction.	C885	1A1; P-1
• Research vehicle service information including fluid type, internal engine operation, vehicle service history, service precautions, and technical service bulletins.	C002	1A2; P-1
• Identify service precautions related to service of the internal combustion of a hybrid vehicle.	C900	1A9; P-2
• Practice Task: Demonstrate the use of the three Cs (concern, cause, and correction).	N/A	N/A

Materials Required

- Blank work order
- Vehicle with available service history records
- Depending on the type of concern, special diagnostic tools may be required. See your supervisor/instructor for instructions to identify what tools may be required.
- Vehicle service information

Some Safety Issues to Consider

- Diagnosis of this fault may require test-driving the vehicle on the school grounds. Attempt this task only with full permission from your instructor and follow all the guidelines exactly.
- When running any vehicles in the shop, make sure you use the shop's exhaust ventilation system to discharge all exhaust gas safely outside.
- Lifting equipment such as vehicle jacks and stands, vehicle hoists, and engine hoists are important tools that increase productivity and make the job easier. However, they can also cause severe injury or death if used improperly. Make sure you follow the manufacturer's operation procedures. Also, make sure you have your supervisor's/instructor's permission to use any particular type of lifting equipment.
- Comply with personal and environmental safety practices associated with clothing; eye protection; hand tools; power equipment; proper ventilation; and the handling, storage, and disposal of chemicals/materials in accordance with local, state, and federal safety and environmental regulations.

Performance Standard

0—No exposure: No information or practice provided during the program; complete training required

1—Exposure only: General information provided with no practice time; close supervision needed; additional training required

2—Limited practice: Has practiced job during training program; additional training required to develop skill

3—Moderately skilled: Has performed job independently during training program; limited additional training may be required

4—Skilled: Can perform job independently with no additional training

TASK Complete work order to include customer information, vehicle identifying information, customer concern, related service history, cause, and correction.

MAST
1A1

Time off_____

Time on_____

Total time_____

CDX Tasksheet Number: C885

1. Using a vehicle with an engine-related customer concern, complete the work order, specifying the following:

   a. Customer information:

   b. Customer concern:

   c. Vehicle identifying information:

   d. Any related service history, etc.:

2. Determine the cause of the concern and list it on the work order.

3. List the action(s) needed to correct the concern, on the work order.

4. Have your supervisor/instructor verify satisfactory completion of the work order, any observations found, and any necessary action(s) recommended.

Performance Rating

CDX Tasksheet Number: C885

0	1	2	3	4

Supervisor/instructor signature _____ Date _____

Research vehicle service information including fluid type, internal engine operation, vehicle service history, service precautions, and technical service bulletins.

Time off_____

Time on_____

Total time_____

CDX Tasksheet Number: C002

1. **Using the VIN for identification, use the appropriate source to access the vehicle's service history in relation to prior related internal engine work or customer concerns.**

    a. **List any related repairs/concerns, and their dates:**

2. **Using the VIN for identification, access any relevant technical service bulletins for the particular vehicle you are working on in relation to any internal engine updates, precautions, or other service issues. List any related service bulletins and their titles:**

3. **Using the appropriate vehicle service information identify and list the correct fluid type for the vehicle.**

    a. **Engine oil**
    b. **Engine coolant**
    c. **Power steering fluid**
    d. **Brake fluid**
    e. **Clutch fluid**
    f. **Transmission fluid**
    g. **Diesel exhaust fluid**
    h. **Windshield washer fluid**

4. Have your supervisor/instructor verify satisfactory completion of this procedure, any observations found, and any necessary action(s) recommended.

> **NOTE** The following sign-off goes along with the first task on this tasksheet and can also be signed off once all of the other tasks in this tasksheet are completed.

MAST
1A9

Time off_____

Time on_____

Total time_____

CDX Tasksheet Number: C900

Vehicle used for this activity:

Year _____ Make _____ Model _____

Odometer _____ VIN _____

1. **Research the precautions when servicing an internal combustion engine on a hybrid vehicle in the appropriate service information. List all precautions:**

2. **Have your supervisor/instructor verify satisfactory completion of the procedure, any observations found, and any necessary action(s) recommended.**

Performance Rating

CDX Tasksheet Number: C900

0	1	2	3	4

Supervisor/instructor signature _____ Date _____

Demonstrate the use of the 3 Cs (concern, cause, and correction).

Time off_____

Time on_____

CDX Tasksheet Number: N/A

Total time_____

1. **Using the following scenario, write up the 3 Cs as listed on most repair orders. Assume that the customer authorized the recommended repairs.**

   An 8-year-old vehicle has been brought to your shop with an engine repair concern. The customer tells you that the vehicle runs rough at all speeds and conditions, and has gotten worse over the past couple of weeks. The malfunction indicator lamp (MIL) is blinking when the engine is running. The customer thought the malfunction was due to bad gas; he ran the tank out and refilled it with good gas from a very reputable station, but the car still runs rough after using half of a tank. The customer authorizes your shop to perform a diagnosis and you find the following:

   a. The vehicle is about 8 years old and has nearly 165,000 miles on it, but is in good overall condition.

   b. There is a diagnostic trouble code P0303, which indicates an engine misfire on cylinder #3.

   c. All of the spark plugs are moderately worn and show signs of moderate oil fouling, and the spark plug wires are original.

   d. Cylinder compression is about 25 psi on cylinder #3. The other cylinders are within specifications, but on the low side.

   e. A cylinder leakage test shows 85% leakage on cylinder #3 past the exhaust valve. The other cylinders show about 25% leakage past the piston rings.

   f. The engine mounts are oil-soaked due to a leaking valve cover and oil pan gaskets.

   g. The rear main seal shows signs of significant leakage.

   h. The oil light sometimes flickers when the engine is fully warmed up and Idling, even though the oil is near the full mark.

   i. The radiator has a small coolant leak in the core.

   > **NOTE** Ask your instructor whether you should use a copy of the shop repair order or the 3 Cs in this manual to record this information.

2. **Concern:**

3. **Cause:**

4. Correction:

5. Other recommended service:

6. Have your supervisor/instructor verify satisfactory completion of this procedure, any observations found, and any necessary action(s) recommended.

Performance Rating

CDX Tasksheet Number: N/A

0	1	2	3	4

Supervisor/instructor signature _____ Date _____

Fastener Repair

Student/Intern Information:

Name_____ Date_____ Class_____

Vehicle used for this activity:

Year _____ Make _____ Model_____

Odometer_____VIN_____

Time off_____

Time on_____

Total time_____

Learning Objective/Task	CDX Tasksheet Number	2017 MAST NATEF Reference Number; Priority Level
• Perform common fastener and thread repair, to include: remove broken bolt, restore internal and external threads, and repair internal threads with thread insert.	C886	1A7; P-1

Materials Required

- Vehicle or simulator with a damaged fastener/thread
- Fastener repair tools specific to the job

Some Safety Issues to Consider

- Power drills are powerful, and the drill bit can grab, especially when enlarging an existing hole. Always follow all safety precautions when drilling.
- Use the proper lubricant when drilling and tapping.
- Comply with personal and environmental safety practices associated with clothing; eye protection; hand tools; power equipment; proper ventilation; and the handling, storage, and disposal of chemicals/materials in accordance with local, state, and federal safety and environmental regulations.

Performance Standard

0—No exposure: No information or practice provided during the program; complete training required

1—Exposure only: General information provided with no practice time; close supervision needed; additional training required

2—Limited practice: Has practiced job during training program; additional training required to develop skill

3—Moderately skilled: Has performed job independently during training program; limited additional training may be required

4—Skilled: Can perform job independently with no additional training

Perform common fastener and thread repair, to include: remove broken bolt, restore internal and external threads, and repair internal threads with thread insert.

MAST
1A7

Time off_____

Time on_____

Total time_____

CDX Tasksheet Number: C886

> **NOTE** Your instructor may prefer that you perform this task on a mock-up or piece of scrap metal. Ask your instructor how he or she would like you to proceed.

1. **Identify the damaged fastener and its location, and list the information here:**

2. **Research the appropriate method of extracting the broken fastener, and list it here:**

3. **Using the appropriate method, remove the broken bolt from its location. List your observation(s):**

4. **Restore internal and external threads as required, and list your results:**

5. **Have your supervisor/instructor check your work. Supervisor's/instructor's initials:** _____

6. **Repair internal threads with a thread insert using the recommended method. List the steps below:**

7. Have your supervisor/instructor verify satisfactory completion of this procedure, any observations found, and any necessary action(s) recommended.

Performance Rating

CDX Tasksheet Number: C886

0	1	2	3	4

Supervisor/instructor signature _____ Date _____

Engine Mechanical Testing

Student/Intern information:

Name_____ Date_____ Class_____

Vehicle used for this activity:

Year _____ Make _____ Model_____

Odometer_____VIN_____

Time off_____

Time on_____

Total time_____

Learning Objective/Task	CDX Tasksheet Number	2017 MAST NATEF Reference Number; Priority Level
• Inspect engine assembly for fuel, oil, coolant, and other leaks; determine needed action.	C004	1A4; P-1
• Verify operation of the instrument panel engine warning indicators.	C898	1A3; P-1
• Perform cranking sound diagnosis.	N/A	N/A
• Perform engine absolute manifold pressure tests (vacuum/boost); determine needed action.	C392	8A5; P-1
• Perform cylinder power balance tests; determine needed action.	C393	8A6; P-2
• Perform cylinder cranking and running compression tests; determine needed action.	C709	8A7; P-1
• Perform cylinder leakage tests; determine needed action.	C395	8A8; P-1

Materials Required

- Vehicle or simulator
- Vacuum gauge
- Tachometer (hand-held if the vehicle is not equipped with an in-dash tachometer)
- Insulated spark plug wire pliers (if using this method to disable the cylinders)
- Scan tool (if using this method to disable the cylinders)
- Compression tester
- Cylinder leakage tester
- Stethoscope
- Flashlight

Some Safety Issues to Consider

- You will be working under the hood of a running vehicle. Keep your hands and fingers away from moving belts, fans, and other parts.
- Be sure to only disconnect the proper vacuum hose. Many other hoses look alike but could carry gasoline or hot coolant under high pressure.
- During this test, you may be disabling the ignition or fuel systems. Be sure you only do so for the minimum amount of time to get your readings. Operating the engine with cylinders disabled may lead to damage of the catalytic converter or other parts. If in doubt, ask your supervisor/instructor.

- If you disable the cylinders by disconnecting the spark plug wires, you may expose yourself to extremely high voltage (up to 100,000 volts). Reduce the possibility of electrical shock by using appropriate insulated spark plug wire pliers.
- When running any vehicles in the shop, make sure you use the shop's exhaust ventilation system to discharge all exhaust gas safely outside.
- Always follow your supervisor's/instructor's directions on how to get the piston to top dead center. Failure to do so could cause injury or damage to the vehicle.
- Use caution when turning the engine to top dead center. If you do this by hand, be sure your fingers, hands, etc. stay clear of belts and pulleys that could cause severe pinching.
- Make sure the ignition switch is in the "off" position and the key is removed from the ignition switch during this job to prevent someone from inadvertently cranking the engine over while you are working on it.
- Comply with personal and environmental safety practices associated with clothing; eye protection; hand tools; power equipment; proper ventilation; and the handling, storage, and disposal of chemicals/materials in accordance with local, state, and federal safety and environmental regulations.

Performance Standard

0—No exposure: No information or practice provided during the program; complete training required

1—Exposure only: General information provided with no practice time; close supervision needed; additional training required

2—Limited practice: Has practiced job during training program; additional training required to develop skill

3—Moderately skilled: Has performed job independently during training program; limited additional training may be required

4—Skilled: Can perform job independently with no additional training

Inspect engine assembly for fuel, oil, coolant, and other leaks; determine needed action.

MAST
1A4

DX Tasksheet Number: C004

NOTE If the vehicle's engine assembly is coated with leaking fluids and road dirt, you may need to pressure wash the engine before inspecting it for leaks. Some very small leaks, or leaks on engines that have a lot of accumulated residue, may be diagnosed with the use of a fluorescent dye and ultraviolet light. Check with your supervisor/instructor about which procedure to perform. Follow the dye check equipment manufacturer's instructions if you are performing this test.

NOTE Fluid leaks can be hard to locate. Remember that gravity tends to pull any leaking fluid down. You will need to identify the highest point of the leak to locate its source. Fluids can also be flung from rotating parts, sprayed under pressure from pinhole leaks, or blown by airflow far from the source. Investigate carefully.

---

1. **Check for fluid leaks under the hood. List any leaks (component leaking and type of fluid):**

2. **Safely raise and secure the vehicle on a hoist.**

3. **Inspect the engine, cooling system, fuel system, transmission/transaxle, and any differentials for leaks. Identify the type of fluid leaking and the source of the leak for the following items:**

    a. **Engine:**

    b. **Fuel system:**

    c. **Cooling system:**

d. Transmission/transaxle:

e. Steering system:

f. Differentials:

4. Determine any necessary action(s):

5. Have your supervisor/instructor verify satisfactory completion of this procedure, any observations found, and any necessary action(s) recommended.

Performance Rating

CDX Tasksheet Number: C004

0	1	2	3	4

Supervisor/instructor signature _____ Date _____

Verify operation of the instrument panel
engine warning indicators.

MAST
1A3

Time off_____

Time on_____

Total time_____

DX Tasksheet Number: C898

1. **Research the operation of instrument panel gauges/indicator lights in the appropriate service information. List each of the warning indicators:**

2. **Turn the ignition to the "run" position (engine not running). List the status of each gauge/indicator:**

3. **Start the engine and allow it to run for a few minutes. List the status of each gauge/indicator:**

4. **List any gauges/indicators that are showing a fault and the fault indicated:**

5. **Have your supervisor/instructor verify satisfactory completion of this procedure, any observations found, and any necessary action(s) recommended.**

Performance Rating

CDX Tasksheet Number: C898

0	1	2	3	4

Supervisor/instructor signature _____ Date _____

Time off_____

Time on_____

Total time_____

CDX Tasksheet Number: N/A

1. **Disable the ignition or fuel system so that the engine will crank, but not start.**

   NOTE Some vehicles can be put into "clear flood" mode by depressing the throttle to the floor before turning the ignition key to the "run" position. This prevents the fuel injectors from being activated. If your vehicle is equipped with this mode, hold the throttle down to the floor and try cranking the engine over (make sure you are prepared to turn off the ignition switch if the engine starts). You can also disable the engine by disconnecting the fuel injectors or ignition coils.

2. **Crank the engine over for approximately 5 seconds and listen to the cranking sound.**

   NOTE The engine should crank over at a normal speed. Too fast could mean low compression caused by bent valves or a slipped timing belt or chain. Too slow could mean a seized piston or bearing, or a faulty starting system. An uneven cranking sound may indicate grossly uneven compression pressures in the cylinders.

3. **List your observation(s):**

4. **Determine any necessary action(s):**

5. **Have your supervisor/instructor verify satisfactory completion of this procedure, any observations found, and any necessary action(s) recommended.**

Performance Rating

CDX Tasksheet Number: N/A

0	1	2	3	4

Supervisor/instructor signature _____ Date _____

Perform engine absolute manifold pressure tests
(vacuum/boost); determine needed action.

MAST
8A5

CDX Tasksheet Number: C392

1. **Find an appropriate vacuum hose to connect into.**

> **NOTE** Make sure the vacuum hose is connected to the intake manifold vacuum and
> you are not disconnecting anything that will affect the operation of the engine. If
> possible, the use of a vacuum tee will allow you to take the reading while allowing
> the vacuum to get to its intended device.

2. **Running Vacuum Test**

    a. **Describe the purpose of this test, the components or functions the test checks, and what the results might indicate:**

    b. **Start the engine, allow it to idle, and note the vacuum reading:**

        i. **Is the vacuum gauge needle relatively steady? Yes: _____**
            No: _____

    c. **Carefully raise the engine rpm to 2000 rpm and note the vacuum reading: _____**

        i. **Is the vacuum gauge needle relatively steady? Yes: _____**
            No: _____

        ii. **The vacuum reading should be higher at 2000 rpm than at idle. Is it?**
            Yes: _____ No: _____

    d. **Determine any necessary action(s):**

3. **Have your supervisor/instructor verify satisfactory completion of this procedure, any observations found, and any necessary action(s) recommended.**

Performance Rating

CDX Tasksheet Number: C392

0	1	2	3	4

Supervisor/instructor signature _____ Date _____

MAST
8A6

CDX Tasksheet Number: C393

1. Research the best option for disabling the cylinders on this vehicle in the appropriate service Information. The list that follows contains the most common methods. Choose the one that you plan on using.

   a. Disconnect individual spark plug wires or ignition coils. _____
   b. Disconnect individual fuel injectors (multi-port fuel injection only). _____
   c. Use a diagnostic scope to disable cylinders through the ignition primary circuit. _____
   d. Use a scan tool on vehicles with power balance capabilities. _____
   e. Use short sections of vacuum hose and a test light (option for waste spark ignition systems). _____

2. Determine from the service information if this vehicle has an idle control system. If it does, list how to best disable the system during this test:

3. Have your supervisor/instructor check the above answers. Supervisor's/instructor's initials: _____

4. If this vehicle is equipped with an idle control system, disable it and set the idle speed to an appropriate rpm.

   a. List the rpm here: _____

5. Disable the cylinders one at a time and record the rpm drop (not the rpm) of each cylinder.

   a. rpm drop: ---_____ ---_____ ---_____ ---_____ ---_____ ---_____ ---_____ ---_____

6. Determine any necessary action(s):

7. Have your supervisor/instructor verify satisfactory completion of this procedure, any observations found, and any necessary action(s) recommended.

Performance Rating

CDX Tasksheet Number: C393

0	1	2	3	4

Supervisor/instructor signature _____ Date _____

Time off_____

Time on_____

Total time_____

DX Tasksheet Number: C709

1. **Research the procedure and specifications for performing both a cranking compression test and a running compression test on this vehicle in the appropriate service information.**

2. **List the conditions that must be met for the cranking compression test to be accurate (you may paraphrase):**

3. **Specifications**
   a. **Minimum compression pressure:** _____ **psi/kPa or %**
   b. **Maximum variation:** _____ **%**

4. **Cranking Compression Test: Perform the cranking compression test following the specified procedure. The top row in the table below is a standard test and the bottom row is a wet test using a small amount of clean engine oil. The wet test would normally be performed on engines that fail the standard test. List the readings obtained for each cylinder in the table.**

Cylinder	#1	#2	#3	#4	#5	#6	#7	#8
Standard test (psi/kPa)								
Wet test(psi/kPa)								

   a. **Calculate the difference between the highest and lowest cylinders (dry test):** _____ **%**

5. **Running Compression Test: Perform the running compression test following the specified procedure. List the readings obtained for each cylinder:**

> **NOTE** Make sure the person snapping the throttle open is ready to turn off the ignition switch if the throttle sticks open.

Cylinder	#1	#2	#3	#4	#5	#6	#7	#8
Idle (psi/kPa)								
Snap throttle (psi/kPa)								

a. Determine any necessary action(s):

6. Have your supervisor/instructor verify satisfactory completion of this procedure, any observations found, and any necessary action(s) recommended.

CDX Tasksheet Number: C709

0	1	2	3	4

Supervisor/instructor signature _____ Date _____

Time off_____

Time on_____

Total time_____

DX Tasksheet Number: C395

1. List all of the possible places where compression can leak out of a cylinder:

2. Remove the appropriate spark plugs to test the cylinder with the lowest compression pressure.

3. Bring that piston up to top dead center on the compression stroke and install the cylinder leakage tester. List the reading you obtained.

   a. Cylinder #: _____

   b. Cylinder leakage: _____ %

   c. Leaking from: _____

4. Perform this test on one other cylinder. List the reading you obtained. Before removing the cylinder leakage tester, call your supervisor/instructor over to verify the reading.

   a. Cylinder #: _____

   b. Cylinder leakage: _____ %

   c. Leaking from: _____

5. Determine any necessary action(s):

6. Have your supervisor/instructor verify satisfactory completion of this procedure, any observations found, and any necessary action(s) recommended.

Performance Rating

CDX Tasksheet Number: C395

0	1	2	3	4

Supervisor/instructor signature _____ Date _____

Engine Removal

Student/Intern information:

Name_____ Date_____ Class_____

Vehicle used for this activity:

Year _____ Make _____ Model_____

Odometer_____VIN_____

Time off_____

Time on_____

Total time_____

Learning Objective/Task	CDX Tasksheet Number	2017 MAST NATEF Reference Number; Priority Level
• Remove and reinstall engine on a newer vehicle equipped with OBD; reconnect all attaching components and restore the vehicle to running condition.	C671	1A10; P-3

Recommended Resource Materials
- CDX Automotive program
- Technical service bulletins, shop manuals, and any other information applicable to the specific vehicle or components you are working on
- Class notes

Materials Required
- Vehicle
- Lift or jack and jack stands
- Fastener storage containers
- Drain pan(s)
- Engine hoist (crane)
- Manufacturer- or job-specific tools

Some Safety Issues to Consider
- This procedure may require cleaning the engine prior to inspection. If so, use the proper equipment and procedures to carry this out safely. Also, get your supervisor's/instructor's permission prior to cleaning.
- You will be working under the hood of a running vehicle. Keep your hands and fingers away from moving belts, fans, and other parts.
- Lifting equipment such as vehicle jacks and stands, vehicle hoists, and engine hoists are important tools that increase productivity and make the job easier. However, they can also cause severe injury or death if used improperly. Make sure you follow the manufacturer's operation procedures. Also, make sure you have your supervisor's/instructor's permission to use any particular type of lifting equipment.
- Comply with personal and environmental safety practices associated with clothing; eye protection; hand tools; power equipment; proper ventilation; and the handling, storage, and disposal of chemicals/materials in accordance with local, state, and federal safety and environmental regulations.

Performance Standard

0–No exposure: No information or practice provided during the program; complete training required

1–Exposure only: General information provided with no practice time; close supervision needed; additional training required

2–Limited practice: Has practiced job during training program; additional training required to develop skill

3–Moderately skilled: Has performed job independently during training program; limited additional training may be required

4–Skilled: Can perform job independently with no additional training

Remove and reinstall engine on a newer vehicle equipped
with OBD; reconnect all attaching components and restore
the vehicle to running condition.

MAST
1A10

DX Tasksheet Number: C671

1. **Research the procedure and specifications for removing and installing the engine in the appropriate service information.**

    a. **List the flat rate time for R&R engine:** _____ hr

    b. **List the flat rate time for R&R engine and O/H:** _____ hr

    c. **List any special tools required for this task:**

    d. **List the specified engine oil:** _____

    e. **List the engine oil capacity:** _____ qt/lt

    f. **List the specified coolant:** _____

    g. **List the cooling system capacity:** _____ qt/lt

    h. **List any precautions specific to replacing the engine in this vehicle:**

2. **Following the specified procedure(s), prepare the vehicle for engine removal by properly locating it in the work stall, draining any appropriate fluids such as engine coolant and oil, and removing any body components such as the hood, inner fender(s), etc.**

3. **Following the specified procedure(s), remove the engine assembly from the vehicle.**

4. **Inspect the assembly for any damaged components, fasteners, etc., and list your observation(s):**

5. **List the amount of time it took to remove the engine assembly:**
   _____ hr

6. **Have your supervisor/instructor verify removal of the engine assembly. Supervisor's/instructor's initials:** _____

NOTE If you are rebuilding the engine, continue on to the Cylinder Head Removal, Inspection, and Installation tasksheet. After completion of those tasks, return here to reinstall the engine assembly.

---

7. Following the specified procedure(s) and specifications, reinstall the engine into the engine compartment.

8. Reconnect all hoses, wiring, belts, cables, and components, being careful to install them in their proper places.

9. Refill the engine with the specified oil. Ensure that the oil filter is installed.

10. Refill the cooling system with the specified coolant and bleed any air from the system.

11. Check all other fluid levels such as power steering fluid and brake fluid. Top off as necessary.

12. Recheck that all fasteners are properly torqued.

13. Perform any other prestart procedures such as charging the vehicle's battery, priming the lubrication system, etc.

14. List any specified break-in/start-up procedures:

15. Have your supervisor/instructor verify that the engine is ready to start. Supervisor's/instructor's initials: _____

NOTE It is good practice to have a fire extinguisher close by in case of a fire.

16. Install the exhaust hose(s). Start the engine and check for proper oil pressure, leaks, and abnormal noises. If any problems arise, shut down the engine and repair any issues. List your observation(s):

17. Verify the proper adjustment of any timing components, if applicable.

18. Continue the break-in/start-up procedure, being careful to monitor the engine temperature, oil pressure, and malfunction indicator lamp (MIL). Stop the engine if any issues arise.

19. Once the initial break-in period is complete, shut down the engine and check for leaks, loose components, etc. List any observation(s):

20. Have your supervisor/instructor verify proper engine operation. Supervisor's/instructor's initials: _____

21. Reinstall any removed items such as the hood and inner fenders. Align as necessary.

22. Recheck the fluid levels and inspect for any leaks.

23. List the amount of time it took to install the engine assembly: _____ hr

24. With your instructor's permission, test drive the vehicle to verify correct operation. List your observation(s):

25. Have your supervisor/instructor verify satisfactory completion of this procedure, any observations found, and any necessary action(s) recommended.

Cylinder Head Removal, Inspection, and Installation

Student/Intern information:

Name_____ Date_____ Class_____

Vehicle used for this activity:

Year_____ Make _____ Model_____

Odometer_____VIN_____

Learning Objective/Task	CDX Tasksheet Number	2017 MAST NATEF Reference Number; Priority Level
• Remove cylinder head; inspect gasket condition; install cylinder head and gasket; tighten according to manufacturer's specification and procedure.	C673	1B1; P-1
• Clean and visually inspect a cylinder head for cracks; check gasket surface areas for warpage and surface finish; check passage condition.	C674	1B2; P-1

Materials Required

- Complete engine
- Harmonic balancer puller
- Harmonic balancer installation kit
- Head stand
- Head gasket set
- Torque wrench
- Torque angle gauge
- Gasket scraper (nonmetallic on aluminum and plastic surfaces)
- Some engines require a liquid gasket remover and chemical metal prep
- Straightedge, piece of glass, or granite comparator surface
- Feeler blade set
- Crack detection equipment (magna-flux for cast iron; Zyglo for aluminum)
- Blowgun/air nozzle
- Vehicle-specific tools

Some Safety Issues to Consider

- This procedure may require cleaning the engine prior to inspection. If so, use the proper equipment and procedures to carry this out safely. Also, get your supervisor's/instructor's permission prior to cleaning.
- Lifting equipment such as vehicle jacks and stands, vehicle hoists, and engine hoists are important tools that increase productivity and make the job easier. However, they can also cause severe injury or death if used improperly. Make sure you follow the manufacturer's operation procedures. Also, make sure you have your supervisor's/instructor's permission to use any particular type of lifting equipment.
- Cylinder heads can be heavy, so make sure you get help when removing and installing them.
- Compressed air can be very dangerous. Never blow it at someone. Never use it to remove dirt or dust from your skin or clothing. Never use it without an OSHA-approved nozzle.
- Comply with personal and environmental safety practices associated with clothing; eye protection; hand tools; power equipment; proper ventilation; and the handling, storage, and disposal of chemicals/materials in accordance with local, state, and federal safety and environmental regulations.

Performance Standard

0—No exposure: No information or practice provided during the program; complete training required

1—Exposure only: General information provided with no practice time; close supervision needed; additional training required

2—Limited practice: Has practiced job during training program; additional training required to develop skill

3—Moderately skilled: Has performed job independently during training program; limited additional training may be required

4—Skilled: Can perform job independently with no additional training

Remove cylinder head; inspect gasket condition; install
cylinder head and gasket; tighten according to
manufacturer's specification and procedure.

MAST
1B1

Time off_____

Time on_____

Total time_____

DX Tasksheet Number: C673

1. **Research the procedure and specifications for removing and installing the cylinder head(s) in the appropriate service information.**

   a. **Does this vehicle use TTY head bolts? Yes: _____ No: _____**

   b. **List or print off and attach to this sheet any special tools required for this task:**

   c. **List or print off and attach to this sheet any special precautions required for this task:**

   d. **List or print off and attach to this sheet the straightness specifications for the head surface:**

   e. **List or print off and attach to this sheet the surface finish requirements for the head surface:**

   f. **List or print off and attach to this sheet the torque procedure for the head bolts:**

g. Draw or print off and attach to this sheet the torque sequence for the head bolts:

2. **Following the specified procedure, remove the cylinder head(s).**

> **NOTE** Be very careful not to damage or scratch the head surface as this could cause a leak. Lay the head down on shop towels, and only use nonmetallic scrapers on aluminum or plastic surfaces.

3. **Inspect the old gasket(s) and list your observation(s):**

> **NOTE** While the head(s) is(are) removed from the engine, it makes sense to perform task C674: Clean and visually inspect a cylinder head for cracks; check gasket surface areas for warpage and surface finish; check passage condition.

4. **Following the procedure in the service information, install the head gasket(s) and cylinder head(s). Make sure you follow the specified procedure and sequence for tightening down the head bolts. Failure to do so could cause the gasket to fail.**

5. **Have your supervisor/instructor verify satisfactory completion of this procedure, any observations found, and any necessary action(s) recommended.**

Performance Rating

CDX Tasksheet Number: C673

0	1	2	3	4

Supervisor/instructor signature _____ Date _____

MAST
1B2

Time off_____

Time on_____

Total time_____

CDX Tasksheet Number: C674

1. **Following the procedure in the service information, clean the head surfaces and prepare them for inspection.**

   NOTE Be very careful not to damage or scratch the head surface as this could cause a leak. Lay the head down on shop towels, and only use nonmetallic scrapers on aluminum or plastic surfaces.

2. **Inspect the heads for signs of any cracks. This may involve magnafluxing or chemical crack detection. List the procedure you used and any observation(s):**

3. **Measure the gasket surfaces for warpage. List your measurements and observation(s):**

4. **Check the surface finish according to the manufacturer's procedure. List your observation(s):**

5. **Inspect the passages for blockage or leakage. List your observation(s):**

6. **Have your supervisor/instructor verify satisfactory completion of this procedure, any observations found, and any necessary action(s) recommended.**

Performance Rating

CDX Tasksheet Number: C674

0	1	2	3	4

Supervisor/instructor signature _____ Date _____

Cylinder Head Disassembly, Inspection, and Repair

Student/Intern information:

Name _____ Date _____ Class _____

Vehicle used for this activity:

Year _____ Make _____ Model _____

Odometer _____ VIN _____

Learning Objective/Task	CDX Tasksheet Number	2017 MAST NATEF Reference Number; Priority Level
• Inspect pushrods, rocker arms, rocker arm pivots, and shafts for wear, bending, cracks, looseness, and blocked oil passages (orifices); determine needed action.	C021	1B3; P-2
• Inspect valve lifters; determine needed action.	C722	1B12; P-2
• Inspect and/or measure camshaft for runout, journal wear, and lobe wear.	C724	1B13; P-3
• Inspect camshaft bearing surface for wear, damage, out-of-round, and alignment; determine needed action.	C027	1B14; P-3
• Inspect valve springs for squareness and free height comparison; determine needed action.	C718	1B7; P-3
• Inspect valve guides for wear; check valve stem-to-guide clearance; determine needed action.	C719	1B9; P-3
• Inspect valves and valve seats; determine needed action.	C720	1B10; P-3
• Check valve spring assembled height and valve stem height; determine needed action.	C721	1B11; P-3
• Establish camshaft position sensor indexing.	C677	1B6; P-1
• Adjust valves (mechanical or hydraulic lifters).	C723	1B4; P-1

Recommended Resource Materials

- CDX Automotive program
- Technical service bulletins, shop manuals, and any other information applicable to the specific vehicle or components you are working on
- Class notes

Materials Required

- Straightedge or piece of glass
- Feeler blades
- Blow gun/air nozzle
- Set of V-blocks
- Valve spring tension gauge
- Square
- Machinist's rule
- Installed height micrometer
- Ball micrometers
- Outside micrometers
- Dial indicator

Some Safety Issues to Consider

- Engine castings and parts can have sharp edges. Be careful when handling them.
- Cleaning parts may bring you in contact with hazardous chemicals. Always wear the appropriate gloves and clothing when working with chemicals. Refer to the safety data sheet (SDS) for further information.
- Used engine oil contains cancer-causing agents. Always avoid oil contact with your hands. Alway wash your hands after completing this task.
- Compressed air can be very dangerous. Never blow it at someone. Never use it to remove dirt or dust from your skin or clothing. Never use it without an OSHA-approved nozzle.
- Comply with personal and environmental safety practices associated with clothing; eye protection; hand tools; power equipment; proper ventilation; and the handling, storage, and disposal of chemicals/materials in accordance with local, state, and federal safety and environmental regulations.

Performance Standard

0–No exposure: No information or practice provided during the program; complete training required

1–Exposure only: General information provided with no practice time; close supervision needed; additional training required

2–Limited practice: Has practiced job during training program; additional training required to develop skill

3–Moderately skilled: Has performed job independently during training program; limited additional training may be required

4–Skilled: Can perform job independently with no additional training

Inspect pushrods, rocker arms, rocker arm pivots, and shafts for wear, bending, cracks, looseness, and blocked oil passages (orifices); determine needed action.

MAST
1B3

Time off_____

Time on_____

CDX Tasksheet Number: CO21

Total time_____

1. **Research the procedure and specifications for disassembling and inspecting the pushrods, rocker arms, pivots, and shafts in the appropriate service information.**

   a. **List, or print off and attach to this sheet, the procedure for inspecting these parts:**

2. **Disassemble the rocker arm assemblies and clean them in a safe and environmentally approved way. This is commonly performed in a hot water spray machine.**

3. **Inspect the following parts:**

   a. **Pushrods: Worn _____ Bent _____ Cracked _____ Blocked passages _____ OK _____ (Check any that apply)**
   b. **Rocker arms: Worn _____ Bent _____ Cracked _____ Blocked passages _____ OK _____ (Check any that apply)**
   c. **Rocker arm studs: Worn _____ Bent _____ Cracked _____ OK _____ (Check any that apply)**
   d. **Pivots/shafts: Worn _____ Bent _____ Cracked _____ Blocked passages _____ OK _____ (Check any that apply)**

4. **Determine any necessary action(s):**

5. **Have your supervisor/instructor verify satisfactory completion of this procedure, any observations found, and any necessary action(s) recommended.**

Performance Rating

CDX Tasksheet Number: CO21

0	1	2	3	4

Supervisor/instructor signature _____ Date _____

MAST
1B12

Time off_____

Time on_____

Total time_____

CDX Tasksheet Number: C722

1. Research the procedure and specifications for inspecting the valve lifters in the appropriate service information.

   a. List the type of lifter this engine is equipped with:
      Hydraulic _____ Solid _____
   b. List, or print off and attach to this sheet, the inspection procedure and any specifications:

2. Inspect the valve lifters and list your observation(s):

3. Determine any necessary action(s):

4. Have your supervisor/instructor verify satisfactory completion of this procedure, any observations found, and any necessary action(s) recommended.

Performance Rating

CDX Tasksheet Number: C722

0	1	2	3	4

Supervisor/instructor signature _____ Date _____

TASK Inspect and/or measure camshaft for runout, journal wear, and lobe wear.

MAST
1B13

DX Tasksheet Number: C724

1. **Research the procedure and specifications for inspecting and measuring the camshaft in the appropriate service information.**

    a. **Specified maximum camshaft journal runout:** _____ in/mm
    b. **Specified camshaft journal diameter:** _____ in/mm
    c. **Specified lobe lift**

       i. **Intake:** _____ in/mm

       ii. **Exhaust:** _____ in/mm

    d. **Specified maximum lobe wear:** _____ in/mm

2. **Visually inspect the condition of the cam lobes for excessive wear. List your observation(s):**

3. **Following the specified procedure, measure the camshaft journal runout. List the measurement. List which journals were supported and which one was measured.**

4. **Following the specified procedure, measure the camshaft journal diameter. List your measurements for each cam journal in the table below.**

Camshaft Journal	#1	#2	#3	#4	#5
Cam #1 (in/mm)					
Cam #2 (in/mm)					
Cam #3 (in/mm)					
Cam #4 (in/mm)					

5. **Calculate the maximum camshaft journal wear:** _____ in/mm

6. **Following the specified procedure, measure the cam lobe lift and list your measurements in the table below.**

	#1	#2	#3	#4	#5	#6	#7	#8
Intake lobes								
Exhaust Lobes								

7. Calculate the maximum lobe wear.

    a. Intake: _____ in/mm

    b. Exhaust: _____ in/mm

8. Determine any necessary action(s):

9. Have your supervisor/instructor verify satisfactory completion of this procedure, any observations found, and any necessary action(s) recommended.

Performance Rating

0	1	2	3	4

Supervisor/instructor signature _____ Date _____

TASK Inspect camshaft bearing surface for wear, damage, out-of-round, and alignment; determine needed action.

MAST
1B14

Time off_____

Time on_____

Total time_____

DX Tasksheet Number: C027

> **NOTE** Perform this task only if the engine is an overhead cam design. If it is a cam-in-block design, the camshaft bearings are inspected during the Block Disassembly, Inspection, and Repair tasksheet.

1. **Research the procedures and specifications for inspecting and measuring the camshaft bearings in the appropriate service information.**
   a. **Specified camshaft bearing inside diameter:** _____ in/mm
   b. **Specified camshaft journal diameter:** _____ in/mm
   c. **Specified camshaft journal bearing clearance:** _____ in/mm

2. **Measure the inside diameter of the camshaft bearings. List your measurements in the table below.**

Camshaft Bearing	#1	#2	#3	#4	#5
Cam #1 (in/mm)					
Cam #2 (in/mm)					
Cam #3 (in/mm)					
Cam #4 (in/mm)					

3. **Measure the diameter of the camshaft journals (or copy them from the previous task). List your measurements in the table below.**

Camshaft Journal	#1	#2	#3	#4	#5
Cam #1 (in/mm)					
Cam #2 (in/mm)					
Cam #3 (in/mm)					
Cam #4 (in/mm)					

4. **Calculate the camshaft journal bearing clearance. List your measurements in the table below.**

Camshaft Journal	#1	#2	#3	#4	#5
Cam #1 (in/mm)					
Cam #2 (in/mm)					
Cam #3 (in/mm)					
Cam #4 (in/mm)					

5. Inspect the bearings and journals for evidence of damage, wear, and misalignment. List your observation(s):

6. Determine any necessary action(s):

7. Have your supervisor/instructor verify satisfactory completion of this procedure, any observations found, and any necessary action(s) recommended.

Performance Rating

0	1	2	3	4

Supervisor/instructor signature _____ Date _____

Time off_____

Time on_____

Total time_____

DX Tasksheet Number: C718

1. **Research the procedure and specifications for checking valve spring squareness and free height in the appropriate service information.**

   a. **List, or print off and attach to this sheet, the procedure for checking squareness:**

   b. **Specified valve spring free height**

      i. **Intake:** _____ in/mm

      ii. **Exhaust:** _____ in/mm

   c. **Specified valve spring installed height**

      i. **Intake:** _____ in/mm

      ii. **Exhaust:** _____ in/mm

   d. **Specified valve spring pressure at the specified installed height**

      i. **Intake:** _____ lb/kg at
         _____ in/mm

      ii. **Exhaust:** _____ lb/kg at
         _____ in/mm

   e. **Specified valve spring pressure at the specified valve open height**

      i. **Intake:** _____ lb/kg at
         _____ in/mm

      ii. **Exhaust:** _____ lb/kg at
         _____ in/mm

> **NOTE** You may want to measure and record the existing valve installed height and valve stem height before grinding the valves or machining the valve seats since specifications are not always available. Since some engines have nonadjustable valve trains, this is a critical measurement when reassembling the valve assemblies.

2. **Disassemble the valve and valve spring assemblies, if not already done.**

3. **Check the valve springs for squareness using the protractor-head square. List your observation(s):**

4. **Measure the free height of each valve spring. List your measurements in the table below.**

Valve Spring	#1	#2	#3	#4	#5	#6	#7	#8
Intake (in/mm)								
Exhaust (in/mm)								

5. **Measure the valve spring pressure at the specified installed height. List your measurements in the table below.**

Valve Spring	#1	#2	#3	#4	#5	#6	#7	#8
Intake (lb/kg)								
Exhaust (lb/kg)								

6. **Measure the valve spring pressure at the specified valve open height. List your measurements in the table below.**

Valve Spring	#1	#2	#3	#4	#5	#6	#7	#8
Intake (lb/kg)								
Exhaust (lb/kg)								

7. **Determine any necessary action(s):**

8. **Have your supervisor/instructor verify satisfactory completion of this procedure, any observations found, and any necessary action(s) recommended.**

Performance Rating

CDX Tasksheet Number: C718

0	1	2	3	4

Supervisor/instructor signature _____ Date _____

MAST
1B9

DX Tasksheet Number: C719

1. Research the procedure and specifications for checking valve guides and clearance in the appropriate service information.

   a. Specified valve guide clearance

      i. Intake: _____ in/mm

      ii. Exhaust: _____ in/mm

   b. Which method of determining valve guide clearance is recommended?
      Micrometer method / Dial indicator method (Circle one)

2. Measure the intake valve guide inner diameter and the intake valve stem diameter; calculate the clearance (micrometer method) or measure the side-to-side play of the valve stem with a dial indicator (dial indicator method). List your measurements in the table below.

Intake Valve	#1	#2	#3	#4	#5	#6	#7	#8
Guide (in/mm)								
Valve (in/mm)								
Clearance (in/mm)								

3. Measure the exhaust valve guide inner diameter and the exhaust valve stem diameter, then calculate the clearance (micrometer method), or measure the side-to-side play of the valve stem with a dial indicator (dial indicator method). List your measurements in the table below.

Exhaust Valve	#1	#2	#3	#4	#5	#6	#7	#8
Guide (in/mm)								
Valve (in/mm)								
Clearance (in/mm)								

4. Determine any necessary action(s):

5. Have your supervisor/instructor verify satisfactory completion of this procedure, any observations found, and any necessary action(s) recommended.

Performance Rating

CDX Tasksheet Number: C719

0	1	2	3	4

Supervisor/instructor signature _____ Date _____

MAST
1B10

Time off_____

Time on_____

Total time_____

CDX Tasksheet Number: C720

1. **Research the procedure and specifications for inspecting valves and valve seats in the appropriate service information.**

    a. **Specified valve stem diameter**

        i. **Intake:** _____ in/mm

        ii. **Exhaust:** _____ in/mm

    b. **Specified valve margin thickness**

        i. **Intake:** _____ in/mm

        ii. **Exhaust:** _____ in/mm

    c. **Specified valve face angle**

        i. **Intake:** _____ degrees

        ii. **Exhaust:** _____ degrees

    d. **Specified valve seat angle**

        i. **Intake:** _____ degrees

        ii. **Exhaust:** _____ degrees

    e. **Specified valve seat width**

        i. **Intake:** _____ in/mm

        ii. **Exhaust:** _____ in/mm

    f. **List, or print off and attach to this sheet, the procedure for inspecting the valves and valve seats:**

2. **Measure the valve stem diameter and check for taper. List your measurements in the table below.**

Valve	#1	#2	#3	#4	#5	#6	#7	#8
Intake (in/mm)								
Exhaust (in/mm)								

3. **Measure the valve margin thickness. List your measurements in the table below.**

Valve	#1	#2	#3	#4	#5	#6	#7	#8
Intake (in/mm)								
Exhaust (in/mm)								

4. Measure the valve seat width. List your measurements in the table below.

Valve Seat	#1	#2	#3	#4	#5	#6	#7	#8
Intake (in/mm)								
Exhaust (in/mm)								

5. Inspect the valves and valve seats according to the manufacturer's procedure. List your observation(s):

6. Determine any necessary action(s):

7. Have your supervisor/instructor verify satisfactory completion of this procedure, any observations found, and any necessary action(s) recommended.

Performance Rating

CDX Tasksheet Number: C720

| 0 | 1 | 2 | 3 | 4 |

Supervisor/instructor signature _____ Date _____

Check valve spring assembled height and valve stem height; determine needed action.

MAST
1B11

CDX Tasksheet Number: C721

1. **Research the procedure and specifications in the appropriate service information for checking the following:**

    a. **Specified valve stem height**

        i. **Intake:** _____ in/mm

        ii. **Exhaust:** _____ in/mm

    b. **Specified valve spring assembled height**

        i. **Intake:** _____ in/mm

        ii. **Exhaust:** _____ in/mm

    c. **List, or print off and attach to this sheet, the procedure for making these measurements:**

2. **Perform this task only if the valves and valve seats are ready to be put back into service.**

    NOTE The valves are ready to be put back into service if they have been reground to meet specifications or if they have been replaced with new valves. This also applies for the valve seats. If you sent the heads out to be machined, the machinist should have ensured that these specifications were met.

3. **Measure the valve stem height. List your measurements in the table below.**

Valve	#1	#2	#3	#4	#5	#6	#7	#8
Intake (in/mm)								
Exhaust (in/mm)								

4. **Measure the valve spring assembled height. List your measurements in the table below.**

    NOTE If the valve springs have been replaced with new ones, double-check the valve spring pressure to make sure they meet specifications. If you are reusing the existing valve springs and they passed this test earlier, continue on.

Valve	#1	#2	#3	#4	#5	#6	#7	#8
Intake (in/mm)								
Exhaust (in/mm)								

5. **Determine any necessary action(s):**

6. **Have your supervisor/instructor verify satisfactory completion of this procedure, any observations found, and any necessary action(s) recommended.**

> **NOTE** NATEF has not specified a task for reassembling the head(s). However, now would be a good time to do so. Follow the specified procedure to reassemble the head(s), but be sure to follow all the necessary precautions.

> **NOTE** Some overhead cam heads with bucket-style cam followers may need to have their valves adjusted at this point with the use of select fit shims. Check the service information to determine if this procedure is required for this engine. If so, adjust the valve at this time. Otherwise, valve adjustment will happen after the head and timing components have been installed.

Performance Rating

CDX Tasksheet Number: C721

0	1	2	3	4

Supervisor/instructor signature _____ Date _____

MAST
1B6

CDX Tasksheet Number: C677

Time off_____

Time on_____

Total time_____

> **NOTE** If not already done, install the timing components following the specified procedure, being careful to line up all timing marks. Also, ensure that all belts/chains are properly tensioned.

1. **Research the procedure and specifications to establish camshaft position indexing in the appropriate service information.**

   a. **List, or print off and attach to this sheet, the procedure for indexing the camshaft position sensor:**

2. **Following the specified procedure, index the camshaft position sensor. List your observation(s):**

3. **Have your supervisor/instructor verify satisfactory completion of this procedure, any observations found, and any necessary action(s) recommended.**

Performance Rating

CDX Tasksheet Number: C677

| 0 | 1 | 2 | 3 | 4 |

Supervisor/instructor signature _____ Date _____

Adjust valves (mechanical or hydraulic lifters).

Time off_____

Time on_____

CDX Tasksheet Number: C723

1. On a vehicle with adjustable valves, research the procedure and specifications for adjusting the valves in the appropriate service information.

   a. List the type of lifters this engine uses: Mechanical: _____
      Hydraulic: _____

Total time_____

   b. How are the valves adjusted on this engine?

   c. Specified valve clearance
      i. Intake: _____ in/mm @ _____ °F/°C
      ii. Exhaust: _____ in/mm @ _____ °F/°C

   d. Valve adjustment locknut torque, if equipped: _____ ft-lb/N·m

2. Following the specified procedure, adjust the valves to specification. List your observation(s):

3. Determine any necessary action(s):

4. Have your supervisor/instructor verify satisfactory completion of this procedure, any observations found, and any necessary action(s) recommended.

Performance Rating

CDX Tasksheet Number: C723

0	1	2	3	4

Supervisor/instructor signature _____ Date _____

Block Disassembly, Inspection, and Repair

Student/Intern information:

Name_____ Date_____ Class_____

Vehicle used for this activity:

Year _____ Make _____ Model_____

Odometer_____VIN_____

Time off_____

Time on_____

Total time_____

Learning Objective/Task	CDX Tasksheet Number	2017 MAST NATEF Reference Number; Priority Level
• Remove, inspect, and/or replace crankshaft vibration damper (harmonic balancer).	C679	1C1; P-1
• Disassemble engine block; clean and prepare components for inspection and reassembly.	C029	1C2; P-1
• Inspect engine block for visible cracks, passage condition, core and gallery plug condition, and surface warpage; determine needed action.	C030	1C3; P-2
• Inspect and measure cylinder walls/sleeves for damage, wear, and ridges; determine needed action.	C726	1C4; P-2
• Inspect and measure piston skirts and ring lands; determine needed action.	C678	1C10; P-2
• Deglaze and clean cylinder walls.	C727	1C5; P-2
• Inspect and measure camshaft bearings for wear, damage, out-of-round, and alignment; determine needed action.	C034	1C6; P-3
• Inspect auxiliary shaft(s) (balance, intermediate, idler, counterbalance, and/or silencer); inspect shaft(s) and support bearings for damage and wear; determine needed action; reinstall and time.	C730	1C13; P-2

Recommended Resource Materials

- CDX Automotive program
- Technical service bulletins, shop manuals, and any other information applicable to the specific vehicle or components you are working on
- Class notes

Materials Required

- Complete engine, simulator, or vehicle
- Harmonic balance puller

Some Safety Issues to Consider

- Lifting equipment such as engine hoists are important tools that increase productivity and make the job easier. However, they can also cause severe injury or death if used improperly. Make sure you follow the manufacturer's operation procedures.
- If using an engine stand, make sure the engine stand is rated for the weight of the engine you are mounting on it. Also, use bolts with the proper strength and length. Severe injury could occur if the engine were to fall due to failure of the engine stand or bolts.
- Compressed air can be very dangerous. Never blow it at someone. Never use it to remove dirt or dust from your skin or clothing. Never use it without an OSHA-approved nozzle.
- Comply with personal and environmental safety practices associated with clothing; eye protection; hand tools; power equipment; proper ventilation; and the handling, storage, and disposal of chemicals/materials in accordance with local, state, and federal safety and environmental regulations.

Performance Standard

0—No exposure: No information or practice provided during the program; complete training required

1—Exposure only: General information provided with no practice time; close supervision needed; additional training required

2—Limited practice: Has practiced job during training program; additional training required to develop skill

3—Moderately skilled: Has performed job independently during training program; limited additional training may be required

4—Skilled: Can perform job independently with no additional training

Remove, inspect, and/or replace crankshaft vibration damper
(harmonic balancer).

MAST
1C1

Time off_____

Time on_____

Total time_____

CDX Tasksheet Number: C679

1. **Research the procedure for removing and inspecting the crankshaft vibration damper in the appropriate service information.**

    a. **Specified crankshaft pulley bolt torque:** _____ **ft-lb/N·m**
    b. **List any special procedures or precautions related to the harmonic balancer:**

2. **Following the specified procedure, remove the harmonic balancer.**

3. **Following the specified procedure, inspect the harmonic balancer. List your observation(s):**

4. **Determine any necessary action(s):**

5. **Have your supervisor/instructor verify removal of the harmonic balancer and your answers. Supervisor/instructor:** _____

    NOTE You may want to continue on with the next task at this point. If so, return to this task after reinstalling the timing components.

6. **Following the specified procedure, reinstall the harmonic balancer.**

7. **Have your supervisor/instructor verify satisfactory completion of this procedure, any observations found, and any necessary action(s) recommended.**

Performance Rating

CDX Tasksheet Number: C679

0	1	2	3	4

Supervisor/instructor signature _____ Date _____

Disassemble engine block; clean and prepare components for inspection and reassembly.

CDX Tasksheet Number: C029

1. **Research the procedure and specifications for disassembling and inspecting the engine block in the appropriate service information.**

    a. **Print off the procedure for disassembling the block and attach it to this sheet.**

    b. **List the specification for crankshaft end play:** _____ **in/mm**

    NOTE Make sure the engine stand is rated for the weight of the engine you are mounting on it. Also, use bolts with the proper strength and length. Severe injury could occur if the engine were to fall due to failure of the engine stand or bolts.
    ---

2. **If not already completed, mount the engine block to an appropriate engine stand. This may require the removal of the flex plate or flywheel.**

3. **Following the specified procedure, measure the crankshaft end play:** _____ **in/mm**

4. **Disassemble the engine block assembly following the specified procedure. Be sure to label all parts to identify where they will be reinstalled. As the engine is being disassembled, visually inspect the parts for obvious damage. List your observation(s):**

    NOTE Be very careful not to damage or scratch any aluminum sealing surfaces since doing so could cause a leak. Do not use metal scrapers, wire brushes, or power abrasive disks to clean aluminum or plastic surfaces.
    ---

5. **Remove any gasket material still stuck to the sealing surfaces with an approved scraper.**

6. **Clean the parts in a safe and environmentally approved way. This is commonly performed in a hot water spray machine.**

7. Visually inspect all parts. List your observation(s):

8. Have your supervisor/instructor verify satisfactory completion of this procedure, any observations found, and any necessary action(s) recommended.

CDX Tasksheet Number: C029

0	1	2	3	4

Supervisor/instructor signature _____ Date _____

Inspect engine block for visible cracks, passage condition, core and gallery plug condition, and surface warpage; determine needed action.

MAST
1C3

CDX Tasksheet Number: C030

1. **Research the procedure and specifications for measuring the engine block for warpage in the appropriate service information.**

    a. **List the specification(s) for block deck warpage:**

2. **Following the specified procedure, carefully inspect the engine block for visible cracks (using magnaflux equipment or penetrating dyes). List your observation(s):**

3. **Inspect the condition of all passages. List your observation(s):**

> **NOTE** Core plugs are normally replaced during engine overhaul, so you may want to remove them at this time. Also, make sure the gallery plugs are removed for the cleaning process.

4. **Inspect the condition of core and gallery plugs. List your observation(s):**

5. Inspect all sealing surfaces for damage. List your observation(s):

6. Determine any necessary action(s):

7. Have your supervisor/instructor verify satisfactory completion of this procedure, any observations found, and any necessary action(s) recommended.

Performance Rating

CDX Tasksheet Number: C030

0	1	2	3	4

Supervisor/instructor signature _____ Date _____

▶ **TASK** Inspect and measure cylinder walls/sleeves for damage, wear, and ridges; determine needed action.

MAST
1C4

Time off_____

Time on_____

Total time_____

CDX Tasksheet Number: C726

1. Research the procedures and specifications for inspecting and measuring the cylinder walls/sleeves in the appropriate service information.

   a. Specified cylinder bore diameter: _____ in/mm
   b. Specified cylinder bore maximum out-of-round: _____ in/mm
   c. Specified cylinder bore maximum taper: _____ in/mm

2. Following the specified procedure, carefully measure the diameter and the maximum out-of-round diameter for each cylinder bore. List your measurements in the table below.

Cylinder	#1	#2	#3	#4	#5	#6	#7	#8
Top (in/mm)								
Bottom (in/mm)								
Taper (in/mm)								
Out-of-round (in/mm)								

3. Following the specified procedure, carefully inspect the cylinder walls/sleeves for damage, wear, and ridges. List your observation(s):

4. Determine any necessary action(s):

5. Have your supervisor/instructor verify satisfactory completion of this procedure, any observations found, and any necessary action(s) recommended.

Performance Rating

CDX Tasksheet Number: C726

0	1	2	3	4

Supervisor/instructor signature _____ Date _____

Engine Repair **149**

Inspect and measure piston skirts and ring lands; determine needed action.

CDX Tasksheet Number: C678

1. **Research the procedures and specifications for inspecting and measuring the piston skirts and ring lands in the appropriate service information.**

    a. **Specified piston skirt diameter:** _____ in/mm
    b. **Specified piston ring groove width**

       i. **Compression (top):** _____ in/mm

       ii. **Compression (bottom):** _____ in/mm

       iii. **Oil:** _____ in/mm

    c. **Specified piston-to-cylinder clearance:** _____ in/mm

2. **Inspect the piston surfaces for obvious signs of damage. List your observation(s):**

3. **Following the specified procedure, carefully measure the diameter, the piston-to-cylinder clearance, and the piston ring groove width (for top compression, bottom compression, and oil rings). List your measurements in the table below.**

Piston	#1	#2	#3	#4	#5	#6	#7	#8
Diameter (in/mm)								
Clearance (in/mm)								
Groove width (top) (in/mm)								
Groove width (bottom) (in/mm)								
Groove width (oil) (in/mm)								

4. **Are the pistons within specified tolerance? Yes: _____ No: _____**

    a. **Why or why not?**

5. **Determine any necessary action(s):**

6. Have your supervisor/instructor verify satisfactory completion of this procedure, any observations found, and any necessary action(s) recommended.

Performance Rating

0	1	2	3	4

Supervisor/instructor signature _____ Date _____

Deglaze and clean cylinder walls.

Time off_____

Time on_____

Total time_____

CDX Tasksheet Number: C727

> **NOTE** This task should be performed only on engines that are not going to be machined over-size. Have your supervisor approve this task based on the results of the previous tasks before you continue.

1. **Is this cylinder block a good candidate for the deglazing process?**
   Yes: _____ No: _____

2. **Do you have your supervisor's approval for this task? Yes: _____ No: _____**

3. **Research the procedures and specifications for deglazing the cylinder walls.**
   a. **Specified coarseness of stones/ball hone:** _____
   b. **Specified deglazing lubricant:** _____
   c. **Specified crosshatch angle/pattern:** _____
   d. **Specified cleaning process after deglazing:** _____

4. **Following the specified procedure, carefully deglaze the cylinder walls using the appropriate honing/deglazing equipment.**

5. **Use the specified cleaning process to clean the cylinder walls and block.**

6. **Inspect the surface of the cylinders for proper deglazing finish. List your observation(s):**

7. **Have your supervisor/instructor verify satisfactory completion of this procedure, any observations found, and any necessary action(s) recommended.**

Performance Rating

CDX Tasksheet Number: C727

0	1	2	3	4

Supervisor/instructor signature _____ Date _____

► TASK Inspect and measure camshaft bearings for wear, damage, out-of-round, and alignment; determine needed action.

MAST
1C6

Time off_____

Time on_____

Total time_____

CDX Tasksheet Number: C034

> NOTE Perform this task only if the engine is a cam-in-block design. If it is an overhead cam design, the camshaft bearings are inspected during the Cylinder Head Disassembly, Inspection, and Repair tasksheet.

1. **Research the procedures and specifications for inspecting and measuring the camshaft bearings in the appropriate service information.**

    a. **Specified camshaft bearing inside diameter:** _____ in/mm
    b. **Specified camshaft journal diameter:** _____ in/mm
    c. **Specified camshaft journal bearing clearance:** _____ in/mm
    d. **Specified camshaft journal out-of-round (max):** _____ in/mm

2. **Inspect the condition of the cam lobes for excessive wear or damage. List your observation(s):**

3. **Measure the inside diameter of the camshaft bearings and the outside diameter of the cam journals. Calculate the bearing clearance and measure the maximum out-of-round reading for each camshaft journal. List your measurements in the table below.**

Cam Bearing or Journal	#1	#2	#3	#4	#5
Cam bearing diameter (in/mm)					
Cam journal diameter (in/mm)					
Bearing clearance (in/mm)					
Out-of-round (in/mm)					

4. **Inspect the bearings and journals for evidence of damage, wear, and misalignment. List your observation(s):**

5. **Determine any necessary action(s):**

6. Have your supervisor/instructor verify satisfactory completion of this procedure, any observations found, and any necessary action(s) recommended.

Performance Rating

CDX Tasksheet Number: C034

0	1	2	3	4

Supervisor/instructor signature _____ Date _____

Inspect auxiliary shaft(s) (balance, intermediate, idler, counterbalance, and/or silencer); inspect shaft(s) and support bearings for damage and wear; determine needed action; reinstall and time.

CDX Tasksheet Number: C730

1. **Research the procedures and specifications to inspect any auxiliary shaft(s) and support bearings in the appropriate service information.**

   a. **List the type of shaft(s) this engine is equipped with:**

   b. **List any appropriate specification(s):**

   c. **List, or print off and attach to this sheet, the installation and timing procedure:**

2. **Inspect the auxiliary shaft(s) and support bearings. List your observation(s):**

3. Determine any necessary action(s):

4. Have your supervisor/instructor check your answers.
   Supervisor/instructor initials: _____

5. Following the specified procedure, reinstall and time the auxiliary shaft(s).

6. Have your supervisor/instructor verify satisfactory completion of this procedure, any observations found, and any necessary action(s) recommended.

Performance Rating

CDX Tasksheet Number: C730

0	1	2	3	4

Supervisor/instructor signature _____ Date _____

Crankshaft and Oil Pump Service

Student/Intern information:

Name_____ Date_____ Class_____

Vehicle used for this activity:

Year_____ Make_____ Model_____

Odometer_____VIN_____

Time off_____

Time on_____

Total time_____

Learning Objective/Task	CDX Tasksheet Number	2017 MAST NATEF Reference Number; Priority Level
• Inspect crankshaft for straightness, journal damage, keyway damage, thrust flange and sealing surface condition, and visual surface cracks; check oil passage condition; measure end play and journal wear; check crankshaft position sensor reluctor ring (where applicable); determine needed action.	C728	1C7; P-1
• Inspect main and connecting rod bearings for damage and wear; determine needed action.	C036	1C8; P-2
• Identify piston and bearing wear patterns that indicate connecting rod alignment and main bearing bore problems; determine needed action.	C729	1C9; P-3
• Inspect oil pump gears or rotors, housing, pressure relief devices, and pump drive; perform needed action.	C733	1D13; P-2

Materials Required

- Engine block, crankshaft, and oil pump
- Engine stand
- Dial indicator
- Straightedge and feeler blade set
- Inside and outside micrometer sets
- Dial bore gauge set

Some Safety Issues to Consider

- Compressed air can be very dangerous. Never blow it at someone. Never use it to remove dirt or dust from your skin or clothing. Never use it without an OSHA-approved nozzle.
- Make sure the engine stand is rated for the weight of the engine you are mounting on it. Also, use bolts with the proper strength and length. Severe injury could occur if the engine were to fall due to failure of the engine stand or bolts.
- Engine castings and parts can have sharp edges. Always exercise extreme caution when working around them. Also, the parts are relatively heavy and can cause serious pinching of fingers. Be careful when handling them.

- Comply with personal and environmental safety practices associated with clothing; eye protection; hand tools; power equipment; proper ventilation; and the handling, storage, and disposal of chemicals/materials in accordance with local, state, and federal safety and environmental regulations.

Performance Standard

0–No exposure: No information or practice provided during the program; complete training required

1–Exposure only: General information provided with no practice time; close supervision needed; additional training required

2–Limited practice: Has practiced job during training program; additional training required to develop skill

3–Moderately skilled: Has performed job independently during training program; limited additional training may be required

4–Skilled: Can perform job independently with no additional training

> **NOTE** In order to easily compare specifications to measurements, space has been provided in each of the sections below to write the specifications.

► **TASK** Inspect crankshaft for straightness, journal damage, keyway damage, thrust flange and sealing surface condition, and visual surface cracks; check oil passage condition; measure end play and journal wear; check crankshaft position sensor reluctor ring (where applicable); determine needed action.

MAST
1C7

Time off_____

Time on_____

Total time_____

CDX Tasksheet Number: C728

1. **Research the procedure and specifications for inspecting the crankshaft and related parts in the appropriate service information.**

2. **Following the specified procedure, measure the crankshaft run-out (straightness).**

   a. **Specs:** _____ in/mm
   b. **Measurement:** _____ in/mm

3. **Following the specified procedure, visually inspect the following for damage, wear, or cracks. List your observations.**

   a. **Crankshaft main bearing journals: Worn _____ Damaged _____ Cracks _____ OK _____ (Check any that apply) Comments:**

   b. **Crankshaft rod bearing journals: Worn _____ Damaged _____ Cracks _____ OK _____ (Check any that apply) Comments:**

   c. **Crankshaft keyway: Worn _____ Damaged _____ Cracks _____ OK _____ (Check any that apply) Comments:**

   d. **Thrust flange: Worn _____ Damaged _____ Cracks _____ OK _____ (Check any that apply) Comments:**

   e. **Rear main bearing sealing surface: Worn _____ Damaged _____ Cracks _____ OK _____ (Check any that apply) Comments:**

f. Oil passages: Worn _____ Damaged _____ Cracks _____ OK _____
(Check any that apply) Comments:

g. Crankshaft position sensor reluctor ring: Worn _____ Damaged _____
Cracks _____ OK _____ (Check any that apply) Comments:

4. Following the specified procedure, measure the crankshaft main bearing journals.
List your measurements in the table below.

Journal	Specs	#1	#2	#3	#4	#5	#6
Diameter (in/mm)							
Out-of-round (in/mm)							
Taper (in/mm)							

5. Following the specified procedure, measure the crankshaft connecting rod
journals. List your measurements in the table below.

Journal	Specs	#1	#2	#3	#4	#5	#6	#7	#8
Diameter (in/mm)									
Out-of-round (in/mm)									
Taper (in/mm)									

6. Determine any necessary action(s):

7. Have your supervisor/instructor verify satisfactory completion of this
procedure, any observations found, and any necessary action(s) recommended.

Performance Rating

CDX Tasksheet Number: C728

0	1	2	3	4

Supervisor/instructor signature _____ Date _____

Inspect main and connecting rod bearings for damage and wear; determine needed action.

MAST
1C8

Time off_____

Time on_____

Total time_____

CDX Tasksheet Number: CO36

1. **Research the procedure and specifications for inspecting the main and connecting rod bearings in the appropriate service information.**

    a. **List, or print off and attach to this sheet, the faults and wear patterns for the various bearing issues:**

2. **Following the specified procedure, inspect the main and connecting rod bearings. List your observations:**

3. **Determine any necessary action(s):**

4. **Have your supervisor/instructor verify satisfactory completion of this procedure, any observations found, and any necessary action(s) recommended.**

Performance Rating

CDX Tasksheet Number: CO36

0	1	2	3	4

Supervisor/instructor signature _____ Date _____

Identify piston and bearing wear patterns that indicate connecting rod alignment and main bearing bore problems; determine needed action.

MAST
1C9

CDX Tasksheet Number: C729

1. **Research the procedure and specifications for inspecting the piston and bearing wear patterns in the appropriate service information.**

   a. **List, or print off and attach to this sheet, the faults and wear patterns for the various connecting rod and main bearing bore issues:**

2. **Following the specified procedure, visually inspect the pistons and bearings for abnormal wear patterns. List your observations:**

3. **Determine any necessary action(s):**

4. **Have your supervisor/instructor verify satisfactory completion of this procedure, any observations found, and any necessary action(s) recommended.**

Performance Rating

CDX Tasksheet Number: C729

0	1	2	3	4

Supervisor/instructor signature _____ Date _____

MAST
1D13

Time off_____

Time on_____

Total time_____

CDX Tasksheet Number: C733

1. **Research the procedure and specifications to disassemble and inspect the oil pump in the appropriate service information.**

    a. Type of oil pump: _____

    b. Regulated oil pressure: _____ psi/kPa

    c. List, or print off and attach to this sheet, the specified clearances for this pump:

2. **Following the specified procedure, disassemble the pump and visually inspect the parts (including the pressure relief device and pump drive). List your observation(s):**

3. **Following the specified procedure, measure the pump clearances. List your findings:**

4. **Determine any necessary action(s):**

5. **Have your supervisor/instructor verify satisfactory completion of this procedure, any observations found, and any necessary action(s) recommended.**

Performance Rating

CDX Tasksheet Number: C733

0	1	2	3	4

Supervisor/instructor signature _____ Date _____

Assemble Engine Block

Student/Intern information:

Name_____ Date_____ Class_____

Vehicle used for this activity:

Year_____ Make_____ Model_____

Odometer_____VIN_____

Time off_____

Time on_____

Total time_____

Learning Objective/Task	CDX Tasksheet Number	2017 MAST NATEF Reference Number; Priority Level
• Verify engine mechanical timing.	C899	1A6; P-1
• Inspect and replace camshaft and drive belt/chain; (includes checking drive gear wear and backlash, endplay, sprocket and chain wear, overhead cam drive sprocket[s], drive belt[s], belt tension, tensioners, camshaft reluctor ring/tone-wheel, and valve timing components); verify correct camshaft timing.	C676	1B5; P-1
• Determine piston-to-bore clearance.	C597	1C11; P-2
• Inspect, measure, and install piston rings.	C040	1C12; P-2
• Assemble engine block.	C731	1C14; P-1

Materials Required

- Engine block, pistons, and piston rings
- Engine stand
- Feeler blade set
- Inside and outside micrometer sets
- Torque wrench
- Plastigauge®
- Piston ring compressor

Some Safety Issues to Consider

- Make sure the engine stand is rated for the weight of the engine you are mounting on it. Also, use bolts with the proper strength and length. Severe injury could occur if the engine were to fall due to failure of the engine stand or bolts.
- Engine castings and parts can have sharp edges. Always exercise extreme caution when working around them. Also, the parts are relatively heavy and can cause serious pinching of fingers. Be careful when handling them.
- Comply with personal and environmental safety practices associated with clothing; eye protection; hand tools; power equipment; proper ventilation; and the handling, storage, and disposal of chemicals/materials in accordance with local, state, and federal safety and environmental regulations.

Performance Standard

0—No exposure: No information or practice provided during the program; complete training required

1—Exposure only: General information provided with no practice time; close supervision needed; additional training required

2—Limited practice: Has practiced job during training program; additional training required to develop skill

3—Moderately skilled: Has performed job independently during training program; limited additional training may be required

4—Skilled: Can perform job independently with no additional training

Time off_____

Time on_____

Total time_____

DX Tasksheet Number: C899

1. Research the procedure and specifications for inspecting and replacing the timing belt components in the appropriate service information.

    a. List the recommended change interval for the timing belt:
        _____ mi/km

    b. List the flat rate time for removing and replacing the timing belt:
        _____ hrs

    c. What other components does the manufacturer recommend changing at the same time as the timing belt?

    d. List or print off and attach the steps for removing and replacing the timing belt:

        i. Supervisor's/instructor's initials verifying approval to remove this timing belt: _____

2. With your instructor's permission, and following the specified steps, remove the timing belt.

3. Inspect the belt, pulleys, tensioner, cam seals, and water pump. List your observations for each:

4. Have your instructor verify removal of the timing belt and your observations:
    _____

5. Following the specified procedure, reinstall the timing belt, making sure the timing marks are properly aligned and the belt is properly tensioned. Do not install the timing cover yet.

6. Have your instructor verify installation of the timing belt and camshaft timing:

   _____

7. Reassemble any removed components and belts being careful to properly tighten all fasteners and accessory drive belts.

8. When everything is back together, carefully turn the engine by hand (ignition key off) at least two complete turns to verify there isn't a piston-to-valve interference.

9. If the engine turns over properly, start the engine, verify it is running properly, and make any timing or other adjustments.

10. Have your supervisor/instructor verify satisfactory completion of this procedure, any observations found, and any necessary action(s) recommended.

Performance Rating

CDX Tasksheet Number: C899

0	1	2	3	4

Supervisor/instructor signature _____ Date _____

Inspect and replace camshaft and drive belt/chain
(includes checking drive gear wear and backlash,
endplay, sprocket and chain wear, overhead cam drive
sprocket[s], drive belt[s], belt tension, tensioners, camshaft
reluctor ring/tone-wheel, and variable valve timing
components); verify correct camshaft timing.

MAST
1B5

Time off_____

Time on_____

Total time_____

CDX Tasksheet Number: C676

1. **Research the procedure and specifications for inspecting and replacing the camshaft and timing components in the appropriate service information.**

    a. **Type of cam drive system used:** _____

    b. **Is this engine equipped with variable valve timing? Yes:** _____
       No: _____

    c. **Camshaft endplay:** _____ in/mm

    d. **Camshaft drive gear backlash, if equipped:** _____ in/mm

    e. **List or print off and attach to this sheet any precautions when performing this task:**

    f. **List or print off and attach to this sheet any measurement and torque specifications for this task:**

2. **Following the specified procedure, remove any timing belt/chain covers. Visually inspect the installed timing components, including belt/chain tensioner. List your observations:**

3. **Following the specified procedure, disassemble the cam drive system. Clean all gasket surfaces.**

4. **Inspect the condition of the following components, if equipped, and list your observations:**

    a. **Timing belt/chain:** _____

    b. **Sprockets:**_____

    c. **Belt/chain tensioners:** _____

    d. Camshaft endplay: _____ in/mm

    e. Camshaft drive-gear backlash: _____ in/mm

    f. Camshaft reluctor ring/tone-wheel: _____

    g. Crank and cam oil seals: _____

    h. Water pump: _____

    i. Variable valve timing components: _____

5. Determine any necessary action(s):

6. Have your instructor verify removal of the timing components and your observations: _____

7. Following the specified procedure, reinstall the timing components, making sure the timing marks are properly aligned and the belt or chain is properly tensioned. Do not install the timing cover yet.

8. Have your instructor verify installation of the timing components and camshaft timing: _____

9. Reassemble any removed components and belts, being careful to properly tighten all fasteners and accessory drive belts.

10. When everything is back together, carefully turn the engine by hand (ignition key off) at least two complete turns to verify there isn't a piston-to-valve interference.

11. If the engine turns over properly, start the engine, verify it is running properly, and make any timing or other adjustments.

12. Have your supervisor/instructor verify satisfactory completion of this procedure, any observations found, and any necessary action(s) recommended.

Performance Rating

CDX Tasksheet Number: C676

0	1	2	3	4

Supervisor/instructor signature _____ Date _____

MAST
1C11

DX Tasksheet Number: C597

1. Research the procedure and specifications for determining the piston-to-bore clearance in the appropriate service information.

    a. Specified piston-to-bore clearance: _____ in/mm

2. Ensure the cylinder block is thoroughly cleaned according to the manufacturer's recommended procedure and is properly protected from rust and/or corrosion.

3. If the pistons have been replaced, follow the specified procedure to measure the piston-to-bore clearance for each piston and cylinder. List your measurements in the table below. If the bore and pistons are being reused, transfer the measurements from task C678, inspect and measure piston skirts and ring lands; determine needed action.

Cylinder	#1	#2	#3	#4	#5	#6	#7	#8
Piston-to-bore clearance (in/mm)								

4. Is the piston-to-bore clearance within the specified tolerance?
   Yes: _____ No: _____

5. Have your supervisor/instructor verify satisfactory completion of this procedure, any observations found, and any necessary action(s) recommended.

Performance Rating

CDX Tasksheet Number: C597

0	1	2	3	4

Supervisor/instructor signature _____ Date _____

MAST
1C12

DX Tasksheet Number: C040

1. **Research the procedure and specifications for inspecting, measuring, and installing piston rings in the appropriate service information.**

   a. **Specified piston ring end gap**

      i.   **Top compression ring:** _____ in/mm
      ii. **Bottom compression ring:** _____ in/mm
      iii. **Oil ring:** _____ in/mm

   b. **List the markings or ring configuration that determine which side of the ring goes up.**

      i.   **Top compression ring:** _____
      ii. **Bottom compression ring:** _____
      iii. **Oil ring:** _____

   c. **Draw, or print off and attach to this sheet, the specified position of each piston ring gap when installed on the piston:**

2. **Following the specified procedure, measure the piston ring end gap for each cylinder. List in the table below.**

Cylinder	#1	#2	#3	#4	#5	#6	#7	#8
Top compression ring (in/mm)								
Bottom compression ring (in/mm)								
Oil ring (in/mm)								

   a. **Do all of the piston ring end gaps meet specifications?**
      Yes: _____ **No:** _____

3. **If the end gaps meet specifications, install piston rings on each piston. Be sure each ring is placed in the proper ring groove and is installed with the correct side up and in the correct orientation around the piston.**

4. **Determine any necessary action(s):**

5. Have your supervisor/instructor verify satisfactory completion of this procedure, any observations found, and any necessary action(s) recommended.

Performance Rating

CDX Tasksheet Number: C040

0	1	2	3	4

Supervisor/instructor signature _____ Date _____

DX Tasksheet Number: C731

> **NOTE** Due to the differences in assembly procedures and specifications, it is recommended that the specified procedure and specifications be printed out and followed exactly.

> **NOTE** Most measurements were taken during the engine disassembly process to determine the necessary actions. Now that the engine is ready to be reassembled, all measurements need to be repeated to verify that parts are within their specified tolerances. Use the Engine Build Sheet to record all of your measurements. When provided to customers, it lends a touch of professionalism to the job.

1. **Reassemble the engine block following all manufacturer specifications and procedures. List the specifications in the CDX Engine Build/Spec Sheet. Be sure to verify the following information.**

   a. **Make sure the camshaft turns freely. If not, check for proper installation of the cam bearings.**
   b. **Check all oil gallery plugs, and make sure they are tightened/installed properly.**
   c. **Check all water jacket soft plugs for proper installation.**
   d. **Check crankshaft main journals for proper clearance, and record on the Engine Build/Spec Sheet.**
   e. **Check crankshaft end play, and record on the Engine Build/Spec Sheet.**
   f. **Clean and lubricate the cylinder walls. Lubricate the pistons and piston rings.**
   g. **Install the pistons with the rings in the proper orientation.**
   h. **Measure the connecting rod bearing clearance, and record on the Engine Build/Spec Sheet.**
   i. **Pack the oil pump with the proper lubricant and install the pump.**

2. **Once the block is assembled, list any observation(s):**

3. Have your supervisor/instructor verify satisfactory completion of this procedure, any observations found, and any necessary action(s) recommended.

> **NOTE** Once the block is assembled, return to the Cylinder Head Disassembly, Inspection, and Repair tasksheet to continue with the installation of the cylinder heads and valve timing components.

Performance Rating

CDX Tasksheet Number: C731

0	1	2	3	4

Supervisor/instructor signature _____ Date _____

Engine Build/Spec Sheet

Year_____ Make_____ Engine size_____

> **NOTE** Bolt Torque–Print out all bolt torque specifications and check them off as you torque each item. Record all measurements on the spec sheet for archival purposes.

Valve guide inside diameter		Valve spring seat pressure	
Valve stem diameter		Valve spring open pressure	
Valve stem clearance		Coil bind	
Valve adjustment intake		Cylinder head torque	
Valve adjustment exhaust		Camshaft cap torque	
Valve stem installed height		Cam bolt torque	

Piston Clearance

Piston	#1	#2	#3	#4	#5	#6	#7	#8
Cylinder bore								
Piston diameter								
Clearance								

Piston-to-valve clearance: Intake: _____ Exhaust: _____
Engine displacement: _____ (Bore^2) $\times$ 0.785 = _____ $\times$
_____ (Stroke) = _____ ci cylinder displacement $\times$ _____
(# of Cylinders) = _____ ci engine displacement

Ring Gap

Cylinder	#1	#2	#3	#4	#5	#6	#7	#8
#1 Compression ring								
#2 Compression ring								
Oil control ring								

Crankshaft Main Journal and Bearing Measurements

Main Bearing	#1	#2	#3	#4	#5	#6
Main bearings (inside diameter)						
Crankshaft mains (outside diameter)						
Clearance						
Plastigauge®						

Crankshaft end play: _____   Main cap torque: _____

Connecting Rod Journal and Bearing Measurements

Connecting Rod	#1	#2	#3	#4	#5	#6	#7	#8
Rod bearing (inside diameter)								
Rod journal (outside diameter)								
Clearance								
Plastigauge®								

Rod side clearance: _____ _____ _____ _____

Rod cap torque: _____ Wrist pin clearance: _____

Build Sheet Parts List

Gasket set brand/part number (PN) _____

Cylinder head brand/PN _____

Intake valve brand/PN _____

Exhaust valve brand/PN _____

Valve guides brand/PN _____

Valve springs brand/PN _____

Valve retainers brand/PN _____

Valve keepers brand/PN _____

Pistons brand/PN _____

Rings brand/PN _____

Crankshaft brand/PN _____

Main bearings brand/PN _____

Rod bearings brand/PN _____

Wrist pin bushings brand/PN _____

Oil pump brand/PN _____

Connecting rod brand/PN _____

Camshaft brand/PN _____

Camshaft duration at 0.050 lift _____

Camshaft centerline degrees _____

Lifters brand/PN _____

Cam bearings brand/PN _____

Timing set brand/PN _____

Intake manifold brand/PN _____

Notes:

Miscellaneous In-Vehicle Engine Tasks

Student/Intern information:

Name _____ Date _____ Class _____

Vehicle used for this activity:

Year _____ Make _____ Model _____

Odometer _____ VIN _____

Learning Objective/Task	CDX Tasksheet Number	2017 MAST NATEF Reference Number; Priority Level
• Install engine covers using gaskets, seals, and sealers as required.	C541	1A5; P-1
• Inspect, remove, and/or replace engine mounts.	C596	1A8; P-2
• Replace valve stem seals on an assembled engine; inspect valve spring retainers, locks/keepers, and valve lock/keeper grooves; determine needed action.	C675	1B8; P-3

Time off _____

Time on _____

Total time _____

Materials Required

- Vehicle
- Gasket scraper (nonabrasive for aluminum and plastic surfaces)
- Seal pullers and installers
- Vehicle hoist
- Engine support or transmission jack
- Valve spring compressor
- Cylinder leakage tester

Some Safety Issues to Consider

- Lifting equipment such as engine hoists are important tools that increase productivity and make the job easier. However, they can also cause severe injury or death if used improperly. Make sure you follow the manufacturer's operation procedures.
- This procedure will require cleaning the components. Use the proper personal protective equipment for the chemicals and processes used.
- Engine castings and parts can have sharp edges. Always exercise extreme caution when working around them. Also, the parts are relatively heavy and can cause serious pinching of fingers. Be careful when handling them.
- Diagnosis of this fault may require test-driving the vehicle on the school grounds. Attempt this task only with full permission from your instructor and follow all the guidelines exactly.
- Comply with personal and environmental safety practices associated with clothing; eye protection; hand tools; power equipment; proper ventilation; and the handling, storage, and disposal of chemicals/materials in accordance with local, state, and federal safety and environmental regulations.

Performance Standard

0—No exposure: No information or practice provided during the program; complete training required

1—Exposure only: General information provided with no practice time; close supervision needed; additional training required

2—Limited practice: Has practiced job during training program; additional training required to develop skill

3—Moderately skilled: Has performed job independently during training program; limited additional training may be required

4—Skilled: Can perform job independently with no additional training

Time off_____

Time on_____

Total time_____

CDX Tasksheet Number: C541

> **NOTE** This task may be completed as part of an engine rebuild or done separately on another vehicle.

1. **List the gaskets and/or seals you are installing:**

2. **Research the procedure and specifications for the gaskets and/or seals you are removing/installing in the appropriate service information.**

   a. **List the recommended sealant required for each gasket/seal, if needed:**

   b. **List or print off and attach to this sheet any torque specifications for the cover(s) you are removing:**

3. **Following the specified procedure, remove the appropriate engine cover.**

4. **Remove any seals and gasket material with the proper tools. Be careful not to gouge or damage the surfaces being cleaned. Also, prepare the sealing surfaces for cover reinstallation according to the service information. List your observation(s):**

5. Have your supervisor/instructor verify that the cover is ready to be reinstalled. Supervisor's/instructor's initials: _____

6. Reinstall the cover following the specified procedure. Torque all fasteners to the proper torque and check for any leakage.

7. Have your supervisor/instructor verify satisfactory completion of this procedure, any observations found, and any necessary action(s) recommended.

Performance Rating

CDX Tasksheet Number: C541

0	1	2	3	4

Supervisor/instructor signature _____ Date _____

MAST
1A8

Time off_____

Time on_____

Total time_____

CDX Tasksheet Number: C596

1. **Research the procedure to inspect and replace the engine mounts in the appropriate service information.**

    a. **List the type of engine mount this vehicle uses:** _____

    b. **List or print off and attach to this sheet the precautions for performing this task:**

    c. **List or print off and attach to this sheet the procedure for inspecting the engine mounts:**

2. **Following the specified procedure, inspect the engine mounts and list your observations:**

3. **Determine any necessary action(s):**

4. **Have your supervisor/instructor verify your answers and initial if correct. Supervisor's/instructor's initials:** _____

5. **With your instructor's permission, remove one or more engine mounts following the specified procedure. Inspect the removed engine mount(s) and list your observations:**

6. Have your supervisor/instructor verify the removal of the mount. Supervisor's/instructor's initials: _____

7. Reinstall the engine mount(s) according to the specified procedure.

8. Determine any necessary action(s):

9. Have your supervisor/instructor verify satisfactory completion of this procedure, any observations found, and any necessary action(s) recommended.

Performance Rating

CDX Tasksheet Number: C596

0	1	2	3	4

Supervisor/instructor signature _____ Date _____

Replace valve stem seals on an assembled engine; inspect valve
spring retainers, locks/keepers, and valve lock/keeper
grooves; determine needed action.

MAST
1B8

Time off_____

Time on_____

Total time_____

CDX Tasksheet Number: C675

1. **Research the procedures and specifications for replacing the valve stem seals while the engine is installed in the vehicle in the appropriate service information.**

   a. **List, or print off and attach to this sheet, the precautions for performing this task:**

   b. **List the type of valve seals this engine is equipped with:** _____

   c. **List the flat rate time to perform this task:** _____ hr

   d. **List the special tools required to perform this task:**

2. **Have your supervisor/instructor verify your answers and initial. Supervisor/ instructor's initials:** _____

3. **Following the specified procedure, prepare the engine for removal of the valve spring keepers and retainer by removing the valve cover and rocker arm or cam follower (some engines may require removal of the cam).**

4. **With the valve firmly held in place with compressed air, tap the valve retainer with a hammer and socket to break the bond between the retainer and keepers. Tap in line with the valve stem; do not tap sideways because that could bend the valve stem.**

5. **Install the valve spring compressor and compress the valve spring. Remove the keepers; be sure not to let them fall into the engine. Remove the valve spring and retainer.**

6. **Check to see if there is a burr on the valve stem near the keeper groove. File it smooth if necessary. Remove the old valve seal. Install the new valve seal according to the specified procedure. This may include using a sleeve that fits over the valve stem to protect the valve seal during installation. Also lubricate the seal before installation. And make sure it is fully seated if it is of the positive seal type.**

7. Reinstall the valve spring, retainer, and keepers. Be sure to seat the keepers fully in the valve stem groove.

8. Have your supervisor/instructor verify correct installation of the valve seals and springs. Supervisor/instructor's initials: _____

9. Reinstall the removed valve cover(s) and other parts.

10. Start the engine and verify correct operation.

11. Have your supervisor/instructor verify satisfactory completion of this procedure, any observations found, and any necessary action(s) recommended.

Performance Rating

CDX Tasksheet Number: C675

0	1	2	3	4

Supervisor/instructor signature _____ Date _____

Lubrication System Service

Student/Intern information:

Name_____ Date_____ Class_____

Vehicle used for this activity:

Year_____ Make_____ Model_____

Odometer_____VIN_____

Time off_____

Time on_____

Total time_____

Learning Objective/Task	CDX Tasksheet Number	2017 MAST NATEF Reference Number; Priority Level
• Perform engine oil and filter change; use proper fluid type per manufacturer specification.	C737	1D10; P-1
• Perform oil pressure tests; determine needed action.	C732	1D9; P-1
• Inspect, test, and replace oil temperature and pressure switches and sensors.	C736	1D12; P-2

Materials Required

- Vehicle or simulator
- Vehicle hoist
- Exhaust hose(s)
- Drain pan
- Wheel chocks
- Oil-change sticker
- Remote oil pressure gauge
- Oil pressure-sensor socket
- DVOM/DMM

Some Safety Issues to Consider

- Changing oil on a hot engine can lead to burns. Always be careful to avoid hot engine oil.
- Used engine oil contains cancer-causing agents. Always avoid oil contact with your hands. Always wash your hands after completing this task.
- Vehicle hoists are important tools that increase productivity and make the job easier. However, they can also cause severe injury or death if used improperly. Make sure you follow the hoist's and vehicle manufacturer's operation procedures. Also, make sure you have your supervisor's/instructor's permission to use a vehicle hoist.
- Comply with personal and environmental safety practices associated with clothing; eye protection; hand tools; power equipment; proper ventilation; and the handling, storage, and disposal of chemicals/materials in accordance with local, state, and federal safety and environmental regulations.

Performance Standard

0–No exposure: No information or practice provided during the program; complete training required

1–Exposure only: General information provided with no practice time; close supervision needed; additional training required

2–Limited practice: Has practiced job during training program; additional training required to develop skill

3–Moderately skilled: Has performed job independently during training program; limited additional training may be required

4–Skilled: Can perform job independently with no additional training

► **TASK** Perform engine oil and filter change; use proper fluid type per manufacturer specification.

Time off_____

Time on_____

Total time_____

CDX Tasksheet Number: C737

1. **Research the following specifications/procedures for this vehicle in the appropriate service information.**

    a. **Oil capacity:** _____ qt/lt

    b. **Oil viscosity:** _____

    c. **API or other specified rating:** _____

    d. **Oil pan drain plug torque:** _____ ft-lb/N·m

    e. **Oil filter part number:** _____

    f. **List any special requirements/procedures for changing the oil and filter on this vehicle:**

NOTE Some vehicles have more than one oil drain plug and/or a special procedure for changing the filter.

---

    g. **Determine that a new filter, and the proper oil, is available for this vehicle before proceeding.   Yes:** _____ **No:** _____

2. **Safely raise and secure the vehicle on a hoist.**

NOTE Removing the oil filler cap may allow the oil to drain faster.

---

3. **Follow the specified procedure for draining the used oil and removing the old oil filter.**

NOTE The oil may be extremely hot. Be sure not to come into contact with the used oil.

---

    a. **Is the drain plug gasket reusable? Yes:** _____ **No:** _____

    b. **Did the oil filter gasket come off with the oil filter? Yes:** _____
       No: _____

    c. **Have your instructor verify these answers by initialing here:** _____

4. **Once the used oil has been drained, follow the manufacturer's procedure for installing the new oil filter (oil the gasket) and reinstalling the drain plug (tighten to the specified torque).**

5. **Lower the vehicle.**

6. **Following the appropriate service information, add the proper amount of new oil.**

7. Prepare to start the vehicle by applying the parking brake and placing exhaust hoses over the exhaust pipe(s). Start the vehicle and check for oil leaks. If oil leaks are found, shut off the engine immediately, locate the source of the leak, and inform your instructor. If no leaks are found, shut off the engine after a minute or two of running.

8. Let the engine oil drain back into the oil pan for a few minutes and then check to see that the oil is at the proper level. Add oil if necessary.

   a. What is the final oil level? _____

9. Dispose of the old oil and filter according to legislative guidelines (national, federal, state, and local).

10. Reset the maintenance reminder system if equipped, or fill out an oil-change reminder sticker and place it on the vehicle according to your shop's policy.

11. Have your supervisor/instructor verify satisfactory completion of this procedure, any observations found, and any necessary action(s) recommended.

Performance Rating

0	1	2	3	4

Supervisor/instructor signature _____ Date _____

CDX Tasksheet Number: C732

1. Research the following specifications/procedures for this vehicle in the appropriate service information.
   a. Oil pressure specification(s): _____
   b. List or print off and attach to this sheet the procedure for performing the oil pressure test:

2. Using the appropriate tools, remove the oil pressure switch/sensor from the engine block and install the mechanical oil pressure gauge fitting to the place where the switch was fitted. Place the gauge in a position where you can easily view it, but out of the way of any moving parts, exhaust pipes, etc.

3. Prepare to start the vehicle by applying the parking brake and placing exhaust hoses over the exhaust pipe(s).

4. With a relatively cold engine, start the car and note the pressure gauge reading at idle: _____ psi/kPa

5. Increase the engine speed and watch the pressure gauge reading. Note the cold readings below.
   a. @ 1000 rpm: _____ psi/kPa
   b. @ 1500 rpm: _____ psi/kPa
   c. @ 2000 rpm: _____ psi/kPa
   d. @ 2500 rpm: _____ psi/kPa

6. Repeat the readings at a normal engine-operating temperature at idle: _____ psi/kPa. Note the hot readings here.
   a. @ 1000 rpm: _____ psi/kPa
   b. @ 1500 rpm: _____ psi/kPa
   c. @ 2000 rpm: _____ psi/kPa
   d. @ 2500 rpm: _____ psi/kPa

7. Do the readings meet the specifications? Yes: _____ No: _____

8. Determine any necessary action(s):

9. Have your supervisor/instructor verify satisfactory completion of this
   procedure, any observations found, and any necessary action(s) recommended.

Performance Rating

CDX Tasksheet Number: C732

0	1	2	3	4

Supervisor/instructor signature _____ Date _____

Inspect, test, and replace oil temperature and pressure switches and sensors.

Time off_____

Time on_____

Total time_____

CDX Tasksheet Number: C736

1. **Research the following specifications/procedures for this vehicle in the appropriate service information.**

    a. **Is this vehicle equipped with an oil temperature sensor?**
    Yes: _____ No: _____

    b. **Is this vehicle equipped with an oil pressure switch (warning light style)?**
    Yes: _____ No: _____

    c. **Is this vehicle equipped with an oil pressure-sending unit (gauge style)?**
    Yes: _____ No: _____

    d. **Is the vehicle equipped with an oil pressure sensor (PCM sensor style)?**
    Yes: _____ No: _____

    e. **List the specification(s) for each sensor/switch the vehicle is equipped with:**

    i. **Oil temperature sensor:**

    ii. **Oil pressure switch:**

    iii. **Oil pressure-sending unit:**

    iv. **Oil pressure sensor:**

2. **Following the appropriate service information procedure, test each switch/sensor (as equipped) and list your findings.**

    a. **Oil temperature sensor:**

b. Oil pressure switch:

c. Oil pressure-sending unit:

d. Oil pressure sensor:

3. Determine any necessary action(s):

4. Have your supervisor/instructor verify satisfactory completion of this procedure, any observations found, and any necessary action(s) recommended.

Performance Rating

CDX Tasksheet Number: C736

0	1	2	3	4

Supervisor/instructor signature _____ Date _____

Cooling System Service

Learning Objective/Task	CDX Tasksheet Number	2017 MAST NATEF Reference Number; Priority Level
• Perform cooling system pressure and dye tests to identify leaks; check coolant condition; inspect and test radiator, pressure cap, coolant recovery tank, heater core, and galley plugs; determine needed action.	C578	1D1; P-1
• Inspect, replace, and/or adjust drive belts, tensioners, and pulleys; check pulley and belt alignment.	C734	1D3; P-1
• Inspect and replace engine cooling and heater system hoses.	N/A	N/A
• Remove, inspect, and replace thermostat and gasket/seal.	C735	1D7; P-1
• Inspect and/or test coolant; drain and recover coolant; flush and refill cooling system; use proper fluid type per manufacturer specification; bleed air as required.	C050	1D4; P-1
• Inspect, remove, and replace water pump.	C680	1D5; P-2
• Remove and replace radiator.	C052	1D6; P-2
• Inspect and test fan(s), fan clutch (electrical or mechanical), fan shroud, and air dams; determine needed action.	C053	1D8; P-1
• Inspect auxiliary coolers; determine needed action.	C871	1D11; P-3
• Identify causes of engine overheating.	C598	1D2; P-1

Time off_____

Time on_____

Total time_____

Materials Required

- Vehicle or simulator
- Cooling system pressure tester
- Antifreeze hydrometer (or refractometer)
- pH test strip or pH tester
- Infrared temperature gun
- DVOM/DMM
- Drain pan
- Gasket scraper

Some Safety Issues to Consider

- Only open the radiator cap (or any other part of the cooling system) when the engine is cool. Opening a radiator cap on a warm or hot engine could cause severe burns.
- Electric fans can turn on at any time. Keep hands and fingers away.
- Remove the ignition key and secure it so the vehicle can't be started. And if the vehicle is equipped with a push button start, keep the key at least 25 feet away from the vehicle.
- Keep away from moving belts and pulleys as they can severely injure or kill you.
- When running any vehicles in the shop, make sure you use the shop's exhaust ventilation system to discharge all exhaust gas safely outside.
- Comply with personal and environmental safety practices associated with clothing; eye protection; hand tools; power equipment; proper ventilation; and the handling, storage, and disposal of chemicals/materials in accordance with local, state, and federal safety and environmental regulations.

Performance Standard

0—No exposure: No information or practice provided during the program; complete training required

1—Exposure only: General information provided with no practice time; close supervision needed; additional training required

2—Limited practice: Has practiced job during training program; additional training required to develop skill

3—Moderately skilled: Has performed job independently during training program; limited additional training may be required

4—Skilled: Can perform job independently with no additional training

▶ **TASK** Perform cooling system pressure and dye tests to identify leaks; check coolant condition; inspect and test radiator, pressure cap, coolant recovery tank, heater core , and galley plugs; determine needed action.

MAST
1D1

Time off_____

Time on_____

Total time_____

CDX Tasksheet Number: C578

1. **Research the following specifications for this vehicle in the appropriate service information.**

    a. **Radiator cap pressure rating:** _____ psi/kPa
    b. **Cooling system capacity:** _____ qt/lt
    c. **Type of coolant:** _____
    d. **Specified pH:** _____

2. **Cooling System Pressure Test: If the vehicle is cold or cool, and the engine is not running, remove the radiator cap. Top off the radiator with the correct type of coolant/water mix if it is not already full. Install the proper adapter on the cooling system access point. Pressurize the cooling system to the specified radiator cap pressure listed above (or a maximum of 2 psi higher). Make sure you leave the system pressurized for a minimum of 10 minutes while you inspect for coolant leaks.**

    > **NOTE** Do not forget to check the heater core and the core plugs.

    a. **List any leaks found and any necessary action(s):**

3. **Coolant Condition: Remove the pressure tester from the radiator. Fit the proper adapter on the tester so that you can check the radiator cap.**

    a. **Pressure-test the cap and check it for the following information.**

        i.   **At what pressure does it vent?** _____ psi/kPa
        ii. **At what pressure does it hold?** _____ psi/kPa
        iii. **Determine any necessary action(s):**

4. **Check Coolant Condition: With the engine cold or cool, and the pressure cap removed, check the condition and level of the coolant.**

    a. **Do a visual inspection of the coolant. List your findings and any necessary action(s).**

    b. **Check the level of the coolant in both the overflow bottle and the radiator. List your findings and any necessary action(s).**

5. **Radiator, Recovery Tank, and Hoses: Inspect the radiator, recovery tank, and hoses for damage or broken/missing pieces. List your findings and any necessary action(s):**

6. **Radiator Test: Reinstall the radiator cap on the radiator. Place the exhaust hose over the vehicle's exhaust pipe(s). Start the vehicle and allow the engine to warm up.**

   a. **Use the infrared temperature gun to measure the temperature across the radiator core. The temperature should show a steady cooling reading as you trace the core tubes from the hot side of the radiator to the cool side. Any tubes that are significantly cooler than the others indicate a plugged tube in the radiator.**

   b. **List your observations and determine any necessary action(s):**

7. **Have your supervisor/instructor verify satisfactory completion of this procedure, any observations found, and any necessary action(s) recommended.**

Performance Rating

CDX Tasksheet Number: C578

0	1	2	3	4

Supervisor/instructor signature _____ Date _____

Inspect, replace, and/or adjust drive belts, tensioners, and pulleys; check pulley and belt alignment.

MAST
1D3

Time off_____

Time on_____

Total time_____

CDX Tasksheet Number: C734

1. **Locate "inspecting, adjusting and or replacing a generator (alternator) drive belts, pulleys, and tensioners; check pulley and belt alignment" in the appropriate service information for the vehicle you are working on.**

   a. List the specified drive belt tension: _____

   b. **List the faults to look for when inspecting drive belts, pulleys, and tensioners:**

   c. **Describe how to check the correct pulley and belt alignment:**

   d. **Locate the belt routing diagram, or draw a picture of the current routing arrangement:**

2. **Remove the vehicle drive belt(s).**

3. **Inspect the vehicle drive belts, pulleys, and tensioners for faults. List your observations for the following parts:**

   a. **Vehicle drive belt(s):**

b. Pulleys:

c. Tensioner(s):

d. Pulley/belt alignment:

4. Have your instructor verify the removal of the belt(s) and the faults found. Supervisor's/instructor's initials: _____

5. Reinstall the vehicle drive belts using the appropriate service information.

6. Re-tension the drive belt(s) using the appropriate service information.

7. Check for the correct pulley, tensioner, and drive belt alignment.

8. Determine any necessary action(s):

9. Have your supervisor/instructor verify satisfactory completion of this procedure, any observations found, and any necessary action(s) recommended.

Performance Rating

CDX Tasksheet Number: C734

0	1	2	3	4

Supervisor/instructor signature _____ Date _____

Additional Task

CDX Tasksheet Number: N/A

1. **Visually inspect the external condition of all the hoses that carry coolant on the vehicle. Also, squeeze each hose and check for soft or brittle conditions. List your observations below.**

   a. **Radiator hose condition:**

   b. **Heater hose condition:**

   c. **Other hoses (bypass hoses, heated intake hoses, etc.):**

2. **Drain an appropriate amount of coolant from the system to lower the coolant level below the level of the hose you are removing.**

3. **Remove the hose. Be careful not to damage the fitting it is connected to.**

> **NOTE** Do not twist the hose to loosen it from the radiator or heater core fittings. You could pull the fitting out of the core. Either carefully slide a tool between the fitting and the hose, or slit the hose on top of the fitting, being careful not to damage the fitting, and peel the hose off of the fitting.

4. **Inspect the inside of the hose. List your observation(s):**

5. **Have your instructor verify the removal and the faults found.**
   Supervisor's/instructor's initials: _____

6. **Replace the hose with a new one, if needed. Be sure to properly route it.**

7. **Refill the system with the proper coolant; perform a pressure or vacuum test to check for leaks.**

8. Apply the vehicle's parking brake and secure the vehicle with wheel chocks to prevent the vehicle from rolling. Also, place the exhaust hose over the exhaust pipe(s).

9. Start the engine and allow it to warm up to a normal operating temperature and recheck for leaks and proper coolant level.

10. Have your supervisor/instructor verify satisfactory completion of this procedure, any observations found, and any necessary action(s) recommended.

Performance Rating

CDX Tasksheet Number: N/A

0	1	2	3	4

Supervisor/instructor signature _____ Date _____

Remove, inspect, and replace thermostat and gasket/seal. **MAST** 1D7

CDX Tasksheet Number: C735

1. **Research the thermostat replacement procedure for this vehicle in the appropriate service information.**

    a. **List any special procedures and/or tools to perform this task:**

    b. **List the thermostat housing bolt torque:** _____ ft-lb/N·m

2. **Look up the flat rate time for this task in a flat rate manual:** _____ hr

3. **Drain enough coolant out of the radiator to lower the level below the thermostat. Save this to put back in the system when the task is finished. Keep it free of dirt and debris.**

4. **Follow the manufacturer's procedure and remove the thermostat.**

5. **Carefully scrape off any old gasket residue from the thermostat housing and mating surface. Be careful not to gouge the sealing surfaces.**

6. **Have your instructor verify removal of the thermostat. Supervisor's/instructor's initials:** _____

> NOTE Ask your supervisor/instructor whether or not to perform the next action before proceeding.

7. **Test the old thermostat in a pan of boiling water to see at what temperature it opens. Suspend the thermostat in a pan of heated water using a piece of wire. The thermostat should be fully immersed in water, but do not allow it to touch the side or bottom of the pan.**

    a. **List the temperature at which the thermostat started to open:** _____ °F/°C

    b. **List the temperature at which the thermostat was fully open:** _____ °F/°C

    c. **How far did the thermostat open?** _____ in/mm

    d. **Did the thermostat operate according to specifications? Yes:** _____ **No:** _____

8. **Install a new thermostat and gasket/seal (or reinstall the old one if your instructor directed you to do so). Torque bolts to the proper torque.**

> NOTE Be careful when bolting down the thermostat housing. Make sure the thermostat is still in its recessed groove. Failure to do so will result in a broken housing and damaged thermostat. If in doubt, ask your supervisor/instructor.

9. Once the thermostat is installed, return the drained antifreeze back into the system.

10. Follow the manufacturer's procedure to bleed any air from the cooling system.

11. Apply the vehicle's parking brake and secure the vehicle with wheel chocks to prevent the vehicle from rolling. Also, place the exhaust hose over the exhaust pipe(s).

12. Start the vehicle and check for any leaks or overheating. Immediately shut off the vehicle if a leak or overheating is found. Repair any leaks, or determine the reason for overheating if present.

13. Return the vehicle to its beginning condition and return any tools that you may have used to their proper locations.

14. Have your supervisor/instructor verify satisfactory completion of this procedure, any observations found, and any necessary action(s) recommended.

Performance Rating

CDX Tasksheet Number: C735

0	1	2	3	4

Supervisor/instructor signature _____ Date _____

Inspect and test coolant; drain and recover coolant; flush and refill cooling system; use proper fluid type per manufacturer specification; bleed air as required.

CDX Tasksheet Number: C050

1. Research the following specifications/procedures for this vehicle in the appropriate service information.

    a. What is the cooling system capacity? _____ qt/lt
    b. What type of antifreeze is required? _____
    c. List or print off and attach to this sheet the cooling system bleeding procedure:

2. Coolant Test:

    a. If the vehicle is cold or cool and not running, remove the radiator cap and test the coolant's freeze protection.

       i. What is the coolant's freeze protection point? _____ °F/°C

    b. List the coolant's boiling point: _____ °F/°C at _____ psi/kPa
    c. Test the coolant's pH reading: _____

       i. Is this within specification? Yes: _____ No: _____

    d. Determine any necessary action(s):

3. Using the appropriate cooling system recycle/flush machine, flush and refill the cooling system with the correct amount of recommended antifreeze. Properly recycle/dispose of any used coolant.

    a. When this procedure is finished, retest the coolant's freeze protection: _____ °F/°C

       i. What is the coolant pH? _____
       ii. Is this within specification? Yes: _____ No: _____

    b. Follow the manufacturer's procedure to bleed air out of the cooling system, if necessary.
    c. Place exhaust hoses on the vehicle's exhaust pipe(s) and wheel chocks to prevent the vehicle from moving. Start the vehicle and monitor the cooling system to make sure that the engine warms up properly and that the thermostat opens at the correct temperature. Also, check that the coolant is at the correct level.

d. Determine any necessary action(s):

4. Return the vehicle to its beginning condition and return any tools that you may have used to their proper locations.

5. Have your supervisor/instructor verify satisfactory completion of this procedure, any observations found, and any necessary action(s) recommended.

Performance Rating

CDX Tasksheet Number: C050

0	1	2	3	4

Supervisor/instructor signature _____ Date _____

DX Tasksheet Number: C680

1. **Research the following specifications/procedures for this vehicle in the appropriate service information.**
   a. Water pump bolt torque: _____ ft-lb/N·m
   b. Type of antifreeze: _____
   c. Draw or print off and attach to this sheet the belt routing diagram:

2. **Drain the coolant out of the radiator. In most situations, the coolant gets replaced/recycled. If your instructor wants you to reuse the coolant, save it in a clean container and keep it free of dirt and debris.**

3. **Following the specified procedure, remove the water pump.**

4. **Inspect the pump for signs of deterioration, leaks, and worn bearings. List your observations:**

5. **Have your instructor verify the removal of the water pump. Supervisor's/instructor's initials:** _____

6. **Replace the water pump with a new water pump, if needed. Torque all fasteners to the proper torque.**

7. **Reinstall the removed coolant (or new coolant) into the radiator. Top off with the correct coolant, if needed.**

8. **Pressure test or vacuum test the cooling system to check for leaks. Repair any leaks found.**

9. **Apply the vehicle's parking brake or secure the vehicle with wheel chocks to prevent the vehicle from rolling. Also, place the exhaust hose over the exhaust pipe(s).**

10. **Start the vehicle and check for any leaks or overheating. Immediately shut off the vehicle if a leak or overheating is found. Repair any leaks, or determine the reason for overheating if present.**

11. **Return the vehicle to its beginning condition and return any tools that you may have used to their proper locations.**

12. Have your supervisor/instructor verify satisfactory completion of this procedure, any observations found, and any necessary action(s) recommended.

Performance Rating

CDX Tasksheet Number: C680

0	1	2	3	4

Supervisor/instructor signature _____ Date _____

Time off_____

Time on_____

Total time_____

CDX Tasksheet Number: C052

1. Research the following specifications/procedures for this vehicle in the appropriate service information.

   a. Cooling system capacity: _____ qt/lt

   b. Type of antifreeze: _____

2. Drain as much coolant from the vehicle as possible into a clean drain pan so that you can reuse the coolant. Also, place the drain pan so that dirt and other debris will not contaminate it while removing the radiator.

3. Follow the specified procedure to remove the radiator.

> **NOTE** Be careful when removing the hoses from the radiator. You will need to slide a thin tool (such as a small screwdriver) carefully between the hose and the radiator fitting to loosen the hose, or slit the hose and carefully peel it off of the fitting. Failure to do this could cause damage to the radiator fitting.

4. Inspect the radiator for any damage and list your observation(s):

5. Have your instructor verify the removal of the radiator.
   Supervisor's/instructor's initials: _____

6. Reinstall the radiator following the specified procedure.

7. Reinstall the removed coolant into the radiator. Top off with the correct coolant, if needed.

8. Pressure test or vacuum test the cooling system to check for leaks. Repair any leaks found.

9. Apply the vehicle's parking brake or secure the vehicle with wheel chocks to prevent the vehicle from rolling. Also, place the exhaust hose over the exhaust pipe(s).

10. Start the vehicle and check for any leaks or overheating. Immediately shut off the vehicle if a leak or overheating is found. Repair any leaks, or determine the reason for overheating if present.

11. **Have your supervisor/instructor verify satisfactory completion of this procedure, any observations found, and any necessary action(s) recommended.**

Performance Rating

0	1	2	3	4

Supervisor/instructor signature _____ Date _____

TASK Inspect and test fan(s), fan clutch (electrical or mechanical), fan shroud, and air dams determine needed action.

MAST
1D8

Time off _____

Time on _____

Total time _____

CDX Tasksheet Number: C053

Mechanical Fans:

1. **Research the fan inspection and testing procedure for this vehicle in the appropriate service information.**

   a. **List or print off and attach to this sheet the inspection and testing procedure for the fan system:**

2. **Visually inspect the fan and fan clutch for damage or wear and list your observations:**

3. **Test the fan clutch according to the specified procedure and list your observations:**

4. **Determine any necessary action(s):**

Electric Fans:

1. **Research the fan inspection and testing procedure for this vehicle in the appropriate service information.**

   a. **List or print off and attach to this sheet the inspection and testing procedure for the fan system:**

   b. **List the temperature at which the electric fan should turn on:** _____ °F/°C

2. Visually inspect the fan for damage or wear and list your observations:

3. Test the fan system according to the specified procedure and list your observations:

4. Determine any necessary action(s):

Fan Shroud and Air Dam:

1. Visually inspect the fan shroud and air dam for any damage, missing parts, or wear and list your observations:

2. Determine any necessary action(s):

3. Return the vehicle to its beginning condition and return any tools that you may have used to their proper locations.

4. Have your supervisor/instructor verify satisfactory completion of this procedure, any observations found, and any necessary action(s) recommended.

Performance Rating

CDX Tasksheet Number: C053

0	1	2	3	4

Supervisor/instructor signature _____ Date _____

MAST
1D11

DX Tasksheet Number: C871

1. Research the auxiliary cooler testing procedure for this vehicle in the appropriate service information. Normally, the coolers are located either in front of the radiator or as part of the cooler end of the radiator.

   a. List the auxiliary cooler(s) this vehicle is equipped with (and the type: air-cooled, liquid cooled, etc.):

   b. List or print off and attach to this sheet the inspection and testing procedure for the cooler(s):

2. Closely examine the unit for leaks or damage that could develop into leaks under normal operating conditions. Make particular note of the condition of any tubes or hoses, and the condition of their fittings. List your test(s) and observation(s):

3. Determine any necessary action(s):

4. Return the vehicle to its beginning condition and return any tools that you may have used to their proper locations.

5. Have your supervisor/instructor verify satisfactory completion of this procedure, any observations found, and any necessary action(s) recommended.

Performance Rating

CDX Tasksheet Number: C871

0	1	2	3	4

Supervisor/instructor signature _____ Date _____

MAST
1D2

DX Tasksheet Number: C598

Vehicle used for this activity:

Year _____ Make _____ Model_____

Odometer_____ VIN_____

1. **List the customer concern in relation to the overheating problem:**

2. **Research the particular concern in the appropriate service information and list the possible causes:**

3. **Inspect the cooling system and engine to determine the cause of the concern. List your tests and results:**

4. **Determine any necessary action(s) to correct the fault:**

5. **Return the vehicle to its beginning condition and return any tools that you may have used to their proper locations.**

6. **Have your supervisor/instructor verify satisfactory completion of this procedure, any observations found, and any necessary action(s) recommended.**

Performance Rating

CDX Tasksheet Number: C598

0	1	2	3	4

Supervisor/instructor signature _____ Date _____

Section A2:
Automatic Transmission and Transaxle

CONTENTS

Vehicle, Customer, and Service Information

Student/Intern information:

Name _____ Date _____ Class

_____

Vehicle used for this activity:

Year _____ Make _____ Model _____

_____

Odometer _____VIN _____

Learning Objective/Task	CDX Tasksheet Number	2017 MAST NATEF Reference Number; Priority Level
• Research vehicle service information, fluid type, vehicle service history, service precautions, and technical service bulletins.	C681	2A2; P-1
• Describe the operational characteristics of a continuously variable transmission (CVT).	C606	2C4; P-3
• Describe the operational characteristics of a hybrid vehicle drive train.	C607	2C5; P-3
• Demonstrate the use of the 3 Cs (concern, cause, and correction).	N/A	N/A

Time off_____

Time on_____

Total time_____

Materials Required

- Blank work order
- Vehicle with available service history records
- Depending on the type of concern, special diagnostic tools may be required. See your supervisor/instructor for instructions to identify what tools may be required.

Some Safety Issues to Consider

- This task may require test-driving the vehicle on the school grounds. Attempt this task only with full permission from your instructor and follow all the guidelines exactly.
- When running any vehicles in the shop, make sure you use the shop's exhaust ventilation system to discharge all exhaust gas safely outside.
- Lifting equipment such as vehicle jacks and stands, vehicle hoists, and engine hoists are important tools that increase productivity and make the job easier. However, they can also cause severe injury or death if used improperly. Make sure you follow the manufacturer's operation procedures. Also, make sure you have your supervisor's/instructor's permission to use any particular type of lifting equipment.

- Comply with personal and environmental safety practices associated with clothing; eye protection; hand tools; power equipment; proper ventilation; and the handling, storage, and disposal of chemicals/materials in accordance with local, state, and federal safety and environmental regulations.

Performance Standard

0–No exposure: No information or practice provided during the program; complete training required

1–Exposure only: General information provided with no practice time; close supervision needed; additional training required

2–Limited practice: Has practiced job during training program; additional training required to develop skill

3–Moderately skilled: Has performed job independently during training program; limited additional training may be required

4–Skilled: Can perform job independently with no additional training

MAST
2A2

Time off_____

Time on_____

Total time_____

DX Tasksheet Number: C681

1. **Using the vehicle VIN for identification, use the appropriate source to access the vehicle's service history in relation to prior related transmission/transaxle work or customer concerns.**

    a. **List any transmission-related repairs/concerns, and their dates:**

2. **List the specified type of fluid for this vehicle:**
   _____

3. **Using the vehicle VIN for identification, access any relevant technical service bulletins for the particular vehicle you are working on in relation to any transmission/transaxle updates, precautions, or other service issues. List any related service bulletins and their titles:**

4. **Have your supervisor/instructor verify satisfactory completion of this procedure, any observations found, and any necessary action(s) recommended.**

Performance Rating

CDX Tasksheet Number: C681

0	1	2	3	4

Supervisor/instructor signature _____ Date _____

TASK Describe the operational characteristics of a
continuously variable transmission (CVT).

MAST
2C4

DX Tasksheet Number: C606

Vehicle used for this activity:

Year_____ Make_____ Model_____

Odometer_____ VIN _____

1. **Research the description and operation of a continuously variable transmission in the appropriate service information.**

   a. **What type of CVT is this transmission?**_____

   b. **How does this CVT achieve reduction?**

   c. **How does this CVT achieve direct drive?**

   d. **How does this CVT achieve neutral?**

   e. **How does this CVT achieve reverse?**

f. What type of fluid does this CVT use? _____

g. What is the fluid capacity? _____ qt/lt

h. What is the service interval for the transmission fluid? _____ mi/
km

i. Look up if there is a fluid condition monitor for the transmission. What is
the procedure to reset the fluid monitor?

2. Have your supervisor/instructor verify satisfactory completion of this
procedure, any observations found, and any necessary action(s) recommended.

Performance Rating

CDX Tasksheet Number: C606

0	1	2	3	4

Supervisor/instructor signature _____ Date _____

MAST
2C5

Time off_____

Time on_____

Total time_____

DX Tasksheet Number: C607

1. **Research the description and operation of a hybrid vehicle drive train in the appropriate service information.**

   a. **What type of hybrid is this vehicle?**

   Series: _____ Parallel: _____ Series-Parallel: _____

   b. **Can this vehicle operate only on the internal combustion engine?**
   Yes: _____ No: _____

   c. **Describe the conditions when the internal combustion engine runs:**

   d. **Can this vehicle operate only on the electric motor?**
   Yes: _____ No: _____

   e. **Describe the conditions when the electric motor operates:**

   f. **Does this vehicle use regeneration?**
   Yes: _____ No: _____

   g. **Describe how regeneration operates in this vehicle:**

2. **Have your supervisor/instructor verify satisfactory completion of this procedure, any observations found, and any necessary action(s) recommended.**

Performance Rating

CDX Tasksheet Number: C607

0	1	2	3	4

Supervisor/instructor signature _____ Date _____

Additional Task

Time off_____

Time on_____

Total time_____

CDX Tasksheet Number: N/A

1. Using the following scenario, write up the three Cs as listed on most repair orders. Assume that the customer authorized the recommended repairs.

   A compact vehicle is brought to your shop with an automatic transaxle concern. The customer tells you that the transmission started slipping a couple of days ago, and it is getting worse. You road test the vehicle and notice that it is slipping in all gears when under moderate load. You pull the vehicle onto a rack and find the following:

   a. The vehicle has 122,000 miles on it, but is in good condition otherwise.
   b. The transmission fluid is dark and smells burnt. The fluid is about two pints too low, but topping it off does not stop the vehicle from slipping when it is stall-tested.
   c. The transmission-pan gasket and both axle seals are seeping heavily.
   d. With the pan removed, there is a lot of band and clutch material in the bottom, but very few metal filings.
   e. The transmission mount is torn.
   f. Both outer CV joint boots are badly cracked and just starting to leak grease, but the joints are still good.

   > **NOTE** Ask your instructor whether you should use a copy of the shop repair order or the three Cs here to record this information.

2. Concern:

3. Cause:

4. Correction:

5. Other recommended service:

6. Have your supervisor/instructor verify satisfactory completion of this task, any observations found, and any necessary action(s) recommended.

Performance Rating

CDX Tasksheet Number: N/A

0	1	2	3	4

Supervisor/instructor signature _____ Date _____

Inspection and Testing

Student/Intern information:

Name _____ Date _____ Class

_____

Vehicle used for this activity:

Year _____ Make _____ Model _____

_____

Odometer _____ VIN _____

Learning Objective/Task	CDX Tasksheet Number	2017 MAST NATEF Reference Number; Priority Level
• Perform pressure tests (including transmissions/transaxles equipped with electronic pressure control); determine needed action.	C740	2A6; P-1
• Perform stall test; determine needed action.	C741	2A8; P-2
• Perform lock-up converter system tests; determine needed action.	C063	2A9; P-3

Time off_____

Time on_____

Total time_____

Materials Required

- Vehicle with automatic transmission/transaxle and lock-up converter
- Vehicle hoist
- Flashlight or shop light
- Optional: fluorescent dye and ultraviolet light
- Transmission pressure gauge set
- Tachometer
- Scan tool
- DVOM/DMM

Some Safety Issues to Consider

- Vehicle hoists are important tools that increase productivity and make the job easier. However, they can also cause severe injury or death if used improperly. Make sure you follow the manufacturer's operation procedures. Also, make sure you have your supervisor's/instructor's permission to use a hoist.
- This procedure may require cleaning the transmission or axle assembly prior to inspection. If so, use the proper equipment and procedures to carry this out safely. Also, get your supervisor's/instructor's permission prior to cleaning.
- **Caution:** Stall testing for more than a few seconds can damage the transmission or other parts of the vehicle. It is also a hazardous task. Perform this task with the utmost care! Note that some manufacturers don't allow a stall test to be performed on their vehicles.
- When running any vehicles in the shop, make sure you use the shop's exhaust ventilation system to discharge all exhaust gas safely outside.

- Diagnosis of this fault may require test-driving the vehicle on the school grounds. Attempt this task only with full permission from your instructor and follow all the guidelines exactly.
- Comply with personal and environmental safety practices associated with clothing; eye protection; hand tools; power equipment; proper ventilation; and the handling, storage, and disposal of chemicals/materials in accordance with local, state, and federal safety and environmental regulations.

Performance Standard

0—No exposure: No information or practice provided during the program; complete training required

1—Exposure only: General information provided with no practice time; close supervision needed; additional training required

2—Limited practice: Has practiced job during training program; additional training required to develop skill

3—Moderately skilled: Has performed job independently during training program; limited additional training may be required

4—Skilled: Can perform job independently with no additional training

Perform pressure tests (including transmissions/transaxles equipped with electronic pressure control); determine needed action.

MAST
2A6

Time off_____

Time on_____

Total time_____

CDX Tasksheet Number: C740

1. Research all applicable pressure specifications and test procedure(s) for this transmission in the appropriate service information.

   a. Line pressure: _____ psi/kPa
   b. Governor pressure: _____ psi/kPa
   c. Throttle pressure:_____ psi/kPa
   d. Low-gear servo/clutch pressure: _____ psi/kPa
   e. Second-gear servo/clutch pressure: _____ psi/kPa
   f. Direct-clutch pressure: _____ psi/kPa
   g. Cooler-circuit pressure: _____ psi/kPa
   h. List any other pressure specifications off to the right side of the above specifications.

2. Perform the applicable transmission-pressure tests. Be sure to follow the specified procedures. Note that a scan tool may need to be used on electronically controlled transmissions. List your observations below.

   a. Line pressure: _____ psi/kPa
   b. Governor pressure: _____ psi/kPa
   c. Throttle pressure: _____ psi/kPa
   d. Low-gear servo/clutch pressure: _____ psi/kPa
   e. Second-gear servo/clutch pressure: _____ psi/kPa
   f. Direct-clutch pressure: _____ psi/kPa
   g. Cooler-circuit pressure: _____ psi/kPa
   h. List any other pressures off to the right side of the above readings.

3. Determine any necessary action(s):

4. Have your supervisor/instructor verify satisfactory completion of this procedure, any observations found, and any necessary action(s) recommended.

Performance Rating

CDX Tasksheet Number: C740

0	1	2	3	4

Supervisor/instructor signature _____ Date _____

Perform stall test; determine needed action.

Time off_____

Time on_____

CDX Tasksheet Number: C741

1. **Research the specifications and procedures to stall test this transmission.**

Total time_____

> **NOTE** Do not perform this test on a transmission if the line pressure is not up to specifications or further damage to the transmission could quickly result. Also, some manufacturers do not want their transmissions stall tested. And on vehicles with electronic throttle control, the PCM may not allow a stall test to be performed without a scan tool.

    a. **Does the manufacturer recommend a stall test? Yes: _____ No: _____**

    b. **Specified stall speed(s) _____**

    c. **List all precautions when performing the stall test:**

2. **Perform the stall test. Be sure to follow all safety precautions. List your observation(s):**

3. **Determine any necessary action(s):**

4. **Have your supervisor/instructor verify satisfactory completion of this procedure, any observations found, and any necessary action(s) recommended.**

Performance Rating

CDX Tasksheet Number: C741

0	1	2	3	4

Supervisor/instructor signature _____ Date _____

Perform lock-up converter system tests; determine
      needed action.

Time off_____

Time on_____

CDX Tasksheet Number: C063

Total time_____

1. **Research the specifications and procedure for testing the lock-up converter.**

   a. **Lock-up converter solenoid resistance:** _____ **ohms**

   b. **List or print off and attach to this sheet the procedure for testing the lock-up converter:**

   c. **Ask your instructor where you are to perform the lock-up converter test:**
      Road test: _____ **Vehicle hoist:** _____

2. **Have your supervisor/instructor approve your answers. Supervisor's/instructor's initials:** _____

3. **Perform the lock-up converter performance test.**

   a. **Prepare the vehicle for this test by following the specified procedure.**

   b. **Test the operation of the lock-up converter system following your instructor's directions. List your observation(s):**

4. **Perform the lock-up converter pinpoint test.**

   a. **Test for the proper electrical signal at the lock-up converter solenoid connector following the specified procedure. List your observation(s):**

   b. **Measure the electrical continuity/resistance of the solenoid:** _____ **ohms**

5. **Determine any necessary action(s):**

6. Have your supervisor/instructor verify satisfactory completion of this procedure, any observations found, and any necessary action(s) recommended.

Performance Rating

CDX Tasksheet Number: C063

0	1	2	3	4

Supervisor/instructor signature _____ Date _____

Diagnosis

Student/Intern information:

Name _____ Date _____ Class _____

Vehicle used for this activity:

Year _____ Make _____ Model_____

Odometer_____VIN_____

Learning Objective/Task	CDX Tasksheet Number	2017 MAST NATEF Reference Number; Priority Level
• Diagnose electronic transmission/transaxle control systems using appropriate test equipment and service information.	C600	2A11; P-1
• Inspect, test, adjust, repair, and/or replace electrical/electronic components and circuits including computers, solenoids, sensors, relays, terminals, connectors, switches, and harnesses; demonstrate understanding of relearn procedure.	C601	2B3; P-1
• Diagnose transmission/transaxle gear reduction/multiplication concerns using driving, driven, and held-member (power flow) principles.	C066	2A10; P-1
• Diagnose pressure concerns in a transmission using hydraulic principles (Pascal's Law).	C747	2A12; P-2
• Diagnose noise and vibration concerns; determine needed action.	C743	2A7; P-2
• Identify and interpret transmission/transaxle concerns, differentiate between engine performance and transmission/transaxle concerns; determine needed action.	C599	2A1; P-1
• Check fluid level in a transmission or a transaxle equipped with a dipstick.	C902	2A4; P-1
• Check fluid level in a transmission or a transaxle not equipped with a dipstick.	C903X	2A5; P-1
• Diagnose fluid loss and condition concerns; determine needed action.	C682	2A3; P-1

Time off_____

Time on_____

Total time_____

Materials Required

- Vehicle with automatic transmission/transaxle
- Vehicle hoist
- Transmission pressure gauge set
- Tachometer
- Scan tool
- DVOM/DMM

Some Safety Issues to Consider

- Vehicle hoists are important tools that increase productivity and make the job easier. However, they can also cause severe injury or death if used improperly. Make sure you follow the manufacturer's operation procedures. Also, make sure you have your supervisor's/instructor's permission to use a hoist.
- When running any vehicles in the shop, make sure you use the shop's exhaust ventilation system to discharge all exhaust gas safely outside.
- Diagnosis of this fault may require test-driving the vehicle on the school grounds. Attempt this task only with full permission from your instructor and follow all the guidelines exactly.
- Always wear the correct protective eyewear and clothing, and use the appropriate safety equipment, as well as fender covers, seat protectors, and floor mat protectors.
- Comply with personal and environmental safety practices associated with clothing; eye protection; hand tools; power equipment; proper ventilation; and the handling, storage, and disposal of chemicals/materials in accordance with local, state, and federal safety and environmental regulations.

Performance Standard

0–No exposure: No information or practice provided during the program; complete training required

1–Exposure only: General information provided with no practice time; close supervision needed; additional training required

2–Limited practice: Has practiced job during training program; additional training required to develop skill

3–Moderately skilled: Has performed job independently during training program; limited additional training may be required

4–Skilled: Can perform job independently with no additional training

Time off_____

Time on_____

Total time_____

CDX Tasksheet Number: C600

1. List the customer concern related to an electronic control system issue:

2. Connect an appropriate scan tool to the data link connector (DLC). Retrieve and list any transmission-related codes:

3. Research the specifications and procedures for diagnosing the code(s).
   a. List the possible cause(s) of the code(s):

   b. List or print off and attach to this sheet the procedure for diagnosing the code(s):

4. Perform the diagnostic tests following the specified procedure using the appropriate test equipment.
   a. List your tests and test results:

b. List the test equipment you used to diagnose this concern:

5. Determine any necessary action(s) to correct the fault:

6. Have your supervisor/instructor verify satisfactory completion of this procedure, any observations found, and any necessary action(s) recommended.

Inspect, test, adjust, repair, and/or replace electrical/electronic components and circuits, including computers, solenoids, sensors, relays, terminals, connectors, switches, and harnesses; demonstrate understanding of relearn procedure.

MAST
2B3

Time off_____

Time on_____

Total time_____

CDX Tasksheet Number: C601

1. **Research the specifications and procedures for inspecting, testing, adjusting, and replacing the electrical/electronic components and sensors.**

    a. **List or print off and attach to this sheet the procedure for inspecting, testing, adjusting, and replacing these components:**

    b. **List any specified precautions:**

2. **Inspect the following components for proper operation and list your observations.**

    a. **Computer:**

    b. **Solenoids/relays:**

    c. **Sensors/switches:**

    d. **Terminals/connectors/harnesses:**

3. **Ask your instructor which components you should replace.**

    a. **Computer: Yes: _____ No: _____**
    b. **Solenoids/relays: Yes: _____ No: _____**
    c. **Sensors/switches: Yes: _____ No: _____**
    d. **Terminals/connectors/harnesses: Yes: _____ No: _____**

4. Remove the appropriate component(s) following the specified procedure. List your observation(s):

5. Have your supervisor/instructor verify removal and your observations. Supervisor's/instructor's initials: _____

6. Replace each component following the specified procedure.

7. Adjust each component following the specified procedure.

8. Have your supervisor/instructor verify satisfactory completion of this procedure, any observations found, and any necessary action(s) recommended.

Performance Rating

CDX Tasksheet Number: C601

0	1	2	3	4

Supervisor/instructor signature _____ Date _____

TASK Diagnose transmission/transaxle gear reduction/multiplication concerns using driving, driven, and held-member (power flow) principles.

Time on_____

Total time_____

CDX Tasksheet Number: C066

Vehicle used for this activity:

Year _____ Make _____ Model_____

Odometer_____ VIN_____

1. List the customer concern:

2. Research the particular transmission/transaxle concern in the appropriate service information, including power flow charts and driving, driven, and held-member charts.
   a. List the possible cause(s) of the concern:

   b. List or print off and attach to this sheet the procedure for diagnosing the concern:

3. Perform the diagnostic tests following the specified procedure.
   a. List your tests and test results:

Automatic Transmission and Transaxle **247**

    b. Describe how you used the diagnostic charts to diagnose the concern:

    4. Determine any necessary action(s) to correct the fault:

    5. Have your supervisor/instructor verify satisfactory completion of this procedure, any observations found, and any necessary action(s) recommended.

Performance Rating

CDX Tasksheet Number: C066

0	1	2	3	4

Supervisor/instructor signature _____ Date _____

Diagnose pressure concerns in a transmission using hydraulic
principles (Pascal's Law).

MAST
2A12

CDX Tasksheet Number: C747

Vehicle used for this activity:

Year _____ Make _____ Model _____

Odometer _____ VIN _____

1. List the transmission/transaxle pressure-related concern:

2. Research the concern in the appropriate service information.

   a. List the possible cause(s) of the concern:

   b. List (or print off and attach) any specified transmission pressures:

3. Write out Pascal's Law in your own words:

4. Describe how you will use Pascal's Law to help you diagnose this concern:

5. Perform the appropriate pressure tests and list your observation(s):

6. Determine any necessary action(s) to correct the fault:

7. Have your supervisor/instructor verify satisfactory completion of this procedure, any observations found, and any necessary action(s) recommended.

Performance Rating

CDX Tasksheet Number: C747

0	1	2	3	4

Supervisor/instructor signature _____ Date _____

Diagnose noise and vibration concerns; determine
needed action.

Time off_____

Time on_____

Total time_____

CDX Tasksheet Number: C743

Vehicle used for this activity:

Year _____ Make _____ Model _____

Odometer _____ VIN _____

1. **List the transmission-noise and vibration-related concern:**

2. **Research the concern in the appropriate service information.**
   a. **List the possible cause(s) of the concern:**

   b. **List or print off and attach to this sheet the specified procedure for diagnosing the concern:**

3. **Perform the appropriate tests, following the specified procedure. List your observation(s):**

4. **List the cause(s) of the concern:**

5. Determine any necessary action(s) to correct the fault:

6. Have your supervisor/instructor verify satisfactory completion of this procedure, any observations found, and any necessary action(s) recommended.

Performance Rating

CDX Tasksheet Number: C743

0	1	2	3	4

Supervisor/instructor signature _____ Date _____

Identify and interpret transmission/transaxle concerns, differentiate between engine performance and transmission/transaxle concerns; determine needed action.

MAST
2A1

Time off_____

Time on_____

Total time_____

CDX Tasksheet Number: C599

1. **Ask your instructor to assign you a vehicle that has a potential transmission/ engine performance concern. List the customer concern(s):**

2. **Research the particular concern in the appropriate service manual.**

   a. **List the possible causes:**

3. **Inspect the vehicle to determine the cause of the concern (differentiate between engine performance and transmission/transaxle concerns).**

   a. **List the steps you took and their results to determine the fault(s):**

4. **List the cause of the concern(s):**

5. **List the necessary action(s) to correct the fault(s):**

6. Have your supervisor/instructor verify satisfactory completion of this procedure, any observations found, and any necessary action(s) recommended.

Performance Rating

CDX Tasksheet Number: C599

0	1	2	3	4

Supervisor/instructor signature _____ Date _____

MAST
2A4

Time off_____

Time on_____

Total time_____

CDX Tasksheet Number: C902

1. **Research the procedure to check the transmission fluid level in the appropriate
   service information. List the specified steps:**

2. **Following the specified steps, check the transmission fluid level. List level:**

3. **Have your supervisor/instructor verify satisfactory completion of this procedure,
   any observations found, and any necessary action(s) recommended.**

Performance Rating

CDX Tasksheet Number: C902

0	1	2	3	4

Supervisor/instructor signature _____ Date _____

MAST
2A5

CDX Tasksheet Number: C903X

Vehicle used for this activity:

Year_____ Make_____ Model_____

Odometer_____ VIN _____

1. **Research the procedure to check the transmission fluid level in a vehicle that doesn't use a transmission dipstick in the appropriate service information. List the specified steps:**

2. **Following the specified steps, check the transmission fluid level. List level:**

3. **Have your supervisor/instructor verify satisfactory completion of this procedure, any observations found, and any necessary action(s) recommended.**

Performance Rating

CDX Tasksheet Number: C903X

0	1	2	3	4

Supervisor/instructor signature _____ Date _____

MAST
2A3

Time off_____

Time on_____

Total time_____

CDX Tasksheet Number: C682

1. List the automatic transmission fluid loss or condition concern:

2. Safely raise and support the vehicle on a hoist. Inspect the transmission for any fluid leaks. List the source of any leaks:

3. Place a few drops of transmission fluid from the transmission on a clean white paper towel. The transmission fluid should have a clean appearance on the towel. If the center portion of the fluid is dirty, then the fluid is dirty. List your observation(s):

4. Smell the transmission fluid. Compare it to a fresh sample of the correct transmission fluid. List your observation(s):

5. If the fluid is in poor condition, ask your instructor if you should change the fluid and filter. If so, inspect the bottom of the pan once it is removed. List your observation(s):

6. Determine any necessary actions to correct the fault(s):

7. Have your supervisor/instructor verify satisfactory completion of this procedure, any observations found, and any necessary action(s) recommended.

Performance Rating

CDX Tasksheet Number: C682

0	1	2	3	4

Supervisor/instructor signature _____ Date _____

Maintenance and Repair

Student/Intern information:

Name_____ Date_____ Class_____

Vehicle used for this activity:

Year _____ Make _____ Model_____

Odometer_____VIN_____

Learning Objective/Task	CDX Tasksheet Number	2017 MAST NATEF Reference Number; Priority Level
• Inspect, adjust, and/or replace external manual-valve shift linkage, transmission-range sensor/switch, and park/neutral position switch.	C683	2B1; P-1
• Inspect for leakage; replace external seals, gaskets, and bushings.	C748	2B2; P-2
• Inspect, replace, and/or align powertrain mounts.	C602	2B5; P-2
• Drain and replace fluid and filter(s); use proper fluid type per manufacturer specification.	C907	2B4; P-1

Time off_____

Time on_____

Total time_____

Materials Required

- Vehicle with automatic transmission/transaxle
- Vehicle hoist
- Scan tool
- DVOM/DMM
- Floor jack
- Drain pan
- Torque wrench
- Specified filter and fluid

Some Safety Issues to Consider

- Vehicle hoists are important tools that increase productivity and make the job easier. However, they can also cause severe injury or death if used improperly. Make sure you follow the manufacturer's operation procedures. Also, make sure you have your supervisor's/instructor's permission to use a hoist.
- When running any vehicles in the shop, make sure you use the shop's exhaust ventilation system to discharge all exhaust gas safely outside.
- Diagnosis of this fault may require test-driving the vehicle on the school grounds. Attempt this task only with full permission from your instructor and follow all the guidelines exactly.

- This procedure may require cleaning the transmission or axle assembly prior to inspection. If so, use the proper equipment and procedures to carry this out safely. Also, get your supervisor's/instructor's permission prior to cleaning.
- Comply with personal and environmental safety practices associated with clothing; eye protection; hand tools; power equipment; proper ventilation; and the handling, storage, and disposal of chemicals/materials in accordance with local, state, and federal safety and environmental regulations.

Performance Standard

0—No exposure: No information or practice provided during the program; complete training required

1—Exposure only: General information provided with no practice time; close supervision needed; additional training required

2—Limited practice: Has practiced job during training program; additional training required to develop skill

3—Moderately skilled: Has performed job independently during training program; limited additional training may be required

4—Skilled: Can perform job independently with no additional training

MAST
2B1

Time off_____

Time on_____

Total time_____

DX Tasksheet Number: C683

1. Research the specifications and procedures for inspecting, adjusting, and replacing the manual valve shift linkage, transmission range sensor/switch, and park/neutral position switch in the appropriate service information.

    a. List or print off and attach to this sheet the procedure for inspecting, adjusting, and replacing these components:

    b. List any specified precautions:

2. Inspect the following components for proper operation. List your observations.

    a. Manual-valve shift linkage:

    b. Transmission-range sensor/switch:

    c. Park/neutral position switch:

3. Ask your instructor which components you should replace.
    a. Manual valve shift linkage: Yes: _____ No: _____
    b. Transmission-range sensor/switch: Yes: _____ No: _____
    c. Park/neutral position switch: Yes: _____ No: _____

4. Remove the appropriate component(s) following the specified procedure. List your observation(s):

5. Have your supervisor/instructor verify removal. Supervisor's/instructor's initials: _____

6. Replace each component following the specified procedure.

7. Adjust each component following the specified procedure.

8. Have your supervisor/instructor verify satisfactory completion of this procedure, any observations found, and any necessary action(s) recommended.

Performance Rating

CDX Tasksheet Number: C683

0	1	2	3	4

Supervisor/instructor signature _____ Date _____

Inspect for leakage; replace external seals, gaskets, and bushings.

Time off_____

Time on_____

Total time_____

DX Tasksheet Number: C748

Vehicle used for this activity:

Year _____ Make _____ Model _____

Odometer _____ VIN _____

1. Safely raise and support the vehicle on a hoist.

2. Inspect the transmission/transaxle seals and gaskets for leaks.

    a. List each external seal, gasket, and bushing; and identify the source of any leak(s):

3. With your instructor's permission, replace any leaking seals or gaskets. List the parts replaced and your observations:

4. Have your supervisor/instructor verify satisfactory completion of this procedure, any observations found, and any necessary action(s) recommended.

Performance Rating

CDX Tasksheet Number: C748

0	1	2	3	4

Supervisor/instructor signature _____ Date _____

Time off_____

Time on_____

DX Tasksheet Number: C602

Vehicle used for this activity:

Year_____ Make _____ Model_____

Odometer_____ VIN _____

Total time_____

1. **Research the procedure to inspect, replace, and align the powertrain mounts in the appropriate service information.**

   a. **List the type of mount(s) this vehicle uses:**
   _____

   b. **List or print off and attach to this sheet the procedure for inspecting the mount(s):**

   c. **List or print off and attach to this sheet the precautions for performing this task:**

2. **Following the specified procedure, inspect each of the powertrain mounts, and list your observations:**

3. **Determine any necessary action(s):**

4. **Have your supervisor/instructor verify your answers. Supervisor's/instructor's initials:** _____

5. **With your supervisor/instructor's permission, remove one or more powertrain mounts following the specified procedure. Inspect the removed mount(s) and list your observations:**

6. Have your supervisor/instructor verify the removal of the mount. Supervisor's/instructor's initials: _____

7. Reinstall and align the powertrain mount(s) according to the specified procedure

8. Determine any necessary action(s):

9. Have your supervisor/instructor verify satisfactory completion of this procedure, any observations found, and any necessary action(s) recommended.

Performance Rating

CDX Tasksheet Number: C602

0	1	2	3	4

Supervisor/instructor signature _____ Date _____

TASK Drain and replace fluid and filter(s); use proper fluid type per manufacturer specification.

MAST
2B4

Time off_____

Time on_____

Total time_____

DX Tasksheet Number: C907

Vehicle used for this activity:

Year _____ Make _____ Model _____

Odometer _____ VIN _____

1. **Research the specifications and procedure in the appropriate service information.**

    a. **Transmission service interval:** _____ mi/km
    b. **Transmission fluid type:** _____
    c. **Transmission fluid capacity:** _____ qt/lt
    d. **Pan bolts torque:** _____ in-lb/ft-lb/N·m
    e. **Filter screw torque, if needed:** _____ in-lb/ft-lb/N·m
    f. **List the steps required to properly check the fluid level:**

2. **Following the specified procedure, remove the transmission pan and filter (filter may be an external filter). Inspect any residue and debris in the bottom of the pan or stuck to the filter. List your observations:**

3. **Determine any necessary action(s):**

4. **Have your supervisor/instructor verify removal of the pan and filter. Supervisor's/instructor's initials:** _____

5. **Clean the pan, magnet, and gasket surfaces.**

6. **Following the specified procedure, install the filter, pan, gasket, initial amount of fluid, and any other removed components.**

> **NOTE** Make sure you fill the transmission with the proper amount of the specified fluid. Most service information lists two fluid capacities: one for a drain and refill, and the second for an overhaul. Make sure you use the proper specification.

7. Follow the specified procedure to circulate the fluid and bleed any air from the system. This usually involves moving the gear selector through each position and then checking the fluid level. Add fluid to bring the fluid to the proper level (do NOT overfill).

8. Verify the correct operation of the transmission. This may require a test drive. Get your supervisor's/instructor's permission before performing this step, and list your observation(s):

9. Have your supervisor/instructor verify satisfactory completion of this procedure, any observations found, and any necessary action(s) recommended.

Performance Rating

CDX Tasksheet Number: C907

0	1	2	3	4

Supervisor/instructor signature _____ Date _____

Transmission Disassembly and Inspection

Student/Intern information:

Name_____ Date_____ Class_____

Vehicle used for this activity:

Year _____ Make _____ Model_____

Odometer_____VIN_____

Learning Objective/Task	CDX Tasksheet Number	2017 MAST NATEF Reference Number; Priority Level
• Disassemble, clean, and inspect transmission/transaxle.	C684	2C6; P-1
• Inspect, measure, and reseal oil pump assembly and components.	C688	2C10; P-2
• Measure transmission/transaxle end play and/or preload; determine needed action.	C689	2C11; P-1
• Inspect and measure planetary gear assembly components; determine needed action.	C752	2C15; P-2
• Inspect bushings; determine needed action.	C751	2C14; P-2
• Inspect, measure, and/or replace thrust washers and bearings.	C750	2C12; P-2
• Inspect one-way clutches, races, rollers, sprags, springs, cages, and retainers; determine needed action.	C759	2C22; P-2
• Inspect oil delivery circuits, including seal rings, ring grooves, and sealing surface areas, feed pipes, orifices, and check valves/balls.	C690	2C13; P-2
• Inspect case bores, passages, bushings, vents, and mating surfaces; determine needed action.	C753	2C16; P-2
• Inspect servo and accumulator bores, pistons, seals, pins, springs, and retainers; determine needed action.	C686	2C8; P-2
• Inspect clutch drum, piston, check balls, springs, retainers, seals, friction plates, pressure plates, and bands; determine needed action.	C756	2C19; P-2
• Measure clutch pack clearance; determine needed action.	C757	2C20; P-1
• Air test operation of clutch and servo assemblies.	C758	2C21; P-1
• Inspect, measure, clean, and replace valve body (includes surfaces, bores, springs, valves, switches, solenoids, sleeves, retainers, brackets, check valves/balls, screens, spacers, and gaskets).	C685	2C7; P-2
• Diagnose and inspect transaxle drive, link chains, sprockets, gears, bearings, and bushings; perform needed action.	C754	2C17; P-2
• Inspect, measure, repair, adjust, or replace transaxle final drive components.	C755	2C18; P-2

Time off_____

Time on_____

Total time_____

Materials Required

- Vehicle with automatic transmission/transaxle
- Vehicle hoist
- Transmission jack
- Dial indicator
- Drain pan
- Cooler flushing equipment
- Torque wrench
- Manufacturer or job specific special tools
- Transmission/transaxle
- Snap ring pliers
- Dial indicator
- Feeler blades
- Straightedge
- Approved air nozzle
- Manufacturer-specific tools

- This procedure may require cleaning the transmission or axle assembly prior to inspection. If so use the proper equipment and procedures to carry this out safely. Also, get your supervisor's/instructor's permission prior to cleaning.
- Automotive transmissions/transaxles are heavy. Make sure they are secured to the transmission jack during removal and installation.
- Comply with personal and environmental safety practices associated with clothing; eye protection; hand tools; power equipment; proper ventilation; and the handling, storage, and disposal of chemicals/materials in accordance with local, state, and federal safety and environmental regulations.
- Castings and machined parts may have sharp edges. Handle these parts with care.
- Many transmission parts are round and can easily roll off of tables and carts. Be sure to place them in a secure manner to prevent component damage or personal injury from falling objects.
- Compressed air can be very dangerous if applied to broken skin or body cavities. Always use approved air nozzles, and never point them at yourself or another person.
- Transmissions, transaxles, and their component assemblies are heavy and can slip easily. Work safely, get help, and do not overextend your abilities.

erformance Standard

-**No exposure:** No information or practice provided during the program; complete training required

-**Exposure only:** General information provided with no practice time; close supervision needed; additional training required

-**Limited practice:** Has practiced job during training program; additional training required to develop skill

-**Moderately skilled:** Has performed job independently during training program; limited additional training may be required

-**Skilled:** Can perform job independently with no additional training

DX Tasksheet Number: C684

1. **Research the disassembly and inspection procedures in the appropriate service information.**

    a. **List any precautions for performing this task:**

    b. **List any special tools required to perform this task:**

2. **Following the specified procedure, disassemble the transmission/transaxle into its unit components, ensuring that you note their location and orientation. Make notes or take pictures as appropriate. Also, lay them out in a logical manner to facilitate reassembly.**

    NOTE Round objects such as clutch drums, ball bearings, roller bearings, and bushings can roll off of the work table if not secured, causing personal injury. This could also lead to damage or loss of the components. Always lay round objects on their side when possible, or store them in a work tray to prevent rolling.

3. **Clean the components according to the specified procedure. Make sure you relocate them in the same logical sequence as before**

4. Perform a preliminary visual inspection of the components. This is an initial inspection designed to identify major issues with the transmission/transaxle. Further inspection of the subunits will occur later. List your observations for each main assembly:

5. Have your supervisor/instructor verify satisfactory completion of this procedure, any observations found, and any necessary action(s) recommended.

Time off_____

Time on_____

Total time_____

DX Tasksheet Number: C688

1. **Research the procedure for disassembling and inspecting the oil pump in the appropriate service information.**

   a. **Type of pump (gerotor, crescent, vane, etc.):**
   _____

   b. **List, or print off and attach to this sheet, the clearance specifications for this pump:**

   c. **Pump housing bolt torque:** _____ **ft-lb/N·m**
   d. **Pump-to-case bolt torque:** _____ **ft-lb/N·m**

2. **Following the specified procedure, disassemble the oil pump. Be sure not to damage any of the surfaces or parts.**

   NOTE You may need to scribe a mark on the pump halves so that you can reassemble the pump in the proper orientation. Refer to the service information to see if this is the case. Also be careful not to damage any of the wear surfaces with a scribe. Use a nondamaging method of marking the components.

3. **Measure the specified clearances. List your readings:**

4. **Determine any necessary action(s):**

5. **Have your supervisor/instructor verify disassembly.**
   Supervisor's/instructor's initials: _____

6. Following the specified procedure, reassemble the oil pump. Be sure to prelubricate the oil pump and replace any seals and bushings as necessary. List your observations:

7. Have your supervisor/instructor verify satisfactory completion of this procedure, any observations found, and any necessary action(s) recommended.

Performance Rating

CDX Tasksheet Number: C688

0	1	2	3	4

Supervisor/instructor signature _____ Date _____

MAST
2C11

DX Tasksheet Number: C689

1. **Research the procedure and specifications to measure the end play or preload.**

   a. **Specified end play or preload:** _____

   b. **List, or print off and attach to this sheet, the steps to perform the end play or preload measurement:**

   c. **How is the end play or preload adjusted on this transmission/transaxle?**

2. **Following the specified procedure, measure the end play or preload:**
   _____

3. **Determine any necessary action(s):**

4. **Have your supervisor/instructor verify satisfactory completion of this procedure, any observations found, and any necessary action(s) recommended.**

Performance Rating

CDX Tasksheet Number: C689

0	1	2	3	4

Supervisor/instructor signature _____ Date _____

Inspect and measure planetary gear assembly components; determine needed action.

MAST 2C15

Time off_____

Time on_____

Total time_____

CDX Tasksheet Number: C752

1. Research the procedure for inspecting and measuring the planetary gear(s) in the appropriate service information.

    a. Type of planetary gear (Simpson, Ravigneaux, etc.): _____
    b. List, or print off and attach to this sheet, the clearance and other specifications for the planetary gear(s):

2. Following the specified procedure, perform any planetary gear assembly measurements. List your observations:

3. Visually inspect the planetary gear assemblies (including the sun gear, ring gear, planetary gears, thrust washers, and carrier assembly) for wear or damage. List your observations:

4. Determine any necessary action(s):

5. Have your supervisor/instructor verify satisfactory completion of this procedure, any observations found, and any necessary action(s) recommended.

Performance Rating

CDX Tasksheet Number: C752

0	1	2	3	4

Supervisor/instructor signature _____ Date _____

MAST
2C14

CDX Tasksheet Number: C751

1. **Research the procedure and any specifications for inspecting the bushings in the appropriate service information.**

   a. **List the name and any specifications for each bushing:**

2. **Following the specified procedure, inspect and/or measure each bushing. List your observations:**

3. **Determine any necessary action(s):**

4. **Have your supervisor/instructor verify satisfactory completion of this procedure, any observations found, and any necessary action(s) recommended.**

Performance Rating

CDX Tasksheet Number: C751

0	1	2	3	4

Supervisor/instructor signature _____ Date _____

TASK Inspect, measure, and/or replace thrust washers and bearings.

MAST 2C12

Time off_____

Time on_____

Total time_____

CDX Tasksheet Number: C750

1. Research the procedure and specifications for inspecting, measuring, and replacing thrust washers and bearings in the appropriate service information.

   a. List the name and specified thickness for each thrust washer and thrust bearing:

   b. Which thrust washer(s) or thrust bearing(s) is the selective fit for obtaining the proper gear train end play?

2. Following the specified procedure, inspect and/or measure each thrust washer and thrust bearing. List your observations:

3. Determine any necessary action(s):

4. Have your supervisor/instructor verify satisfactory completion of this procedure, any observations found, and any necessary action(s) recommended.

Performance Rating

CDX Tasksheet Number: C750

| 0 | 1 | 2 | 3 | 4 |

Supervisor/instructor signature _____ Date _____

Automatic Transmission and Transaxle **285**

TASK Inspect one-way clutches, races, rollers, sprags, springs, cages, and retainers; determine needed action.

Time off_____

Time on_____

Total time_____

CDX Tasksheet Number: C759

1. Research the procedure and any specifications for inspecting the one-way clutch assemblies in the appropriate service information.

   a. List the device that each roller or sprag clutch holds:

   b. List, or print off and attach to this sheet, any inspection procedures for these components:

2. Following the specified procedure, inspect each one-way clutch (including races, rollers, sprags, springs, cages, and retainers). List your observations:

3. Determine any necessary action(s):

4. Have your supervisor/instructor verify satisfactory completion of this procedure, any observations found, and any necessary action(s) recommended.

Performance Rating

CDX Tasksheet Number: C759

0	1	2	3	4

Supervisor/instructor signature _____ Date _____

MAST
2C13

CDX Tasksheet Number: C690

1. Research the procedure and any specifications for inspecting the oil delivery circuits, including seal rings, ring grooves, and sealing surface areas; feed pipes; orifices; and check valves/balls.

   a. List any specifications for the above components:

2. Following the specified procedure, inspect the oil delivery circuits (including the components above). List your observations:

3. Determine any necessary action(s):

4. Have your supervisor/instructor verify satisfactory completion of this procedure, any observations found, and any necessary action(s) recommended.

Performance Rating

CDX Tasksheet Number: C690

0	1	2	3	4

Supervisor/instructor signature _____ Date _____

Inspect case bores, passages, bushings, vents, and mating surfaces; determine needed action.

MAST
2C16

Time off_____

Time on_____

Total time_____

CDX Tasksheet Number: C753

1. Research the procedure and any specifications for inspecting case bores, passages, bushings, vents, and mating surfaces.

    a. List any specifications for the above components:

2. Following the specified procedure, inspect case bores, passages, bushings, vents, and mating surfaces. List your observations:

3. Determine any necessary action(s):

4. Have your supervisor/instructor verify satisfactory completion of this procedure, any observations found, and any necessary action(s) recommended.

Performance Rating

CDX Tasksheet Number: C753

0	1	2	3	4

Supervisor/instructor signature _____ Date _____

MAST
2C8

Time off_____

Time on_____

Total time_____

CDX Tasksheet Number: C686

1. **Research the procedure and any specifications for inspecting servo and accumulator bores, pistons, seals, pins, springs, and retainers.**

   a. **List any specifications for the above components:**

2. **If not already completed, disassemble each servo and accumulator.**

3. **Following the specified procedure, inspect servo and accumulator bores, pistons, seals, pins, springs, and retainers. List your observations:**

4. **Determine any necessary action(s):**

5. **Have your supervisor/instructor verify satisfactory completion of this procedure, any observations found, and any necessary action(s) recommended.**

Performance Rating

CDX Tasksheet Number: C686

0	1	2	3	4

Supervisor/instructor signature _____ Date _____

Inspect clutch drum, piston, check balls, springs, retainers, seals, friction plates, pressure plates, and bands; determine needed action.

MAST
2C19

CDX Tasksheet Number: C756

1. **Research the procedure and specifications for inspecting the clutch drum, piston, check balls, springs, retainers, seals, and friction and pressure plates for each clutch.**

    a. **In the table below, list the name of each clutch this transmission/ transaxle is equipped with and the number of steel plates and friction plates it contains.**

Name of Clutch	Number of Steel Plates	Number of Friction Plates

    b. **List, or print off and attach to this sheet, any specifications related to the clutch drum, piston, check balls, springs, retainers, seals, and friction and pressure plates:**

    c. **Research the procedure and specifications for inspecting the bands.**

        i. **List each band and the gear(s) each band is applied in:**

ii. List any specifications for each band:

2. Following the specified procedure, disassemble and inspect the components for each clutch assembly. List your observations for each clutch:

3. Following the specified procedure, inspect each band for wear or damage. List your observations:

4. Determine any necessary action(s):

5. Have your supervisor/instructor verify satisfactory completion of this procedure, any observations found, and any necessary action(s) recommended.

Performance Rating

CDX Tasksheet Number: C756

0	1	2	3	4

Supervisor/instructor signature _____ Date _____

▶ **TASK** Measure clutch pack clearance; determine needed action.

MAST
2C20

Time off_____

Time on_____

Total time_____

CDX Tasksheet Number: C757

1. Research the procedure and specifications for measuring clutch pack clearance in the appropriate service information.

   a. List the specified clutch pack clearance for each clutch in the table below.

Name of Clutch	Specified Clearance (in/mm)

   b. List how each clutch pack clearance is adjusted on this transmission/transaxle:

2. If not already completed, reassemble each clutch following the specified procedure.

3. Following the specified procedure, measure the clutch pack clearance for each clutch. List your measurements in the table below.

Name of Clutch	Measured Clearance (in/mm)

4. Determine any necessary action(s):

5. Have your supervisor/instructor verify satisfactory completion of this procedure, any observations found, and any necessary action(s) recommended.

Performance Rating

CDX Tasksheet Number: C757

0	1	2	3	4

Supervisor/instructor signature _____ Date _____

▶ **TASK** Air test operation of clutch and servo assemblies.

MAST
2C21

Time off_____

Time on_____

Total time_____

CDX Tasksheet Number: C758

> **NOTE** Most clutch assemblies can usually be air tested outside of the transmission once they are completely assembled with the clutch pack. Therefore, now would be a good time to perform that task for each self-contained clutch pack. Servos, which operate bands, must usually be tested with the gear train and bands installed. You may have to come back to this task for supervisor/instructor sign-off when it is appropriate to air test any servos during the assembly of the transmission/transaxle.

1. **Research the procedure for air testing each clutch and servo assembly.**

    a. **List any special tools needed for this procedure:**

2. **Following the specified procedure, air test each clutch assembly. List your observations for each one in the table below.**

Name of Clutch	Observations

3. **Have your supervisor/instructor verify the above results. Supervisor's/instructor's initials:** _____

4. **Once the transmission/transaxle is assembled far enough to air test the servos, test each one following the specified procedure. List your observations in the table below.**

Name of Servo	Observations

a. Determine any necessary action(s):

5. Have your supervisor/instructor verify satisfactory completion of this procedure, any observations found, and any necessary action(s) recommended.

Performance Rating

CDX Tasksheet Number: C758

0	1	2	3	4

Supervisor/instructor signature _____ Date _____

Inspect, measure, clean, and replace valve body (includes surfaces, bores, springs, valves, switches, solenoids, sleeves, retainers, brackets, check valves/balls, screens, spacers, and gaskets).

MAST
2C7

Time off_____

Time on_____

CDX Tasksheet Number: C685

Total time_____

1. **Research the procedure and specifications to inspect, measure, clean, and replace the valve body.**

   a. **List, or print off and attach to this sheet, any precautions for this task:**

   b. **List, or print off and attach to this sheet, any specifications related to this task:**

   c. **List, or print off and attach to this sheet, the torque specifications for the valve body bolts, screws, and fasteners:**

2. **Following the specified procedure, disassemble, clean, measure, and inspect the valve body components. List your observations for each.**

   a. **Valve body and plate surfaces:**

   b. **Bores, valves, and sleeves:**

c. Springs:

d. Retainers, spacers, and brackets:

e. Check valves and check balls:

f. Gaskets and screens:

3. Have your supervisor/instructor verify disassembly of the valve body. Supervisor's/instructor's initials: _____

4. Following the specified procedure, reassemble the valve body. Be careful to install all valves, springs, check balls, and gaskets in the proper orientation. Also, be sure to torque all fasteners in the correct sequence and to the proper torque.

5. Have your supervisor/instructor verify satisfactory completion of this procedure, any observations found, and any necessary action(s) recommended.

Performance Rating

CDX Tasksheet Number: C685

0	1	2	3	4

Supervisor/instructor signature _____ Date _____

Diagnose and inspect transaxle drive, link chains, sprockets, gears, bearings, and bushings; perform needed action.

MAST
2C17

Time off_____

Time on_____

Total time_____

CDX Tasksheet Number: C754

1. **Research the procedure and specifications to inspect the transaxle drive, link chains, sprockets, gears, bearings, and bushings.**

   a. **List, or print off and attach to this sheet, any precautions for this task:**

   b. **List, or print off and attach to this sheet, any specifications related to this task:**

2. **Following the specified procedure, inspect the following components. List your observations.**

   a. **Link chains:**

   b. **Sprockets:**

   c. **Gears:**

   d. **Bearings:**

e. Bushings:

3. Determine any necessary action(s):

4. Have your supervisor/instructor verify satisfactory completion of this procedure, any observations found, and any necessary action(s) recommended.

Inspect, measure, repair, adjust, or replace transaxle final drive
components.

MAST
2C18

CDX Tasksheet Number: C755

1. **Research the procedure and specifications to inspect, measure, repair, adjust, or replace transaxle final drive components.**

    a. **List, or print off and attach to this sheet, any precautions for this task:**

    b. **List any special tools required to complete this task:**

    c. **List, or print off and attach to this sheet, any specifications related to this task:**

2. **Following the specified procedure, inspect, measure, repair, adjust, or replace the following components. List your observations.**

    a. **Link chains:**

    b. **Sprockets:**

c. Gears:

d. Bearings:

e. Bushings:

3. Determine any necessary action(s):

4. Have your supervisor/instructor verify satisfactory completion of this procedure, any observations found, and any necessary action(s) recommended.

Transmission Removal and Replacement

Student/Intern information:

Name_____ Date_____ Class_____

Vehicle used for this activity:

Year _____ Make _____ Model_____

Odometer_____VIN_____

Learning Objective/Task	CDX Tasksheet Number	2017 MAST NATEF Reference Number; Priority Level
• Remove and reinstall transmission/transaxle and torque converter; inspect engine core plugs, rear crankshaft seal, dowel pins, dowel pin holes, and mating surfaces.	C604	2C1; P-2
• Inspect, leak test, flush and/or replace transmission/transaxle oil cooler, lines, and fittings.	C749	2C2; P-1
• Inspect converter flex (drive) plate, converter attaching bolts, converter pilot, converter pump drive surfaces, converter end play, and crankshaft pilot bore.	C605	2C3; P-2

Time off_____

Time on_____

Total time_____

Materials Required

- Blank work order
- Vehicle with available service history records
- Depending on the type of concern, special diagnostic tools may be required. See your supervisor/instructor for instructions to identify what tools may be required.

Some Safety Issues to Consider

- This task may require test-driving the vehicle on the school grounds. Attempt this task only with full permission from your instructor and follow all the guidelines exactly.
- When running any vehicles in the shop, make sure you use the shop's exhaust ventilation system to discharge all exhaust gas safely outside.
- Lifting equipment such as vehicle jacks and stands, vehicle hoists, and engine hoists are important tools that increase productivity and make the job easier. However, they can also cause severe injury or death if used improperly. Make sure you follow the manufacturer's operation procedures. Also, make sure you have your supervisor's/instructor's permission to use any particular type of lifting equipment.
- Comply with personal and environmental safety practices associated with clothing; eye protection; hand tools; power equipment; proper ventilation; and the handling, storage, and disposal of chemicals/materials in accordance with local, state, and federal safety and environmental regulations.

Performance Standard

0–No exposure: No information or practice provided during the program; complete training required

1–Exposure only: General information provided with no practice time; close supervision needed; additional training required

2–Limited practice: Has practiced job during training program; additional training required to develop skill

3–Moderately skilled: Has performed job independently during training program; limited additional training may be required

4–Skilled: Can perform job independently with no additional training

■ **TASK** Remove and reinstall transmission/transaxle and torque
converter; inspect engine core plugs, rear crankshaft seal,
dowel pins, dowel pinholes, and mating surfaces.

MAST
2C1

Time off_____

Time on_____

Total time_____

DX Tasksheet Number: C604

1. Research the following torque specifications and transmission/transaxle removal
   and installation procedure in the appropriate service information.
   a. Flexplate-to-crankshaft bolt torque: _____ ft-lb/N·m
   b. Torque converter-to-flexplate bolt torque: _____ ft-lb/N·m
   c. Transmission-to-block bolt torque: _____ ft-lb/N·m
   d. Transmission fluid type: _____
   e. Transmission fluid capacity: _____ qt/lt
   f. List or print off and attach to this sheet the procedure for removing and
      installing the transmission/transaxle:

2. Following the specified procedure, remove the transmission/transaxle from the
   vehicle.

3. Inspect the following components and list your observations.
   a. Engine core plugs:

   b. Rear crankshaft seal:

   c. Dowel pins and holes:

   d. Engine and bell-housing mating surfaces:

4. Have your supervisor/instructor verify your observations. Supervisor's/instructor's initials:_____

> **NOTE** At this time, you may want to overhaul the transmission/transaxle or perform other tasks such as inspecting/replacing the torque converter or flushing the transmission/transaxle cooler lines. Once any related tasks are completed and it is time to reinstall the transmission/transaxle, return to this page to complete the task and have it signed off.

5. Prepare the transmission to be reinstalled. Ensure that the torque converter is fully engaged in the transmission. Failure to do so may cause severe damage to the transmission/transaxle and the converter.

6. Have your instructor check that the converter is installed properly. Supervisor's/instructor's initials: _____

7. Position all wires, hoses, and tubes out of the way and in their specified positions. Secure them temporarily if necessary.

> **NOTE** It is easy for wires and hoses to fall down and get pinched between the engine and bell housing. This will cause electrical issues in the vehicle as well as alignment issues with the transmission.

8. Following the specified procedure, reinstall the transmission/transaxle. Be sure to tighten all fasteners to the proper torque.

9. Refill the transmission/transaxle to the proper level.

10. Check that all cooler lines, electrical wires, linkages, and other removed components are properly installed and adjusted.

11. Have your instructor verify that the vehicle is ready to be started. Supervisor's/instructor's initials: _____

12. Place exhaust hose(s) over the exhaust pipe(s) and set the parking brake.

13. Start the vehicle and move the transmission selector through each gear. Check the transmission fluid level and top off as necessary.

14. Check for leaks, loose parts, or anything that isn't right with the transmission and the related parts. List your observation(s):

15. With your supervisor's/instructor's permission, test drive the vehicle to ensure the transmission operates correctly. List your observations:

16. Double check your work and verify that there are no leaks and that everything is back in its proper place. List your observations:

17. Have your supervisor/instructor verify satisfactory completion of this procedure, any observations found, and any necessary action(s) recommended.

MAST
2C2

Time off_____

Time on_____

Total time_____

CDX Tasksheet Number: C749

1. Research the procedure to inspect, test, flush, and replace the cooler lines and fittings.

   a. List or print off and attach to this sheet the steps to test, flush, and replace the cooler lines:

2. Following the specified procedure, perform the following tasks. List your observations.

   a. Inspect the cooler, lines, and fittings for damage or wear:

   b. Test the cooler, lines, and fittings for leaks:

   c. Flush or replace the cooler and lines:

3. Have your supervisor/instructor verify satisfactory completion of this procedure, any observations found, and any necessary action(s) recommended.

Performance Rating

CDX Tasksheet Number: C749

0	1	2	3	4

Supervisor/instructor signature _____ Date _____

Inspect converter flex (drive) plate, converter-attaching bolts, converter pilot, converter pump-drive surfaces, converter end play, and crankshaft pilot bore.

MAST
2C3

Time off_____

Time on_____

Total time_____

DX Tasksheet Number: C605

1. **Research the procedure and specifications for inspecting the torque converter, flexplate, and crankshaft pilot bore.**

    a. Torque converter-to-flexplate bolt torque: _____ ft-lb/N·m
    b. Flexplate-to-crankshaft bolt torque: _____ ft-lb/N·m
    c. Converter end play: _____ in/mm
    d. Converter pilot diameter, if specified: _____ in/mm
    e. Crankshaft pilot bore, if specified: _____ in/mm

2. **Following the specified procedure, inspect each of the listed items below. List your observations.**

    a. Flexplate (cracks, warpage, elongated holes, starter ring-gear wear, etc.):

    b. Converter-attaching bolts (worn, stretched, rounded heads, etc.):

    c. Converter pilot (gouges, excessive rust, etc.):

    d. Crankshaft pilot bore (gouges, excessive rust, etc.):

    e. Converter pump-drive surface (wear, nicks, burrs, etc.):

    f. Converter end play: _____ in/mm

3. Determine any necessary action(s):

4. Have your supervisor/instructor verify satisfactory completion of this procedure, any observations found, and any necessary action(s) recommended.

Performance Rating　　　　　**CDX Tasksheet Number: C605**

0	1	2	3	4

Supervisor/instructor signature _____ Date _____

Assemble Transmission

Student/Intern information:

Name _____ Date _____ Class _____

Vehicle used for this activity:

Year _____ Make _____ Model _____

Odometer _____ VIN _____

Learning Objective/Task	CDX Tasksheet Number	2017 MAST NATEF Reference Number; Priority Level
• Assemble transmission/transaxle.	C083	2C9; P-1

Time off_____

Time on_____

Total time_____

Materials Required

- Transmission/transaxle
- Torque wrenches of appropriate size
- Feeler blades
- Approved air nozzle
- Dial indicator
- Specified assembly lubricant
- Manufacturer-specific tools

Some Safety Issues to Consider

- Castings and machined parts may have sharp edges. Handle these parts with care.
- Many transmission parts are round and can easily roll off of tables and carts. Be sure to place them in a secure manner to prevent component damage or personal injury from falling objects.
- Compressed air can be very dangerous if applied to broken skin or body cavities. Always use approved air nozzles, and never point them at yourself or another person.
- Transmissions, transaxles, and their component assemblies are heavy and can slip easily. Work safely, get help, and do not overextend your abilities.
- Comply with personal and environmental safety practices associated with clothing; eye protection; hand tools; power equipment; proper ventilation; and the handling, storage, and disposal of chemicals/materials in accordance with local, state, and federal safety and environmental regulations.

Performance Standard

0—No exposure: No information or practice provided during the program; complete training required

1—Exposure only: General information provided with no practice time; close supervision needed; additional training required

2—Limited practice: Has practiced job during training program; additional training required to develop skill

3—Moderately skilled: Has performed job independently during training program; limited additional training may be required

4—Skilled: Can perform job independently with no additional training

DX Tasksheet Number: C083

1. **Research the reassembly procedure for this transmission/transaxle in the appropriate service information.**

    a. **List the specified assembly lubricant:**

    _____

    b. **List the special tools required to perform this task:**

    c. **Transmission/transaxle end play:** _____ **in/mm**

    > **NOTE** All of the component assemblies should already be properly reassembled. If they are not, reassemble them according to the specified procedures as listed in previous tasks. Ensure that they meet all specifications.

2. **Following the specified procedure, reassemble the transmission, making sure all components are seated properly. Perform all specified checks along the way. List your observations:**

3. **Once the transmission/transaxle gear train and pump are fully installed, adjust any bands if necessary.**

    a. **Air check each servo and clutch. List each clutch and servo and your observations:**

NOTE Your instructor may want to approve the servo air check from task C758, "Air test operation of clutch and servo assemblies," after you perform it here.

    b. Measure the gear train end play: _____ in/mm

4. **Following the specified procedure, reinstall the valve body, linkage, filter, and pan(s).**

5. **Complete any other specified procedures related to the assembly process.**

6. **Have your supervisor/instructor verify satisfactory completion of this procedure, any observations found, and any necessary action(s) recommended.**

Performance Rating

CDX Tasksheet Number: C083

0	1	2	3	4

Supervisor/instructor signature _____ Date _____

Section A3:
Manual Drive Train and Axles

CONTENTS

Vehicle, Customer, and Service Information

Student/Intern information:

Name _____ Date _____ Class _____

Vehicle used for this activity:

Year _____ Make _____ Model_____

Odometer_____VIN_____

Learning Objective/Task	CDX Tasksheet Number	2017 MAST NATEF Reference Number; Priority Level
• Research vehicle service information including fluid type, vehicle service history, service precautions, and technical service bulletins.	C102	3A2; P-1
• Identify and interpret drive train concerns; determine needed action.	C101	3A1; P-1
• Describe the operational characteristics of an electronically controlled manual transmission/transaxle.	C611	3C2; P-2
• Demonstrate the use of the 3 Cs (concern, cause, and correction).	N/A	N/A

Time off_____

Time on_____

Total time_____

Materials Required

- Blank work order
- Vehicle with available service history records
- Depending on the type of concern, special diagnostic tools may be required. See your supervisor/instructor for instructions to identify what tools may be required.

Some Safety Issues to Consider

- Diagnosis of this fault may require test-driving the vehicle on the school grounds. Attempt this task only with full permission from your instructor and follow all the guidelines exactly.
- When running any vehicles in the shop, make sure you use the shop's exhaust ventilation system to discharge all exhaust gas safely outside.
- Lifting equipment such as vehicle jacks and stands, vehicle hoists, and engine hoists are important tools that increase productivity and make the job easier. However, they can also cause severe injury or death if used improperly. Make sure you follow the manufacturer's operation procedures. Also, make sure you have your supervisor's/instructor's permission to use any particular type of lifting equipment.
- Comply with personal and environmental safety practices associated with clothing; eye protection; hand tools; power equipment; proper ventilation; and the handling, storage, and disposal of chemicals/materials in accordance with local, state, and federal safety and environmental regulations.

Performance Standard

0–No exposure: No information or practice provided during the program; complete training required

1–Exposure only: General information provided with no practice time; close supervision needed; additional training required

2–Limited practice: Has practiced job during training program; additional training required to develop skill

3–Moderately skilled: Has performed job independently during training program; limited additional training may be required

4–Skilled: Can perform job independently with no additional training

MAST
3A2

DX Tasksheet Number: C102

1. **Using the vehicle VIN for identification, use the appropriate source to access the vehicle's service history in relation to prior related drive train system work or customer concerns.**

   a. **List any related repairs/concerns, and their dates:**

2. **List the specified type of transmission fluid for this vehicle:** _____

3. **Using the vehicle VIN for identification, access any relevant technical service bulletins for the particular vehicle you are working on in relation to any drive train system updates, precautions, or other service issues. List any related service bulletins:**

4. **Have your supervisor/instructor verify satisfactory completion of this procedure, any observations found, and any necessary action(s) recommended.**

Performance Rating

CDX Tasksheet Number: C102

0	1	2	3	4

Supervisor/instructor signature _____ Date _____

MAST
3A1

DX Tasksheet Number: C101

1. List the customer's transmission-related concern(s):

2. Research the particular concern in the appropriate service information. List the possible causes:

3. Inspect the vehicle to determine the cause of the concern. List the steps you took to determine the fault(s):

4. List the cause of the concern(s):

5. List the necessary action(s) to correct the fault(s):

6. Have your supervisor/instructor verify satisfactory completion of this procedure, any observations found, and any necessary action(s) recommended.

Performance Rating

CDX Tasksheet Number: C101

0	1	2	3	4

Supervisor/instructor signature _____ Date _____

Time off_____

Time on_____

Total time_____

CDX Tasksheet Number: C611

Vehicle used for this activity:

Year _____ Make _____ Model_____

Odometer_____ VIN_____

1. **Research the description and operation of an electronically controlled manual transmission/transaxle in the appropriate service information.**

    a. **How many forward speeds does this transmission have?**

    b. **How do the electronics interface with the transmission to control the transmission?**

    c. **How does this transmission achieve neutral?**

    d. **What type of fluid does this transmission use?** _____

    e. **What is the fluid capacity?** _____ qt/lt

    f. **What type of clutch(es) does this transmission use?**

2. **Have your supervisor/instructor verify satisfactory completion of this procedure, any observations found, and any necessary action(s) recommended.**

Performance Rating

CDX Tasksheet Number: C611

0	1	2	3	4

Supervisor/instructor signature _____ Date _____

Additional Task

Time off_____

Time on_____

Total time_____

CDX Tasksheet Number: N/A

1. **Using the following scenario, write up the 3 Cs as listed on most repair orders. Assume that the customer authorized the recommended repairs.**
   A late model half-ton pickup truck is brought to your shop with a manual transaxle concern. The customer tells you that the transmission started slipping a couple of days ago after his brother used it to haul several loads of gravel. You road test the vehicle and notice that it is slipping in all gears when under a moderate load. Also, the clutch pedal seems softer than normal, and there is a burning smell when you get back to the shop. You pull the vehicle onto a rack, and find the following:

   a. **The vehicle has 91,000 miles on it, but otherwise is in good condition.**
   b. **The transmission fluid is full and looks good.**
   c. **The slave cylinder is seeping brake fluid slightly from the dust boot, and the clutch master cylinder fluid level is a bit low.**
   d. **With the clutch inspection cover removed, there is a lot of clutch material and the burning smell is very strong.**
   e. **The rear shocks are leaking badly past the shaft seal.**

   > **NOTE** Ask your instructor whether you should use a copy of the shop repair order or the 3 Cs below to record this information.

2. **Concern:**

3. **Cause:**

4. **Correction:**

5. **Other recommended service:**

6. **Have your supervisor/instructor verify satisfactory completion of this procedur** any observations found, and any necessary action(s) recommended.

Transmission/Transaxle Maintenance

Student/Intern information:

Name _____ Date _____ Class _____

Vehicle used for this activity:

Year _____ Make _____ Model _____

Odometer _____ VIN _____

Learning Objective/Task	CDX Tasksheet Number	2017 MAST NATEF Reference Number; Priority Level
• Check fluid condition; check for leaks; determine needed action.	C691	3A3; P-1
• Drain and refill manual transmission/transaxle and final drive unit; use proper fluid type per manufacturer specification.	C105	3A4; P-1

Time off_____

Time on_____

Total time_____

Materials Required

- Vehicle with manual transmission/transaxle
- Vehicle hoist
- Drain pan
- Flashlight or shop light
- Fluorescent dye and ultraviolet light (optional)
- Specified fluid

Some Safety Issues to Consider

- Vehicle hoists are important tools that increase productivity and make the job easier. However, they can also cause severe injury or death if used improperly. Make sure you follow the manufacturer's operation procedures. Also, make sure you have your supervisor's/instructor's permission to use any particular type of lifting equipment.
- When running any vehicles in the shop, make sure you use the shop's exhaust ventilation system to discharge all exhaust gas safely outside.
- This procedure may require cleaning the engine prior to inspection. If so, use the proper equipment and procedures to carry this out safely. Also, get your supervisor's/instructor's permission prior to cleaning.
- Comply with personal and environmental safety practices associated with clothing; eye protection; hand tools; power equipment; proper ventilation; and the handling, storage, and disposal of chemicals/materials in accordance with local, state, and federal safety and environmental regulations.

Performance Standard

0–No exposure: No information or practice provided during the program; complete training required

1–Exposure only: General information provided with no practice time; close supervision needed; additional training required

2–Limited practice: Has practiced job during training program; additional training required to develop skill

3–Moderately skilled: Has performed job independently during training program; limited additional training may be required

4–Skilled: Can perform job independently with no additional training

MAST
3A3

Time off_____

Time on_____

Total time_____

DX Tasksheet Number: C691

1. **List the transmission designation for this vehicle:** _____

2. **Research the following specifications for this vehicle in the appropriate service information.**

    a. **Fluid type:** _____

    b. **Fluid capacity:** _____ **qt/lt**

    c. **How is the fluid level checked?**

3. **Safely raise and secure the vehicle on a hoist.**

4. **Following the specified procedure, check the fluid level and list your observation(s):**

5. **Inspect the condition of the fluid. Look for contaminants, metal shavings, and degraded fluid condition. List your observation(s):**

6. **Inspect the transmission/transaxle assembly for leaks.**

    a. **Identify and list the source of any leak(s):**

7. **Determine any necessary action(s):**

8. **Have your supervisor/instructor verify satisfactory completion of this procedure, any observations found, and any necessary action(s) recommended.**

Performance Rating

CDX Tasksheet Number: C691

0	1	2	3	4

Supervisor/instructor signature _____ Date _____

Drain and refill manual transmission/transaxle and final drive unit; use proper fluid type per manufacturer specification.

MAST 3A4

CDX Tasksheet Number: C105

1. **Research the following specifications and procedure in the appropriate service information.**

    a. **Transmission/transaxle service interval:** _____ km/mi
    b. **Transmission/transaxle fluid type:** _____
    c. **Transmission/transaxle fluid capacity:** _____ qt/lt
    d. **Final drive service interval:** _____ km/mi
    e. **Final drive fluid type:** _____
    f. **Final drive fluid capacity:** _____ qt/lt

2. **Following the specified procedure, drain the transmission/transaxle fluid into a clean drain pan. Inspect any residue and debris in the bottom of the drain pan. List your observations:**

3. **Determine any necessary action(s):**

4. **Drain the final drive unit (if separate from the transmission) into a clean drain pan. Inspect any residue and debris in the bottom of the drain pan. List your observations:**

5. **Have your supervisor/instructor verify fluid removal and your answers. Supervisor's/instructor's initials:** _____

6. **Following the specified procedure, refill the transmission/transaxle and final drive unit. Replace all fill plugs and tighten them to the proper torque. List your observations:**

7. **Have your supervisor/instructor verify satisfactory completion of this procedure, any observations found, and any necessary action(s) recommended.**

Performance Rating

CDX Tasksheet Number: C105

0	1	2	3	4

Supervisor/instructor signature _____ Date _____

Clutch Maintenance

Student/Intern information:

Name _____ Date _____ Class _____

Vehicle used for this activity:

Year _____ Make _____ Model _____

Odometer _____ VIN _____

Learning Objective/Task	CDX Tasksheet Number	2017 MAST NATEF Reference Number; Priority Level
• Inspect clutch pedal linkage, cables, automatic adjuster mechanisms, brackets, bushings, pivots, and springs; perform needed action.	C107	3B2; P-1
• Check and adjust clutch master cylinder fluid level; check for leaks; use proper fluid type per manufacturer specification.	C938	3B5; P-1
• Bleed clutch hydraulic system.	C111	3B4; P-1

Time off_____

Time on_____

Total time_____

Materials Required

- Vehicle with manual transmission/transaxle
- Vehicle hoist
- Flashlight or shop light
- Ruler
- Brake/clutch bleeding kit
- Drain pan
- Line or flare wrench set
- Specified fluid

Some Safety Issues to Consider

- Vehicle hoists are important tools that increase productivity and make the job easier. However, they can also cause severe injury or death if used improperly. Make sure you follow the manufacturer's operation procedures. Also, make sure you have your supervisor's/instructor's permission to use any particular type of lifting equipment.
- When running any vehicles in the shop, make sure you use the shop's exhaust ventilation system to discharge all exhaust gas safely outside.
- Diagnosis of this fault may require test-driving the vehicle on the school grounds. Attempt this task only with full permission from your instructor and follow all the guidelines exactly.

- Brake fluid can damage painted surfaces. Avoid spills and splashes, and rinse off with water immediately.
- Comply with personal and environmental safety practices associated with clothing; eye protection; hand tools; power equipment; proper ventilation; and the handling, storage, and disposal of chemicals/materials in accordance with local, state, and federal safety and environmental regulations.

Performance Standard

0—No exposure: No information or practice provided during the program; complete training required

1—Exposure only: General information provided with no practice time; close supervision needed; additional training required

2—Limited practice: Has practiced job during training program; additional training required to develop skill

3—Moderately skilled: Has performed job independently during training program; limited additional training may be required

4—Skilled: Can perform job independently with no additional training

Inspect clutch pedal linkage, cables, automatic adjuster mechanisms, brackets, bushings, pivots, and springs; perform needed action.

MAST
3B2

CDX Tasksheet Number: C107

1. **Research the procedure and specifications for inspecting and adjusting the clutch linkage in the appropriate service information.**

   a. **Clutch pedal height:** _____ in/mm
   b. **Clutch pedal free play:** _____ in/mm
   c. **Is this an adjustable clutch? Yes:** _____ **No:** _____
   d. **If yes, how is it adjusted?**

2. **Following the specified procedure, inspect the following parts for damage, wear, or missing components. List your observations for each.**

   a. **Clutch pedal linkage:**

   b. **Cable(s):**

   c. **Automatic adjuster mechanism, if equipped:**

   d. **Brackets:**

   e. **Bushings/guides/pivots:**

    f. Springs:

3. Measure the clutch pedal height: _____ in/mm

4. Measure the clutch pedal free play: _____ in/mm

5. Determine any necessary action(s):

6. Have your supervisor/instructor verify your answers.
   Supervisor's/instructor's initials: _____

7. Perform any necessary action(s) and list your observations:

8. Have your supervisor/instructor verify satisfactory completion of this
   procedure, any observations found, and any necessary action(s) recommended.

Performance Rating

CDX Tasksheet Number: C107

0	1	2	3	4

Supervisor/instructor signature _____ Date _____

Check and adjust clutch master cylinder fluid level; check for leaks; use proper fluid type per manufacturer specification.

MAST
3B5

Time off_____

Time on_____

Total time_____

CDX Tasksheet Number: C938

1. **Research the procedure and specifications for checking and adjusting the master cylinder fluid level in the appropriate service information.**

    a. **Specified clutch master cylinder fluid:** _____

    b. **Specified clutch master cylinder fluid replacement interval:**
    _____ **mi/km/mo**

2. **Check the clutch master cylinder fluid level and condition.**
   List your observations:

3. **Inspect the following clutch hydraulic system components for leaks.**
   List your observations:

    a. **Clutch master cylinder:**

    b. **Clutch slave cylinder (look under the dust boot):**

    c. **Hydraulic clutch lines and hoses:**

4. **Have your supervisor/instructor verify satisfactory completion of this procedure, any observations found, and any necessary action(s) recommended.**

Performance Rating

CDX Tasksheet Number: C938

0	1	2	3	4

Supervisor/instructor signature _____ Date _____

MAST
3B4

CDX Tasksheet Number: C111

Vehicle used for this activity:

Year _____ Make _____ Model _____

Odometer _____ VIN _____

1. **Research the procedure and specifications for bleeding the clutch hydraulic system in the appropriate service information.**

    a. **Specified fluid:** _____

    b. **List or print off and attach to this sheet the steps to bleed the system:**

    c. **List any special tools needed for this task:**

2. **Following the specified procedure, inspect the following parts for damage, wear, or missing components. List your observations for each.**

    a. **Clutch master cylinder:**

    b. **Clutch slave cylinder:**

    c. **Lines (steel or plastic):**

d. Hoses (flexible):

3. Following the specified procedure, bleed the hydraulic clutch system, being careful not to run the reservoir low. List your observation(s):

4. Have your supervisor/instructor verify satisfactory completion of this procedure, any observations found, and any necessary action(s) recommended.

Performance Rating

CDX Tasksheet Number: C111

0	1	2	3	4

Supervisor/instructor signature _____ Date _____

Clutch Diagnosis and Repair

Student/Intern information:

Name _____ Date _____ Class _____

Vehicle used for this activity:

Year _____ Make _____ Model _____

Odometer _____ VIN _____

Learning Objective/Task	CDX Tasksheet Number	2017 MAST NATEF Reference Number; Priority Level
• Diagnose clutch noise, binding, slippage, pulsation, and chatter; determine needed action.	C106	3B1; P-1
• Measure flywheel runout and crankshaft end play; determine needed action.	C848	3B7; P-2
• Inspect flywheel and ring gear for wear, cracks, and discoloration; determine needed action.	C847	3B6; P-1
• Inspect and/or replace clutch pressure plate assembly, clutch disc, release (throw-out) bearing, linkage, and pilot bearing/bushing (as applicable).	C608	3B3; P-1

Time off _____

Time on _____

Total time _____

Materials Required

- Vehicle with manual transmission/transaxle
- Vehicle hoist
- Transmission jack
- Flashlight or shop light
- Dial indicator
- Flywheel wrench (holding tool)
- 1/8" to 3/16" pin punch
- Clutch alignment tool
- Torque wrench

Some Safety Issues to Consider

- Only students who have their supervisor's/instructor's direct permission should perform this task due to the safety concerns involved.
- Diagnosis of this fault may require test-driving the vehicle on the school grounds. Attempt this task only with full permission from your instructor and follow all the guidelines exactly.
- **Caution**: Clutch dust may contain asbestos, which has been determined to cause cancer when inhaled or ingested. Treat all clutch dust as if it contains asbestos and use OSHA-approved asbestos removal equipment. DO NOT allow clutch dust to become airborne by using anything that would disturb the dust. Also, wear protective gloves during this procedure and dispose of or clean them in an approved manner.
- Vehicle hoists are important tools that increase productivity and make the job easier. However, they can also cause severe injury or death if used improperly. Make sure you follow the manufacturer's operation procedures. Also, make sure you have your supervisor's/instructor's permission to use any particular type of lifting equipment.
- Comply with personal and environmental safety practices associated with clothing; eye protection; hand tools; power equipment; proper ventilation; and the handling, storage, and disposal of chemicals/materials in accordance with local, state, and federal safety and environmental regulations.

Performance Standard

0—No exposure: No information or practice provided during the program; complete training required

1—Exposure only: General information provided with no practice time; close supervision needed; additional training required

2—Limited practice: Has practiced job during training program; additional training required to develop skill

3—Moderately skilled: Has performed job independently during training program; limited additional training may be required

4—Skilled: Can perform job independently with no additional training

Diagnose clutch noise, binding, slippage, pulsation, and chatter; determine needed action.

Time off_____

Time on_____

Total time_____

CDX Tasksheet Number: C106

1. **List the customer concern(s) related to the conditions listed above:**

2. **If your instructor approves, test-drive the vehicle to verify the concern. List your observation(s):**

> **NOTE** If the clutch is spongy, you may need to do some preliminary checks such as checking the level of fluid in the hydraulic clutch master cylinder before test-driving the vehicle.

3. **Research the concern in the appropriate service information. List or print off and attach to this sheet the possible causes:**

    a. **List or print off and attach to this sheet the steps to diagnose this concern:**

4. Following the specified procedure, diagnose the cause of the customer concern. List your steps and the results obtained:

5. Determine any necessary action(s) to correct the fault:

6. Have your supervisor/instructor verify satisfactory completion of this procedure, any observations found, and any necessary action(s) recommended.

Performance Rating

CDX Tasksheet Number: C106

| 0 | 1 | 2 | 3 | 4 |

Supervisor/instructor signature _____ Date _____

Measure flywheel runout and crankshaft end play; determine needed action.

Time off_____

Time on_____

Total time_____

CDX Tasksheet Number: C848

1. **Research the specifications and procedure for measuring flywheel runout and crankshaft end play in the appropriate service information.**

   a. Flywheel runout: _____ in/mm
   b. Crankshaft end play: _____ in/mm

2. **If not already completed, following the specified procedure, remove the transmission/transaxle. List any observations:**

3. **Following the specified procedure, remove the pressure plate and clutch disc.**

   > **NOTE** It is good practice to remove the pressure plate bolts evenly. This requires backing each bolt out a turn or two at a time to avoid warping the pressure plate. Also, have an assistant hold the pressure plate and clutch disc when they get close to becoming loose to avoid dropping them on the floor and damaging them or injuring your feet.

4. **Clean up any debris using an approved method for disposing of hazardous dust.**

5. **Following the specified procedure, measure the following.**

   a. Flywheel runout: _____ in/mm
   b. Crankshaft end play: _____ in/mm

6. **Determine any necessary action(s):**

7. **Have your supervisor/instructor verify satisfactory completion of this procedure, any observations found, and any necessary action(s) recommended.**

Performance Rating

CDX Tasksheet Number: C848

0	1	2	3	4

Supervisor/instructor signature _____ Date _____

Inspect flywheel and ring gear for wear, cracks, and discoloration; determine needed action.

MAST
3B6

CDX Tasksheet Number: C847

1. **Research the procedure for inspecting the flywheel and ring gear in the appropriate service information. List any specifications or specific instructions for inspection:**

2. **Inspect the flywheel for wear, cracks, and discoloration. List your observations:**

3. **Inspect the ring gear for wear, chipped teeth, and cracks. List your observations:**

> **NOTE** It is common for the ring gear teeth to be worn in a pattern. For example, a four-cylinder engine will have greater wear every 180°, a six-cylinder engine every 120°, and an eight-cylinder engine every 90°. Therefore, be sure to inspect all of the teeth, not just a few of them.

4. **Determine any necessary action(s):**

5. **Have your supervisor/instructor verify satisfactory completion of this procedure, any observations found, and any necessary action(s) recommended.**

Performance Rating

CDX Tasksheet Number: C847

0	1	2	3	4

Supervisor/instructor signature _____ Date _____

Inspect and/or replace clutch pressure plate assembly, clutch disc, release (throw-out) bearing, linkage, and pilot bearing/bushing (as applicable).

MAST
3B3

Time off_____

Time on_____

Total time_____

CDX Tasksheet Number: C608

1. **Research the procedure and any specifications for inspecting the clutch assembly.**

   a. **List any specifications or specific instructions for inspection:**

   b. **Flywheel-to-crankshaft bolt torque:** _____ ft-lb/N·m

      i. **Threadlock required: Yes:** _____ **No:** _____

   c. **Pressure plate-to-flywheel bolt torque:** _____ ft-lb/N·m

   d. **Pilot bushing/bearing lubricant, if applicable:** _____

2. **Inspect each of the following and list your observations.**

   a. **Pressure plate assembly:**

   b. **Clutch disc:**

   c. **Release (throw-out) bearing and linkage:**

   d. **Pilot bearing/bushing:**

3. Determine any necessary action(s):

4. Have your supervisor/instructor verify your observations and recommendations and initial below.

    a. Supervisor's/instructor's initials: _____

5. With your instructor's permission, replace any worn parts with new/remanufactured components.

6. Following the specified procedure, install the pilot bushing/bearing, if removed. Lubricate it with the specified lubricant, if applicable.

7. Following the specified procedure, install the flywheel. Be sure to torque the flywheel bolts.

8. Following the specified procedure, install the clutch disc and pressure plate. Use an appropriate clutch alignment tool to ensure proper positioning of the clutch disc.

> **NOTE** The pressure plate bolts should be tightened down evenly. This is usually done by tightening each bolt a turn or two, one at a time, until the pressure plate is evenly seated on the flywheel surface. Then, torque each bolt according to the specified torque and sequence.

9. Install the release (throw-out) bearing and linkage.

10. List any observation(s):

11. Have your supervisor/instructor verify satisfactory completion of this procedure, any observations found, and any necessary action(s) recommended.

Performance Rating

CDX Tasksheet Number: C608

0	1	2	3	4

Supervisor/instructor signature _____ Date _____

Transmission/Transaxle Diagnosis

Student/Intern information:

Name _____ Date _____ Class _____

Vehicle used for this activity:

Year _____ Make _____ Model_____

Odometer_____VIN_____

Learning Objective/Task	CDX Tasksheet Number	2017 MAST NATEF Reference Number; Priority Level
• Diagnose noise concerns through the application of transmission/ transaxle powerflow principles.	C609	3C3; P-2
• Diagnose hard shifting and jumping out of gear concerns; determine needed action.	C693	3C4; P-2
• Diagnose transaxle final drive assembly noise and vibration concerns; determine needed action.	C887	3C5; P-3

Time off_____

Time on_____

Total time_____

Materials Required

- Vehicle(s) with specific concern(s)
- Vehicle hoist
- Powerflow flowcharts
- Stethoscope
- Job-specific tools
- Manufacturer-specific tools

Some Safety Issues to Consider

- Vehicle hoists are important tools that increase productivity and make the job easier. However, they can also cause severe injury or death if used improperly. Make sure you follow the manufacturer's operation procedures. Also, make sure you have your supervisor's/instructor's permission to use any particular type of lifting equipment.
- When running any vehicles in the shop, make sure you use the shop's exhaust ventilation system to discharge all exhaust gas safely outside.
- Diagnosis of this fault may require test-driving the vehicle on the school grounds. Attempt this task only with full permission from your instructor and follow all the guidelines exactly.
- Castings and machined parts may have sharp edges. Handle these parts with care.
- Comply with personal and environmental safety practices associated with clothing; eye protection; hand tools; power equipment; proper ventilation; and the handling, storage, and disposal of chemicals/materials in accordance with local, state, and federal safety and environmental regulations.

Performance Standard

0–No exposure: No information or practice provided during the program; complete training required

1–Exposure only: General information provided with no practice time; close supervision needed; additional training required

2–Limited practice: Has practiced job during training program; additional training required to develop skill

3–Moderately skilled: Has performed job independently during training program; limited additional training may be required

4–Skilled: Can perform job independently with no additional training

MAST
3C3

DX Tasksheet Number: C609

1. List the transmission/transaxle noise-related customer concern:

2. Research the concern in the appropriate service information and list the possible causes:

3. Following the specified procedure, use powerflow flowcharts to identify the cause of the noise concern. List your tests and observations:

4. List the cause of the noise concern:

5. Determine any necessary action(s) to correct the fault:

6. Have your supervisor/instructor verify satisfactory completion of this procedure, any observations found, and any necessary action(s) recommended.

Performance Rating

CDX Tasksheet Number: C609

0	1	2	3	4

Supervisor/instructor signature _____ Date _____

TASK Diagnose hard shifting and jumping out of gear concerns; determine needed action.

MAST
3C4

Time off_____

Time on_____

Total time_____

CDX Tasksheet Number: C693

Vehicle used for this activity:

Year _____ Make _____ Model _____

Odometer _____ VIN _____

1. List the hard shifting or jumping out of gear customer concern:

2. Research the concern in the appropriate service information and list the possible causes:

3. Following the specified procedure, diagnose the fault. List your tests and observations:

4. List the cause of the hard shifting or jumping out of gear concern:

5. Determine any necessary action(s) to correct the fault:

6. Have your supervisor/instructor verify satisfactory completion of this procedure, any observations found, and any necessary action(s) recommended.

Performance Rating

CDX Tasksheet Number: C693

0	1	2	3	4

Supervisor/instructor signature _____ Date _____

MAST
3C5

Time off_____

Time on_____

Total time_____

CDX Tasksheet Number: C887

Vehicle used for this activity:

Year _____ Make _____ Model_____

Odometer_____ VIN_____

1. List the final drive noise or vibration customer concern:

2. Research the concern in the appropriate service information and list the possible causes:

3. Following the specified procedure, diagnose the fault. List your tests and observations:

4. List the cause of the noise or vibration concern:

5. Determine any necessary action(s) to correct the fault:

6. Have your supervisor/instructor verify satisfactory completion of this procedure, any observations found, and any necessary action(s) recommended.

Performance Rating

CDX Tasksheet Number: C887

0	1	2	3	4

Supervisor/instructor signature _____ Date _____

Transmission/Transaxle Repair

Student/Intern information:

Name_____ Date_____ Class_____

Vehicle used for this activity:

Year _____ Make _____ Model_____

Odometer_____VIN_____

Learning Objective/Task	CDX Tasksheet Number	2017 MAST NATEF Reference Number; Priority Level
• Inspect, adjust, lubricate, and/or replace shift linkages, brackets, bushings, cables, pivots, and levers.	C768	3C1; P-2
• Disassemble, inspect, clean, and reassemble internal transmission/transaxle components.	C910	3C6; P-2

Time off_____

Time on_____

Total time_____

Materials Required

- Vehicle/simulator
- Parts trays
- Manufacturer-specific tools

Some Safety Issues to Consider

- Castings and machined parts may have sharp edges. Handle these parts with care.
- Comply with personal and environmental safety practices associated with clothing; eye protection; hand tools; power equipment; proper ventilation; and the handling, storage, and disposal of chemicals/materials in accordance with local, state, and federal safety and environmental regulations.

Performance Standard

0—No exposure: No information or practice provided during the program; complete training required

1—Exposure only: General information provided with no practice time; close supervision needed; additional training required

2—Limited practice: Has practiced job during training program; additional training required to develop skill

3—Moderately skilled: Has performed job independently during training program; limited additional training may be required

4—Skilled: Can perform job independently with no additional training

TASK Inspect, adjust, lubricate, and/or replace shift linkages, brackets, bushings, cables, pivots, and levers.

MAST
3C1

Time off_____

Time on_____

Total time_____

CDX Tasksheet Number: C768

1. Research the procedure and specifications for inspecting, adjusting, lubricating, and replacing shift linkages in the appropriate service information.

   a. List or print off and attach to this sheet the procedure for adjusting the shift linkages, if applicable:

2. Following the specified procedure, inspect and lubricate the shift linkage components. List your observations for each component.

   a. Shift linkages:

   b. Brackets:

   c. Bushings:

   d. Cables:

e. Pivots:

f. Levers:

3. Following the specified procedure, replace and/or adjust each shift linkage. List your observations:

4. Have your supervisor/instructor verify satisfactory completion of this procedure, any observations found, and any necessary action(s) recommended.

Performance Rating

CDX Tasksheet Number: C768

0	1	2	3	4

Supervisor/instructor signature _____ Date _____

DX Tasksheet Number: C910

1. **Research the procedure to disassemble, clean, and reassemble the transmission/transaxle in the appropriate service information.**

   a. **List any special tools required for this task:**

   b. **List, or print off and attach to this sheet, the procedure to disassemble and reassemble the transmission/transaxle:**

2. **Following the specified procedure, disassemble the transmission/transaxle, ensuring that you note their location and orientation. Make notes or take pictures as appropriate. Lay them out in a logical manner to facilitate reassembly.**

   > **NOTE** Round objects such as gears, shafts, ball bearings, roller bearings, and bushings can roll off of the work table if not secured, causing personal injury. This could also lead to damage or loss of the components. Always lay round objects on their side when possible, or store them in a work tray to prevent rolling.

3. **Clean the components according to the specified procedure. Make sure you relocate them in the same logical sequence as before.**

4. **Perform a preliminary visual inspection of the components. This is an initial inspection designed to identify major issues with the transmission/transaxle. Further inspection of the subunits and parts will occur as you perform the next several tasks.**
   List your observations:

5. **Have your supervisor/instructor verify the initial disassembly and your observations.**

   a. **Supervisor's/instructor's initials: _____ Date: _____**

Drive Shaft, Half Shaft, Universal, and Constant-Velocity Joint Diagnosis and Repair

Student/Intern information:

Name _____ Date _____ Class _____

Vehicle used for this activity:

Year _____ Make _____ Model _____

Odometer _____ VIN _____

Learning Objective/Task	CDX Tasksheet Number	2017 MAST NATEF Reference Number; Priority Level
• Diagnose constant-velocity (CV) joint noise and vibration concerns; determine needed action.	C132	3D1; P-1
• Inspect, service, and/or replace shafts, yokes, boots, and universal/CV joints.	C849	3D4; P-1
• Inspect, remove, and/or replace bearings, hubs, and seals.	C134	3D3; P-1
• Diagnose universal joint noise and vibration concerns; perform needed action.	C133	3D2; P-2
• Check shaft balance and phasing; measure shaft runout; measure and adjust driveline angles.	C779	3D5; P-2

Time off _____

Time on _____

Total time _____

Materials Required

- Vehicle hoist
- Dial indicator
- Driveline angle gauge
- Hydraulic press
- U-joint press or equivalent
- Torque wrench
- Manufacturer-specific tools

Some Safety Issues to Consider

- Diagnosis of this fault may require test-driving the vehicle on the school grounds. Attempt this task only with full permission from your instructor and follow all the guidelines exactly.
- Vehicle hoists are important tools that increase productivity and make the job easier. However, they can also cause severe injury or death if used improperly. Make sure you follow the manufacturer's operation procedures. Also, make sure you have your supervisor's/instructor's permission to use any particular type of lifting equipment.

- Lug nuts must always be tightened to the proper torque. Always use a properly calibrated torque wrench.
- CV joints may contain grease made with lead, which can be harmful to your health. Avoid getting it on your skin and hands. Wash your hands thoroughly before eating.
- Comply with personal and environmental safety practices associated with clothing; eye protection; hand tools; power equipment; proper ventilation; and the handling, storage, and disposal of chemicals/materials in accordance with local, state, and federal safety and environmental regulations.

Performance Standard

0—No exposure: No information or practice provided during the program; complete training required

1—Exposure only: General information provided with no practice time; close supervision needed; additional training required

2—Limited practice: Has practiced job during training program; additional training required to develop skill

3—Moderately skilled: Has performed job independently during training program; limited additional training may be required

4—Skilled: Can perform job independently with no additional training

Diagnose constant-velocity (CV) joint noise and vibration concerns; determine needed action.

Time off_____

Time on_____

Total time_____

DX Tasksheet Number: C132

1. **List the CV-related customer concern:**

2. **With your instructor's permission, test-drive the vehicle in an open area on a firm surface. Turn the steering wheel to its maximum lock position and drive smoothly in a tight circle. Listen for a distinctive clicking or knocking noise coming from one or more corners of the vehicle. List your observations:**

3. **Repeat step 2, turning the steering wheel in the other direction while driving in a tight circle. List your observations:**

4. **Safely raise and secure the vehicle on a hoist and visually inspect the CV joint boots for splits and tears, or signs of grease leakage from the boot or joint housing. List your observations:**

5. **Check for excessive play or binding in the inboard and outboard CV joints. List your observations:**

6. **Determine any necessary action(s):**

7. Have your supervisor/instructor verify satisfactory completion of this procedure, any observations found, and any necessary action(s) recommended.

Performance Rating

CDX Tasksheet Number: C132

0	1	2	3	4

Supervisor/instructor signature _____ Date _____

Inspect, service, and/or replace shafts, yokes, boots, and universal/CV joints.

MAST
3D4

DX Tasksheet Number: C849

1. **Research the procedure and specifications to inspect, service, and replace shafts, yokes, boots, and universal/CV joints in the appropriate service information.**

    a. **List any special tools required to perform this task:**

    b. **List any specific precautions when performing this task:**

    c. **List or print off and attach to this sheet the procedure for servicing universal/CV joints, shafts, and boots:**

2. **If not already done, safely raise and support the vehicle on a hoist and inspect the half shafts and boots. List your observations:**

3. **Following the specified procedure, remove the worn half shaft(s).**

4. **With your instructor's permission, disassemble the half shaft(s) following the specified procedure.**

5. **Clean and inspect all parts. List your observations for each.**

    a. **Shaft(s):**

    b. **Yoke(s):**

   c. Boots (and clamps):

   d. CV joint(s) (including any balls or rollers):

6. **Determine any necessary action(s):**

7. **Have your supervisor/instructor verify disassembly and your observations. Supervisor's/instructor's initials:** _____

> **NOTE** You may want to continue on with the next task once the half shaft(s) are reassembled and removed. If so, return here to complete this task once you are ready to reinstall the half shaft(s).

8. **Perform any necessary actions to service the half shaft(s) and reinstall them in the vehicle following the specified procedure. List your observations:**

> **NOTE** Be sure to tighten all fasteners to the proper torque.

9. **Have your supervisor/instructor verify satisfactory completion of this procedure, any observations found, and any necessary action(s) recommended.**

Performance Rating

CDX Tasksheet Number: C849

0	1	2	3	4

Supervisor/instructor signature _____ Date _____

CDX Tasksheet Number: C134

1. Research the procedure and specifications for removing and replacing the FWD wheel bearing, hub, and seals in the appropriate service information.

   a. List any special tools required to perform this task:

   b. List any specific precautions when performing this task:

   c. List or print off and attach to this sheet the procedure for replacing the wheel bearing, seal, and hub:

2. If not already done, safely raise and support the vehicle on a hoist and remove the wheel bearing following the specified procedure.

3. Inspect the bearing, shaft, and hub for damage or wear. List your observations:

4. Determine any necessary action(s):

5. Have your supervisor/instructor verify removal and your observations. Supervisor's/instructor's initials: _____

6. Following the specified procedure, replace the wheel bearing, seal, and hub. Make sure the bearing is fully seated and retained in the hub. List your observations:

> NOTE Be sure to tighten all fasteners to the proper torque.

7. Have your supervisor/instructor verify satisfactory completion of this procedure, any observations found, and any necessary action(s) recommended.

Performance Rating

CDX Tasksheet Number: C134

0	1	2	3	4

Supervisor/instructor signature _____ Date _____

CDX Tasksheet Number: C133

Vehicle used for this activity:

Year _____ Make _____ Model _____

Odometer _____ VIN _____

1. List the universal joint-related customer concern:

2. With your instructor's permission, test-drive the vehicle in an open area on a firm surface. Listen for a distinctive squeaking noise or clunking sound coming from under the vehicle, which is usually worse at low speeds. Universal joints can also cause a vibration at low speeds due to intermittent binding, or at higher speeds due to causing the drive shaft to be located off center. List your observations:

3. Safely raise and secure the vehicle on a hoist and inspect the universal joints for looseness, wear, and damage. List your observations:

NOTE Make sure the parking brake is not applied and the transmission is in neutral. This will allow you to turn the drive shaft to check it for play and binding in various positions.

4. Determine any necessary action(s):

5. Have your supervisor/instructor verify your observations and diagnosis. Supervisor's/instructor's initials: _____

6. **Perform any necessary action(s) following the specified procedure. List your observations:**

NOTE Be sure to tighten all fasteners to the proper torque.

---

7. **Have your supervisor/instructor verify satisfactory completion of this procedure, any observations found, and any necessary action(s) recommended.**

Performance Rating

0	1	2	3	4

Supervisor/instructor signature _____ Date _____

MAST
3D5

Time off_____

Time on_____

Total time_____

CDX Tasksheet Number: C779

Vehicle used for this activity:

Year _____ Make _____ Model_____

Odometer_____ VIN_____

1. **Research the procedure and specifications for inspecting, measuring, and adjusting the driveline balance, phasing, and angles in the appropriate service information.**

    a. **List any special tools required to perform this task:**

    b. **List any specific precautions when performing this task:**

    c. **List any specifications for balance, phasing, runout, and driveline angles:**

    d. **List or print off and attach to this sheet the procedure for inspecting, measuring, and adjusting the driveline balance, phasing, and angles:**

2. **Safely raise and secure the vehicle on a hoist. Make sure the parking brake is released and the transmission is in neutral.**

3. Check the drive shaft for phasing. List your observation(s):

4. Measure drive shaft runout: _____ in/mm

5. Measure driveline angles.

   a. Front: _____ degrees
   b. Center (if specified): _____ degrees
   c. Rear: _____ degrees

6. Check the drive shaft for balance. List your observation(s):

7. Determine any necessary action(s):

8. Have your supervisor/instructor verify satisfactory completion of this procedure, any observations found, and any necessary action(s) recommended.

Performance Rating

CDX Tasksheet Number: C779

0	1	2	3	4

Supervisor/instructor signature _____ Date _____

Drive Axle Diagnosis and Repair

Ring and Pinion Gears and Differential Case Assembly

Student/Intern information:

Name _____ Date _____ Class _____

Vehicle used for this activity:

Year _____ Make _____ Model_____

Odometer_____VIN_____

Learning Objective/Task	CDX Tasksheet Number	2017 MAST NATEF Reference Number; Priority Level
• Check and adjust differential case fluid level; use proper fluid type per manufacturer specification.	C911	3E1:2; P-1
• Drain and refill differential case; use proper fluid type per manufacturer specification.	C912	3E1:3; P-1
• Clean and inspect differential case; check for leaks; inspect housing vent.	C785	3E1:1, P-1
• Inspect and replace companion flange and/or pinion seal; measure companion flange runout.	C889	3E1:5; P-2
• Diagnose noise and vibration concerns; determine needed action.	C138	3E1:4; P-2
• Inspect ring gear and measure runout; determine needed action.	C780	3E1:6; P-3
• Remove, inspect, reinstall, and/or replace drive pinion and ring gear, spacers, sleeves, and bearings.	C890	3E1:7; P-3
• Disassemble, inspect, measure, adjust, and/or replace differential pinion gears (spiders), shaft, side gears, side bearings, thrust washers, and case.	C147	3E1:12; P-3
• Measure and adjust drive pinion depth.	C781	3E1:8; P-3
• Measure and adjust drive pinion bearing preload.	C782	3E1:9; P-3
• Reassemble and reinstall differential case assembly; measure runout; determine needed action.	C148	3E1:13; P-3
• Measure and adjust side bearing preload and ring and pinion gear total backlash and backlash variation on a differential carrier assembly (threaded cup or shim types).	C145	3E1:10; P-3
• Check ring and pinion tooth contact patterns; perform needed action.	C783	3E1:11; P-3

Time off_____

Time on_____

Total time_____

Materials Required

- Drive axle assembly
- Dial indicator
- Prussian Blue or gear paste
- Puller set
- Seal puller
- Torque wrenches
- Manufacturer-specific tools

Some Safety Issues to Consider

- Vehicle hoists are important tools that increase productivity and make the job easier. However, they can also cause severe injury or death if used improperly. Make sure you follow the manufacturer's operation procedures. Also, make sure you have your supervisor's/instructor's permission to use any particular type of lifting equipment.
- When running any vehicles in the shop, make sure you use the shop's exhaust ventilation system to discharge all exhaust gas safely outside.
- Diagnosis of this fault may require test-driving the vehicle on the school grounds. Attempt this task only with full permission from your instructor and follow all the guidelines exactly.
- Castings and machined parts may have sharp edges. Handle these parts with care.
- Comply with personal and environmental safety practices associated with clothing; eye protection; hand tools; power equipment; proper ventilation; and the handling, storage, and disposal of chemicals/materials in accordance with local, state, and federal safety and environmental regulations.

Performance Standard

0—No exposure: No information or practice provided during the program; complete training required

1—Exposure only: General information provided with no practice time; close supervision needed; additional training required

2—Limited practice: Has practiced job during training program; additional training required to develop skill

3—Moderately skilled: Has performed job independently during training program; limited additional training may be required

4—Skilled: Can perform job independently with no additional training

TASK Check and adjust differential case fluid level; use proper fluid type per manufacturer specification.

MAST
3E1:2

Time off_____

Time on_____

Total time_____

CDX Tasksheet Number: C911

1. List the drive axle designation for this vehicle: _____

2. Research the following specifications for this vehicle in the appropriate service information.

    a. Fluid type:_____

    b. Fluid capacity: _____ qt/lt

    c. How is the fluid level checked?

    d. Are any additives required? Yes: _____ No: _____

      i. If yes, what additive? _____

3. Safely raise and secure the vehicle on a hoist.

4. Check the fluid level and adjust as necessary with the proper fluid. List your observation(s):

5. Inspect the drive axle assembly for leaks.

    a. Identify and list the source of any leak(s):

6. Inspect the condition of the fluid. Look for contaminants, metal shavings, and degraded fluid condition. List your observation(s):

7. Determine any necessary action(s):

8. Have your supervisor/instructor verify satisfactory completion of this procedure, any observations found, and any necessary action(s) recommended.

Performance Rating

CDX Tasksheet Number: C911

0   1   2   3   4

Supervisor/instructor signature _____ Date _____

MAST
3E1:3

Time off_____

Time on_____

Total time_____

CDX Tasksheet Number: C912

Vehicle used for this activity:

Year _____ Make _____ Model _____

Odometer _____ VIN _____

1. **Research the following specifications for this vehicle in the appropriate service information.**
   a. **Fluid type:** _____
   b. **Fluid capacity:** _____ qt/lt
   c. **Differential fluid service interval:** _____ mi/km
   d. **How is fluid drained from this differential housing?**

2. **Safely raise and secure the vehicle on a hoist.**

3. **Following the specified procedure, drain the fluid from the differential housing. List your observations:**

4. **Have your supervisor/instructor verify removal of the fluid, and your observations. Supervisor's/instructor's initials:** _____

5. **Replace the drain plug or rear cover making sure the plug or bolts are tightened properly.**

6. **Fill the differential housing to the proper level with the specified lubricant.**

> **NOTE** Some differentials require special additives. Always check the service information to determine the proper fluid or additives.

7. **Have your supervisor/instructor verify satisfactory completion of this procedure, any observations found, and any necessary action(s) recommended.**

Performance Rating

CDX Tasksheet Number: C912

0	1	2	3	4

Supervisor/instructor signature _____ Date _____

Clean and inspect differential case; check for leaks; inspect
housing vent.

MAST
3E1:1

CDX Tasksheet Number: C785

Vehicle used for this activity:

Year _____ Make _____ Model_____

Odometer_____ VIN_____

1. **Research the procedure and specifications for cleaning and inspecting the differential housing and vent in the appropriate service information.**

    a. **Specified lubricant and/or additive:** _____
    b. **Differential lubricant capacity:** _____ qt/lt
    c. **Differential fluid service interval:** _____ mi/km
    d. **How is the lubricant level checked in this vehicle?**

2. **Safely raise and secure the vehicle on a hoist.**

3. **Inspect the differential housing for leaks or damage. List your observation(s):**

4. **Inspect the vent and make sure it is clear of any obstructions, and connected to its vent hose if equipped. List your observations:**

5. **Determine any necessary action(s):**

6. Have your supervisor/instructor verify satisfactory completion of this procedure, any observations found, and any necessary action(s) recommended.

Performance Rating

CDX Tasksheet Number: C785

0	1	2	3	4

Supervisor/instructor signature _____ Date _____

Inspect and replace companion flange and/or pinion seal; measure companion flange runout.

MAST
3E1:5

Time off_____

Time on_____

Total time_____

CDX Tasksheet Number: C889

Vehicle used for this activity:

Year _____ Make _____ Model_____

Odometer_____ VIN_____

1. Research the procedure and specifications for inspecting and replacing the companion flange and pinion seal in the appropriate service information.

   a. Maximum allowable companion flange runout (if specified): _____ in/mm
   b. Companion flange nut torque: _____ ft-lb/N·m
   c. Drive shaft-to-drive axle bolt torque: _____ ft-lb/N·m

2. Safely raise and secure the vehicle on a hoist.

3. Perform an initial visual inspection of the companion flange and pinion seal. List your observation(s):

4. Following the specified procedure, remove the drive shaft.

5. Measure the companion flange runout, if possible: _____ in/mm

6. Following the specified procedure, remove the companion flange and pinion seal. Inspect the following components for damage or wear.

   a. Companion flange:

   b. Pinion seal:

   c. Pinion shaft sealing surface:

7. Determine any necessary action(s):

8. Have your supervisor/instructor verify removal and your observations.
   Supervisor's/instructor's initials: _____

> NOTE If you are tasked with disassembling the drive axle assembly, continue on
> with the following tasks and return here when you are ready to reinstall the pinion
> seal and companion flange.

9. Following the specified procedure, replace the pinion seal and companion flange.
   Be sure to properly tighten the companion flange nut. Once torqued, check the
   turning effort required to rotate the companion flange. List your observation(s):

10. Re-measure the companion flange runout: _____ in/mm
    a. If the runout is not within specifications, inform your instructor.

11. Reinstall the drive shaft and any other removed components. Torque all
    fasteners to specifications.

12. Have your supervisor/instructor verify satisfactory completion of this procedure,
    any observations found, and any necessary action(s) recommended.

Performance Rating

CDX Tasksheet Number: C889

0	1	2	3	4

Supervisor/instructor signature _____ Date _____

MAST
3E1:4

Time off_____

Time on_____

Total time_____

CDX Tasksheet Number: C138

1. List the drive axle noise and vibration-related customer concern:

2. Research the concern in the appropriate service information.

    a. List the possible causes of the concern:

    b. List, or print off and attach to this sheet, the specified procedure for diagnosing the concern:

3. Perform the appropriate tests, following the specified procedure. List your observation(s):

4. List the cause of the concern:

5. Determine any necessary action(s) to correct the fault:

6. Have your supervisor/instructor verify satisfactory completion of this procedure, any observations found, and any necessary action(s) recommended.

Performance Rating

CDX Tasksheet Number: C138

0	1	2	3	4

Supervisor/instructor signature _____ Date _____

Inspect ring gear and measure runout; determine
    needed action.

MAST
3E1:6

CDX Tasksheet Number: C780

Vehicle used for this activity:

Year _____ Make _____ Model _____

Odometer _____ VIN _____

1. **Research the procedure and specifications for inspecting and measuring ring gear runout in the appropriate service information.**
    a. **Maximum allowable ring gear runout:** _____ **in/mm**
    b. **Type of drive axle: Integral/Unitized or Removable Carrier (Circle one)**
    c. **Does this vehicle have a removable rear differential cover?**
       Yes/No (Circle one)

2. **Following the specified procedure, remove the appropriate components to gain access to the ring gear assembly.**

3. **Visually inspect the ring gear for wear and damage. List your observation(s):**

4. **Using a dial indicator, measure the ring gear runout:** _____ **in/mm**

5. **Determine any necessary action(s):**

6. **Have your supervisor/instructor verify satisfactory completion of this procedure, any observations found, and any necessary action(s) recommended.**

Performance Rating

CDX Tasksheet Number: C780

☐	☐	☐	☐	☐
0	1	2	3	4

Supervisor/instructor signature _____ Date _____

Remove, inspect, reinstall, and/or replace drive pinion and ring gear, spacers, sleeves, and bearings.

MAST
3E1:7

Time off_____

Time on_____

Total time_____

CDX Tasksheet Number: C890

1. **Research the procedure and specifications for removing, inspecting, and replacing the drive pinion and ring gear in the appropriate service information.**

   a. **Ring gear bolt torque:** _____ **ft-lb/N·m**

   b. **List any special tools required for this task:**

   c. **List, or print off and attach to this sheet, the steps to perform this task:**

2. **Following the specified procedure, remove the drive pinion and ring gear.**

3. **Inspect the following components for wear or damage. List your observations for each.**

   a. **Drive pinion:**

   b. **Ring gear:**

   c. **Spacers and sleeves:**

   d. **Bearings:**

4. Determine any necessary action(s):

5. Have your supervisor/instructor verify satisfactory completion of this procedure, any observations found, and any necessary action(s) recommended.

Performance Rating

CDX Tasksheet Number: C890

0	1	2	3	4

Supervisor/instructor signature _____ Date _____

MAST
3E1:12

Time off_____

Time on_____

Total time_____

CDX Tasksheet Number: C147

1. **Research the procedure and specifications for disassembling, inspecting, measuring, and replacing the differential gears and associated parts.**

   a. **List any measurements or specifications for this task:**

   b. **List any special tools required for this task:**

   c. **List, or print off and attach to this sheet, the steps for performing this task:**

2. **Following the specified procedure, disassemble the differential pinion gears and associated parts.**

3. **Inspect and measure the following parts. List your observations for each.**

   a. **Differential pinion gears:**

   b. **Shaft:**

   c. **Side gears:**

d. Side bearings:

e. Thrust washers:

f. Case:

4. **Determine any necessary action(s):**

5. **Have your supervisor/instructor verify satisfactory completion of this procedure any observations found, and any necessary action(s) recommended.**

MAST
3E1:8

CDX Tasksheet Number: C781

1. Research the procedure and specifications for measuring and adjusting drive pinion depth in the appropriate service information.

   a. Specified drive pinion depth: _____ in/N·m
   b. How is the drive pinion depth adjusted on this drive axle?

   c. List any special tools required for this task:

   d. List, or print off and attach to this sheet, the steps to perform this task:

2. Following the specified procedure, measure the drive pinion depth: _____ in/N·m

   a. Is this within specifications? Yes: _____ No: _____

3. If outside of specifications, adjust the drive pinion depth.

   a. Final measurement: _____ in/N·m

4. Have your supervisor/instructor verify satisfactory completion of this procedure, any observations found, and any necessary action(s) recommended.

Performance Rating

CDX Tasksheet Number: C781

0	1	2	3	4

Supervisor/instructor signature _____ Date _____

MAST
3E1:9

CDX Tasksheet Number: C782

1. **Research the procedure and specifications for measuring and adjusting drive pinion preload in the appropriate service information.**

    a. **Specified drive pinion preload:** _____ **in-lb/N·m**

    b. **How is the drive pinion preload adjusted on this drive axle?**

    c. **List any special tools required for this task:**

2. **Following the specified procedure, measure the drive pinion preload:** _____ **in-lb/N·m**

    a. **Is this within specifications? Yes:** _____ **No:** _____

3. **If outside of specifications, adjust the drive pinion preload.**

    a. **Final measurement:** _____ **in-lb/N·m**

4. **Have your supervisor/instructor verify satisfactory completion of this procedure, any observations found, and any necessary action(s) recommended.**

Performance Rating

CDX Tasksheet Number: C782

0	1	2	3	4

Supervisor/instructor signature _____ Date _____

TASK Reassemble and reinstall differential case assembly;
measure runout; determine needed action.

MAST
3E1:13

Time off_____

Time on_____

Total time_____

CDX Tasksheet Number: C148

1. **Research the procedure and specifications for reassembling the differential case assembly in the appropriate service information.**

    a. **Specified maximum differential case runout:** _____ **in/mm**

    b. **List, or print off and attach to this sheet, any other specifications for this task:**

2. **Following the specified procedure, reassemble and reinstall the differential case assembly.**

3. **Measure the differential case runout:** _____ **in/mm**

4. **Determine any necessary action(s):**

5. **Have your supervisor/instructor verify satisfactory completion of this procedure, any observations found, and any necessary action(s) recommended.**

Performance Rating

CDX Tasksheet Number: C148

0	1	2	3	4

Supervisor/instructor signature _____ Date _____

TASK Measure and adjust side bearing preload and ring and pinion gear total backlash and backlash variation on a differential carrier assembly (threaded cup or shim types).

MAST
3E1:10

Time off_____

Time on_____

Total time_____

CDX Tasksheet Number: C145

1. **Research the procedure and specifications to measure and adjust backlash on a differential carrier assembly in the appropriate service information.**

    a. Side bearing preload: _____ in-lb/N·m

    b. Ring and pinion gear total backlash: _____ in/mm

    c. Backlash variation: _____ in/mm

    d. List, or print off and attach to this sheet, the steps to perform this task:

2. **Following the specified procedure, perform the following measurements.**

    a. Side bearing preload: _____ in-lb/N·m

    b. Ring and pinion gear total backlash: _____ in/mm

    c. Backlash variation: _____ in/mm

3. **Determine any necessary action(s):**

4. **If outside of specifications, adjust the preload and backlash. List your final measurements.**

    a. Side bearing preload: _____ in-lb/N·m

    b. Ring and pinion gear total backlash: _____ in/mm

    c. Backlash variation: _____ in/mm

5. **Have your supervisor/instructor verify satisfactory completion of this procedure, any observations found, and any necessary action(s) recommended.**

Performance Rating

CDX Tasksheet Number: C145

0	1	2	3	4

Supervisor/instructor signature _____ Date _____

Check ring and pinion tooth contact patterns;
perform needed action.

MAST
3E1:11

Time off_____

Time on_____

Total time_____

CDX Tasksheet Number: C783

1. Research the procedure and specifications to check and correct ring and pinion gear tooth patterns in the appropriate service information.

   a. Draw, or print off and attach to this sheet, the correct ring and pinion gear tooth pattern for both the drive and coast sides:

2. Following the specified procedure, check the ring and pinion gear tooth patterns. List your observations:

3. Determine any necessary action(s):

4. Have your supervisor/instructor verify your observations.
   Supervisor's/instructor's initials: _____

5. Perform any necessary action(s). List your observation(s):

6. Do the patterns meet specifications? Yes: _____ No: _____

7. Have your supervisor/instructor verify satisfactory completion of this procedure, any observations found, and any necessary action(s) recommended.

Performance Rating

CDX Tasksheet Number: C783

0	1	2	3	4

Supervisor/instructor signature _____ Date _____

Limited Slip Differential

Student/Intern information:

Name _____ Date _____ Class _____

Vehicle used for this activity:

Year _____ Make _____ Model_____

Odometer_____VIN_____

Learning Objective/Task	CDX Tasksheet Number	2017 MAST NATEF Reference Number; Priority Level
• Diagnose noise, slippage, and chatter concerns; determine needed action.	C784	3E2:1; P-3
• Measure rotating torque; determine needed action.	C786	3E2:2; P-3

Time off_____

Time on_____

Total time_____

Materials Required

- Drive axle with limited slip differential
- Specified lubricant and/or additive
- Drain pan
- Torque wrenches
- Manufacturer-specific tools

Some Safety Issues to Consider

- Vehicle hoists are important tools that increase productivity and make the job easier. However, they can also cause severe injury or death if used improperly. Make sure you follow the manufacturer's operation procedures. Also, make sure you have your supervisor's/instructor's permission to use any particular type of lifting equipment.
- When running any vehicles in the shop, make sure you use the shop's exhaust ventilation system to discharge all exhaust gas safely outside.
- Diagnosis of this fault may require test-driving the vehicle on the school grounds. Attempt this task only with full permission from your instructor and follow all the guidelines exactly.
- Castings and machined parts may have sharp edges. Handle these parts with care.
- Comply with personal and environmental safety practices associated with clothing; eye protection; hand tools; power equipment; proper ventilation; and the handling, storage, and disposal of chemicals/materials in accordance with local, state, and federal safety and environmental regulations.

Performance Standard

0-No exposure: No information or practice provided during the program; complete training required

1-Exposure only: General information provided with no practice time; close supervision needed; additional training required

2-Limited practice: Has practiced job during training program; additional training required to develop skill

3-Moderately skilled: Has performed job independently during training program; limited additional training may be required

4-Skilled: Can perform job independently with no additional training

MAST
3E2:1

Time off_____

Time on_____

Total time_____

DX Tasksheet Number: C784

1. **List the limited slip differential customer concern:**

2. **Research the procedure and specifications to diagnose noise, slipping, and chatter concerns in the appropriate service information.**

   a. **List or print off and attach to this sheet the steps to diagnose this concern:**

   b. **List the specified lubricant and/or additive:** _____

3. **Following the specified procedure, diagnose the customer concern. List your tests and results:**

4. **List the cause(s) of the concern:**

5. **List the necessary action(s) to correct the concern:**

6. **Have your supervisor/instructor verify satisfactory completion of this procedure, any observations found, and any necessary action(s) recommended.**

Performance Rating

CDX Tasksheet Number: C784

0	1	2	3	4

Supervisor/instructor signature _____ Date _____

MAST
3E2:2

DX Tasksheet Number: C786

1. Research the procedure and specifications for measuring the rotating torque on the limited slip differential in the appropriate service information.

    a. Specified breakaway torque: _____ ft-lb/N·m
    b. List, or print off and attach to this sheet, the steps for measuring the rotating torque:

2. Following the specified procedure, measure the rotating torque: _____ ft-lb/N·m

    a. Is this within specifications? Yes/No (Circle one)

3. Determine any necessary action(s):

4. Have your supervisor/instructor verify satisfactory completion of this procedure, any observations found, and any necessary action(s) recommended.

Performance Rating

CDX Tasksheet Number: C786

0	1	2	3	4

Supervisor/instructor signature _____ Date _____

Drive Axle Shaft

Student/Intern information:

Name _____ Date _____ Class _____

Vehicle used for this activity:

Year _____ Make _____ Model _____

Odometer_____VIN_____

Learning Objective/Task	CDX Tasksheet Number	2017 MAST NATEF Reference Number; Priority Level
• Diagnose drive axle shafts, bearings, and seals for noise, vibration, and fluid leakage concerns; determine needed action.	C153	3E3:5; P -2
• Inspect and replace drive axle wheel studs.	C154	3E3:1; P-1
• Measure drive axle flange runout and shaft end play; determine needed action.	C850	3E3:4; P-2
• Remove and replace drive axle shafts.	C155	3E3:2; P-1
• Inspect and replace drive axle shaft seals, bearings, and retainers.	C156	3E3:3; P-2

Time off_____

Time on_____

Total time_____

Materials Required

- Dial indicator
- Stethoscope
- Hydraulic press
- Seal puller
- Torque wrenches
- Manufacturer-specific tools

Some Safety Issues to Consider

- Diagnosis of this fault may require test-driving the vehicle on the school grounds. Attempt this task only with full permission from your instructor and follow all the guidelines exactly.
- Vehicle hoists are important tools that increase productivity and make the job easier. However, they can also cause severe injury or death if used improperly. Make sure you follow the manufacturer's operation procedures. Also, make sure you have your supervisor's/instructor's permission to use any particular type of lifting equipment.
- Lug nuts must always be tightened to the proper torque. Always use a properly calibrated torque wrench.
- This task may require you to run the vehicle on the hoist. Attempt this only with your instructor's permission.
- Comply with personal and environmental safety practices associated with clothing; eye protection; hand tools; power equipment; proper ventilation; and the handling, storage, and disposal of chemicals/materials in accordance with local, state, and federal safety and environmental regulations.

Performance Standard

0–No exposure: No information or practice provided during the program; complete training required

1–Exposure only: General information provided with no practice time; close supervision needed; additional training required

2–Limited practice: Has practiced job during training program; additional training required to develop skill

3–Moderately skilled: Has performed job independently during training program; limited additional training may be required

4–Skilled: Can perform job independently with no additional training

TASK Diagnose drive axle shafts, bearings, and seals for noise, vibration, and fluid leakage concerns; determine needed action.

MAST
3E3:5

Time off_____

Time on_____

Total time_____

CDX Tasksheet Number: C153

1. **List the customer concern:**

2. **With your instructor's permission, test-drive the vehicle in an open area with minimal noise on a smooth road surface. Listen for excessive noise while gradually increasing speed. List your observation(s):**

> **NOTE** A worn wheel bearing will usually make noise in a manner proportional to speed. When you are traveling at a speed that is making the noise, it is good practice to put the vehicle in neutral and allow the vehicle to coast. If the wheel bearing(s) is (are) worn, this will cause no considerable difference in sound. Also, try different transmission gears to rule out transmission- and clutch-related noises.

3. **Safely raise and secure the vehicle on a hoist.**

4. **Perform a visual inspection for obvious damage or leaks, paying particular attention to the brake backing plates and center differential. List your observation(s):**

5. **With your instructor's permission, run the vehicle in gear on the hoist while listening to the wheel bearings with a stethoscope. Make sure the vehicle is very secure on the hoist. List your observation(s):**

6. **Determine any necessary action(s):**

Manual Drive Train and Axles **419**

7. Have your supervisor/instructor verify satisfactory completion of this procedure, any observations found, and any necessary action(s) recommended.

Performance Rating

| 0 | 1 | 2 | 3 | 4 |

Supervisor/instructor signature _____ Date _____

DX Tasksheet Number: C154

Vehicle used for this activity:

Year _____ Make _____ Model _____

Odometer _____ VIN _____

1. **Research the procedure and specifications for replacing the axle shaft wheel studs in the appropriate service information.**

    a. **There are generally two standard procedures for replacing wheel studs. One is to remove the hub from the vehicle and use a hydraulic press to remove and install the studs. The other is to use a hammer to drive out the old stud, and then use washers and the flat side of the lug nut to draw the new stud into the hub. Which method does the service information describe for this vehicle?**

    b. **List any special tools or procedures for this task:**

    c. **Lug nut torque: _____ ft-lb/N·m**

2. **Safely raise and secure the vehicle on a hoist.**

3. **Remove the wheel assembly and inspect the lug nuts and wheel studs. List your observations and any necessary actions:**

4. **Have your supervisor/instructor verify your observations. Supervisor's/instructor's initials: _____**

5. **Remove the damaged wheel stud(s) from the hub. Supervisor's/instructor's initials: _____**

6. **Install the new wheel stud(s) in the hub, following all service information instructions.**

7. Have your supervisor/instructor verify satisfactory completion of this procedure, any observations found, and any necessary action(s) recommended.

Performance Rating

CDX Tasksheet Number: C154

0	1	2	3	4

Supervisor/instructor signature _____ Date _____

▶ TASK Measure drive axle flange runout and shaft end play; determine needed action.

MAST
3E3:4

Time off_____

Time on_____

Total time_____

DX Tasksheet Number: C850

Vehicle used for this activity:

Year _____ Make _____ Model _____

Odometer _____ VIN _____

1. **Research the procedure and specifications for measuring the drive axle flange and shaft end play in the appropriate service information.**
   a. **Maximum specified axle flange runout: _____ in/mm**
   b. **Specified axle shaft end play: _____ in/mm**

2. **Perform an initial visual inspection of the axle flange. List your observation(s):**

3. **Following the specified procedure, measure the axle flange runout: _____ in/mm**

4. **Following the specified procedure, measure the axle shaft end play: _____ in/mm**

5. **Determine any necessary action(s):**

6. **Have your supervisor/instructor verify satisfactory completion of this procedure, any observations found, and any necessary action(s) recommended.**

Performance Rating

CDX Tasksheet Number: C850

0	1	2	3	4

Supervisor/instructor signature _____ Date _____

MAST
3E3:2

Time off_____

Time on_____

CDX Tasksheet Number: C155

Vehicle used for this activity:

Year _____ Make _____ Model_____

Odometer_____ VIN_____

Total time_____

1. **Research the procedure and specifications for replacing the drive axle shafts in the appropriate service information.**

    a. **Specified retainer bolt torque, if equipped: _____ ft-lb/N·m**
    b. **List or print off and attach to this sheet the steps to replace the axle shaft:**

2. **Following the specified procedure, remove the axle shaft. List your observation(s):**

3. **Have your supervisor/instructor verify removal and your observations. Supervisor's/instructor's initials: _____**

    > **NOTE** You may want to skip ahead to the next task while the axle shaft is removed. Return here once that task is completed to reinstall the axle shaft.

4. **Following the specified procedure, reinstall the axle shaft. Be sure to tighten all fasteners to the specified torque. List your observation(s):**

5. **Have your supervisor/instructor verify satisfactory completion of this procedure, any observations found, and any necessary action(s) recommended.**

Performance Rating

CDX Tasksheet Number: C155

0	1	2	3	4

Supervisor/instructor signature _____ Date _____

MAST
3E3:3

CDX Tasksheet Number: C156

Vehicle used for this activity:

Year _____ Make _____ Model _____

Odometer _____ VIN _____

1. **Research the procedure and specifications for inspecting and replacing the seals, bearings, and retainers in the appropriate service information.**

   a. **List or print off and attach to this sheet the steps for performing this task:**

2. **Following the specified procedure, inspect each component and list your observations.**

   a. **Seal(s):**

   b. **Bearing(s):**

   c. **Retainer(s):**

3. **Remove the bearing(s), seal(s), and retainer(s). List your observations:**

4. **Have your supervisor/instructor verify removal and your observations. Supervisor's/instructor's initials: _____**

5. Reinstall the bearing(s), seal(s), and retainer(s). List your observations:

6. Have your supervisor/instructor verify satisfactory completion of this procedure, any observations found, and any necessary action(s) recommended.

Performance Rating

CDX Tasksheet Number: C156

0	1	2	3	4

Supervisor/instructor signature _____ Date _____

Four-Wheel Drive/All-Wheel Drive Component Diagnosis and Repair

Student/Intern information:

Name _____ Date _____ Class _____

Vehicle used for this activity:

Year _____ Make _____ Model _____

Odometer _____ VIN _____

Learning Objective/Task	CDX Tasksheet Number	2017 MAST NATEF Reference Number; Priority Level
• Diagnose noise, vibration, and unusual steering concerns; determine needed action.	C787	3F5; P-3
• Inspect, adjust, and repair shifting controls (mechanical, electrical, and vacuum), bushings, mounts, levers, and brackets.	C788	3F1; P-3
• Disassemble, service, and reassemble transfer case and components.	C875	3F7; P-2
• Inspect locking hubs; determine needed action(s).	C876	3F2; P-3
• Check for leaks at drive assembly and transfer case seals; check vents; check fluid level; use proper fluid type per manufacturer specification.	C914	3F3; P-3
• Diagnose, test, adjust, and/or replace electrical/electronic components of four-wheel drive/ all-wheel drive systems.	C878	3F6; P-2
• Identify concerns related to variations in tire circumference and/or final drive ratios.	C613	3F4; P-2

Time off_____

Time on_____

Total time_____

Materials Required

- 4WD/AWD-equipped vehicle
- Stethoscope
- Transmission jack
- Seal puller
- Wheel-bearing socket set
- Specified wheel-bearing grease
- Torque wrenches
- Tape measure
- DMM/DVOM
- Manufacturer-specific tools

Some Safety Issues to Consider

- Vehicle hoists are important tools that increase productivity and make the job easier. However, they can also cause severe injury or death if used improperly. Make sure you follow the manufacturer's operation procedures. Also, make sure you have your supervisor's/instructor's permission to use any particular type of lifting equipment.
- When running any vehicles in the shop, make sure you use the shop's exhaust ventilation system to discharge all exhaust gas safely outside.
- Diagnosis of this fault may require test-driving the vehicle on the school grounds. Attempt this task only with full permission from your instructor and follow all the guidelines exactly.
- Castings and machined parts may have sharp edges. Handle these parts with care.
- Comply with personal and environmental safety practices associated with clothing; eye protection; hand tools; power equipment; proper ventilation; and the handling, storage, and disposal of chemicals/materials in accordance with local, state, and federal safety and environmental regulations.

Performance Standard

0—No exposure: No information or practice provided during the program; complete training required

1—Exposure only: General information provided with no practice time; close supervision needed; additional training required

2—Limited practice: Has practiced job during training program; additional training required to develop skill

3—Moderately skilled: Has performed job independently during training program; limited additional training may be required

4—Skilled: Can perform job independently with no additional training

MAST
3F5

Time off_____

Time on_____

Total time_____

CDX Tasksheet Number: C787

1. List the four-wheel drive/all-wheel drive steering-related customer concern:

2. Research the concern in the appropriate service information and list the possible causes:

3. Following the specified procedure, diagnose the fault. List your tests and observations:

4. List the cause of the noise, vibration, or steering concern:

5. Determine any necessary action(s) to correct the fault:

6. Have your supervisor/instructor verify satisfactory completion of this procedure, any observations found, and any necessary action(s) recommended.

TASK Inspect, adjust, and repair shifting controls (mechanical, electrical, and vacuum), bushings, mounts, levers, and brackets.

MAST
3F1

Time off_____

Time on_____

Total time_____

CDX Tasksheet Number: C788

1. **Research the procedure and specifications for inspecting, adjusting, and repairing the shifting controls in the appropriate service information.**

    a. **What type of controls does this vehicle use?** _____

    b. **List or print off and attach to this sheet the steps to inspect and adjust the four-wheel drive shift controls:**

2. **Safely raise and support the vehicle on a hoist and inspect the following. List your observations for each.**

    a. **Linkage:**

    b. **Bushings:**

    c. **Mounts:**

    d. **Levers:**

    e. **Brackets:**

    f. Electric controls (if equipped):

    g. Vacuum controls (if equipped):

3. Determine any necessary action(s):

4. Have your supervisor/instructor verify satisfactory completion of this procedure, any observations found, and any necessary action(s) recommended.

Performance Rating

CDX Tasksheet Number: C788

0	1	2	3	4

Supervisor/instructor signature _____ Date _____

Time off_____

Time on_____

Total time_____

CDX Tasksheet Number: C875

1. **Research the procedure and specifications for disassembling, servicing, and reassembling the transfer case in the appropriate service information.**

    a. **List any special tools required for this task:**

    b. **List the flat rate time for this task:** _____ **hr**

    c. **List or print off and attach to this sheet the steps to disassemble and reassemble the transfer case:**

2. **Following the specified procedure, disassemble the transfer case.**

    NOTE It is good practice to lay out the components on a workbench or parts tray in a logical manner to facilitate reassembly.

3. **Following the specified procedure, inspect the components for wear or damage. List your observations:**

4. **Determine any necessary action(s):**

5. Have your supervisor/instructor verify disassembly and observations. Supervisor's/instructor's initials: _____

6. Following the specified procedure, service the transfer case components and list your actions:

7. Have your supervisor/instructor verify that the transfer case is ready to be reassembled and initial below.

   a. Supervisor's/instructor's initials: _____

8. Following the specified procedure, reassemble the transfer case. Be sure to tighten all fasteners to the proper torque. List your observations:

9. Have your supervisor/instructor verify satisfactory completion of this procedure, any observations found, and any necessary action(s) recommended.

Performance Rating

0	1	2	3	4

Supervisor/instructor signature _____ Date _____

▶ **TASK** Inspect locking hubs; determine needed action(s).

MAST
3F2

Time off_____

Time on_____

Total time_____

CDX Tasksheet Number: C876

1. **Research the procedure and specifications for servicing the wheel bearings and locking hubs in the appropriate service information.**
   a. List the specified wheel-bearing lubricant: _____
   b. List or print off and attach to this sheet the procedure for adjusting the wheel bearings:

2. **Safely raise and support the vehicle on a hoist or jack stands.**

3. **Following the specified procedure, remove the locking hub(s) and wheel bearings (inner and outer). List your observation(s):**

4. **Following the specified procedure, disassemble the locking hub(s). Clean all parts in an environmentally safe way and re-inspect each component. List your observation(s):**

> **NOTE** There are various views on whether a wheel bearing should be cleaned with solvents, as it could leave solvent-laden grease in the bearing. See your instructor or the service information for the recommended procedure for cleaning and packing wheel bearings.

5. **Determine any necessary action(s):**

6. **Have your supervisor/instructor verify disassembly and observations.**
   Supervisor's/instructor's initials: _____

7. **Following the specified procedure, repack the wheel bearings and lubricate the locking hub components.**

8. **Following the specified procedure, reassemble the wheel bearings. Make sure you properly adjust the wheel bearings.**

> **NOTE** Most wheel bearings require a three-step adjustment procedure. First, apply a large initial torque to the wheel-bearing adjustment nut to seat the wheel bearings. Second, back off the adjustment nut. Third, readjust with a much smaller torque to provide the proper bearing preload. Do not leave the bearings torqued to the higher torque or damage to the bearings will result. Also, remember to use a new cotter pin if that is the method used to retain the adjustment nut.

9. **Have your supervisor/instructor verify correct bearing adjustment. Supervisor's/instructor's initials:** _____

10. **Following the specified procedure, reassemble the locking hubs. List your observation(s):**

11. **Have your supervisor/instructor verify satisfactory completion of this procedure, any observations found, and any necessary action(s) recommended.**

Performance Rating

CDX Tasksheet Number: C876

0	1	2	3	4

Supervisor/instructor signature _____ Date _____

MAST
3F3

CDX Tasksheet Number: C914

1. **Research the procedure and specifications for this task in the appropriate service information.**

   a. List the specified lube for the drive axle: _____

   b. List the specified fluid for the transfer case: _____

2. **Following the specified procedure, perform a visual inspection of the drive assembly seals and vents. List your observation(s) for each.**

   a. **Drive assembly seals:**

   b. **Vents:**

3. **Following the specified procedure, check the level of the drive axle lubricant. List your observations:**

4. **Following the specified procedure, perform a visual inspection of the transfer case assembly seals and vents. List your observation(s) for each.**

   a. **Transfer case seals:**

   b. **Vents:**

5. Following the specified procedure, check the level of the transfer case fluid. List your observations:

6. Have your supervisor/instructor verify satisfactory completion of this procedure, any observations found, and any necessary action(s) recommended.

▶ TASK Diagnose, test, adjust, and/or replace electrical/electronic
components of four-wheel drive/all-wheel drive systems.

MAST
3F6

Time off_____

Time on_____

Total time_____

CDX Tasksheet Number: C878

Vehicle used for this activity:

Year _____ Make _____ Model _____

Odometer _____ VIN _____

1. **List the related customer concern:**

2. **Research the possible cause(s) of the concern in the appropriate service information. List the possible cause(s):**

3. **Following the specified procedure, diagnose the cause of the concern. List your tests and observation(s):**

4. **List the cause of the concern:**

5. **Determine any necessary action(s) to correct the fault:**

6. **Have your supervisor/instructor verify satisfactory completion of this procedure, any observations found, and any necessary action(s) recommended.**

Performance Rating

CDX Tasksheet Number: C878

0	1	2	3	4

Supervisor/instructor signature _____ Date _____

Manual Drive Train and Axles **441**

Identify concerns related to variations in tire circumference and/or final drive ratios.

MAST
3F4

Time off_____

Time on_____

Total time_____

CDX Tasksheet Number: C613

1. Research the effects of variations in tire circumference and final drive ratios on the operation of a four-wheel drive/all-wheel drive vehicle in the appropriate service information.

2. What would the customer concern be for a four-wheel drive/all-wheel drive vehicle equipped with different size tires?

3. What would the customer concern be for a vehicle equipped with different final drive ratios?

4. Set the tire pressure to the specified pressure. Measure the tire circumference for each tire and list below:

   a. Left front tire circumference: _____ in/mm
   b. Right front tire circumference: _____ in/mm
   c. Right rear tire circumference: _____ in/mm
   d. Left rear tire circumference: _____ in/mm

5. How much difference in circumference is generally allowable? _____ in/mm

6. Determine the final drive ratios for each axle assembly:

   a. Rear axle ratio: _____
   b. Front axle ratio: _____

7. Determine any necessary action(s):

8. Have your supervisor/instructor verify satisfactory completion of this procedure, any observations found, and any necessary action(s) recommended.

Performance Rating

CDX Tasksheet Number: C613

0	1	2	3	4

Supervisor/instructor signature _____ Date _____

Section A4: Suspension and Steering Systems

CONTENTS

Vehicle, Customer, and Service Information

Student/Intern information:

Name _____ Date _____ Class _____

Vehicle used for this activity:

Year _____ Make _____ Model _____

Odometer _____ VIN _____

Learning Objective/Task	CDX Tasksheet Number	2017 MAST NATEF Reference Number; Priority Level
• Research vehicle service information including fluid type, vehicle service history, service precautions, and technical service bulletins.	C166	4A1; P-1
• Identify and interpret suspension and steering system concerns; determine needed action.	C851	4A2; P-1
• Demonstrate the use of the three Cs (concern, cause, correction)	N/A	N/A

Time off _____

Time on _____

Total time _____

Materials Required

- Blank work order
- Vehicle with available service history records
- Depending on the type of concern, special diagnostic tools may be required. See your supervisor/instructor for instructions to identify what tools may be required.

Some Safety Issues to Consider

- Diagnosis of this fault may require test-driving the vehicle on the school grounds. Attempt this task only with full permission from your instructor and follow all the guidelines exactly.
- When running any vehicles in the shop, make sure you use the shop's exhaust ventilation system to discharge all exhaust gas safely outside.
- Lifting equipment such as vehicle jacks and stands, vehicle hoists, and engine hoists are important tools that increase productivity and make the job easier. However, they can also cause severe injury or death if used improperly. Make sure you follow the manufacturer's operation procedures. Also, make sure you have your supervisor's/instructor's permission to use any particular type of lifting equipment.
- Comply with personal and environmental safety practices associated with clothing; eye protection; hand tools; power equipment; proper ventilation; and the handling, storage, and disposal of chemicals/materials in accordance with local, state, and federal safety and environmental regulations.

Performance Standard

0—No exposure: No information or practice provided during the program; complete training required

1—Exposure only: General information provided with no practice time; close supervision needed; additional training required

2—Limited practice: Has practiced job during training program; additional training required to develop skill

3—Moderately skilled: Has performed job independently during training program; limited additional training may be required

4—Skilled: Can perform job independently with no additional training

► TASK Research vehicle service information including
fluid type, vehicle service history, service precautions,
and technical service bulletins.

MAST
4A1

CDX Tasksheet Number: C166

1. **Using the VIN for identification, use the appropriate source to access the vehicle's service history in relation to prior related suspension and steering system work or customer concerns.**

   a. **List any related steering and suspension system repairs/concerns and their dates:**

2. **Using the VIN for identification, access any relevant technical service bulletins for the particular vehicle you are working on in relation to steering and suspension updates or other service issues.**

   a. **List any steering and suspension system-related service bulletins and their titles:**

3. **Research the type of front and rear suspension used on this vehicle and list here:**

4. **Research the type of steering system used on this vehicle and list here:**

5. **Research the type of steering fluid required for this vehicle and list it here:**

6. Have your supervisor/instructor verify satisfactory completion of this procedure, any observations found, and any necessary action(s) recommended.

Performance Rating

0	1	2	3	4

Supervisor/instructor signature _____ Date _____

Identify and interpret suspension and steering system
concerns; determine needed action.

MAST
4A2

Time off_____

Time on_____

Total time_____

CDX Tasksheet Number: C851

1. **List the customer concern:**

2. **Research the particular concern in the appropriate service information.**

   a. **List the possible causes:**

3. **Inspect the steering and suspension system to determine the cause of the concern. List the steps you took to determine the fault:**

4. **List the cause of the concern:**

5. **List the necessary action(s) to correct this fault:**

6. **Have your supervisor/instructor verify satisfactory completion of this procedure, any observations found, and any necessary action(s) recommended.**

Performance Rating

CDX Tasksheet Number: C851

0	1	2	3	4

Supervisor/instructor signature _____ Date _____

Demonstrate the use of the three Cs (concern, cause, correction). **Additional Task**

CDX Tasksheet Number: N/A

1. **Using the following scenario, write up the three Cs as listed on most repair orders. Assume that the customer authorized the recommended repairs.**

   A vehicle is brought to your shop with a steering or suspension concern. The customer tells you that the vehicle has been pulling to the right ever since he hit a big pothole on a recent trip. The vehicle also has a vibration that is very noticeable when driving and is getting worse. He would like an estimate before the end of the day, because he will be leaving on a two-week vacation in the morning, and he would like the vehicle repaired while he is away. You test-drive the vehicle to verify the concerns, pull the vehicle up on the alignment hoist, and find the following:

   a. The tires are only a few months old, but the right front tire has broken belts as evidenced by the bulge in one edge.
   b. The right front wheel has a bent flange.
   c. The wheel alignment machine shows improper toe-out on turns that, upon further inspection, are shown to be caused by a bent right front steering arm on the steering knuckle.
   d. The rear struts are excessively worn and don't dampen like they should.
   e. The vehicle is about 1000 miles past its scheduled oil and filter change.
   f. The serpentine belt is showing excessive wear.

   > **NOTE** Ask your instructor if you should use the shop's repair order to complete this task, or the three Cs listed here.

2. **Concern/complaint:**

3. **Cause:**

4. **Correction:**

5. Other recommended service:

6. Have your supervisor/instructor verify satisfactory completion of this procedure, any observations found, and any necessary action(s) recommended.

Performance Rating

0	1	2	3	4

Supervisor/instructor signature _____ Date _____

Wheel and Tire Maintenance

Student/Intern information:

Name _____ Date _____ Class _____

Vehicle used for this activity:

Year _____ Make _____ Model_____

Odometer_____VIN_____

Learning Objective/Task	CDX Tasksheet Number	2017 MAST NATEF Reference Number; Priority Level
• Inspect tire condition; identify tire wear patterns; check for correct size, application (load and speed ratings), and air pressure as listed on the information placard/label.	C619	4F1; P-1
• Rotate tires according to manufacturer's recommendations including vehicles equipped with tire pressure monitoring systems (TPMS).	C222	4F3; P-1
• Dismount, inspect, and remount tire on wheel; balance wheel and tire assembly.	C620	4F6; P-1
• Demonstrate knowledge of steps required to remove and replace sensors in a tire pressure monitoring system (TPMS) including relearn procedure.	C936	4F11; P-1
• Dismount, inspect, and remount tire on wheel equipped with tire pressure monitoring system sensor.	C621	4F7; P-1

Time off_____

Time on_____

Total time_____

Materials Required

- Worn tire assigned by supervisor/instructor
- Tread-depth gauge
- Tire-pressure gauge
- Tire inflator
- Tire valve core tool
- Wheel weight hammer
- Vehicle hoist
- Lug wrench (or impact wrench with appropriate impact socket)
- Torque wrench and appropriate socket
- Tire mounting and balancing equipment
- Depending on the type of concern, special diagnostic tools may be required. See your supervisor/instructor for instructions to identify what tools may be required.

Some Safety Issues to Consider

- Worn or damaged tires may have steel cords sticking out of the tire. These wires are very sharp and will severely cut you. Do not rub your hand across a tire without checking first for exposed cords.
- Vehicle hoists are important tools that increase productivity and make the job easier. However, they also can cause severe injury or death if used improperly. Make sure you follow the hoist and vehicle manufacturer's operation procedures. Also make sure you have your supervisor's/ instructor's permission to use a vehicle hoist.
- Compressed air can be very dangerous. Never blow it at someone. Never use it to remove dirt or dust from your skin or clothing. Never use it without an OSHA-approved nozzle.
- Over-inflating tires could cause the tire to explode with great force. Never exceed the maximum tire pressure for the tire you are working on. Use a tire cage when inflating a tire that has been removed from a rim or repaired.
- Tires, even if they have good tread, only have a safe life of 6–10 years depending on type, condition, and environment. Check your state and local regulations about the age that tires should be replaced, and do not repair/service a tire older than that.
- Lug nuts must always be torqued to the proper torque. Always use a properly calibrated torque wrench. Never use an impact wrench to tighten lug nuts. This could cause the wheel to come loose and fall off if under-tightened. Or, if over-tightened, the lug studs might get damaged which could also cause the wheel to fall off the vehicle. It could also cause the brake rotors to become warped.
- Comply with personal and environmental safety practices associated with clothing; eye protection; hand tools; power equipment; proper ventilation; and the handling, storage, and disposal of chemicals/materials in accordance with local, state, and federal safety and environmental regulations.

Performance Standard

0–No exposure: No information or practice provided during the program; complete training required

1–Exposure only: General information provided with no practice time; close supervision needed; additional training required

2–Limited practice: Has practiced job during training program; additional training required to develop skill

3–Moderately skilled: Has performed job independently during training program; limited additional training may be required

4–Skilled: Can perform job independently with no additional training

TASK Inspect tire condition; identify tire wear patterns; check for correct size, application (load and speed ratings), and air pressure as listed on the tire information placard/label.

MAST
4F1

Time off_____

Time on_____

Total time_____

CDX Tasksheet Number: C619

1. **Research tread wear patterns in the appropriate information.**

2. **Research the following tire specifications on the vehicle's tire decal and on the sidewall of the tire itself:**

   a. **Tire decal (usually located on the vehicle door, door pillar, or glove box lid):**
      Recommended tire designation: _____
      Maximum load on front axle: _____ lb/kg
      Maximum load on rear axle: _____ lb/kg
      Required tire speed rating: _____
      Maximum speed for this rating: _____ mph/kph
      Recommended tire pressure: Front: _____ psi/kPa
      Rear: _____ psi/kPa

   b. **Information on sidewall of tire:**
      Tire designation: _____
      Maximum load: _____ lb/kg
      Speed rating: _____ Speed tire is safe for: _____ mph/kph
      Maximum tire pressure: _____ psi/kPa
      Tread wear rating: _____
      Traction rating: _____
      Temperature rating: _____
      DOT date of manufacture code: _____ Age of tire today: ___ (yrs/mos)

3. **On the most-worn tire, measure the tread depth across the tire tread and list your measurements below:**

   a. **Tread depth (inside of tread):** _____ in/mm
   b. **Tread depth (center of tread):** _____ in/mm
   c. **Tread depth (outside of tread):** _____ in/mm

4. **Check to make sure there are no exposed steel cords. Carefully run your hand across the tread and feel for a feathered condition. Also, run your hand in line with the tread to feel for lumps and bulges.**

   a. **Is the tire feathered? Yes:** _____ **No:** _____
   b. **Are there any bulges? Yes:** _____ **No:** _____

5. **Based on your observations and measurements, determine what, if any, wear patterns exist and list them here:**

6. **Measure the pressure in the tire(s) and record it here:** _____ psi/kPa

7. If the tire is not at the correct pressure, increase or decrease pressure.

   a. Record final pressure: _____ psi/kPa

8. Determine any necessary action(s):

9. Have your supervisor/instructor verify satisfactory completion of this procedure, any observations found, and any necessary action(s) recommended.

Rotate tires according to manufacturer's recommendations including vehicles equipped with tire pressure monitoring systems (TPMS).

MAST
4F3

Time off_____

Time on_____

Total time_____

CDX Tasksheet Number: C222

1. **Research the following specifications in the appropriate service information.**

    > **NOTE** Vehicles equipped with a tire pressure monitoring system (TPMS) may need the system reset after rotating the tires. Verify that you have all the necessary tools and manufacturer's procedure prior to removing the wheels on these vehicles.

    a. **Is this vehicle equipped with TPMS? Yes: _____ No: _____**

        i. **If yes, do you have the specified tools and procedures to reset the TPMS system? Yes: _____ No: _____**

    b. **Lug nut torque: _____ ft-lb/N·m**

    c. **Manufacturer's recommended tire rotation pattern. Draw diagram below.**

    d. **Manufacturer's recommended lug nut torque sequence. Draw diagram below.**

2. **Remove the wheel/tire assemblies from the vehicle.**

    > **NOTE** When removing hubcaps and wheels, please store them in such a manner so as not to damage the visible side of the hubcap or wheel. Laying them face down will cause them to become scratched and damaged. Also, store the lug nuts so they will not get lost or kicked.

3. **Have your supervisor/instructor verify removal. Supervisor's/instructor's initials: _____**

4. Rotate the tires according to the manufacturer's recommendation. As part of this procedure, check the tire pressure. If a tire is found to be under-inflated, check the tire for a leak. If a leak is found, notify your supervisor/instructor for further directions. Also, inspect each tire for nails or other foreign objects. Notify your supervisor/instructor if a problem is found. List your observations:

5. Torque the lug nuts to manufacturer's specifications in the specified sequence.

    a. Record torque: _____ ft-lbs/N·m

6. Reset TPMS if necessary. Follow manufacturer's procedure.

7. Reinstall hubcaps, if equipped. Make sure they are fully seated to prevent them from falling off while driving. If in doubt, ask your supervisor/instructor.

8. Have your supervisor/instructor verify satisfactory completion of this procedure, any observations found, and any necessary action(s) recommended.

Performance Rating

CDX Tasksheet Number: C222

0	1	2	3	4

Supervisor/instructor signature _____ Date _____

TASK Dismount, inspect, and remount tire on wheel; balance wheel and tire assembly.

MAST
4F6

Time off_____

Time on_____

Total time_____

DX Tasksheet Number: C620

> **NOTE** Verify that this wheel is NOT equipped with TPMS.

1. **List the customer concern, if any:**

2. **Prepare the vehicle and remove the wheel concerned.**

3. **Inspect the outer surface of the entire wheel and tire assembly. List your observations:**

4. **Using the correct procedure, dismount the tire from the wheel.**

5. **Inspect the inside of the tire, the tire bead, the inside of the rim, and the valve stem. List your observations:**

6. **Have your supervisor/instructor verify removal.**
   Supervisor's/instructor's initials: _____

7. **Remount tire on the wheel using the correct equipment and procedure.**

8. **Balance wheel and tire assembly (static and dynamic) and draw a diagram of the position and size of the weights:**

9. Determine any necessary action(s):

10. Have your supervisor/instructor verify satisfactory completion of this procedure, any observations found, and any necessary action(s) recommended.

Performance Rating

0	1	2	3	4

Supervisor/instructor signature _____ Date _____

Demonstrate knowledge of steps required to remove
and replace sensors in a tire pressure monitoring system (TPMS)
including relearn procedure.

MAST
4F11

Time off _____

Time on _____

Total time _____

DX Tasksheet Number: C936

1. **Research the procedure for replacing TPMS sensors on at least 3 vehicles (1 domestic car, 1 imported car, and 1 all-wheel drive vehicle) in the appropriate service information.**

   a. **Vehicle year, make, and model:** _____

      i. **Summarize the steps to replace the TPMS sensor:**

      ii. **List any precautions when replacing the TPMS sensor:**

      iii. **List the procedure to calibrate or relearn the TPMS system:**

   b. **Vehicle year, make, and model:** _____

      i. **Summarize the steps to replace the TPMS sensor:**

      ii. **List any precautions when replacing the TPMS sensor:**

iii. List the procedure to calibrate or relearn the TPMS system:

    c. Vehicle year, make, and model: _____

       i. Summarize the steps to replace the TPMS sensor:

       ii. List any precautions when replacing the TPMS sensor:

       iii. List the procedure to calibrate or relearn the TPMS system:

2. Have your supervisor/instructor verify satisfactory completion of this procedure, any observations found, and any necessary action(s) recommended.

Performance Rating

CDX Tasksheet Number: C936

0	1	2	3	4

Supervisor/instructor signature _____ Date _____

464   Suspension and Steering Systems

Dismount, inspect, and remount tire on wheel equipped
with tire pressure monitoring system sensor.

Time off_____

Time on_____

Total time_____

DX Tasksheet Number: C621

Vehicle used for this activity:

Year _____ Make _____ Model _____

Odometer _____ VIN _____

1. List the customer concern, if any:

2. Research the following in the appropriate service information:

    a. Tire removal/installation on TPMS-equipped vehicles. List the proper
        positioning of the wheel on the tire machine when removing the tire:

    b. TPMS maintenance needs and service. List any maintenance that can be
        performed on the TPMS sensors:

    c. TPMS reset procedure, if necessary. List the steps to reset the TPMS
        sensors:

3. Prepare the vehicle and remove the wheel concerned.

4. Inspect the outer surface of the entire wheel and tire assembly. List your
    observations:

5. Using the correct procedure, dismount the tire from the wheel. Be careful not to
    damage the TPMS sensor.

6. Inspect the inside of the tire, the tire bead, the inside of the rim, the valve stem, and the TPMS sensor. List your observations:

7. Have your supervisor/instructor verify removal.
   Supervisor's/instructor's initials: _____

8. Perform any needed maintenance/service on the TPMS system.
   List your actions:

9. Remount tire on wheel using the correct equipment and procedure. Be careful not to damage the TPMS sensor.

10. Balance wheel and tire assembly, if necessary, and draw a diagram of the position and size of the weights:

11. Reinstall wheel/tire assembly on the vehicle and torque lug nuts to the proper torque in the proper sequence.

12. If necessary, reset the TPMS according to the specified procedure. List your observations:

13. Determine any necessary action(s):

14. Have your supervisor/instructor verify satisfactory completion of this procedure, any observations found, and any necessary action(s) recommended.

Wheel and Tire Diagnosis

Student/Intern information:

Name _____ Date _____ Class _____

Vehicle used for this activity:

Year _____ Make _____ Model _____

Odometer_____ VIN _____

Learning Objective/Task	CDX Tasksheet Number	2017 MAST NATEF Reference Number; Priority Level
• Inspect tire and wheel assembly for air loss; perform needed action.	C580	4F8; P-1
• Repair tire following vehicle manufacturer approved procedure.	C552	4F9; P-1
• Measure wheel, tire, axle flange, and hub runout; determine needed action.	C701	4F4; P-2
• Identify indirect and direct tire pressure monitoring system (TPMS); calibrate system; verify operation of instrument panel lamps.	C937	4F10; P-1
• Diagnose wheel/tire vibration, shimmy, and noise; determine needed action.	C855	4F2; P-2
• Diagnose tire pull problems; determine needed action.	C796	4F5; P-1

Time off_____

Time on_____

Total time_____

Materials Required

- Leaky tire assigned by supervisor/instructor
- Tire-pressure gauge
- Tire inflator
- Tire valve core tool
- Vehicle hoist or floor jack and jack stand(s)
- Lug wrench (or impact wrench with appropriate impact socket)
- Tire dunk tank or soapy water in a spray bottle
- Torque wrench and appropriate socket
- Tire patching tools and supplies
- Dial indicator
- Depending on the type of concern, special diagnostic tools may be required. See your supervisor/instructor for instructions to identify what tools may be required.

Some Safety Issues to Consider

- Worn or damaged tires may have steel cords sticking out of the tire. These wires are very sharp and will severely cut you. Do not rub your hand across a tire without checking first for exposed cords.
- Vehicle hoists are important tools that increase productivity and make the job easier. However, they also can cause severe injury or death if used improperly. Make sure you follow the hoist and vehicle manufacturer's operation procedures. Also make sure you have your supervisor's/instructor's permission to use a vehicle hoist.
- Compressed air can be very dangerous. Never blow it at someone. Never use it to remove dirt or dust from your skin or clothing. Never use it without an OSHA-approved nozzle.
- Over-inflating tires could cause the tire to explode with great force. Never exceed the maximum tire pressure for the tire you are working on. Use a tire cage when inflating a tire that has been removed from a rim or repaired.
- Lug nuts must always be torqued to the proper torque. Always use a properly calibrated torque wrench. Never use an impact wrench to tighten lug nuts. This could cause the wheel to come loose and fall off if under-tightened. Or, if over-tightened, the lug studs might get damaged which could also cause the wheel to fall off the vehicle. It could also cause the brake rotors to become warped.
- Comply with personal and environmental safety practices associated with clothing; eye protection; hand tools; power equipment; proper ventilation; and the handling, storage, and disposal of chemicals/materials in accordance with local, state, and federal safety and environmental regulations.

Performance Standard

0—No exposure: No information or practice provided during the program; complete training required

1—Exposure only: General information provided with no practice time; close supervision needed; additional training required

2—Limited practice: Has practiced job during training program; additional training required to develop skill

3—Moderately skilled: Has performed job independently during training program; limited additional training may be required

4—Skilled: Can perform job independently with no additional training

TASK Inspect tire and wheel assembly for air loss; perform needed action.

Time off_____

Time on_____

Total time_____

CDX Tasksheet Number: C580

1. **Research the following specifications in the appropriate service information.**
   a. **Lug nut torque:** _____ **ft-lb/N·m**
   b. **Is this vehicle equipped with TPMS? Yes:** _____ **No:**_____
   c. **If yes, do you have the specified tools and procedures to reset the TPMS system? Yes:** _____ **No:** _____

2. **Remove wheel/tire assembly from vehicle and check it for any leaks using soapy water or a dunk tank. List your observations:**

> **NOTE** When removing hubcaps and wheels, please store them in such a manner as not to damage the visible side of the hubcap or wheel. Laying them face down will cause them to become scratched and damaged. Also store the lug nuts so they will not get lost or kicked.

3. **Mark the position of all wheel weights and the valve stem on the tire with a tire crayon. This is so you can reinstall the tire and weights on the wheel in the same position so rebalancing is unnecessary.**

4. **Using the correct procedure, dismount the tire from the wheel. Be careful not to damage the TPMS, if equipped.**

5. **Inspect the wheel and tire for any damage, rust, or other defects and list them here:**

6. **Are the defects repairable? Yes:** _____ **No:** _____

7. **Have your supervisor/instructor verify your observations, and ask permission to make any repairs. Supervisor's/instructor initials:** _____

8. **With supervisor/instructor approval, repair all defects found.**

> **NOTE** If the tire has a leak that can be repaired with an integrated plug-patch or internal patch, skip ahead to task C552: Repair tire following vehicle manufacturer approved procedure, and return here once the task has been completed.

9. Remount the tire on the wheel, positioning the tire and weights in their original positions on the wheel to restore existing tire balance.

10. Recheck the wheel/tire assembly for leaks. If there are none, reinstall it on the vehicle and torque the lug nuts to the proper specification and in the proper sequence.

11. Have your supervisor/instructor verify satisfactory completion of this procedure any observations found, and any necessary action(s) recommended.

Performance Rating

CDX Tasksheet Number: C580

0	1	2	3	4

Supervisor/instructor signature _____ Date _____

MAST
4F9

CDX Tasksheet Number: C552

1. Inspect the tire for remaining tread life and ensure that any repair undertaken will meet all legislative requirements.

    a. Measure the minimum tread depth: _____ in/mm
    b. Is the tread depth above the legal limit? Yes: _____ No: _____
    c. Is the hole within the repairable zone of the tread?
       Yes: _____ No: _____
    d. Is the diameter of the hole within patching limits? Yes: _____
       No: _____
    e. What type of internal patch are you using? Standard internal patch:
       _____ Integrated plug patch: _____

2. Using a recommended method, prepare the tire for repair, (perform all steps except applying glue and the patch). List your steps and observations here:

3. Have your instructor verify the proper preparation for the patch.
   Supervisor's/instructor initials: _____

4. Determine any necessary action(s), and undertake the repair by applying the glue and patch in accordance with the manufacturer's recommendations and process (most tire patch glues MUST be allowed to fully dry before applying the patch).

5. Have your supervisor/instructor verify satisfactory completion of this procedure, any observations found, and any necessary action(s) recommended.

Performance Rating

CDX Tasksheet Number: C552

0	1	2	3	4

Supervisor/instructor signature _____ Date _____

Measure wheel, tire, axle flange, and hub runout; determine needed action.

MAST
4F4

Time off_____

Time on_____

Total time_____

CDX Tasksheet Number: C701

Vehicle used for this activity:

Year _____ Make _____ Model _____

Odometer _____ VIN _____

1. List the customer concern; if applicable:

2. **Research the procedure for measuring tire, wheel, and hub runout in the appropriate service information. List the following specifications:**

    a. Tire pressure: _____ psi/kPa
    b. Tire designation: _____
    c. Maximum tire runout: _____ in/mm
    d. Maximum wheel runout: _____ in/mm
    e. Maximum axle flange/hub runout: _____ in/mm

3. **Check and adjust the tire pressures according to specifications.**

4. **Inspect each tire and list its designation:**

    a. LF tire:_____
    b. RF tire:_____
    c. RR tire:_____
    d. LR tire:_____
    e. Does each tire meet the manufacturer's recommendations?
       Yes: _____ No: _____

5. **Properly raise the front of the vehicle and support it securely.**

6. **Following the manufacturer's procedure, measure runout of the following:**

    a. LF tire: _____ in/mm
    b. RF tire: _____ in/mm
    c. LF wheel: _____ in/mm
    d. RF wheel: _____ in/mm
    e. LF hub: _____ in/mm
    f. RF hub: _____ in/mm

7. **Determine any necessary action(s):**

8. Have your supervisor/instructor verify satisfactory completion of this procedure, any observations found, and any necessary action(s) recommended.

Performance Rating

0	1	2	3	4

Supervisor/instructor signature _____ Date _____

Identify indirect and direct tire pressure monitoring system
(TPMS); calibrate system; verify operation of instrument
panel lamps.

MAST
4F10

Time off_____

Time on_____

Total time_____

DX Tasksheet Number: C937

Vehicle used for this activity:

Year _____ Make _____ Model _____

Odometer _____ VIN _____

1. **Research the TPMS system in the appropriate service information.**

   a. **Choose the type of TMPS system: Indirect: _____ Direct: _____**

   b. **List or print off and attach to this sheet the process for calibrating the TPMS system:**

   c. **List how the instrument panel warning lamps should behave if the system is operating normally:**

   d. **List how the instrument panel warning lamps should behave if the system is NOT operating normally:**

2. **Describe how an indirect TPMS system detects a tire with low tire pressure:**

3. **Describe how a direct TPMS system detects a tire with low tire pressure:**

4. Check the operation of the TPMS warning lamp and list your observations:

5. Swap the two front-wheel assemblies and calibrate the TPMS system in accordance with the manufacturer's instructions. List your steps and observations here:

6. Have your supervisor/instructor verify satisfactory completion of this procedur any observations found, and any necessary action(s) recommended.

Diagnose wheel/tire vibration, shimmy, and noise; determine
needed action.

MAST
4F2

Time off_____

Time on_____

Total time_____

CDX Tasksheet Number: C855

Vehicle used for this activity:

Year _____ Make _____ Model _____

Odometer _____ VIN _____

1. List the wheel/tire-related customer concern(s):

2. Research the concern in the appropriate service information and any technical
   service bulletins that may apply.

   a. List any applicable service bulletins:

   b. List or print off and attach to this sheet the procedure for diagnosing the
      concern:

3. With the supervisor's/instructor's permission, test-drive the vehicle. Listen and
   feel for any unusual noises and vibrations. List your observations:

4. Using the recommended procedure, inspect and diagnose any vibration, shimmy,
   or noise concerns. List your tests and results here:

5. List the cause of the concern:

6. Determine any necessary action(s) to correct the fault:

7. Have your supervisor/instructor verify satisfactory completion of this procedure, any observations found, and any necessary action(s) recommended.

Performance Rating

0	1	2	3	4

Supervisor/instructor signature _____ Date _____

Diagnose tire pull problems; determine needed action.

MAST
4F5

Time off_____

Time on_____

CDX Tasksheet Number: C796

Vehicle used for this activity:

Year _____ Make _____ Model _____

Odometer _____ VIN _____

Total time_____

1. List the tire pull-related customer concern(s):

2. Research the configuration of this vehicle in the appropriate service information and any technical service bulletins that may apply.

   a. List any applicable service bulletins and their titles:

   b. List or print off and attach to this sheet the procedure for diagnosing the concern:

3. With the supervisor's/instructor's permission, test-drive the vehicle. Check for any tire pull problems. List your observations:

4. Using the recommended procedure, inspect and diagnose any tire pull problems. List your tests and results here:

5. List the cause of the concern:

6. Determine any necessary action(s) to correct the fault:

7. Have your supervisor/instructor verify satisfactory completion of this procedure, any observations found, and any necessary action(s) recommended.

Performance Rating

0	1	2	3	4

Supervisor/instructor signature _____ Date _____

Power Steering Pump Maintenance and Service

Student/Intern information:

Name _____ Date _____ Class _____

Vehicle used for this activity:

Year _____ Make _____ Model_____

Odometer_____VIN_____

Learning Objective/Task	CDX Tasksheet Number	2017 MAST NATEF Reference Number; Priority Level
• Inspect power steering fluid level and condition.	C177	4B9; P-1
• Flush, fill, and bleed power steering system; use proper fluid type per manufacturer specification.	C178	4B10; P-2
• Remove, inspect, replace, and/or adjust power steering pump drive belt.	C180	4B12; P-1
• Inspect for power steering fluid leakage; determine needed action.	C179	4B11; P-1
• Inspect, remove, and/or replace power steering hoses and fittings.	C183	4B15; P-2
• Test power steering pressure; determine needed action.	C1001	4B20; P-2
• Remove and reinstall power steering pump.	C181	4B13; P-2
• Remove and reinstall press fit power steering pump pulley; check pulley and belt alignment.	C699	4B14; P-2

Time off_____

Time on_____

Total time_____

Materials Required

- Vehicle or simulator, equipped with power steering
- Correct power steering fluid
- White piece of paper
- Power steering flush machine or drain pan
- Funnel
- Belt-tension gauge
- Power steering pump pulley remover/installer tool
- Depending on the type of concern, special diagnostic tools may be required. See your supervisor/instructor for instructions to identify what tools may be required.
- Special tools for Stretch Fit belts
- Power steering pressure gauge or analyzer

Some Safety Issues to Consider

- You will be working under the hood of a running vehicle. Keep your hands and fingers away from moving belts, fans, and other parts.
- When running any vehicles in the shop, make sure you use the shop's exhaust ventilation system to discharge all exhaust gas safely outside.
- Lifting equipment such as vehicle jacks and stands, vehicle hoists, and engine hoists are important tools that increase productivity and make the job easier. However, they can also cause severe injury or death if used improperly. Make sure you follow the manufacturer's operation procedures. Also make sure you have your supervisor's/instructor's permission to use any particular type of lifting equipment.
- Caution must be exercised when working around the power steering pump, especially if the vehicle has been driven recently or the engine is at operating temperature. The power steering fluid can be extremely hot and can burn if it comes in contact with unprotected skin. When operating the power steering system, it can be under high hydraulic pressure.
- Comply with personal and environmental safety practices associated with clothing; eye protection; hand tools; power equipment; proper ventilation; and the handling, storage, and disposal of chemicals/materials in accordance with local, state, and federal safety and environmental regulations.

Performance Standard

0–No exposure: No information or practice provided during the program; complete training required

1–Exposure only: General information provided with no practice time; close supervision needed; additional training required

2–Limited practice: Has practiced job during training program; additional training required to develop skill

3–Moderately skilled: Has performed job independently during training program; limited additional training may be required

4–Skilled: Can perform job independently with no additional training

MAST
4B9

CDX Tasksheet Number: C177

1. **Research specified power steering fluid for this vehicle using the appropriate service information.**

    a. **Specified fluid:** _____

    b. **When should the fluid be checked? Hot:** _____ **Cold:** _____
       Either: _____

    c. **If the service information lists a procedure for flushing the power steering fluid, list the main steps (you can paraphrase, or print off the procedure):**

2. **Follow the manufacturer's procedure to check the fluid level.**

   > **NOTE** If power steering fluid is below the minimum level, it could mean there is a leak in the system. Investigate this possibility and report it to your supervisor/ instructor.

3. **Locate the power steering-fluid reservoir.**

    a. **List the level of the power steering fluid:** _____

4. **Place a small amount of the fluid from the reservoir on a white piece of paper and describe its condition:**

5. **Determine any necessary action(s):**

6. **Have your supervisor/instructor verify satisfactory completion of this procedure, any observations found, and any necessary action(s) recommended.**

Performance Rating

CDX Tasksheet Number: C177

0	1	2	3	4

Supervisor/instructor signature _____ Date _____

▶ **TASK** Flush, fill, and bleed power steering system; use proper fluid type per manufacturer specification.

MAST
4B10

Time off_____

Time on_____

Total time_____

CDX Tasksheet Number: C178

1. **Follow the specified procedure to flush the power steering fluid. If no procedure is specified, ask your supervisor/instructor to approve the following procedure:** _____

   a. **With the engine off, place a drain pan under the power steering pump return hose and out of the way of the fan or other moving parts.**

   b. **Remove the return hose from the power steering pump. Place the return hose in the drain pan. Plug the return line fitting in the power steering pump with an appropriate plug or cap.**

   c. **Determine the proper fluid per manufacturer specification. Fill the reservoir to the proper level with new fluid. Have an assistant start the engine and slowly turn the steering wheel to flush out the old fluid. At the same time, continue to add fluid to the reservoir (with the funnel) to keep it approximately full. Continue this until clean fluid comes out of the return line and then turn off the vehicle.**

   d. **Reinstall the return line and fill the reservoir to the proper level.**

   e. **Start the vehicle again and turn the steering wheel a few times from lock to lock. Check the fluid level and top off as necessary.**

   f. **If a buzzing noise is heard, there is probably air trapped in the system. In this case, turn off the engine, raise the front wheels off the ground (support the vehicle on jack stands or a hoist), and turn the wheels from lock to lock with the engine off. Do this several times. Check the fluid level and top off if necessary. Lower the vehicle. Restart the engine and listen and feel for proper operation. Repeat if necessary.**

   g. **Properly dispose of the old power steering fluid.**

   h. **List your observations:**

2. **Have your supervisor/instructor verify satisfactory completion of this procedure, any observations found, and any necessary action(s) recommended.**

Performance Rating

CDX Tasksheet Number: C178

| 0 | 1 | 2 | 3 | 4 |

Supervisor/instructor signature _____ Date _____

Remove, inspect, replace, and/or adjust power
steering pump drive belt.

CDX Tasksheet Number: C180

1. Using the service information, list the following:

    a. Type of power steering fluid:
    _____

    b. Type of belt: V-belt: _____ Serpentine belt: _____
    Stretch Fit belt: _____ Toothed belt: _____

    c. Belt-adjustment mechanism: N/A: _____ Manual: _____
    Automatic: _____

    d. Belt tension, if specified: _____

    e. Draw or print off and attach to this sheet the belt-routing diagram:

2. Following the recommended procedure, loosen the adjustment mechanism and
   remove the power steering pump drive belt. If equipped with a Stretch Fit belt it
   may be necessary to cut the old belt.

3. Examine the belt for cracks, splints, frayed surfaces, and distorted
   configurations (including stretching). Record your observation(s):

4. Examine the drive pulleys for any damage. Record your observation(s):

5. Have your supervisor/instructor verify removal. Supervisor's/instructor's
   initials: _____

> NOTE You may want to skip ahead and perform the next task C181: Remove and
> reinstall power steering pump while you have the belt removed. If so, return to
> this point when you are ready to reinstall the drive belt.

6. Following the specified procedure, replace the drive belt. If equipped with a Stretch Fit belt you will need a special installation tool, follow the manufacturer's instructions carefully.

7. Check the drive belt alignment in relation to the drive pulleys. List your observation(s):

8. Adjust the drive belt tension to the shop manufacturer's specifications (on the manually adjusted system).

    a. Measure the belt tension: _____

9. Check the fluid level in the power steering reservoir. Top off with the proper fluid, if necessary.

10. Start the engine and turn the steering wheel from lock to lock. Check for the following:

    a. Binding: Yes: _____ No: _____
    b. Excessive steering effort: Yes: _____ No: _____
    c. Uneven steering effort: Yes: _____ No: _____

11. Turn the engine off.

12. Re-measure the drive belt tension and list here: _____

13. Have your supervisor/instructor verify satisfactory completion of this procedure, any observations found, and any necessary action(s) recommended.

Performance Rating

CDX Tasksheet Number: C180

0	1	2	3	4

Supervisor/instructor signature _____ Date _____

Inspect for power steering fluid leakage; determine needed action.

MAST
4B11

Time off_____

Time on_____

CDX Tasksheet Number: C179

Vehicle used for this activity:

Year _____ Make _____ Model_____

Odometer_____ VIN_____

Total time_____

> **NOTE** If the vehicle's engine assembly is coated with leaking fluids and road dirt, you may need to pressure wash the engine compartment before inspecting for leaks. Get your instructor's permission before performing a cleaning operation.

> **NOTE** Some very small leaks, or leaks in engines that have a lot of accumulated residue, may be best diagnosed with the use of a fluorescent dye and ultraviolet light. Check with your instructor if this vehicle is a good candidate for that procedure. If so, follow the dye check equipment manufacturer's instructions for performing this test.

1. **Using a good light, inspect under the hood for any power steering fluid leaks. Inspect the reservoir, pump (including shaft seal), hoses, and fittings. List your observation(s):**

> **NOTE** Remember that gravity tends to pull any leaking fluid down. You may need to identify the highest point of the leak to locate the source.

2. **Safely raise and support the vehicle on the hoist.**

3. **Inspect the power steering pump, hoses, and gear box for leaks. Identify and list the source(s) of any leak(s):**

4. **Determine necessary action(s):**

5. **Have your supervisor/instructor verify satisfactory completion of this procedure, any observations found, and any necessary action(s) recommended.**

Performance Rating

CDX Tasksheet Number: C179

0	1	2	3	4

Supervisor/instructor signature _____ Date _____

MAST
4B15

Time off_____

Time on_____

Total time_____

CDX Tasksheet Number: C183

1. Research the procedure to remove and install the power steering hoses and fittings. List the steps or print off the procedure:

2. Following the specified procedure, drain the power steering fluid into a clean container for proper disposal according to environmental guidelines and regulations.

3. Disconnect power steering hoses from both the power steering pump and the power steering box or rack. Plug any exposed fittings to prevent entry of dirt or debris.

4. Disconnect any retaining clips.

5. Remove power steering hoses from the vehicle and place on your workbench.

6. Examine the flexible hoses for cracks, splits, chafed surfaces, and distorted configurations (including hardening and loss of flexibility). List your observation(s):

7. Examine any steel tubes and fittings, check for heat damage, splits, kinking, damaged threads, or restrictions. List your observation(s):

8. Have your supervisor/instructor verify removal. Supervisor's/instructor's initials: _____

9. Following the specified procedure, reinstall the power steering hoses being careful not to cross-thread any fittings or damage any hoses or tubes.

10. Have your supervisor/instructor verify satisfactory completion of this procedure, any observations found, and any necessary action(s) recommended.

Performance Rating

CDX Tasksheet Number: C183

0	1	2	3	4

Supervisor/instructor signature _____ Date _____

MAST
4B20

CDX Tasksheet Number: C1001

1. Research the procedure to pressure test the power steering system. List the steps or print off the procedure:

2. Following the recommended procedure, prepare the vehicle to perform the power steering system pressure test.

3. Connect the pressure tester to the vehicle.

4. With the pressure gauge control valve open, start the engine and run at idle until the air is purged from the system. Turn the engine off. Check the fluid level and check for leaks.

5. Start the engine and record the initial pressure _____ and flow _____ readings on the gauge. Close and open the pressure gauge control valve two or three times. (Never hold the valve closed more than five seconds.) Record the highest pressure indicated on the gauge. _____ psi/kPa

6. With the control valve open, turn the steering wheel to the extreme left and to the extreme right. Record the highest indicated pressure. _____ psi/kPa

7. Compare these readings to the specifications, and take the results to your supervisor.

8. Remove the analyzer from the vehicle. (CAUTION: The fluid may be extremely hot.) Reconnect the hoses using new O-rings.

9. Top off the power steering reservoir and follow the manufacturer's procedure to bleed any air from the system.

10. Check the power steering system for any leaks.

11. Determine any needed action.

12. Have your supervisor/instructor verify satisfactory completion of this proce→dure, any observations found, and any necessary action(s) recommended.

Performance Rating

CDX Tasksheet Number: C1001

0	1	2	3	4

Supervisor/instructor signature _____ Date _____

▶ TASK Remove and reinstall power steering pump.

MAST
4B13

Time off_____

Time on_____

Total time_____

CDX Tasksheet Number: C181

1. **Research the procedure to remove and install the power steering pump. List the steps or print off the procedure:**

2. **Following the specified procedure, remove the power steering pump being careful not to damage any fittings or hoses. Also, pay close attention to the positioning of any brackets and spacers.**

3. **Inspect the pump and pulley. List your observation(s):**

4. **Have your supervisor/instructor verify removal. Supervisor's/instructor's initials: _____**

> **NOTE** You may want to skip ahead and perform the next task C699: Remove and reinstall press fit power steering pump pulley; check pulley and belt alignment while you have the pump removed. If so, return to this point when you are ready to reinstall the pump.

5. **Following the specified procedure, reinstall the power steering pump. Be careful to properly align all brackets, fittings, and hoses. Also, tighten all fasteners to their specified torque.**

6. **Have your supervisor/instructor verify satisfactory completion of this procedure, any observations found, and any necessary action(s) recommended.**

> **NOTE** Return to step 6 of task C180: Remove, inspect, replace, and/or adjust power steering pump drive belt to complete that task.

Performance Rating

CDX Tasksheet Number: C181

0	**1**	**2**	**3**	**4**

Supervisor/instructor signature _____ Date _____

Suspension and Steering Systems **497**

► TASK Remove and reinstall press fit power steering pump pulley; check pulley and belt alignment.

MAST
4B14

CDX Tasksheet Number: C699

1. **Research the procedure to remove and install the power steering pump pulley in the appropriate service information. List the steps or print off the procedure:**

2. **Using the appropriate tools, remove the press fit power steering pump drive pulley from the drive shaft and inspect the pulley for any damage. List your observation(s):**

3. **Inspect the pump drive shaft and shaft seal for any damage. List your observation(s):**

4. **Have your supervisor/instructor verify removal. Supervisor's/instructor's initials: _____**

5. **Reinstall the press fit drive pulley on the power steering pump using the appropriate tool(s).**

> NOTE Return to task **C180: Remove, inspect, replace, and/or adjust power steering pump drive belt** step 6 to complete that task.

6. **Have your supervisor/instructor verify satisfactory completion of this procedure, any observations found, and any necessary action(s) recommended.**

Performance Rating

CDX Tasksheet Number: C699

0	1	2	3	4

Supervisor/instructor signature _____ Date _____

Steering Gear Service

Learning Objective/Task	CDX Tasksheet Number	2017 MAST NATEF Reference Number; Priority Level	
• Inspect rack and pinion steering gear inner tie rod ends (sockets) and bellows boots; replace as needed.	C883	4B8; P-1	Time off_____
• Remove and replace rack and pinion steering gear; inspect mounting bushings and brackets.	C882	4B7; P-2	Time on_____ Total time_____

Materials Required

- Vehicle hoist
- Vehicle with rack and pinion steering gear system
- Inner tie rod socket removal tool
- Depending on the type of concern, special diagnostic tools may be required. See your supervisor/instructor for instructions to identify what tools may be required.

Some Safety Issues to Consider

- Lifting equipment such as vehicle jacks and stands, vehicle hoists, and engine hoists are important tools that increase productivity and make the job easier. However, they can also cause severe injury or death if used improperly. Make sure you follow the manufacturer's operation procedures. Also, make sure you have your supervisor's/instructor's permission to use any particular type of lifting equipment.
- Comply with personal and environmental safety practices associated with clothing; eye protection; hand tools; power equipment; proper ventilation; and the handling, storage, and disposal of chemicals/materials in accordance with local, state, and federal safety and environmental regulations.

Performance Standard

0–No exposure: No information or practice provided during the program; complete training required

1–Exposure only: General information provided with no practice time; close supervision needed; additional training required

2–Limited practice: Has practiced job during training program; additional training required to develop skill

3–Moderately skilled: Has performed job independently during training program; limited additional training may be required

4–Skilled: Can perform job independently with no additional training

MAST
4B8

Time off_____

Time on_____

Total time_____

CDX Tasksheet Number: C883

1. Following the service information procedure, inspect the tie rod ends (sockets)
   and bellows boots. List your observation(s):

2. Determine which inner tie rod end your supervisor/instructor would like you to
   remove:

3. Remove the bellows boot to gain access to the inner tie rod.

4. Following the service information procedure, extend the rack (by turning the
   pinion shaft) to expose the locking nut of the inner tie rod socket. Using the
   appropriate tools, loosen the inner tie rod socket and unscrew the tie rod end.

5. Inspect the components and list your observations:

6. Have your supervisor/instructor verify removal. Supervisor's/instructor's
   initials: _____

7. Following the service information procedure, reassemble the inner tie rod socket
   and torque to the manufacturer's specifications.

8. Have your supervisor/instructor verify proper torque. Supervisor's/instructor's
   initials: _____

9. Reassemble the bellows boot and secure it according to the manufacturer's
   procedure.

10. Have your supervisor/instructor verify satisfactory completion of this
    procedure, any observations found, and any necessary action(s) recommended.

Performance Rating

CDX Tasksheet Number: C883

0	1	2	3	4

Supervisor/instructor signature _____ Date _____

Remove and replace rack and pinion steering gear; inspect
mounting bushings and brackets.

MAST
4B7

CDX Tasksheet Number: C882

1. **Research the following procedures and specifications in the appropriate service information.**

    a. **R & R rack and pinion flat rate time:** _____ hrs

    b. **R & R inner tie rod end (either side) flat rate time:** _____ hrs

    c. **Type of power steering fluid:**
    _____

    d. **Rack and pinion steering gear removal. List the main steps (you can paraphrase or print off the procedure):**

2. **Start the engine and straighten the wheels. Turn the engine off and lock the steering column. This will keep the clock spring centered.**

3. **Follow the service information procedure to remove the rack and pinion steering gear. Be careful not to damage any lines, tubes, or fittings. Plug any lines or fittings to prevent entry of dirt or debris.**

4. **Inspect the condition of the mounting bushings and brackets. List your observations:**

    a. **Have your supervisor/instructor verify removal. Supervisor's/ instructor's initials** _____

    NOTE You may want to skip to task **C883: Inspect rack and pinion steering gear inner tie rod ends (sockets) and bellows boots; replace as needed**. This task will be much easier to perform with the rack and pinion removed from the vehicle. If so, return to this point when you are ready to reinstall the rack and pinion.

5. **Follow the service information procedure to reinstall the rack and pinion steering gear. Be careful not to damage any lines, tubes, or fittings. Also, unless the manufacturer directs otherwise, make sure the rack is centered in its travel so that the clock spring will be indexed to the rack.**

6. **Torque all fasteners and fittings.**

7. **Check the fluid level in the power steering reservoir. Top off with the proper fluid.**

8. **Start the engine and bleed any air from the power steering system. Top off fluid as necessary.**

9. With the engine running, turn the steering wheel from lock to lock. Check for the following:

    a. Binding: Yes: _____ No: _____

    b. Excessive steering effort: Yes: _____ No: _____

    c. Uneven steering effort: Yes: _____ No: _____

10. Have your supervisor/instructor verify satisfactory completion of this procedure, any observations found, and any necessary action(s) recommended.

Performance Rating

CDX Tasksheet Number: C882

0	1	2	3	4

Supervisor/instructor signature _____ Date _____

Steering Linkage Service

Student/Intern information:

Name _____ Date _____ Class _____

Vehicle used for this activity:

Year _____ Make _____ Model _____

Odometer _____ VIN _____

Learning Objective/Task	CDX Tasksheet Number	2017 MAST NATEF Reference Number; Priority Level
• Inspect, remove and/or replace pitman arm, relay (centerlink/intermediate) rod, idler arm, mountings, and steering linkage damper.	C184	4B16; P-2
• Inspect, replace, and/or adjust tie rod ends (sockets), tie rod sleeves, and clamps.	C185	4B17; P-1

Time off_____

Time on_____

Total time_____

Materials Required

- Vehicle hoist
- Vehicle with recirculating ball steering gear system
- Pitman arm puller
- Depending on the type of concern, special diagnostic tools may be required. See your supervisor/instructor for instructions to identify what tools may be required.

Some Safety Issues to Consider

- Lifting equipment such as vehicle jacks and stands, vehicle hoists, and engine hoists are important tools that increase productivity and make the job easier. However, they can also cause severe injury or death if used improperly. Make sure you follow the manufacturer's operation procedures. Also, make sure you have your supervisor's/instructor's permission to use any particular type of lifting equipment.
- Comply with personal and environmental safety practices associated with clothing; eye protection; hand tools; power equipment; proper ventilation; and the handling, storage, and disposal of chemicals/materials in accordance with local, state, and federal safety and environmental regulations.

Performance Standard

0—No exposure: No information or practice provided during the program; complete training required

1—Exposure only: General information provided with no practice time; close supervision needed; additional training required

2—Limited practice: Has practiced job during training program; additional training required to develop skill

3—Moderately skilled: Has performed job independently during training program; limited additional training may be required

4—Skilled: Can perform job independently with no additional training

TASK Inspect, remove, and/or replace pitman arm, relay (centerlink/
intermediate) rod, idler arm, mountings, and steering
linkage damper.

Time off_____

Time on_____

Total time_____

DX Tasksheet Number: C184

1. **Research the following specifications and procedures in the appropriate service information.**

    a. **Maximum allowable play in each of the steering linkage joints:**

2. **Lift and support the vehicle according to the procedure listed in the service information.**

3. **Follow the manufacturer's procedure and inspect the steering system parts listed. List your observation(s):**

    a. **Pitman arm:**

    b. **Relay (centerlink/intermediate) rod:**

    c. **Idler arm and mountings:**

    d. **Steering linkage damper, if equipped:**

    e. **Tie rod ends:**

f. Tie rod sleeves and clamps:

4. Following the manufacturer's procedure, mark the location of the pitman arm shaft and pitman arm splines. Disconnect the pitman arm from the relay (centerlink/intermediate) rod steering linkage.

5. Remove the pitman arm-retaining nut and, using the manufacturer's recommended removal tool, remove the pitman arm.

6. If the vehicle is fitted with a steering damper, remove the steering damper and place it on your workbench.

7. Disconnect the relay (centerlink/intermediate) rod steering linkage.

8. Remove idler arm assembly.

9. Remove tie rod ends from steering knuckles.

> **NOTE** The use of a pickle fork will damage the dust boots. Only use this tool on joints you will be replacing. On joints you will be reusing, try the hammer method to break the joint free. See your instructor for details.

10. Loosen the tie rod adjusting sleeve clamp bolts. Remove tie rod ends from sleeves

> **NOTE** Count the number of turns as you back out each tie rod from its sleeve so you can reinstall it in approximately the same position. This will assist in making the wheel alignment easier to perform.

11. Inspect all components and list your observations:

12. Have your supervisor/instructor verify removal. Supervisor's/instructor's initials: _____

13. Reassemble all components following the manufacturer's recommended procedure, being sure to torque all fasteners and secure all joints with new cotter pins (or other approved method).

    a. List the torque you tightened the tie rod nuts to: _____ ft-lb/N·m
    b. List the torque you tightened the tie rod adjusting sleeve nuts to: _____ ft-lb/N·m
    c. Did you replace all removed cotter pins with new cotter pins?
       Yes: _____ No: _____

14 **Start the vehicle and check for binding or improper steering operation. List your observations:**

> **NOTE** Before this vehicle can be driven, it MUST have a wheel alignment performed. Failure to do so means this is an unsafe vehicle, which could result in substantial injury or even death.

15. **Have your supervisor/instructor verify satisfactory completion of this procedure, any observations found, and any necessary action(s) recommended.**

Performance Rating   **CDX Tasksheet Number: C184**

0	1	2	3	4

Supervisor/instructor signature _____ Date _____

Time off_____

Time on_____

Total time_____

DX Tasksheet Number: C185

1. **Research the following specifications and procedures in the appropriate service information.**

    a. **Maximum allowable play in the tie rod ends:**

2. **Lift and support the vehicle according to the procedure listed in the service information.**

3. **Follow the manufacturer's procedure and inspect the steering system parts listed. List your observation(s):**

    a. **Tie rod ends:**

    b. **Tie rod sleeves and clamps:**

4. **Determine any necessary actions:**

5. **Remove tie rod ends from steering knuckles.**

    NOTE The use of a pickle fork will damage the dust boots. Only use this tool on joints you will be replacing. On joints you will be reusing, try the hammer method to break the joint free. See your instructor for details.

6. **Loosen the tie rod adjusting sleeve clamp bolts. Remove tie rod ends from sleeves.**

    NOTE Count the number of turns as you back out each tie rod from its sleeve so you can reinstall it in approximately the same position. This will assist in making the wheel alignment easier to perform.

7. Inspect all components and list your observations:

8. Have your supervisor/instructor verify removal. Supervisor's/instructor's initials: _____

9. Reassemble all components following the manufacturer's specified procedure, being sure to torque all fasteners and secure all joints with new cotter pins (or other approved method).

   a. List the torque you tightened the tie rod nuts to: _____ ft-lb/N·m
   b. List the torque you tightened the tie rod adjusting sleeve nuts to: _____ ft-lb/N·m
   c. Did you replace all removed cotter pins with new cotter pins?
      Yes: _____ No: _____

10. Start the vehicle and check for binding or improper steering operation. List your observations:

NOTE Before this vehicle can be driven, it MUST have a wheel alignment performed. Failure to do so means this is an unsafe vehicle which could result in substantial injury or even death.

11. Have your supervisor/instructor verify satisfactory completion of this procedure, any observations found, and any necessary action(s) recommended.

Performance Rating

CDX Tasksheet Number: C185

0	1	2	3	4

Supervisor/instructor signature _____ Date _____

Steering Gear Diagnosis

Student/Intern information:

Name _____ Date _____ Class _____

Vehicle used for this activity:

Year _____ Make _____ Model _____

Odometer _____ VIN _____

Learning Objective/Task	CDX Tasksheet Number	2017 MAST NATEF Reference Number; Priority Level	
• Diagnose power steering gear (non-rack and pinion) binding, uneven turning effort, looseness, hard steering, and noise concerns; determine needed action.	C884	4B4; P-2	Time off_____
• Diagnose power steering gear (rack and pinion) binding, uneven turning effort, looseness, hard steering, and noise concerns; determine needed action.	C880	4B5; P-2	Time on_____ Total time_____

Materials Required

- Vehicle hoist
- Vehicle with rack and pinion steering gear system concern
- Vehicle with non-rack and pinion steering gear system concern
- Depending on the type of concern, special diagnostic tools may be required. See your supervisor/instructor for instructions to identify what tools may be required.

Some Safety Issues to Consider

- Diagnosis of this fault may require test-driving the vehicle on the school grounds. Attempt this task only with full permission from your instructor and follow all the guidelines exactly.
- You will be working under the hood of a running vehicle. Keep your hands and fingers away from moving belts, fans, and other parts.
- When running any vehicles in the shop, make sure you use the shop's exhaust ventilation system to discharge all exhaust gas safely outside.
- Lifting equipment such as vehicle jacks and stands, vehicle hoists, and engine hoists are important tools that increase productivity and make the job easier. However, they can also cause severe injury or death if used improperly. Make sure you follow the manufacturer's operation procedures. Also, make sure you have your supervisor's/instructor's permission to use any particular type of lifting equipment.
- Comply with personal and environmental safety practices associated with clothing; eye protection; hand tools; power equipment; proper ventilation; and the handling, storage, and disposal of chemicals/materials in accordance with local, state, and federal safety and environmental regulations.

Performance Standard

0–No exposure: No information or practice provided during the program; complete training required

1–Exposure only: General information provided with no practice time; close supervision needed; additional training required

2–Limited practice: Has practiced job during training program; additional training required to develop skill

3–Moderately skilled: Has performed job independently during training program; limited additional training may be required

4–Skilled: Can perform job independently with no additional training

Diagnose power steering gear (non-rack and pinion) binding, uneven turning effort, looseness, hard steering, and noise concerns; determine needed action.

Time off_____

Time on_____

Total time_____

CDX Tasksheet Number: C884

1. **List the power steering system-related customer concern:**

2. **Verify the concern and list your observations here:**

3. **Research the possible causes for this concern in the appropriate service information.**

    a. **List or print off and attach to this sheet the possible causes:**

    b. **List or print off and attach to this sheet the procedure for diagnosing the concern:**

4. **Follow the specified procedure to diagnose the concern. List your tests and results here:**

5. **List the cause of the concern:**

6. Determine any necessary action(s) to correct the fault:

7. Have your supervisor/instructor verify satisfactory completion of this procedure, any observations found, and any necessary action(s) recommended.

TASK Diagnose power steering gear (rack and pinion) binding, uneven turning effort, looseness, hard steering, and noise concerns; determine needed action.

MAST
4B5

Time off_____

Time on_____

Total time_____

CDX Tasksheet Number: C880

Vehicle used for this activity:

Year _____ Make _____ Model_____

Odometer_____ VIN_____

1. List the power steering system-related customer concern:

2. Verify the concern and list your observations here:

3. Research the possible causes for this concern in the appropriate service information.

   a. List or print off and attach to this sheet the possible causes:

   b. List or print off and attach to this sheet the procedure for diagnosing the concern:

4. Follow the specified procedure to diagnose the concern. List your tests and results here:

5. List the cause of the concern:

6. Determine any necessary action(s) to correct the fault:

7. Have your supervisor/instructor verify satisfactory completion of this procedure, any observations found, and any necessary action(s) recommended.

Performance Rating

0	1	2	3	4

Supervisor/instructor signature _____ Date _____

Steering Column Service

Learning Objective/Task	CDX Tasksheet Number	2017 MAST NATEF Reference Number; Priority Level	
• Disable and enable supplemental restraint system (SRS); verify indicator lamp operation.	C168	4B1; P-1	Time off_____
• Remove and replace steering wheel; center/time supplemental restraint system (SRS) coil (clock spring).	C169	4B2; P-1	Time on_____
• Inspect steering shaft universal joint(s), flexible coupling(s), collapsible column, lock cylinder mechanism, and steering wheel; determine needed action.	C173	4B6; P-2	Total time_____
• Diagnose steering column noises, looseness, and binding concerns (including tilt/telescoping mechanisms); determine needed action.	C170	4B3; P-2	

Materials Required

- Vehicle fitted with supplemental restraint system (SRS)
- Steering wheel puller
- Manufacturer- and job-specific tools
- Masking tape

Some Safety Issues to Consider

- Working on the airbag system can be very dangerous. Consult the service information for the vehicle you are working on and ensure all safety precautions are followed.
- Accidental deployment of the airbag system could happen if you inadvertently probe the wrong wire. Most manufacturers use yellow-colored wiring to denote wiring for the airbag system. Always be aware of the system/circuit you are working on.
- Comply with personal and environmental safety practices associated with clothing; eye protection; hand tools; power equipment; proper ventilation; and the handling, storage, and disposal of chemicals/materials in accordance with local, state, and federal safety and environmental regulations.

Performance Standard

0–No exposure: No information or practice provided during the program; complete training required

1–Exposure only: General information provided with no practice time; close supervision needed; additional training required

2–Limited practice: Has practiced job during training program; additional training required to develop skill

3–Moderately skilled: Has performed job independently during training program; limited additional training may be required

4–Skilled: Can perform job independently with no additional training

Disable and enable supplemental restraint system (SRS); verify indicator lamp operation.

MAST
4B1

CDX Tasksheet Number: C168

1. **Locate "disable vehicle SRS system" in the appropriate service information for the vehicle you are working on.**

    a. **List or print off and attach to this sheet the safety precautions to be taken when disabling the SRS system:**

    b. **List or print off and attach to this sheet the steps to disable the SRS system:**

    c. **List or print off and attach to this sheet the steps to enable the SRS system:**

2. **Have your supervisor/instructor verify your listed procedures. Supervisor's/instructor's initials: _____**

3. **Disarm the SRS system.**

4. **Have your supervisor/instructor verify that the SRS is disabled. Supervisor's/instructor's initials: _____**

> **NOTE** You may want to consider skipping to task C169: Remove and replace steering wheel; center/time supplemental restraint system (SRS) coil (clock spring) since it requires disabling the SRS. Return to this step when you complete that task and re-enable the SRS.

5. **Following the specified procedure, enable the vehicle's SRS.**

6. **Following the specified procedure, verify indicator lamp operation.**

7. Have your supervisor/instructor verify satisfactory completion of this procedure, any observations found, and any necessary action(s) recommended.

Performance Rating

CDX Tasksheet Number: 168

0	1	2	3	4

Supervisor/instructor signature _____ Date _____

Remove and replace steering wheel; center/time supplemental restraint system (SRS) coil (clock spring).

MAST
4B2

Time off_____

Time on_____

Total time_____

CDX Tasksheet Number: C169

1. **Locate "remove and replace steering wheel" and "center/time SRS clock spring" procedures in the appropriate service information.**

   a. **List or print off and attach to this sheet the procedures for removing and replacing the steering wheel:**

   b. **List or print off and attach to this sheet the procedure to center/time the SRS clock spring:**

2. **Have your supervisor/instructor verify your listed procedures. Supervisor's/instructor's initials: _____**

3. **Following the specified procedures and precautions, remove the steering wheel.**

4. **Following the specified procedures and precautions, remove the clock spring.**

5. **Inspect the components and list your observation(s):**

6. **Have your supervisor/instructor verify the removal of these components. Supervisor's/instructor's initials: _____**

7. **Reassemble the steering column. Be sure to follow all manufacturer-recommended procedures and precautions.**

> **NOTE** Return to task step 5 of C168: Disable and enable supplemental restraint system (SRS); verify indicator lamp operation to enable the SRS.

8. **Have your supervisor/instructor verify satisfactory completion of this procedure, any observations found, and any necessary action(s) recommended.**

Performance Rating

CDX Tasksheet Number: C169

0	1	2	3	4

Supervisor/instructor signature _____ Date _____

Inspect steering shaft universal joint(s), flexible coupling(s), collapsible column, lock cylinder mechanism, and steering wheel; determine needed action.

MAST
4B6

Time off_____

Time on_____

Total time_____

CDX Tasksheet Number: C173

1. If the vehicle is fitted with an SRS, disable it according to the manufacturer's procedure and precautions.

2. Safely raise and support the vehicle so the tires are a few inches off the floor.

3. With the steering column lock activated, try to turn the steering wheel from side to side.

   a. Is the locking mechanism working? Yes: _____ No: _____
   b. List your observation(s):

4. With the engine ignition key in the "off" position, ensure the steering lock is not engaged and have an assistant rock the steering wheel from side to side (just enough to move the road wheels slightly). While the steering wheel is being rocked, check for any wear or looseness in the shaft universal joint(s) or flexible coupling(s).

   a. List your observation(s):

5. Following the specified procedure, check that the steering column collapsible action has not been compromised.

   a. List your observation(s):

6. Check the steering wheel for the following and list any observation(s):

   a. Looseness on the steering shaft:

   b. Structural damage:

    c. SRS airbag is intact and has appropriate pad/cover:

    d. Size and appropriateness for the make and model of the vehicle (refer to the service information):

7. Have your supervisor/instructor verify your observations. Supervisor's/instructor's initials: _____

8. Perform any necessary action(s) and list them here:

9. Following the specified procedure, enable the SRS.

10. Have your supervisor/instructor verify satisfactory completion of this procedure, any observations found, and any necessary action(s) recommended.

Performance Rating

CDX Tasksheet Number: C173

0	1	2	3	4

Supervisor/instructor signature _____ Date _____

Diagnose steering column noises, looseness, and binding concerns (including tilt/telescoping mechanisms); determine needed action.

MAST
4B3

Time off_____

Time on_____

Total time_____

CDX Tasksheet Number: C170

Vehicle used for this activity:

Year _____ Make _____ Model _____

Odometer _____ VIN _____

1. **List the steering column-related customer concern:**

2. **Verify the concern and list your observations here:**

3. **Research the possible causes for this concern in the appropriate service information.**

    a. **List or print off and attach to this sheet the possible causes:**

    b. **List or print off and attach to this sheet the procedure for diagnosing the concern:**

    c. **List the precautions when working on this steering column:**

4. Follow the specified procedure to diagnose the concern. List your tests and results here:

5. List the cause of the concern:

6. Determine any necessary action(s) to correct this fault:

7. Have your supervisor/instructor verify satisfactory completion of this procedure, any observations found, and any necessary action(s) recommended.

Performance Rating

CDX Tasksheet Number: C170

0	1	2	3	4

Supervisor/instructor signature _____ Date _____

Front Suspension Service—Long and Short Arm

Student/Intern information:

Name _____ Date _____ Class _____

Vehicle used for this activity:

Year _____ Make _____ Model_____

Odometer_____VIN_____

Learning Objective/Task	CDX Tasksheet Number	2017 MAST NATEF Reference Number; Priority Level
• Inspect, remove, and/or replace front/rear stabilizer bar (sway bar) bushings, brackets, and links.	C793	4C9; P-3
• Inspect, remove, and/or replace short and long arm suspension system coil springs and spring insulators.	C193	4C7; P-3
• Inspect, remove, and/or replace steering knuckle assemblies.	C192	4C6; P-3
• Inspect, remove, and/or replace upper and lower control arms, bushings, shafts, and rebound bumpers.	C790	4C3; P-3
• Inspect, remove, and/or replace strut rods and bushings.	C791	4C4: P-3
• Inspect, remove, and/or replace upper and/or lower ball joints (with or without wear indicators).	C792	4C5; P-2

Time off_____

Time on_____

Total time_____

Materials Required

- Vehicle equipped with short and long arm suspension
- Dial indicator
- Spring compressor
- Ball Joint press
- Torque wrench
- Manufacturer- and job-specific tools
- Grease gun with specified grease

Some Safety Issues to Consider

- Lifting equipment such as vehicle jacks and stands, vehicle hoists, and engine hoists are important tools that increase productivity and make the job easier. However, they can also cause severe injury or death if used improperly. Make sure you follow the manufacturer's operation procedures. Also, make sure you have your supervisor's/instructor's permission to use any particular type of lifting equipment.
- Some suspension systems are electronically controlled, and can raise or lower without notice. Please familiarize yourself with the manufacturer's safety precautions related to these procedures.
- Vehicle springs store a lot of energy, which, if released improperly, can cause injury or death. Please familiarize yourself with the manufacturer's safety precautions related to these procedures.

- Comply with personal and environmental safety practices associated with clothing; eye protection; hand tools; power equipment; proper ventilation; and the handling, storage, and disposal of chemicals/materials in accordance with local, state, and federal safety and environmental regulations.

Performance Standard
0–No exposure: No information or practice provided during the program; complete training required

1–Exposure only: General information provided with no practice time; close supervision needed; additional training required

2–Limited practice: Has practiced job during training program; additional training required to develop skill

3–Moderately skilled: Has performed job independently during training program; limited additional training may be required

4–Skilled: Can perform job independently with no additional training

Inspect, remove, and/or replace front/rear stabilizer bar (sway bar) bushings, brackets, and links.

MAST
4C9

Time off_____

Time on_____

Total time_____

CDX Tasksheet Number: C793

1. **Research the disassembly and inspection procedure for the stabilizer bar, bushings, brackets, and links in the appropriate service information.**

    a. **List any precautions:**

    b. **List or print off and attach to this sheet the steps to disassemble the stabilizer bar system.**

2. **Safely raise and support the vehicle.**

3. **Following the specified procedure outlined in the service information, inspect, dismantle, clean, and re-inspect the stabilizer bar, bushings, and links. List your observation(s):**

    a. **Stabilizer bar:**

    b. **Bushing(s):**

    c. **Link(s):**

4. **Determine any necessary action(s):**

5. Have your supervisor/instructor verify satisfactory completion of this procedure, any observations found, and any necessary action(s) recommended.

Performance Rating

CDX Tasksheet Number: C793

0	1	2	3	4

Supervisor/instructor signature _____ Date _____

Inspect, remove, and/or replace short and long arm
suspension system coil springs and spring insulators.

MAST
4C7

Time off_____

Time on_____

Total time_____

CDX Tasksheet Number: C193

1. **Research the removal and inspection procedure for the coil springs and spring insulators in the appropriate service information.**

   a. **List any precautions:**

   b. **List or print off and attach to this sheet the steps to remove the coil springs.**

2. **Have your supervisor/instructor verify your listed precautions and procedures. Supervisor's/instructor's initials: _____**

3. **Following the specified procedure outlined in the service information, inspect, remove, clean, and re-inspect the coil spring and spring insulators. List your observation(s):**

   a. **Coil spring:**

   b. **Spring insulators:**

4. **Determine any necessary action(s):**

5. Have your supervisor/instructor verify satisfactory completion of this procedure, any observations found, and any necessary action(s) recommended.

Performance Rating

0	1	2	3	4

Supervisor/instructor signature _____ Date _____

Inspect, remove, and/or replace steering knuckle assemblies.

MAST
4C6

Time off_____

Time on_____

Total time_____

CDX Tasksheet Number: C192

1. Research the removal and inspection procedure for the steering knuckle assembly in the appropriate service information.

    a. List any precautions:

    b. List or print off and attach to this sheet the steps to remove the steering knuckle assembly.

2. Following the specified procedure outlined in the service information, inspect, remove, clean, and re-inspect the steering knuckle assembly. List your observation(s):

    a. Steering knuckle:

3. Determine any necessary action(s):

4. Have your supervisor/instructor verify satisfactory completion of this procedure, any observations found, and any necessary action(s) recommended.

Performance Rating

CDX Tasksheet Number: C192

0	1	2	3	4

Supervisor/instructor signature _____ Date _____

Inspect, remove, and/or replace upper and lower control arms, bushings, shafts, and rebound bumpers.

Time off_____

Time on_____

Total time_____

CDX Tasksheet Number: C790

1. **Research the removal and inspection procedure for the upper and lower control arms, bushings, shafts, and rebound bumpers in the appropriate service information.**

    a. **List any precautions:**

    b. **List or print off and attach to this sheet the steps to remove the control arms.**

2. **Following the specified procedure outlined in the service information, inspect, remove, clean, and re-inspect the upper and lower control arms, bushings, shafts, and rebound bumpers. List your observation(s):**

    a. **Upper control arm:**

    b. **Lower control arm:**

    c. **Bushings:**

    d. **Shafts:**

    e. **Rebound bumper(s):**

3. Determine any necessary action(s):

4. Have your supervisor/instructor verify satisfactory completion of this procedure, any observations found, and any necessary action(s) recommended.

Inspect, remove, and/or replace strut rods and bushings.

MAST
4C4

Time off_____

Time on_____

Total time_____

CDX Tasksheet Number: C791

1. **Research the inspection and disassembly procedure for the strut rods and bushings in the appropriate service information.**

    a. **List any precautions:**

    b. **List or print off and attach to this sheet the steps to inspect and disassemble the strut rods and bushings:**

2. **Following the specified procedure outlined in the service information, remove the strut rods and bushings from the vehicle. List your observation(s):**

    a. **Strut rod:**

    b. **Bushings:**

3. **Determine any necessary action(s):**

4. **Have your supervisor/instructor verify satisfactory completion of this procedure, any observations found, and any necessary action(s) recommended.**

Performance Rating

CDX Tasksheet Number: C791

0	1	2	3	4

Supervisor/instructor signature _____ Date _____

Inspect, remove, and/or replace upper and/or lower ball joints
(with or without wear indicators).

MAST
4C5

CDX Tasksheet Number: C792

1. **Research the inspection and disassembly procedure for the upper and/or lower ball joints in the appropriate service information.**

    a. **Maximum allowable play in the lower ball joint:** _____ **in/mm**

    b. **Maximum allowable play in the upper ball joint; if applicable:** _____ **in/mm**

    c. **Which ball joint is the load-bearing ball joint? Lower:** _____
        Upper: _____

    d. **List any precautions:**

    e. **List or print off and attach to this sheet the steps to inspect the lower and/or upper ball joints.**

    f. **List or print off and attach to this sheet the steps to disassemble the lower and/or upper ball joints.**

2. **Following the specified procedure, measure the play in the lower and/or upper ball joint(s). List your observation(s):**

    a. **Measure the play in the lower ball joint: Left** _____ **in/mm**
        Right: _____ **in/mm**

    b. **Measure the play in the upper ball joints: Left:** _____ **in/mm**
        Right: _____ **in/mm.**

3. **Following the specified procedure, remove, clean, and re-inspect the lower and/or upper ball joints. List your observation(s):**

4. **Determine any necessary action(s):**

5. **Have your instructor verify the removal of all suspension components and check your observations and necessary actions. Get permission to reassemble the assembly. Supervisor's/instructor's initials:** _____

> **NOTE** At this time, replace/reinstall all removed suspension components following the manufacturer's procedures and precautions. Be sure to tighten all fasteners to their specified torque and replace any retaining devices such as cotter pins (with new ones) and nylon locking nuts. Be careful to route all wires, hoses, and tubes in their original factory position.

6. **Inspect the reassembled suspension unit for any loose fasteners, improperly installed components, etc. List your observations here:**

7. **Determine any necessary action(s):**

8. **Have your supervisor/instructor verify satisfactory completion of this procedure, any observations found, and any necessary action(s) recommended.**

Performance Rating

CDX Tasksheet Number: C792

| 0 | 1 | 2 | 3 | 4 |

Supervisor/instructor signature _____ Date _____

Front Suspension Service—Strut and Torsion Bar

Student/Intern information:

Name _____ Date _____ Class _____

Vehicle used for this activity:

Year _____ Make _____ Model _____

Odometer_____ VIN _____

Learning Objective/Task	CDX Tasksheet Number	2017 MAST NATEF Reference Number; Priority Level
• Inspect, remove, and/or replace strut cartridge or assembly, strut coil spring, insulators (silencers), and upper-strut bearing mount.	C794	4C10; P-3
• Inspect, remove, and/or replace track bar, strut rods/radius arms, and related mounts and bushings.	C934	4C11; P-3
• Inspect, remove, and/or replace torsion bars and mounts.	C194	4C8; P-3

Materials Required

- Vehicle equipped with strut suspension
- Vehicle with torsion bar suspension
- Strut compressor
- Torque wrench
- Manufacturer- and job-specific tools

Some Safety Issues to Consider

- Lifting equipment such as vehicle jacks and stands, vehicle hoists, and engine hoists are important tools that increase productivity and make the job easier. However, they can also cause severe injury or death if used improperly. Make sure you follow the manufacturer's operation procedures. Also, make sure you have your supervisor's/instructor's permission to use any particular type of lifting equipment.
- Some suspension systems are electronically controlled, and can raise or lower without notice. Please familiarize yourself with the manufacturer's safety precautions related to these procedures.
- Vehicle springs store a lot of energy, which, if released improperly, can cause injury or death. Please familiarize yourself with the manufacturer's safety precautions related to these procedures.
- Comply with personal and environmental safety practices associated with clothing; eye protection; hand tools; power equipment; proper ventilation; and the handling, storage, and disposal of chemicals/materials in accordance with local, state, and federal safety and environmental regulations.

Performance Standard

0—No exposure: No information or practice provided during the program; complete training required

1—Exposure only: General information provided with no practice time; close supervision needed; additional training required

2—Limited practice: Has practiced job during training program; additional training required to develop skill

3—Moderately skilled: Has performed job independently during training program; limited additional training may be required

4—Skilled: Can perform job independently with no additional training

TASK Inspect, remove, and/or replace strut cartridge or assembly, strut coil spring, insulators (silencers), and upper-strut bearing mount.

MAST
4C10

Time off_____

Time on_____

Total time_____

CDX Tasksheet Number: C794

1. Research the disassembly and inspection procedure for the strut cartridge or assembly, strut coil spring, insulators (silencers), and upper-strut bearing mount in the appropriate service information.

    a. List any precautions:

    b. List or print off and attach to this sheet the steps to inspect, remove, and disassemble the strut assembly:

2. Have your supervisor/instructor verify your listed precautions and procedures. Supervisor's/instructor's initials: _____

3. Safely raise and support the vehicle.

4. Following the specified procedure outlined in the service information, inspect the struts on the vehicle. List your observations:

5. Following the specified procedure, remove the strut assembly from the vehicle.

> **NOTE** On some vehicles, it makes sense to mark the position of the adjustable components so they can be reinstalled into their original positions.

6. Following the specified procedure outlined in the service information, disassemble the strut. Improperly removing the spring can cause severe injury or death.

7. Clean and inspect the strut cartridge or assembly, strut coil spring, insulators (silencers), and upper-strut bearing mount. List your observation(s):

    a. Strut cartridge or assembly:

    b. Strut coil spring:

    c. Spring insulators:

    d. Upper-strut bearing mount:

8. Determine any necessary action(s):

9. Have your instructor verify the removal and disassembly of the strut, and check your observations and necessary actions. Get permission to reassemble the strut. Supervisor's/instructor's initials: _____

10. Reassemble the strut according to the manufacturer's procedure and precautions. Be careful when compressing and installing the spring as it can cause severe injury or death if installed improperly.

11. Reinstall the strut into the vehicle. Be sure to tighten all fasteners to their specified torque and replace any retaining devices such as cotter pins and nylon locking nuts. Be careful to route all wires, hoses, and tubes in their original factory positions.

12. Inspect the reassembled strut assembly for any loose fasteners, improperly installed components, etc. List your observations here:

13. Have your supervisor/instructor verify satisfactory completion of this procedure, any observations found, and any necessary action(s) recommended.

Performance Rating

CDX Tasksheet Number: C794

0	1	2	3	4

Supervisor/instructor signature _____ Date _____

Inspect, remove, and/or replace track bar, strut rods/radius arms, and related mounts and bushings.

MAST
4C11

CDX Tasksheet Number: C934

1. **Research the inspection and disassembly procedure for the track bars, strut rods/radius arms, mounts, and bushings in the appropriate service information.**

    a. **List or print off and attach to this sheet the steps to inspect and disassemble the track bars, strut rods/radius arms, mounts, and bushings:**

2. **Following the specified procedure outlined in the service information, remove the track bars, strut rods/radius arms, mounts, and bushings from the vehicle. List your observation(s):**

    a. **Track bars:**

    b. **Strut rod/radius arms:**

    c. **Mounts:**

    d. **Bushings:**

3. **Determine any necessary action(s):**

4. **Have your instructor verify the removal and disassembly of the track bars, strut rod/radius arms, mounts, and bushings, and check your observations and necessary actions. Also, have your instructor sign off on the disassembly of the strut in the previous task. Supervisor's/instructor's initials:** _____

5. Reassemble the strut rods, mounts, and bushings according to the manufacturer's procedure and precautions.

6. Have your supervisor/instructor verify satisfactory completion of this procedure, any observations found, and any necessary action(s) recommended.

Performance Rating

CDX Tasksheet Number: C934

0	1	2	3	4

Supervisor/instructor signature _____ Date _____

TASK Inspect, remove, and/or replace torsion bars and mounts.

MAST
4C8

Time off_____

Time on_____

Total time_____

CDX Tasksheet Number: C194

Vehicle used for this activity:

Year_____ Make_____ Model_____

Odometer_____ VIN _____

1. **Research the disassembly and inspection procedure for the torsion bars and mounts in the appropriate service information.**

    a. **List any precautions:**

    b. **List or print off and attach to this sheet the steps to remove the torsion bar:**

    c. **List the flat rate time to remove and install one torsion bar:** _____ **hrs**
    d. **Specified ride height:** _____

2. **Have your supervisor/instructor verify your answers.**
    Supervisor's/instructor's initials: _____

3. **Measure and record vehicle ride height. Note your findings here:**

4. **Safely raise and support the vehicle.**

5. **Following the specified procedure outlined in the service information, remove one torsion bar from the vehicle. List your observation(s):**

    a. **Torsion bar:**

    b. **Mounts:**

    c. **Height-adjustment mechanism:**

    d. **Bushing(s):**

Suspension and Steering Systems **551**

6. Determine any necessary action(s):

7. Have your instructor verify the removal and disassembly of the torsion bar, and check your observations and necessary actions.
Supervisor's/instructor's initials: _____

8. Reinstall the torsion bar according to the manufacturer's procedure and precautions. Be careful when installing and compressing the spring as it can cause severe injury or death if installed improperly.

9. Torque all retaining bolts to the manufacturer's specifications.

10. Following the manufacturer's procedure, adjust the ride height of the vehicle to meet specifications.

11. Inspect the suspension for any loose fasteners, improperly installed components, etc. List your observations here:

12. Determine any necessary action(s):

13. Have your supervisor/instructor verify satisfactory completion of this procedure, any observations found, and any necessary action(s) recommended.

Performance Rating

CDX Tasksheet Number: C194

0	1	2	3	4

Supervisor/instructor signature _____ Date _____

Front-Suspension Diagnosis

Student/Intern information:

Name _____ Date _____ Class _____

Vehicle used for this activity:

Year _____ Make _____ Model _____

Odometer _____ VIN _____

Learning Objective/Task	CDX Tasksheet Number	2017 MAST NATEF Reference Number; Priority Level
• Diagnose short and long arm suspension system noises, body sway, and uneven ride height concerns; determine needed action.	C852	4C1; P-1
• Diagnose strut suspension system noises, body sway, and uneven ride height concerns; determine needed action.	C853	4C2; P-1

Time off_____

Time on_____

Total time_____

Materials Required

- Vehicle hoist
- Vehicle with short- and long-arm suspension system concern
- Vehicle with strut suspension system concern
- Depending on the type of concern, special diagnostic tools may be required. See your supervisor/instructor for instructions to identify what tools may be required.

Some Safety Issues to Consider

- When running any vehicles in the shop, make sure you use the shop's exhaust ventilation system to discharge all exhaust gas safely outside.
- Lifting equipment such as vehicle jacks and stands, vehicle hoists, and engine hoists are important tools that increase productivity and make the job easier. However, they can also cause severe injury or death if used improperly. Make sure you follow the manufacturer's operation procedures. Also, make sure you have your supervisor's/instructor's permission to use any particular type of lifting equipment.
- Vehicle springs store a lot of energy, which, if released improperly, can cause injury or death. Please familiarize yourself with the manufacturer's safety precautions related to these procedures.
- Some suspension systems are electronically controlled and can raise or lower without notice. Please familiarize yourself with the manufacturer's safety precautions related to these procedures.
- Comply with personal and environmental safety practices associated with clothing; eye protection; hand tools; power equipment; proper ventilation; and the handling, storage, and disposal of chemicals/materials in accordance with local, state, and federal safety and environmental regulations.

Performance Standard

0—No exposure: No information or practice provided during the program; complete training required

1—Exposure only: General information provided with no practice time; close supervision needed; additional training required

2—Limited practice: Has practiced job during training program; additional training required to develop skill

3—Moderately skilled: Has performed job independently during training program; limited additional training may be required

4—Skilled: Can perform job independently with no additional training

Diagnose short and long arm suspension system noises, body sway, and uneven ride height concerns; determine needed action.

MAST
4C1

CDX Tasksheet Number: C852

1. List the short and long arm suspension system-related customer concern:

2. Verify the concern and list your observations here:

3. Research the possible causes for this concern in the appropriate service information:

   a. List or print off and attach to this sheet the possible causes:

   b. List or print off and attach to this sheet the procedure for diagnosing the concern:

4. Follow the service-specified procedure to diagnose the concern. List your tests and results here:

5. List the cause of the concern:

6. Determine any necessary action(s) to correct the fault:

7. Have your supervisor/instructor verify satisfactory completion of this procedure, any observations found, and any necessary action(s) recommended.

MAST
4C2

CDX Tasksheet Number: C853

Vehicle used for this activity:

Year _____ Make _____ Model_____

Odometer_____ VIN_____

1. **List the strut suspension system-related customer concern:**

2. **Verify the concern and list your observations here:**

3. **Research the possible causes for this concern in the appropriate service
   information.**

   a. **List or print off and attach to this sheet the possible causes:**

   b. **List or print off and attach to this sheet the procedure for diagnosing the
      concern:**

4. **Follow the specified procedure to diagnose the concern. List your tests and
   results here:**

5. List the cause of the concern:

6. Determine any necessary action(s) to correct the fault:

7. Have your supervisor/instructor verify satisfactory completion of this procedure, any observations found, and any necessary action(s) recommended.

Performance Rating

0	1	2	3	4

Supervisor/instructor signature _____ Date _____

Rear Suspension Service

Student/Intern information:

Name _____ Date _____ Class _____

Vehicle used for this activity:

Year _____ Make _____ Model_____

Odometer_____VIN_____

Learning Objective/Task	CDX Tasksheet Number	2017 MAST NATEF Reference Number; Priority Level
• Inspect, remove, and/or replace shock absorbers; inspect mounts and bushings.	C202	4D1; P-1
• Inspect rear suspension system leaf spring(s), spring insulators (silencers), shackles, brackets, bushings, center pins/bolts, and mounts.	C854	4C12; P-1
• Remove, inspect, service, and/or replace front and rear wheel bearings.	C203	4D2; P-1

Time off_____

Time on_____

Total time_____

Materials Required

- Vehicle with hydraulic shock absorbers and leaf springs
- Vehicle lifting equipment
- Safety stands
- Manufacturer- and job-specific tools
- Specified wheel-bearing grease
- New cotter pin(s), depending on application

Some Safety Issues to Consider

- Vehicle hoists are important tools that increase productivity and make the job easier. However, they also can cause severe injury or death if used improperly. Make sure you follow the hoist and vehicle manufacturer's operation procedures. Also make sure you have your supervisor's/instructor's permission to use a vehicle hoist.
- Shock absorbers may be the primary fastening device for holding the suspension, or axle assembly, in the vehicle. Be sure to support the suspension with the appropriate safety stands.
- Some shock absorbers are pressurized with nitrogen gas. Keep your fingers from being pinched by an expanding shock absorber.
- Some shock absorbers have overload springs attached to them. Be careful not to accidentally release the spring. Serious pinching could occur.
- Some shock absorbers are electronically controlled and can extend or retract without notice. Please familiarize yourself with the manufacturer's safety precautions related to these procedures.
- Always wear the correct protective eyewear and clothing, and use the appropriate safety equipment, as well as fender covers, seat protectors, and floor mat protectors.

- Make sure you understand and observe all legislative and personal safety procedures when carrying out practical assignments. If you are unsure of what these are, ask your supervisor/instructor.

Performance Standard

0–No exposure: No information or practice provided during the program; complete training required

1–Exposure only: General information provided with no practice time; close supervision needed; additional training required

2–Limited practice: Has practiced job during training program; additional training required to develop skill

3–Moderately skilled: Has performed job independently during training program; limited additional training may be required

4–Skilled: Can perform job independently with no additional training

TASK Inspect, remove, and/or replace shock absorbers; inspect mounts and bushings.

MAST
4D1

Time off_____

Time on_____

Total time_____

DX Tasksheet Number: C202

1. Research the shock absorber removal and installation procedure in the appropriate service information. Follow all directions.

    a. Shock absorber fastener torque: _____ ft-lb/N·m
    b. List the flat rate time for this job: _____ hrs

2. Carefully bounce check the shock absorbers by pushing on each corner of the bumpers. Let go at the bottom of the travel and observe how many oscillations it takes for the vehicle to come to a stop. List your observations:

3. Safely raise and support the vehicle on a hoist. Check to see that the vehicle is secure on the hoist, and then remove the shock absorbers following the service information procedures.

    NOTE Be sure to support the suspension, or axle assembly, with safety stands before removing the shocks.

4. Inspect the shock absorbers, rubber bushings (bushes), and mounts and list your observations:

    a. Shock absorbers:

    b. Rubber bushings (bushes):

    c. Shock mounts:

5. Determine any necessary action(s):

6. Have your supervisor/instructor verify the removal and your observations. Supervisor's/instructor's initials: _____

7. Reinstall the shock absorbers according to the specified procedure. Be sure to torque all fasteners properly.

8. Have your supervisor/instructor verify satisfactory completion of this procedure, any
observations found, and any necessary action(s) recommended.

Performance Rating

CDX Tasksheet Number: C202

0	1	2	3	4

Supervisor/instructor signature _____ Date _____

TASK Inspect rear suspension system leaf spring(s), spring insulators (silencers), shackles, brackets, bushings, center pins/bolts, and mounts.

MAST
4C12

Time off_____

Time on_____

Total time_____

DX Tasksheet Number: C854

Vehicle used for this activity:

Year _____ Make _____ Model_____

Odometer _____ VIN_____

1. **Research the leaf-spring inspection procedure in the appropriate service information. Follow all directions.**
   a. **U-bolt torque:** _____ **ft-lb/N·m**
   b. **Shackle bolt torque:** _____ **ft-lb/N·m**

2. **Safely raise and support the vehicle. Support the axle assembly with safety stands.**

3. **Following the specified procedure, inspect and record the condition of each of the following:**
   a. **Rear-shackle bushings:**

   b. **Front-shackle bushings:**

   c. **Spring-leaf insulators:**

   d. **U-bolts and nuts:**

   e. **Rubber-bump stops:**

f. Spring shackles and plates:

g. Leaf-spring pack:

4. Determine any necessary action(s):

5. Have your supervisor/instructor verify satisfactory completion of this procedure, any observations found, and any necessary action(s) recommended.

Performance Rating

0	1	2	3	4

Supervisor/instructor signature _____ Date _____

TASK Remove, inspect, service, and/or replace front and
rear wheel bearings.

MAST
4D2

Time off_____

Time on_____

Total time_____

CDX Tasksheet Number: C203

Vehicle used for this activity:

Year _____ Make _____ Model_____

Odometer_____ VIN_____

1. Which wheel bearing are you servicing? _____

2. What type of bearing is this vehicle equipped with? Serviceable: _____
   Sealed: _____

3. Research the wheel-bearing removal, service, and installation procedure in the
   appropriate service information. Follow all directions.

   a. List the bearing adjustment procedure, if applicable:

   b. Specified wheel-bearing grease: _____
   c. Lug nut torque: _____ ft-lb/N·m
   d. List the flat rate time for this job: _____ hrs

4. Safely raise and support the vehicle.

5. Following the specified procedure, dismantle, clean, and inspect wheel bearing
   and race. List your observation(s):

   a. Wheel bearing:

   b. Race:

   c. Spindle:

Suspension and Steering Systems **565**

    d. Hub:

    e. Grease seal:

    f. Are these parts serviceable? Yes: _____ No: _____

6. **Determine any necessary action(s):**

7. **Have your supervisor/instructor verify the removal and your observations. Supervisor's/instructor's initials: _____**

8. **Repack (if applicable) the wheel bearings with the specified grease.**

9. **Following the specified procedure, reinstall and adjust the wheel-bearing assembly. Before locking the adjustment nut, have your supervisor/ instructor verify the wheel-bearing adjustment. Supervisor's/instructor's initials: _____**

10. **Following the specified procedure, lock the wheel-bearing adjustment nut with the specified retaining device. Always replace disposable devices such as cotter pins with new parts.**

11. **Return the vehicle to its beginning condition and clean and return any tools that you may have used to their proper locations.**

12. **Have your supervisor/instructor verify satisfactory completion of this procedure, any observations found, and any necessary action(s) recommended.**

Performance Rating

CDX Tasksheet Number: C203

0	1	2	3	4

Supervisor/instructor signature _____ Date _____

Electronically Controlled Steering and Suspension Service

Student/Intern information:

Name _____ Date _____ Class _____

Vehicle used for this activity:

Year _____ Make _____ Model _____

Odometer _____ VIN _____

Learning Objective/Task	CDX Tasksheet Number	2017 MAST NATEF Reference Number; Priority Level
• Inspect, test, and diagnose electrically assisted power steering systems (including using a scan tool); determine needed action.	C186	4B18; P-2
• Describe the function of suspension and steering control systems and components (i.e. active suspension and stability control).	C931	4D3; P-3
• Identify hybrid vehicle power steering system electrical circuits and safety precautions.	C551	4B19; P-2

Time off_____

Time on_____

Total time_____

Materials Required

- Vehicle with electronically controlled steering system
- Scan tool
- DMM/DVOM
- Manufacturer- and job-specific tools

Some Safety Issues to Consider

- Diagnosis of this fault may require test-driving the vehicle on the school grounds. Attempt this task only with full permission from your instructor and follow all guidelines and policies exactly.
- Lifting equipment such as vehicle jacks and stands, vehicle hoists, and engine hoists are important tools that increase productivity and make the job easier. However, they can also cause severe injury or death if used improperly. Make sure you follow the manufacturer's operation procedures. Also, make sure you have your supervisor's/instructor's permission to use any particular type of lifting equipment.
- Vehicle springs store a lot of energy, which, if released improperly, can cause injury or death. Please familiarize yourself with the manufacturer's safety precautions related to these procedures.
- Some suspension systems are electronically controlled, and can raise or lower without notice. Please familiarize yourself with the manufacturer's safety precautions related to these procedures.
- Comply with personal and environmental safety practices associated with clothing; eye protection; hand tools; power equipment; proper ventilation; and the handling, storage, and disposal of chemicals/materials in accordance with local, state, and federal safety and environmental regulations.

Performance Standard

0—No exposure: No information or practice provided during the program; complete training required

1—Exposure only: General information provided with no practice time; close supervision needed; additional training required

2—Limited practice: Has practiced job during training program; additional training required to develop skill

3—Moderately skilled: Has performed job independently during training program; limited additional training may be required

4—Skilled: Can perform job independently with no additional training

Inspect, test, and diagnose electrically assisted power
steering systems (including using a scan tool); determine
needed action.

Time off_____

Time on_____

Total time_____

CDX Tasksheet Number: C186

Vehicle used for this activity:

Year _____ Make _____ Model_____

Odometer_____ VIN_____

1. List the electronically controlled steering system-related customer concern:

2. Verify the concern and list your observations:

3. Retrieve any DTCs with a scan tool and list those DTCs:

4. Research the possible causes for this concern in the appropriate service
   information.

   a. List or print off and attach to this sheet the possible causes:

   b. List or print off and attach to this sheet the procedure for diagnosing the
      concern:

5. Follow the specified procedure to diagnose the concern. List your tests and
   results:

6. List the cause of the concern:

7. Determine any necessary action(s) to correct the fault:

8. Have your supervisor/instructor verify satisfactory completion of this procedure, any observations found, and any necessary action(s) recommended.

Performance Rating

CDX Tasksheet Number: C186

0	1	2	3	4

Supervisor/instructor signature _____ Date _____

► TASK Describe the function of suspension and steering control systems and components (i.e. active suspension and stability control).

MAST
4D3

Time off_____

Time on_____

Total time_____

CDX Tasksheet Number: C931

Vehicle used for this activity:

Year _____ Make _____ Model _____

Odometer _____ VIN _____

1. **Research the function of the active suspension and stability control systems in the appropriate service information.**

   a. **Describe, in your own words, the function of the active suspension and stability control systems:**

2. **Have your supervisor/instructor verify satisfactory completion of your answers.**

Performance Rating

CDX Tasksheet Number: C931

0	1	2	3	4

Supervisor/instructor signature _____ Date _____

Identify hybrid vehicle power steering system electrical circuits and safety precautions.

MAST
4B19

Time off_____

Time on_____

Total time_____

CDX Tasksheet Number: C551

Vehicle used for this activity:

Year _____ Make _____ Model _____

Odometer _____ VIN _____

1. **Research the location and safety precautions for the power steering system the vehicle is equipped with in the appropriate service information.**

    a. **List the voltage that the power steering system operates at:** _____ **V**
    b. **List any safety precautions when working on or around the power steering systems and circuits:**

2. **What color wires are used on the hybrid vehicle power steering system electrical circuits?**

3. **On the vehicle, locate and point out the power steering electrical circuits and components to your instructor.**

4. **Have your supervisor/instructor verify satisfactory completion of your answers.**

Performance Rating

CDX Tasksheet Number: C551

0	1	2	3	4

Supervisor/instructor signature _____ Date _____

Wheel Alignment Diagnosis, Adjustment, and Repair

Student/Intern information:

Name _____ Date _____ Class _____

Vehicle used for this activity:

Year _____ Make _____ Model _____

Odometer _____ VIN _____

Learning Objective/Task	CDX Tasksheet Number	2017 MAST NATEF Reference Number; Priority Level	
• Diagnose vehicle wander, drift, pull, hard steering, bump steer, memory steer, torque steer, and steering return concerns; determine needed action.	C206	4E1; P-1	Time off_____
• Perform prealignment inspection and measure vehicle ride height; determine needed action.	C617	4E2; P-1	Time on_____
• Prepare vehicle for wheel alignment on alignment machine; perform four-wheel alignment by checking and adjusting front and rear wheel caster, camber, and toe as required; center steering wheel.	C618	4E3; P-1	Total time_____
• Check toe-out-on-turns (turning radius); determine needed action.	C213	4E4; P-2	
• Check steering axis inclination (SAI) and included angle; determine needed action.	C214	4E5; P-2	
• Check rear wheel thrust angle; determine needed action.	C216	4E6; P-1	
• Check for front wheel setback; determine needed action.	C217	4E7; P-2	
• Check front and/or rear cradle (subframe) alignment; determine needed action.	C795	4E8; P-3	
• Reset steering angle sensor.	C940	4E9; P-2	

Materials Required

- Vehicle with alignment concern
- Tire-pressure gauge and inflator
- Tape measure
- Wheel-alignment machine
- Manufacturer- or job-specific tools

Some Safety Issues to Consider

- Diagnosis of this fault may require test-driving the vehicle on the school grounds. Attempt this task only with full permission from your instructor and follow all guidelines and policies exactly.
- Lifting equipment such as vehicle jacks and stands, vehicle hoists, and engine hoists are important tools that increase productivity and make the job easier. However, they can also cause severe injury or death if used improperly. Make sure you follow the manufacturer's operation procedures. Also, make sure you have your supervisor's/instructor's permission to use any particular type of lifting equipment.
- Vehicle springs store a lot of energy, which, if released improperly, can cause injury or death. Please familiarize yourself with the manufacturer's safety precautions related to these procedures.
- Some suspension systems are electronically controlled, and can raise or lower without notice. Please familiarize yourself with the manufacturer's safety precautions related to these procedures.
- Comply with personal and environmental safety practices associated with clothing; eye protection; hand tools; power equipment; proper ventilation; and the handling, storage, and disposal of chemicals/materials in accordance with local, state, and federal safety and environmental regulations.

Performance Standard

0—No exposure: No information or practice provided during the program; complete training required

1—Exposure only: General information provided with no practice time; close supervision needed; additional training required

2—Limited practice: Has practiced job during training program; additional training required to develop skill

3—Moderately skilled: Has performed job independently during training program; limited additional training may be required

4—Skilled: Can perform job independently with no additional training

Diagnose vehicle wander, drift, pull, hard steering, bump steer, memory steer, torque steer, and steering return concerns; determine needed action.

MAST
4E1

CDX Tasksheet Number: C206

1. **List the wheel alignment-related customer concern:**

2. **Verify the concern and list your observations here:**

3. **Research the possible causes for this concern in the appropriate service information.**

   a. **List or print off and attach to this sheet the possible causes:**

   b. **List or print off and attach to this sheet the procedure for diagnosing the concern:**

4. **Reflecting back over these tasks, complete the three Cs, which you stated previously.**

   a. **List the customer concern(s):**

b. List the cause(s) of the concern(s):

c. List the action(s) necessary to correct the fault(s):

5. Have your supervisor/instructor verify satisfactory completion of this procedure, any observations found, and any necessary action(s) recommended.

Performance Rating

CDX Tasksheet Number: C206

0	1	2	3	4

Supervisor/instructor signature _____ Date _____

Perform prealignment inspection and measure vehicle
ride height; determine needed action.

MAST
4E2

Time off_____

Time on_____

Total time_____

CDX Tasksheet Number: C617

1. **Research the prealignment process for this vehicle in the appropriate service information.**

    a. **List the ride-height specifications:**

    b. **Can the ride height be manually adjusted on this vehicle?**
       Yes: _____ No: _____
       i. **If yes, what is the specified adjustment procedure?**

    c. **List the specified tire size:** _____
    d. **List the specified tire pressure(s):** _____ psi/kPa
    e. **List any other manufacturer-specified checks:**

2. **Following the specified procedure, inspect the vehicle.**

    a. **Is the vehicle abnormally loaded? Yes:** _____ **No:** _____
    b. **Are the specified tires installed on the vehicle?**
       Yes: _____ No: _____
    c. **List the condition and wear of each tire as you inflate the tires to proper pressure:**

       Left front: (Initial psi): _____ psi; Condition:_____
       Right front: (Initial psi): _____ psi; Condition:_____
       Right rear: (Initial psi): _____ psi; Condition:_____
       Left rear: (Initial psi): _____ psi; Condition:_____
    d. **Does the vehicle meet the specified ride height?**
       Yes: _____ No: _____
    e. **List the results of other specified checks:**

3. Perform any necessary action(s) and list your results:

4. Does the vehicle meet the prealignment inspection requirements for an alignment? Yes: _____ No: _____

5. Have your supervisor/instructor verify satisfactory completion of this procedure, any observations found, and any necessary action(s) recommended.

Performance Rating

CDX Tasksheet Number: C617

0	1	2	3	4

Supervisor/instructor signature _____ Date _____

Prepare vehicle for wheel alignment on alignment machine; perform four-wheel alignment by checking and adjusting front and rear wheel caster, camber, and toe as required; center steering wheel.

MAST
4E3

Time off_____

Time on_____

Total time_____

CDX Tasksheet Number: C618

1. **Prepare the vehicle for wheel alignment on the alignment machine.**

2. **Perform four-wheel alignment measurements and list the following readings:**
   Front wheels:
   a. **Caster: LF:** _____ **RF:** _____ **Specs:** _____
   b. **Cross caster: Measured:** _____ **Specs:** _____
   c. **Camber: LF:** _____ **RF:** _____ **Specs:** _____
   d. **Cross camber: Measured:** _____ **Specs:** _____
   e. **Toe: LF:** _____ **RF:** _____ **Specs:** _____
   f. **Total toe: Measured:** _____ **Specs:** _____

   Rear wheels:
   g. **Caster: LF:** _____ **RF:** _____
      Specs: _____
   h. **Cross caster: Measured:** _____ **Specs:** _____
   i. **Camber: LF:** _____ **RF:** _____ **Specs:** _____
   j. **Cross camber: Measured:** _____ **Specs:** _____
   k. **Toe: LF:** _____ **RF:** _____ **Specs:** _____
   l. **Total toe: Measured:** _____ **Specs:** _____

3. **Determine any necessary action(s):**

4. **Have your supervisor/instructor verify satisfactory completion of this procedure, any observations found, and any necessary action(s) recommended.**

Performance Rating

CDX Tasksheet Number: C618

0	1	2	3	4

Supervisor/instructor signature _____ Date _____

Check toe-out-on-turns (turning radius);
determine needed action.

MAST
4E4

Time off_____

Time on_____

CDX Tasksheet Number: C213

Total time_____

1. **Following the manufacturer's procedure, measure toe-out-on-turns.**
   a. **LF wheel set at: _____ degrees**
   b. **RF wheel measures: _____ degrees**
   c. **RF wheel set at: _____ degrees**
   d. **LF wheel measures: _____ degrees**

2. **Determine any necessary action(s):**

3. **Have your supervisor/instructor verify satisfactory completion of this procedure, any observations found, and any necessary action(s) recommended.**

Performance Rating

CDX Tasksheet Number: C213

0	1	2	3	4

Supervisor/instructor signature _____ Date _____

Check steering axis inclination (SAI) and included angle;
determine needed action.

MAST
4E5

Time off_____

Time on_____

Total time_____

CDX Tasksheet Number: C214

1. **Following the manufacturer's procedure, measure SAI (steering axis inclination) and included angle.**
   a. **SAI: LF:** _____ **Specs:** _____
   b. **SAI: RF:** _____ **Specs:** _____
   c. **Included angle: LF:** _____ **Specs:** _____
   d. **Included angle: RF:** _____ **Specs:** _____

2. **Determine any necessary action(s):**

3. **Have your supervisor/instructor verify satisfactory completion of this procedure, any observations found, and any necessary action(s) recommended.**

Performance Rating

CDX Tasksheet Number: C214

0	1	2	3	4

Supervisor/instructor signature _____ Date _____

Check rear wheel thrust angle; determine needed action.

MAST
4E6

Time off_____

Time on_____

CDX Tasksheet Number: C216

1. **Following the manufacturer's procedure, measure the rear wheel thrust angle.**
   a. **Manufacturer's specifications:** _____
   b. **Measured thrust angle:** _____

Total time_____

2. **Determine any necessary action(s):**

3. **Have your supervisor/instructor verify satisfactory completion of this procedure, any observations found, and any necessary action(s) recommended.**

Performance Rating

CDX Tasksheet Number: C216

0	1	2	3	4

Supervisor/instructor signature _____ Date _____

Time off_____

Time on_____

CDX Tasksheet Number: C217

Total time_____

1. **Following the manufacturer's procedure, check for front wheel setback.**

    a. **Manufacturer's specifications:** _____

    b. **Measured setback:** _____

2. **Determine any necessary action(s):**

3. **Have your supervisor/instructor verify all of your measurements and necessary actions for all of the previous tasks. Get permission to perform the necessary action(s). Supervisor's/instructor's initials:** _____

4. **Perform all of the adjustments necessary for a four-wheel alignment as listed in the previous tasks.**

5. **When finished, remeasure all alignment angles to make sure they are within specifications.**

6. **List or print off and attach to this sheet the post-alignment measurements. Front wheels:**

    a. **Caster: LF:** _____ **RF:** _____ **Specs:** _____
    b. **Cross caster: Measured:** _____ **Specs:** _____
    c. **Camber: LF:** _____ **RF:** _____ **Specs:** _____
    d. **Cross camber: Measured:** _____ **Specs:** _____
    e. **Toe: LF:** _____ **RF:** _____ **Specs:** _____
    f. **Total toe: Measured:** _____ **Specs:** _____

    Rear wheels:

    a. **Caster: LF:** _____ **RF:** _____ **Specs:** _____
    b. **Cross caster: Measured:** _____ **Specs:** _____
    c. **Camber: LF:** _____ **RF:** _____ **Specs:** _____
    d. **Cross camber: Measured:** _____ **Specs:** _____
    e. **Toe: LF:** _____ **RF:** _____ **Specs:** _____
    f. **Total toe: Measured:** _____ **Specs:** _____

    Toe-out-on-turns:

    a. **LF wheel set at:** _____ **degrees**
    b. **RF wheel measures:** _____ **degrees**
    c. **RF wheel set at:** _____ **degrees**
    d. **LF wheel measures:** _____ **degrees**

7. **SAI:** _____ **degrees**

8. **Included angle:** _____ **degrees**

9. **Rear wheel thrust angle:** _____ **degrees**

10. List the measurement(s) for front wheel setback: _____

11. Is the steering wheel centered? Yes: _____ No: _____

12. Do all the angles meet the manufacturer's specifications?
    Yes: _____ No: _____

13. Determine any further necessary action(s), such as resetting the steering angle sensor:

14. Inspect the vehicle for any loose or missing fasteners or improper repairs. List your observation(s):

15. Have your supervisor/instructor verify satisfactory completion of this procedure, any observations found, and any necessary action(s) recommended.

Performance Rating

CDX Tasksheet Number: C217

☐	☐	☐	☐	☐
0	1	2	3	4

Supervisor/instructor signature _____ Date _____

Check front and/or rear cradle (subframe) alignment; determine needed action.

MAST
4E8

Time off _____

Time on _____

Total time _____

CDX Tasksheet Number: C795

Vehicle used for this activity:

Year _____ Make _____ Model _____

Odometer _____ VIN _____

1. **Following the manufacturer's procedure, check front and rear cradle alignment.**

    a. **Manufacturer's specifications:**

    b. **Measured cradle alignment:**

2. **Determine any necessary action(s):**

3. **Have your supervisor/instructor verify satisfactory completion of this procedure, any observations found, and any necessary action(s) recommended.**

Performance Rating

CDX Tasksheet Number: C795

0	1	2	3	4

Supervisor/instructor signature _____ Date _____

MAST
4E9

CDX Tasksheet Number: C940

1. Research the steering angle sensor reset procedure for this vehicle in the appropriate service information.

    a. List, or print out and attach, the steps to reset the sensor:

    b. List any special tools required for this procedure:

2. If possible, list the current steering angle: _____

3. Following the specified procedure, reset the steering angle sensor. List any observation(s):

4. List the final steering angle: _____

5. Have your supervisor/instructor verify satisfactory completion of this procedure, any observations found, and any necessary action(s) recommended.

Performance Rating

CDX Tasksheet Number: C940

0	1	2	3	4

Supervisor/instructor signature _____ Date _____

Section A5:
Brakes

CONTENTS

Vehicle, Customer, and Service Information

_____

Student/Intern information:

Name _____ Date _____ Class _____
_____

Vehicle used for this activity:

Year _____ Make _____ Model_____

Odometer_____VIN_____

Learning Objective/Task	CDX Tasksheet Number	2017 MAST NATEF Reference Number; Priority Level	
• Research vehicle service information including fluid type, vehicle service history, service precautions, and technical service bulletins.	C230	5A2; P-1	Time off_____
• Identify and interpret brake system concerns; determine needed action.	C229	5A1; P-1	Time on_____
• Describe procedure for performing a road test to check brake system operation, including an anti-lock brake system (ABS).	C944	5A3; P-1	Total time_____
• Demonstrate the use of the three Cs (concern, cause, and correction).	N/A	N/A	

Materials Required

- Blank work order
- Vehicle with available service history records
- Depending on the type of concern, special diagnostic tools may be required. See your supervisor/instructor for instructions to identify what tools may be required.

Some Safety Issues to Consider

- If you need to start the vehicle, you should ensure that the parking brake is firmly applied; if necessary, use wheel chocks to prevent the vehicle from moving when the vehicle is started to verify the completion of these tasks.
- Diagnosis of this fault may require test-driving the vehicle on the school grounds. Attempt this task only with full permission from your supervisor/instructor and follow all the guidelines exactly.
- Lifting equipment such as vehicle jacks and stands, vehicle hoists, and engine hoists are important tools that increase productivity and make the job easier. However, they can also cause severe injury or death if used improperly. Make sure you follow the manufacturer's operation procedures. Also make sure you have your supervisor's/instructor's permission to use any particular type of lifting equipment.
- **Caution:** Most types of brake fluid are harmful to painted surfaces. Be sure to prevent brake fluid from coming into contact with a vehicle's paint. Use fender covers to minimize this risk and be sure to wipe up any spilled brake fluid immediately with a wet rag.

- **Caution:** Brake dust may contain asbestos, which has been determined to cause cancer when inhaled or ingested. Treat all brake dust as if it contains asbestos and use OSHA-approved asbestos removal equipment. Do not allow brake dust to become airborne by using anything that would disturb the dust. Also, wear protective gloves during this procedure and dispose of or clean them in an approved manner.
- Comply with personal and environmental safety practices associated with clothing; eye protection; hand tools; power equipment; proper ventilation; and the handling, storage, and disposal of chemicals/materials in accordance with local, state, and federal safety and environmental regulations.

Performance Standard

0–No exposure: No information or practice provided during the program; complete training required

1–Exposure only: General information provided with no practice time; close supervision needed; additional training required

2–Limited practice: Has practiced job during training program; additional training required to develop skill

3–Moderately skilled: Has performed job independently during training program; limited additional training may be required

4–Skilled: Can perform job independently with no additional training

TASK Research vehicle service information including fluid type, vehicle service history, service precautions, and technical service bulletins.

MAST
5A2

Time off_____

Time on_____

Total time_____

CDX Tasksheet Number: C230

1. Using the VIN for identification, use the appropriate source to access the vehicle's service history in relation to prior braking system work or customer concerns.

    a. List any related repairs/concerns, and their dates:

    b. List any service precautions related to brake system diagnosis and repair:

2. List the specified type of brake fluid for this vehicle: _____

3. Using the VIN for identification, access any relevant technical service bulletins for the particular vehicle you are working on in relation to braking system updates or other service issues. List related TSBs and their description(s):

4. Have your supervisor/instructor verify satisfactory completion of this procedure, any observations found, and any necessary action(s) recommended.

Performance Rating

CDX Tasksheet Number: C230

0	1	2	3	4

Supervisor/instructor signature _____ Date _____

Identify and interpret brake system concerns;
determine needed action.

Time off_____

Time on_____

Total time_____

CDX Tasksheet Number: C229

1. List the customer concern:

2. Research the particular concern in the appropriate service information.

   a. List the possible causes:

3. Inspect the braking system to determine the cause of the concern, and list the steps you took to determine the fault:

4. List the cause of the concern/complaint:

5. List the necessary action(s) to correct this fault:

6. Have your supervisor/instructor verify satisfactory completion of this procedure, any observations found, and any necessary action(s) recommended.

Performance Rating

CDX Tasksheet Number: C229

0	1	2	3	4

Supervisor/instructor signature _____ Date _____

MAST
5A3

Time off_____

Time on_____

Total time_____

DX Tasksheet Number: C944

1. **Research the shop policies for performing a road test to check brake system operation. List the shop policies:**

2. **List the precautions that should be taken before road testing brakes:**

3. **List the precautions that should be taken during road testing of brakes, including testing of the ABS:**

4. **Have your supervisor/instructor verify satisfactory completion of this procedure, any observations found, and any necessary action(s) recommended.**

Performance Rating

CDX Tasksheet Number: C944

0	1	2	3	4

Supervisor/instructor signature _____ Date _____

CDX Tasksheet Number: N/A

1. **Using the following scenario, write up the three Cs as listed on most repair orders. Assume that the customer authorized the recommended repairs. A vehicle is brought to your shop with a brake concern. The customer tells you that the brakes make a grinding noise that comes from the front wheels when the brakes are applied. The vehicle has been doing this for about two weeks, but the customer was too busy to bring the car in for repairs. You remove the wheels, inspect all of the brakes, and find the following:**

   a. **The brake pads on the left front are worn down to metal and have scored the rotor badly. The rotor is worn down to the point that it is 0.043 of an inch under the minimum specified thickness.**

   b. **The right side brake pads are worn well below minimum specifications but have not worn down to metal. The rotor is about 0.040 of an inch thicker than the minimum thickness specified.**

   c. **Both front calipers appear to be original and the pistons do not move as freely as they should; the brake fluid is very dark and dirty.**

   d. **The rear brake shoes are in like-new condition, but wet with brake fluid.**

> **NOTE** Ask your instructor whether you should use a copy of the shop repair order, or the three Cs here, to record this information.

2. **Concern/complaint:**

3. **Cause:**

4. **Correction:**

5. **Other recommended service:**

6. Have your supervisor/instructor verify satisfactory completion of this procedure, any observations found, and any necessary action(s) recommended.

Performance Rating

0	1	2	3	4

Supervisor/instructor signature _____ Date _____

Fluid Testing and Maintenance

Learning Objective/Task	CDX Tasksheet Number	2017 MAST NATEF Reference Number; Priority Level
• Select, handle, store, and fill brake fluids to proper level; use proper fluid type per manufacturer specification.	C239	5B9; P-1
• Test brake fluid for contamination.	C625	5B13; P-1
• Bleed and/or flush brake system.	C705	5B12; P-1

Time off_____

Time on_____

Total time_____

Materials Required

- Vehicle or brake system simulator
- Specified brake fluid
- DVOM/DMM or brake fluid tester/test strip
- Brake bleeder wrenches
- Suction gun or brake fluid removal device
- Brake bleeder

Some Safety Issues to Consider

- **Caution:** Most types of brake fluid are harmful to painted surfaces. Be sure to prevent brake fluid from coming into contact with a vehicle's paint. Use fender covers to minimize this risk and be sure to wipe up any spilled brake fluid immediately with a wet rag.
- Do not mix DOT 5 brake fluid with a DOT 3 or 4 glycol-based fluid. They are incompatible.
- If you need to start the vehicle, you should ensure that the parking brake is firmly applied. If necessary, use wheel chocks to prevent the vehicle from moving when the vehicle is started to verify the completion of these tasks.
- Before moving a vehicle that has had any brake system or hydraulic system repairs, make sure the brake pedal is firm. If not, do not move the vehicle.
- When running any vehicles in the shop, make sure you use the shop's exhaust ventilation system to discharge all exhaust gas safely outside.
- Completion of this task may require test-driving the vehicle on the school grounds. Attempt this task only with full permission from your supervisor/instructor and follow all the guidelines exactly.
- Comply with personal and environmental safety practices associated with clothing; eye protection; hand tools; power equipment; proper ventilation; and the handling, storage, and disposal of chemicals/materials in accordance with local, state, and federal safety and environmental regulations.

Performance Standard

0–No exposure: No information or practice provided during the program; complete training required

1–Exposure only: General information provided with no practice time; close supervision needed; additional training required

2–Limited practice: Has practiced job during training program; additional training required to develop skill

3–Moderately skilled: Has performed job independently during training program; limited additional training may be required

4–Skilled: Can perform job independently with no additional training

Select, handle, store, and fill brake fluids to proper level; use proper fluid type per manufacturer specification.

MAST
5B9

Time off_____

Time on_____

Total time_____

DX Tasksheet Number: C239

1. **Research the specified brake fluid and the bleeding/flushing procedure for this vehicle using the appropriate service information.**

   a. **Specified fluid:**_____

   b. **Bleeding/flushing sequence:**_____

   c. **Bleeding/flushing precautions:**

2. **Locate the master cylinder reservoir.**

   a. **List the level of the brake fluid:**_____

   > **NOTE** If the brake fluid is below the minimum level, it could mean there is a leak in the system or the disc brake pads are worn. Investigate these possibilities and report them to your supervisor/instructor.

3. **If appropriate, add the appropriate type of brake fluid to the master cylinder reservoir to bring it to the full mark.**

4. **Knowledge Check: What precautions should be taken when brake fluid is stored?**

5. **Knowledge Check: List the different types of brake fluid available:**

6. **Have your supervisor/instructor verify satisfactory completion of this procedure, any observations found, and any necessary action(s) recommended.**

Performance Rating

CDX Tasksheet Number: C239

0	1	2	3	4

Supervisor/instructor signature _____ Date _____

MAST
5B13

Time off_____

Time on_____

CDX Tasksheet Number: C625

Total time_____

1. **Test the fluid using one of the following procedures:**

   a. **DVOM/DMM–Galvanic Reaction Test**
      i. **Remove the master cylinder cap.**
      ii. **Set the DVOM/DMM to DC volts.**
      iii. **Place the red voltmeter lead in the reservoir brake fluid.**
      iv. **Place the black lead on the metal housing of the master cylinder.**
      v. **List the voltage reading obtained:**_____ **V**

   > **NOTE** If reading is above 0.3V, this indicates a galvanic reaction and means there is an unacceptable level of moisture in the brake fluid.

   Determine any necessary actions:

   b. **Brake Fluid Tester**
      i. **Follow the directions for the tester you have and test the brake fluid.**
      ii. **List your findings:**

   c. **Brake Fluid Test Strip**
      i. **Follow the directions for the test strip you have and test the brake fluid.**
      ii. **List your findings:**

2. **Have your supervisor/instructor verify satisfactory completion of this procedure, any observations found, and any necessary action(s) recommended.**

Performance Rating

CDX Tasksheet Number: C625

0	1	2	3	4

Supervisor/instructor signature _____ Date _____

Bleed and/or flush brake system.

Time off_____

Time on_____

CDX Tasksheet Number: C705

Total time_____

1. Which method of bleeding/flushing will you use?_____

2. In what order will you be bleeding the brakes?_____

3. Remove all old brake fluid from the master cylinder reservoir using the suction gun. Dispose of the fluid properly.

4. Refill the master cylinder reservoir using the specified brake fluid.

5. Using the appropriate equipment, bleed/flush each brake assembly until clean fluid comes out, making sure you keep the master cylinder reservoir from running low on fluid. Carefully tighten the bleeder screw and replace the bleeder screw dust cap when each wheel assembly is finished.

    a. List the condition of the removed fluid:

6. Start the engine and apply the brakes to make sure the pedal is still firm. List the pedal feel:_____

7. Refill the master cylinder reservoir to the proper level.

8. List any necessary action(s):

9. Return the vehicle to its beginning condition and return any tools you used to their proper locations.

10. Have your supervisor/instructor verify satisfactory completion of this procedure, any observations found, and any necessary action(s) recommended.

Performance Rating

CDX Tasksheet Number: C705

0	1	2	3	4

Supervisor/instructor signature _____ Date _____

Master Cylinder Testing and Service

Student/Intern information:

Name _____ Date _____ Class _____

Vehicle used for this activity:

Year _____ Make _____ Model_____

Odometer_____VIN_____

Learning Objective/Task	CDX Tasksheet Number	2017 MAST NATEF Reference Number; Priority Level
• Measure brake pedal height, travel, and free play (as applicable); determine needed action.	C622	5B2; P-1
• Check master cylinder for internal/external leaks and proper operation; determine needed action.	C704	5B3; P-1
• Remove, bench bleed, and reinstall master cylinder.	C235	5B4; P-1
• Measure and adjust master cylinder pushrod length.	C556	5E5; P-3

Time off_____

Time on_____

Total time_____

Materials Required

- Depending on the type of concern, special diagnostic tools may be required. See your supervisor/instructor for instructions to identify what tools may be required.
- Tape measure
- Vehicle or simulator
- Work light and shop rag
- Line wrenches

Some Safety Issues to Consider

- If you need to start the vehicle, you should ensure that the parking brake is firmly applied; if necessary, use wheel chocks to prevent the vehicle from moving when the vehicle is started to verify the completion of these tasks.
- When running any vehicles in the shop, make sure you use the shop's exhaust ventilation system to discharge all exhaust gas safely outside.
- Only students who have their supervisor's/instructor's direct permission should perform this task due to the safety concerns involved.
- Diagnosis of this fault may require test-driving the vehicle on the school grounds. Attempt this task only with full permission from your supervisor/instructor and follow all the guidelines exactly.
- **Caution:** Most types of brake fluid are harmful to painted surfaces. Be sure to prevent brake fluid from coming into contact with a vehicle's paint. Use fender covers to minimize this risk and be sure to wipe up any spilled brake fluid immediately with a wet rag.
- Comply with personal and environmental safety practices associated with clothing; eye protection; hand tools; power equipment; proper ventilation; and the handling, storage, and disposal of chemicals/materials in accordance with local, state, and federal safety and environmental regulations.

Performance Standard

0—No exposure: No information or practice provided during the program; complete training required

1—Exposure only: General information provided with no practice time; close supervision needed; additional training required

2—Limited practice: Has practiced job during training program; additional training required to develop skill

3—Moderately skilled: Has performed job independently during training program; limited additional training may be required

4—Skilled: Can perform job independently with no additional training

Measure brake pedal height, travel, and free play (as applicable); determine needed action.

MAST
5B2

Time off_____

Time on_____

Total time_____

CDX Tasksheet Number: C622

1. Research the description and operation of the brake system for this vehicle in the appropriate service information. Also research the master cylinder diagnostic procedure and removal/installation procedures. Check off the systems in the list below that this vehicle is equipped with:

   a. Power assist: Yes: _____ No: _____
   b. ABS: Yes: _____ No: _____
   c. Four-wheel ABS: Yes: _____ No: _____
   d. Rear-wheel ABS: Yes: _____ No: _____
   e. Traction control: Yes: _____ No: _____
   f. Front-/rear-split hydraulic system: Yes: _____ No: _____
   g. Diagonal-split hydraulic system: Yes: _____ No: _____
   h. Brake pedal height: _____ in/mm
   i. Brake pedal free play: _____ in/mm
   j. Brake pedal reserve height: _____ in/mm

2. Brake pedal height

   a. Following the service procedure, measure the brake pedal height. Record your readings here: _____ in/mm
   b. Within specifications? Yes: _____ No: _____
   c. If not as specified, determine any necessary actions:

3. Reserve pedal height/pedal travel

   a. Following the service procedure, start the vehicle and apply the brake pedal with moderate foot pressure. Measure the reserve pedal height/ pedal travel and record the measurement: _____ in/mm
   b. If not as specified, determine any necessary actions:

4. Brake pedal free play

   a. Following the service procedure, measure the brake pedal free play and record the measurement here: _____ in/mm
   b. Within specifications? Yes: _____ No: _____
   c. If not as specified, determine any necessary actions:

5. Have your supervisor/instructor verify satisfactory completion of this
   procedure, any observations found, and any necessary action(s) recommended.

Performance Rating

0	1	2	3	4

Supervisor/instructor signature _____ Date _____

Check master cylinder for internal/external leaks
and proper operation; determine needed action.

Time off_____

Time on_____

Total time_____

CDX Tasksheet Number: C704

1. Research the description and operation of the brake system for this vehicle
in the appropriate service information. Also research the master cylinder
diagnostic procedure and removal/installation procedures.

   a. Master cylinder pushrod length: _____ in/mm
   b. Master cylinder nut/bolt torque: _____ ft/lb or N·m

2. Inspect the master cylinder for external leaks.

   a. Check the brake fluid level in the reservoir. Record your reading here:

      _____

   b. Inspect the master cylinder for obvious signs of leakage. Be sure to check
   all brake line fittings, sensor connections, reservoir seal(s), and the areas
   at the rear of the master cylinder near the seal. Also check the inside of
   the vacuum hose to the power booster.

   > NOTE If fluid is found on the inside of the hose, the rear seal in the master cylinder
   > may be leaking fluid into the booster.

   c. List your observations:

2. Check the master cylinder for proper operation.

   a. Start the vehicle, apply the brake pedal beginning with a very light
   pressure, and gradually increasing the pressure. The brake pedal should
   hold its position with very little travel beyond its applied height. If the
   pedal continues to sink, the system may have an external or internal
   leak. Do this test several times with various pedal pressures and time
   elements. Be sure you hold foot pressure on the system for at least one
   minute.
   b. List your observations:

3. Inspect the master cylinder for internal leaks.

   a. Remove the master cylinder reservoir cap.
   b. Have an assistant apply the brake pedal firmly and hold it. Watch the
   fluid in the reservoir; it should have an initial spurt of fluid from each of
   the two compensating ports as the brake pedal is first moved.

> **NOTE** The brake fluid level should not rise in the reservoir as the brake pedal is held down. If it does, this indicates an internal leak in one or more of the master cylinder seals and it will need to be serviced. On quick take-up type master cylinders, the quick take-up valve vents excess fluid to the rear half of the reservoir.

    c. **List your observations:**

4. **Determine any necessary action(s):**

5. **Have your supervisor/instructor verify satisfactory completion of this procedure, any observations found, and any necessary action(s) recommended.**

Performance Rating

CDX Tasksheet Number: C704

0	1	2	3	4

Supervisor/instructor signature _____ Date _____

MAST
5B4

CDX Tasksheet Number: C235

1. Following the specified procedure, perform the following steps to remove the master cylinder.

   a. If the master cylinder is being replaced with a new or rebuilt unit, compare the new unit to the old one to verify that it is the correct replacement. If not, inform your supervisor/instructor.

   b. Use a suction gun to remove as much brake fluid from the master cylinder reservoir as possible. Do not drip brake fluid on any painted surface of the vehicle.

   NOTE Be careful to avoid getting brake fluid on any painted surface of the vehicle.

   c. Using flare nut or line wrenches, loosen the brake line fittings. Also use the double wrench method of loosening the fittings if fitted with an adapter. Place a rag under the fittings to catch any leaking brake fluid.

   d. Unbolt the master cylinder from the power booster and remove the master cylinder, being careful to avoid getting brake fluid on any painted surface of the vehicle.

2. Bench bleed the master cylinder.

3. Install the master cylinder, being careful not to cross-thread the fittings.

   NOTE It is good practice to start the fittings by finger before the bolts holding the master cylinder in place are tightened. This helps prevent cross-threading of the fittings in the master cylinder, especially on aluminum master cylinders.

4. Bleed any remaining air from the hydraulic brake system.

5. Verify the correct brake pedal travel and feel.

6. Return the vehicle to its beginning condition and return any tools you used to their proper locations.

7. Have your supervisor/instructor verify satisfactory completion of this procedure, any observations found, and any necessary action(s) recommended.

Performance Rating

CDX Tasksheet Number: C235

0	1	2	3	4
□	□	□	□	□

Supervisor/instructor signature _____ Date _____

Measure and adjust master cylinder pushrod length.

Time off_____

Time on_____

Total time_____

CDX Tasksheet Number: C556

1. Research the specifications and procedure for measuring and adjusting pushrod length in the appropriate service information.

    a. Master cylinder pushrod length: _____ in/mm
    b. Master cylinder nut/bolt torque: _____ ft/lb or N·m

2. Measure the pushrod length according to the manufacturer's procedure.

    a. List measurement here: _____ in/mm

3. Determine any necessary action(s): Knowledge Check: What would be the customer concern if the pushrod length were too long and caused the master cylinder piston seal to cover one or both of the compensating ports? List your answer.

4. Knowledge Check: What would be the customer concern if the pushrod length were substantially shorter than specifications? List your answer.

5. Have your supervisor/instructor verify satisfactory completion of this procedure, any observations found, and any necessary action(s) recommended.

Performance Rating

CDX Tasksheet Number: C556

0	1	2	3	4

Supervisor/instructor signature _____ Date _____

Brake Lines and Hoses Inspection and Repair

Student/Intern information:

Name _____ Date _____ Class _____

Vehicle used for this activity:

Year _____ Make _____ Model _____

Odometer_____ VIN _____

Learning Objective/Task	CDX Tasksheet Number	2017 MAST NATEF Reference Number; Priority Level
• Inspect brake lines, flexible hoses, and fittings for leaks, dents, kinks, rust, cracks, bulging, wear, and loose fittings and supports; determine needed action.	C237	5B6; P-1
• Replace brake lines, hoses, fittings, and supports.	C623	5B7; P-2
• Fabricate brake lines using proper material and flaring procedures (double flare and ISO types).	C624	5B8; P-2

Time off_____

Time on_____

Total time_____

Materials Required

- Vehicle or brake system simulator
- Vehicle hoist
- Flare nut wrenches
- Flaring tool set of the correct type
- Brake tubing to flare
- Specified brake fluid

Some Safety Issues to Consider

- If you need to start the vehicle, you should ensure that the parking brake is firmly applied; if necessary, use wheel chocks to prevent the vehicle from moving when the vehicle is started to verify the completion of these tasks.
- When running any vehicles in the shop, make sure you use the shop's exhaust ventilation system to discharge all exhaust gas safely outside.
- Only students who have their supervisor's/instructor's direct permission should perform this task due to the safety concerns involved.
- Diagnosis of this fault may require test-driving the vehicle on the school grounds. Attempt this task only with full permission from your supervisor/instructor and follow all the guidelines exactly.
- Comply with personal and environmental safety practices associated with clothing; eye protection; hand tools; power equipment; proper ventilation; and the handling, storage, and disposal of chemicals/materials in accordance with local, state, and federal safety and environmental regulations.

Performance Standard

0–No exposure: No information or practice provided during the program; complete training required

1–Exposure only: General information provided with no practice time; close supervision needed; additional training required

2–Limited practice: Has practiced job during training program; additional training required to develop skill

3–Moderately skilled: Has performed job independently during training program; limited additional training may be required

4–Skilled: Can perform job independently with no additional training

Inspect brake lines, flexible hoses, and fittings for leaks, dents, kinks, rust, cracks, bulging, wear, and loose fittings and supports; determine needed action.

MAST
5B6

Time off_____

Time on_____

Total time_____

CDX Tasksheet Number: C237

1. **Safely raise and secure the vehicle on the hoist, then trace all brake lines from the master cylinder to each wheel's brake assembly. Inspect the steel brake lines for the following defects and list each defect's location and cause:**

   a. **Leaks:**

   b. **Dents:**

   c. **Kinks:**

   d. **Rust:**

   e. **Cracks:**

   f. **Wear:**

   g. **Loose fittings or supports:**

2. **Inspect all flexible brake lines for the following defects and list each defect's location and cause:**

   a. **Cracks:**

   b. **Bulging:**

   c. **Wear:**

   d. **Loose fittings or supports:**

3. **Determine any necessary action(s):**

4. **Have your supervisor/instructor verify satisfactory completion of this procedure, any observations found, and any necessary action(s) recommended.**

Performance Rating

CDX Tasksheet Number: C237

0	1	2	3	4

Supervisor/instructor signature _____ Date _____

Replace brake lines, hoses, fittings, and supports.

MAST
5B7

Time off_____

Time on_____

Total time_____

CDX Tasksheet Number: C623

1. **Safely raise and secure the vehicle on the hoist and, where appropriate, drain the brake line of fluid and safely dispose of it.**

   NOTE You may be able to use a brake pedal depressor to hold down the brake pedal slightly. This will close off the compensating ports in the master cylinder and therefore minimize the amount of fluid draining out of the system. Just remember that the brake lights will stay on continuously while the pedal is depressed.

2. **Carefully remove (using flare nut wrenches) any brake lines, hoses, fittings, and supports that are to be replaced.**

3. **Have your instructor initial to verify removal:** _____

4. **Replace any removed flexible hoses, fittings, and supports in accordance with the service manual procedure.**

   NOTE Be sure to properly route the lines and tighten adequately.

5. **Fill the master cylinder reservoir with the specified fluid.**

6. **Bleed the system in accordance with the recommended procedure.**

7. **Test the system for leaks and integrity. List your observations:**

8. **Have your supervisor/instructor verify satisfactory completion of this procedure, any observations found, and any necessary action(s) recommended.**

Performance Rating

CDX Tasksheet Number: C623

0	1	2	3	4

Supervisor/instructor signature _____ Date _____

Fabricate brake lines using proper material and flaring procedures (double flare and ISO types).

MAST
5B8

Time off_____

Time on_____

Total time_____

CDX Tasksheet Number: C624

1. **Safely raise and secure the vehicle on the hoist and, where appropriate, drain the brake line of fluid and safely dispose of it.**

   NOTE You may be able to use a brake pedal depressor to hold down the brake pedal slightly. This will close off the compensating ports in the master cylinder and therefore minimize the amount of fluid draining out of the system. Just remember that the brake lights will stay on continuously while the pedal is depressed.

2. **Carefully remove (using flare nut wrenches) any brake lines and supports that are to be replaced. List the type of flare used on this brake line:**

3. **Fabricate (using the correct equipment and procedure) any brake lines that are to be replaced using proper material and flaring procedures (double flare and ISO types). The old ones can be used for patterns in this regard.**

4. **List the type of tube material used:**_____

5. **Have your instructor inspect the flare. Supervisor's/instructor's initials:**
   _____

6. **Replace any removed brake lines, fittings, and supports in accordance with the service information procedure.**

   NOTE Be sure to route the lines properly and tighten adequately.

7. **Fill the master cylinder reservoir with the specified fluid.**

8. **Bleed the system in accordance with the recommended procedure.**

9. **Test the system for leaks and integrity. List your observations:**

10. **Have your supervisor/instructor verify satisfactory completion of this procedure, any observations found, and any necessary action(s) recommended.**

Performance Rating

CDX Tasksheet Number: C624

0	1	2	3	4

Supervisor/instructor signature _____ Date _____

Disc Brake Inspection, Maintenance, and Service

Learning Objective/Task	CDX Tasksheet Number	2017 MAST NATEF Reference Number; Priority Level
• Diagnose poor stopping, noise, vibration, pulling, grabbing, dragging, or pulsation concerns; determine needed action.	C708	5D1; P-1
• Remove and clean caliper assembly; inspect for leaks, damage, and wear; determine needed action.	C802	5D2; P-1
• Inspect caliper mounting and slides/pins for proper operation, wear, and damage; determine needed action.	C803	5D3; P-1
• Check brake pad wear indicator; determine needed action.	C632	5D11; P-1
• Remove, inspect, and/or replace brake pads and retaining hardware; determine needed action.	C627	5D4; P-1
• Lubricate and reinstall caliper, brake pads, and related hardware; seat brake pads and inspect for leaks.	C805	5D5; P-1
• Retract and readjust caliper piston on an integrated parking brake system.	C631	5D10; P-2
• Describe the importance of operating vehicle to burnish/break in replacement brake pads according to manufacturer's recommendations.	C948	5D12; P-1

Time off_____

Time on_____

Total time_____

Materials Required

- Vehicle or simulator with disc brake concern
- Vehicle lifting equipment
- Asbestos removal equipment
- Work light and shop rag
- Line wrench
- Caliper lube
- Torque wrench(es)
- Feeler gauge set

Some Safety Issues to Consider

- If you need to start the vehicle, you should ensure that the parking brake is firmly applied; if necessary, use wheel chocks to prevent the vehicle from moving when the vehicle is started to verify the completion of these tasks.
- When running any vehicles in the shop, make sure you use the shop's exhaust ventilation system to discharge all exhaust gas safely outside.
- Only students who have their supervisor's/instructor's direct permission should perform this task due to the safety concerns involved.
- Diagnosis of this fault and verification of repairs may require test driving the vehicle on the school grounds. Attempt this task only with full permission from your supervisor/instructor and follow all the guidelines exactly.
- Vehicle hoists are important tools that increase productivity and make the job easier. However, they can also cause severe injury or death if used improperly. Make sure you follow the hoist's and vehicle manufacturers' operation procedures. Also make sure you have your supervisor's/instructor's permission to use a vehicle hoist.
- **Caution:** Brake dust may contain asbestos, which has been determined to cause cancer when inhaled or ingested. Treat all brake dust as if it contains asbestos and use OSHA-approved asbestos removal equipment. Do not allow brake dust to become airborne by using anything that would disturb the dust. Also, wear protective gloves during this procedure and dispose of or clean them in an approved manner.
- **Caution:** Most types of brake fluid are harmful to painted surfaces. Be sure to prevent brake fluid from coming in contact with a vehicle's paint. Use fender covers to minimize this risk and be sure to wipe up any spilled brake fluid immediately with a wet rag.
- Comply with personal and environmental safety practices associated with clothing; eye protection; hand tools; power equipment; proper ventilation; and the handling, storage, and disposal of chemicals/materials in accordance with local, state, and federal safety and environmental regulations.

Performance Standard

0—No exposure: No information or practice provided during the program; complete training required

1—Exposure only: General information provided with no practice time; close supervision needed; additional training required

2—Limited practice: Has practiced job during training program; additional training required to develop skill

3—Moderately skilled: Has performed job independently during training program; limited additional training may be required

4—Skilled: Can perform job independently with no additional training

Diagnose poor stopping, noise, vibration, pulling, grabbing, dragging, or pulsation concerns; determine needed action.

MAST
5D1

Time off_____

Time on_____

Total time_____

CDX Tasksheet Number: C708

1. **List the brake-related customer complaints/concerns:**

2. **Research the description and operation of the brake system for this vehicle in the appropriate service information. Also, research the disc brake diagnostic procedure and removal/installation procedures.**

    a. **List the possible cause(s) of the complaint/concern:**

    b. **Minimum brake pad thickness:** _____ in/mm
    c. **Caliper bore-to-piston clearance (maximum):** _____ in/mm
    d. **List specified caliper slide lubricant:** _____
    e. **Caliper bolt torque:** _____ ft-lb/ N·m
    f. **Lug nut torque:** _____ ft-lb/ N·m
    g. **Draw the lug nut torque pattern for this vehicle:**

3. **With instructor permission, test-drive the vehicle to verify the complaint.**

    NOTE Be sure to follow all shop policies regarding test drives.

    a. **List your observations:**

4. **Reflecting back on this job, list the cause(s) of the customer concerns as listed at the beginning of this tasksheet:**

5. Document the correction(s) required to fix the customer concern:

6. Did you repair the vehicle? Yes: _____ No: _____

7. List any additional necessary action(s):

8. Return the vehicle to its beginning condition and return any tools you used to their proper locations.

9. Have your supervisor/instructor verify satisfactory completion of this procedure, any observations found, and any necessary action(s) recommended.

Performance Rating

CDX Tasksheet Number: C708

0	1	2	3	4

Supervisor/instructor signature _____ Date _____

Remove and clean caliper assembly; inspect for leaks, damage, and wear; determine needed action.

MAST
5D2

Time off_____

Time on_____

Total time_____

CDX Tasksheet Number: C802

1. **Raise the vehicle and support it properly. Remove the wheel and tire assembly.**

2. **Break loose or open the bleeder screw (then close it) to ensure that it is not seized in place and is able to open. Failure to find this out now could waste a lot of time later trying to repair a bleeder screw that has broken off, if it is seized. Also, if replacing the caliper, it is good practice to bleed all of the old brake fluid out of the brake system at this time, so that old brake fluid isn't run though the new caliper.**

3. **Remove the caliper assembly from its mountings, following the specified procedure. If removing the caliper completely, be careful not to lose the two copper sealing rings when removing the brake line, if applicable.**

4. **Inspect the caliper for leaks or damage, being careful to avoid dislodging brake dust, which may contain asbestos. List your observations:**

   a. **Leaks:**

   b. **Damage/wear:**

5. **Following the specified procedure, clean the caliper assembly.**

6. **Based on your observations, determine any necessary action(s):**

7. **Have your supervisor/instructor verify satisfactory completion of this procedure, any observations found, and any necessary action(s) recommended.**

Performance Rating

CDX Tasksheet Number: C802

0	1	2	3	4

Supervisor/instructor signature _____ Date _____

Inspect caliper mounting and slides/pins for proper operation, wear, and damage; determine needed action.

MAST
5D3

Time off_____

Time on_____

Total time_____

CDX Tasksheet Number: C803

1. Following the specified procedure, clean the caliper mounts and slides/pins.

2. Inspect the caliper mounts, slides/pins, and any threads for operation, wear, and damage. List your observations:

   a. Operation:
   b. Wear:
   c. Damage:

3. Based on your observations, determine any necessary action(s):

4. Have your supervisor/instructor verify satisfactory completion of this procedure, any observations found, and any necessary action(s) recommended.

Performance Rating

CDX Tasksheet Number: C803

| 0 | 1 | 2 | 3 | 4 |

Supervisor/instructor signature _____ Date _____

Check brake pad wear indicator; determine needed
action.

MAST
5D12

CDX Tasksheet Number: C632

1. **List what type of wear indicator system this vehicle uses:**

2. **Check the brake pad wear indicator. How much brake pad thickness remains until the indicator contacts the surface of the rotor?**

   Note your measurement: _____ in/mm

3. **Determine any necessary action(s):**

4. **Have your supervisor/instructor verify satisfactory completion of this procedure, any observations found, and any necessary action(s) recommended.**

Performance Rating

CDX Tasksheet Number: C632

0	1	2	3	4

Supervisor/instructor signature _____ Date _____

Remove, inspect, and/or replace brake pads and retaining hardware; determine needed action.

MAST
5D4

Time off_____

Time on_____

Total time_____

CDX Tasksheet Number: C627

1. **Remove and inspect pads and retaining hardware in accordance with the correct procedure.**

2. **Measure the remaining brake pad thickness:** _____ in/mm

3. **Inspect the brake pads and retaining hardware. List condition(s) found:**

4. **Determine any necessary action(s):**

5. **Have your supervisor/instructor verify satisfactory completion of this procedure, any observations found, and any necessary action(s) recommended.**

> **NOTE** Because you have the rotor exposed, go to the "Rotor Inspection and Service" tasksheet and complete the tasks listed there. This will save you time and effort. Return to this tasksheet and pick up here once you are done with the rotor.

Performance Rating

CDX Tasksheet Number: C627

0	1	2	3	4

Supervisor/instructor signature _____ Date _____

Lubricate and reinstall caliper, brake pads, and related hardware; seat brake pads and inspect for leaks.

MAST
5D5

Time off_____

Time on_____

Total time_____

CDX Tasksheet Number: C805

1. **Make sure the rotor has been properly installed on the hub/spindle.**

2. **Reassemble the pads, hardware, and caliper on caliper mounts using the specified lubricant.**

   NOTE Torque all bolts to specified torque.

4. **If removed, reinstall the brake line fittings using two copper washers (if equipped). Place one between the brake line fitting and the head of the banjo bolt and the other between the brake line fitting and the caliper.**

   NOTE Before performing the next step, ensure that all brake assemblies are completely reassembled, including all brake drums. This will prevent damage to wheel cylinders, brake shoes, and pads.

5. **Seat the pads by applying the brake pedal several times. This will force the brake caliper pistons to adjust to the proper clearance for proper brake application.**

   NOTE Failure to perform this step could lead to no brake application when the vehicle is first moved.

6. **If the brake pedal is spongy, you will need to bleed the brakes of any trapped air in the system. See the appropriate CDX tasksheet for guidance.**

7. **If the brake pedal is firm and does not sink over time, there could still be a small leak that would cause a brake failure at some point in time. Inspect the system for any brake fluid leaks, no matter how small; if found, inform your supervisor/ instructor.**

   a. **Are there any leaks in the system? Yes: _____ No: _____**
   b. **If yes, where?**

8. **Have your supervisor/instructor verify satisfactory completion of this procedure, any observations found, and any necessary action(s) recommended.**

Performance Rating

CDX Tasksheet Number: C805

0	1	2	3	4

Supervisor/instructor signature _____ Date _____

Retract and readjust caliper piston on an integrated parking brake system.

MAST
5D10

Time off_____

Time on_____

Total time_____

CDX Tasksheet Number: C631

1. Research the proper method of retracting and readjusting the caliper piston on an integrated parking brake system in the appropriate service information. List any precautions below.

2. Following the recommended process, retract the caliper piston. Instructor initials: _____

3. Reinstall the caliper and readjust the caliper piston. Instructor initials: _____

4. Determine any necessary action(s):

5. Have your supervisor/instructor verify satisfactory completion of this procedure, any observations found, and any necessary action(s) recommended.

Performance Rating

CDX Tasksheet Number: C631

0	1	2	3	4

Supervisor/instructor signature _____ Date _____

TASK Describe the importance of operating vehicle to burnish/break in replacement brake pads according to manufacturer's recommendations.

MAST
5D12

Time on_____

Total time_____

CDX Tasksheet Number: C948

1. **Research the brake pad burnishing/break in process for the vehicle you are working on, in the appropriate service information. List the process here (or print off and attach to this sheet):**

2. **Describe in your own words why it is important to properly burnish/break in brake pads after installation:**

3. **Have your supervisor/instructor verify satisfactory completion of this procedure, any observations found, and any necessary action(s) recommended.**

Performance Rating

CDX Tasksheet Number: C948

0	1	2	3	4

Supervisor/instructor signature _____ Date _____

Rotor Inspection and Service

Student/Intern information:

Name _____ Date _____ Class _____

Vehicle used for this activity:

Year _____ Make _____ Model _____

Odometer _____ VIN _____

Learning Objective/Task	CDX Tasksheet Number	2017 MAST NATEF Reference Number; Priority Level
• Clean and inspect rotor and mounting surface; measure rotor thickness, thickness variation, and lateral runout; determine needed action.	C628	5D6; P-1
• Remove and reinstall/replace rotor.	C806	5D7; P-1
• Refinish rotor off vehicle; measure final rotor thickness and compare with specification.	C630	5D9; P-1
• Refinish rotor on vehicle; measure final rotor thickness and compare with specification.	C629	5D8; P-1
• Inspect and replace wheel studs.	C274	5F8; P-1

Time off _____

Time on _____

Total time _____

Materials Required

- Vehicle or simulator with disc brake concern
- Vehicle lifting equipment
- Asbestos removal equipment
- Torque wrench/es
- Micrometer
- Dial indicator
- Off-car brake lathe
- On-car brake lathe
- Hydraulic press or hammer and flat washers

Some Safety Issues to Consider

- Vehicle hoists are important tools that increase productivity and make the job easier. However, they can also cause severe injury or death if used improperly. Make sure you follow the hoist's and vehicle manufacturers' operation procedures. Also make sure you have your supervisor's/instructor's permission to use a vehicle hoist.
- **Caution:** Brake dust may contain asbestos, which has been determined to cause cancer when inhaled or ingested. Treat all brake dust as if it contains asbestos and use OSHA-approved asbestos removal equipment. Do not allow brake dust to become airborne by using anything that would disturb the dust. Also, wear protective gloves during this procedure and dispose of or clean them in an approved manner.

- **Caution:** Most types of brake fluid are harmful to painted surfaces. Be sure to prevent brake fluid from coming into contact with a vehicle's paint. Use fender covers to minimize this risk and be sure to wipe up any spilled brake fluid immediately with a wet rag.
- Only students who have their supervisor's/instructor's direct permission should perform this task due to the safety concerns involved.
- Brake lathes are very powerful. Follow all manufacturer instructions when setting up and operating a brake lathe.
- On-car brake lathes typically spin both rotors/wheels on an axle. Make sure the opposite rotor/wheel is free to spin and people stay away from it while refinishing the other rotor.
- Diagnosis of this fault, or verification after repair, may require test-driving the vehicle on the school grounds. Attempt this task only with full permission from your supervisor/instructor and follow all the guidelines exactly.
- Comply with personal and environmental safety practices associated with clothing; eye protection; hand tools; power equipment; proper ventilation; and the handling, storage, and disposal of chemicals/materials in accordance with local, state, and federal safety and environmental regulations.

Performance Standard

0—No exposure: No information or practice provided during the program; complete training required

1—Exposure only: General information provided with no practice time; close supervision needed; additional training required

2—Limited practice: Has practiced job during training program; additional training required to develop skill

3—Moderately skilled: Has performed job independently during training program; limited additional training may be required

4—Skilled: Can perform job independently with no additional training

TASK Clean and inspect rotor and mounting surface; measure rotor thickness, thickness variation, and lateral runout; determine needed action.

MAST
5D6

Time off_____

Time on_____

Total time_____

CDX Tasksheet Number: C628

1. **Research rotor inspection, refinishing, removal, and installation procedure in the appropriate service information. Follow all directions.**

    a. **Minimum rotor thickness:** _____ in/mm
    b. **Maximum thickness variation:** _____ in/mm
    c. **Maximum lateral runout:** _____ in/mm

2. **If you haven't already done so, remove the caliper assembly, brake pads, and any hardware following the manufacturer's procedure.**

3. **Clean the rotor with approved asbestos removal equipment.**

4. **Inspect/measure the rotor for the following:**

    a. **Hard spots/hot spots: Yes:** _____ **No:** _____
    b. **Cracks: Yes:** _____ **No:** _____
    c. **Rotor thickness:** _____ in/mm
    d. **Thickness variation (maximum variation) (check in 6-8 places):** _____ in/mm
    e. **Lateral runout:** _____ in/mm
    f. **Is the rotor machinable? Yes:** _____ **No:** _____

5. **Determine any necessary action(s):**

6. **Have your supervisor/instructor verify satisfactory completion of this procedure, any observations found, and any necessary action(s) recommended.**

> **NOTE** If you are refinishing this rotor on the vehicle, skip down to task C629. Refinish rotor on vehicle; measure final rotor thickness and compare with specifications. If you are refinishing this rotor off the vehicle, continue on to the next task.

Performance Rating

CDX Tasksheet Number: C628

0	1	2	3	4

Supervisor/instructor signature _____ Date _____

Remove and reinstall/replace rotor.

MAST
5D7

CDX Tasksheet Number: C806

1. **Remove the rotor following the specified procedure.**

2. **Now would be a good time to inspect the rotor, if you haven't already, and consider refinishing it. Ask your supervisor/instructor if you are to inspect and/or refinish the rotor. If so, proceed to task C630.**

3. **If you are to reinstall this rotor, have your supervisor/instructor confirm removal. Supervisor's/instructor's initials:** _____

4. **When appropriate (most likely after refinishing), reinstall the rotor according to the manufacturer's recommendations.**

5. **If you had to remove the wheel bearing during disassembly, have your supervisor/instructor verify proper adjustment of the bearings.**

    a. **Supervisor's/instructor's initials:** _____

6. **Have your supervisor/instructor verify satisfactory completion of this procedure, any observations found, and any necessary action(s) recommended.**

NOTE If you came to this tasksheet from the "Disc Brake Inspection and Service" tasksheet, return to that tasksheet and continue where you left off.

Performance Rating

CDX Tasksheet Number: C806

0	1	2	3	4

Supervisor/instructor signature _____ Date _____

MAST
5D9

DX Tasksheet Number: C630

1. Mount the rotor on the brake lathe following the manufacturer's procedure and set it up, ready to make a cut (but don't yet).

2. Measure or list the existing rotor thickness: _____ in/mm

3. Have your instructor verify proper set-up and initial here:

4. Using the correct procedure, refinish the brake rotor to within allowable tolerances.

5. Give the rotor a non-directional finish using sandpaper or an appropriate sanding wheel.

6. Measure the refinished rotor thickness: _____ in/mm

7. Calculate the amount of material that was removed: _____ in/mm

8. Is the rotor fit for return to service? Yes: _____ No: _____

9. Determine any necessary action(s):

10. Have your supervisor/instructor verify satisfactory completion of this procedure, any observations found, and any necessary action(s) recommended.

> **NOTE** If the rotor is serviceable, skip down to task C806: Remove and reinstall/replace rotor.

Performance Rating

CDX Tasksheet Number: C630

0	1	2	3	4

Supervisor/instructor signature _____ Date _____

MAST
5D8

Time off_____

Time on_____

Total time_____

CDX Tasksheet Number: C629

1. Set up the on-car brake lathe following the manufacturer's procedure, ready to make a cut (but don't yet).

2. Measure or list the existing rotor thickness: _____ in/mm

3. Have your instructor verify proper setup and initial here: _____

4. Using the correct procedure, refinish the brake rotor to within allowable tolerances. If necessary, give the rotor a non-directional finish using sandpaper or a sanding disc.

5. Measure the refinished rotor thickness: _____ in/mm

6. Calculate the amount of material that was removed: _____ in/mm

7. Is the rotor fit for return to service? Yes: _____ No: _____

8. Determine any necessary action(s):

9. Have your supervisor/instructor verify satisfactory completion of this procedure, any observations found, and any necessary action(s) recommended.

Performance Rating

CDX Tasksheet Number: C629

0	1	2	3	4

Supervisor/instructor signature _____ Date _____

MAST
5F8

CDX Tasksheet Number: C274

1. Research the wheel stud removal and installation procedure in the appropriate service manual. Follow all directions carefully.

   a. There are generally two standard procedures for replacing wheel studs. One is to remove the hub from the vehicle and use a hydraulic press to remove and install the studs. The other is to use a hammer to drive out the old stud, then use washers and the flat side of the lug nut to draw the new stud into the hub. Which method does the service manual describe for this vehicle? _____

   b. List any special tools or procedures for this task:

   c. Lug nut torque: _____ ft-lb/ N·m

2. Safely raise the vehicle on a hoist. Check to see that the vehicle is secure on the hoist.

3. Remove the wheel assembly and inspect the lug nuts and wheel studs. List your observations and any necessary actions:

4. Have your supervisor/instructor verify your observations. Supervisor/ instructor's initials: _____

5. Remove the damaged wheel stud/s from the hub, being careful to follow the specified procedure. List your observations:

6. Have your supervisor/instructor verify removal. Supervisor/instructor's initials: _____

7. Install a new wheel stud/s in the hub, following the specified procedure. Make sure the stud is fully seated in the hub. List your observations:

8. Have your supervisor/instructor verify the installation. Supervisor/instructor's initials: _____

> NOTE If you came to this tasksheet from the "Disc Brake Inspection and Service" tasksheet, return to that tasksheet and continue where you left off.

9. Reinstall the hub on the vehicle if it was removed. Reinstall the wheel assembly. Torque lug nuts to proper torque.

10. Have your supervisor/instructor verify satisfactory completion of this procedure, any observations found, and any necessary action/s recommended.

Performance Rating

0	1	2	3	4

Supervisor/instructor signature _____ Date _____

Drum Brake Inspection, Maintenance, and Service

Student/Intern information:

Name _____ Date _____ Class _____

Vehicle used for this activity:

Year _____ Make _____ Model_____

Odometer_____VIN_____

Learning Objective/Task	CDX Tasksheet Number	2017 MAST NATEF Reference Number; Priority Level
• Diagnose poor stopping, noise, vibration, pulling, grabbing, dragging, or pedal pulsation concerns; determine needed action.	C706	5C1; P-1
• Remove, clean, and inspect brake drum; measure brake drum diameter; determine serviceability.	C800	5C2; P-1
• Refinish brake drum and measure final drum diameter; compare to specification.	C626	5C3; P-1
• Remove, clean, inspect, and/or replace brake shoes, springs, pins, clips, levers, adjusters/self-adjusters, other related brake hardware, and backing support plates; lubricate and reassemble.	C248	5C4; P-1
• Inspect wheel cylinders for leaks and proper operation; remove and replace as needed.	C707	5C5; P-2
• Pre-adjust brake shoes and parking brake; install brake drums or drum/hub assemblies and wheel bearings; make final checks and adjustments.	C801	5C6; P-1
• Install wheel and torque lug nuts.	C251	5A4; P-1

Time off_____

Time on_____

Total time_____

Materials Required

- Vehicle or simulator with drum brakes
- Vehicle lifting equipment
- Asbestos removal equipment
- Drum brake micrometer
- Brake Lathe
- Brake spring tools
- Micrometer or dial caliper
- Flare nut wrench to fit brake line fitting
- Brake spoon
- Lubriplate

Some Safety Issues to Consider

- Diagnosis of this fault may require test-driving the vehicle on the school grounds or on a hoist, both of which carry severe risks. Attempt this task only with full permission from your supervisor/instructor and follow all the guidelines exactly.
- **Caution:** Brake dust may contain asbestos, which has been determined to cause cancer when inhaled or ingested. Treat all brake dust as if it contains asbestos and use OSHA-approved asbestos removal equipment. Do not allow brake dust to become airborne by using anything that would disturb the dust. Also, wear protective gloves during this procedure and dispose of or clean them in an approved manner.
- Brake springs can fly off with much force. Always wear safety glasses, and grip the springs firmly when removing and installing them.
- Brake lathes are very powerful. Follow all manufacturer instructions when setting up and operating a brake lathe.
- Lifting equipment such as vehicle jacks and stands, vehicle hoists, and engine hoists are important tools that increase productivity and make the job easier. However, they can also cause severe injury or death if used improperly. Make sure you follow the manufacturer's operation procedures. Also make sure you have your supervisor's/instructor's permission to use any particular type of lifting equipment.
- Comply with personal and environmental safety practices associated with clothing; eye protection; hand tools; power equipment; proper ventilation; and the handling, storage, and disposal of chemicals/materials in accordance with local, state, and federal safety and environmental regulations.

Performance Standard

0—No exposure: No information or practice provided during the program; complete training required

1—Exposure only: General information provided with no practice time; close supervision needed; additional training required

2—Limited practice: Has practiced job during training program; additional training required to develop skill

3—Moderately skilled: Has performed job independently during training program; limited additional training may be required

4—Skilled: Can perform job independently with no additional training

Diagnose poor stopping, noise, vibration, pulling, grabbing, dragging, or pedal pulsation concerns; determine needed action.

MAST
5C1

CDX Tasksheet Number: C706

1. List the drum brake-related customer complaint/concern:

2. Research the description and operation of the brake system for this vehicle in the appropriate service information. Also research the drum brake diagnostic procedure and removal/installation procedures.

    a. List the possible cause(s) of the complaint/concern:

3. With instructor permission, test-drive the vehicle to verify the concern. Be sure to follow all shop policies regarding test drives. List your observations:

4. Reflecting back on this job, list the causes of the customer concern as listed at the beginning of this tasksheet:

5. Document the correction(s) required to correct the customer concern:

6. Did you repair the vehicle? Yes: _____ No: _____

7. List any additional necessary action(s):

8. Have your supervisor/instructor verify satisfactory completion of this procedure, any observations found, and any necessary action(s) recommended.

Performance Rating

0	1	2	3	4

Supervisor/instructor signature _____ Date _____

Remove, clean, and inspect brake drum; measure
brake drum diameter; determine serviceability.

MAST
5C2

Time off_____

Time on_____

Total time_____

CDX Tasksheet Number: C800

1. **Research the description and operation of the brake system for this vehicle in the appropriate service information. Also research the drum brake removal/ installation procedures.**

   a. Maximum drum diameter: _____ in/mm
   b. Maximum drum out-of-round: _____ in/mm
   c. Minimum lining thickness: (Primary) _____ in/mm;
      (Secondary) _____ in/mm
   d. Parking brake adjustment specification: _____
   e. Lug nut torque: _____ ft-lb/ N·m
      i. Draw lug nut-torque pattern:

2. **Remove the brake drum following the specified procedure, being careful not to disturb any brake dust. Clean the brake drum using equipment/procedures for dealing with asbestos/dust.**

3. **Inspect the drum.**

   a. Measure and record the diameter: _____ in/mm
   b. Measure and record the amount of out-of-round: _____ in/mm

   > **NOTE** Measure in at least three places equally spaced around the drum.

   c. Hot spots? Yes: _____ No: _____
   d. Cracks? Yes: _____ No: _____
   e. Other defects? List if found:

4. **Based on your observations/measurements, determine any necessary action(s):**

5. Have your supervisor/instructor verify satisfactory completion of this procedure any observations found, and any necessary action(s) recommended.

Refinish brake drum and measure final drum diameter; compare to specification.

MAST
5C3

Time off_____

Time on_____

Total time_____

CDX Tasksheet Number: C626

1. **Mount the brake drum on the brake lathe following the brake lathe manufacturer's procedure, and set it up for a cut, BUT DON'T MAKE A CUT!**

2. **Have your instructor verify proper setup. Supervisor/Instructor initials:** _____

3. **Using the correct equipment and procedure, refinish the brake drum to within allowable tolerances.**

4. **Measure the final drum diameter and note your measurement here:** _____ **in/mm**

5. **Calculate the amount of material removed by the refinishing process:** _____ **in/mm**

6. **Does the drum meet specifications to be safely put back into service?**
   Yes: _____ **No:** _____

   a. **Why or why not?**

7. **Have your supervisor/instructor verify satisfactory completion of this procedure, any observations found, and any necessary action(s) recommended.**

Performance Rating

CDX Tasksheet Number: C626

0	1	2	3	4

Supervisor/instructor signature _____ Date _____

Remove, clean, inspect, and/or replace brake shoes, springs, pins, clips, levers, adjusters/self-adjusters, other related brake hardware, and backing support plates; lubricate and reassemble.

MAST
5C4

Time off_____

Time on_____

Total time_____

CDX Tasksheet Number: C248

1. **Clean brake shoes, hardware, and backing plates using equipment and procedures for dealing with asbestos/dust.**

2. **Disassemble the brake shoes and hardware from the backing plate, being careful not to lose any parts and remembering how they go back together.**

   a. **Measure lining thickness: (Primary)** _____ **in/mm;**
      (Secondary) _____ **in/mm**
   b. **Inspect and clean hardware:**
      i. **Springs:**
         Damaged: _____ **Missing:** _____
         Weak: _____ **Okay:** _____
      ii. **Pins:**
         Damaged: _____ **Missing:** _____
         Okay: _____
      iii. **Levers and adjusters:**
         Damaged: _____ **Missing:** _____
         Okay: _____
      iv. **Backing plate:**
         Damaged: _____ **Worn:** _____
         Okay: _____
      v. **Other hardware:**
         Damaged: _____ **Missing:** _____
         Okay: _____

3. **Determine any necessary action(s):**

4. **Have your instructor initial to verify condition of hardware:** _____

> **NOTE** Many vehicles use a primary shoe toward the front of the vehicle and a secondary shoe toward the rear of the vehicle. Refer to the manufacturer's procedure to install the shoes, springs, and hardware correctly.

5. **Following the manufacturer's procedure, lightly lubricate the support pads on the backing plate and reassemble the brake assembly (shoes, springs, hardware, etc.).**

> **NOTE** The brake shoe support pads on the backing plate require a thin film of the proper lubricant applied to their contact surface. This will reduce the wear on the backing plate as the side of the brake shoe rubs against the backing plate as the brakes are operated. Lubriplate (or in some cases, antiseize) is commonly used for this purpose. Just make sure that it only goes on light enough so you can see through it. If too much lubricant is used, it can contaminate the brake linings, which can cause the brakes to grab.

6. Are the springs seated correctly? Yes: _____ No: _____

7. Does the self-adjuster operate properly? Yes: _____ No: _____

8. List any necessary action(s):

9. Have your supervisor/instructor verify satisfactory completion of this procedure any observations found, and any necessary action(s) recommended.

CDX Tasksheet Number: C248

0	1	2	3	4

Supervisor/instructor signature _____ Date _____

Inspect wheel cylinders for leaks and proper operation; remove and replace as needed.

Time off_____

Time on_____

Total time_____

CDX Tasksheet Number: C707

1. **Inspect the wheel cylinder for leaks or damages dust boots. List your observations:**

2. **Place one thumb in each end of the wheel cylinder. Try to move both pistons side-to-side. This will indicate whether the pistons are stuck in their bores. List your observations:**

3. **Remove the wheel cylinder following the specified procedure.**

   NOTE To prevent twisting the brake line, it is common practice to loosen the brake line fitting before unbolting the wheel cylinder from the backing plate.

4. **Ask your instructor if you should disassemble the wheel cylinder. If no, skip to step #4. If yes, disassemble, clean, and inspect the wheel cylinder for damage, wear, or missing pieces.**

   a. **Bore:**
      Damaged: _____ Okay: _____

   b. **Pistons:**
      Damaged: _____ Missing: _____
      Okay: _____

   c. **Seals:**
      Damaged: _____ Missing: _____
      Okay: _____

   d. **Dust boots:**
      Damaged: _____ Missing: _____
      Okay: _____

   e. **Spring(s):**
      Damaged: _____ Missing: _____
      Okay: _____

5. **List any necessary action(s):**

6. Have your supervisor/instructor inspect the removed or disassembled wheel cylinder and determine whether it should be rebuilt, replaced with new, or reinstalled:

    a. Rebuild: _____ Replace: _____
       Reinstall: _____ (Choose one, then instructor initial)

    b. If rebuilding the wheel cylinder, use new seals, dust boots, springs, and expanders.

7. Reinstall the wheel cylinder on the backing plate.

> **NOTE** It is usually best to start the brake line fitting into the wheel cylinder before bolting the cylinder down. This will allow the threads of the brake line fitting to align with the threads in the wheel cylinder, helping to prevent cross-threading of the parts.

8. Have your supervisor/instructor verify satisfactory completion of this procedure, any observations found, and any necessary action(s) recommended.

Performance Rating

CDX Tasksheet Number: C707

0	1	2	3	4
☐	☐	☐	☐	☐

Supervisor/instructor signature _____ Date _____

Pre-adjust brake shoes and parking brake; install brake drums or drum/hub assemblies and wheel bearings; make final checks and adjustments.

MAST
5C6

Time off_____

Time on_____

Total time_____

CDX Tasksheet Number: C801

1. **Following the specified procedure, pre-adjust the brake shoes and parking brake.**

2. **If this vehicle uses serviceable wheel bearings, see the "Wheel Bearing Service" tasksheet and clean, inspect, service, reinstall, and adjust them according to manufacturer's procedure.**

3. **Install the brake drum.**

   a. **Does the brake drum turn without excessive drag? Yes:** _____
      No: _____

   b. **If equipped with adjustable wheel bearings, are they adjusted properly?**
      Yes: _____ **No:** _____

   > **NOTE** The brakes may need air bled out of the wheel cylinders if they were removed from the vehicle. If they were, consider bleeding all wheel cylinders once all drums and calipers are back in place. Failure to have all drums and calipers installed could cause damage to the wheel cylinders, calipers, brake shoes, and pads. Ask your instructor if you are unclear about this.

4. **Check to see that the brake master cylinder has the proper amount of brake fluid in it.**

   a. **Is it at the proper level? Yes:** _____ **No:** _____

      i. **If no, refill with the proper fluid.**

5. **Start the engine and apply the brake pedal (only when all drums and calipers are installed). List brake pedal feel:**

6. **Shut off the engine and check wheel cylinders and brake line fittings for signs of leakage. List your observations:**

7. Have your supervisor/instructor verify satisfactory completion of this procedure, any observations found, and any necessary action(s) recommended.

Performance Rating

CDX Tasksheet Number: C801

0	1	2	3	4

Supervisor/instructor signature _____ Date _____

MAST
5A4

CDX Tasksheet Number: C251

1. **Install the wheel(s), place lug nuts on studs with the proper side facing the wheel, and torque them to proper torque in the specified sequence.**

> **NOTE** The lug nut contact face MUST match the contact face in the wheel. If the wheel contact face is tapered, the lug nut contact face MUST also be tapered to match. If the contact face in the wheel is flat, the contact face of the lug nut MUST be flat. If in doubt about which way the lug nuts should face, ask your instructor.

2. **To what torque did you tighten the lug nuts?** _____ **ft-lb/ N·m**

3. **Reinstall any wheel covers that have been removed.**

4. **Have your supervisor/instructor feel brake pedal application and determine whether a test drive is necessary to final adjust the brakes and verify satisfactory operation of brakes.**

Performance Rating

CDX Tasksheet Number: C251

0	1	2	3	4

Supervisor/instructor signature _____ Date _____

Parking Brake Inspection and Service

Learning Objective/Task	CDX Tasksheet Number	2017 MAST NATEF Reference Number; Priority Level
• Check parking brake system and components for wear, binding, and corrosion; clean, lubricate, adjust, and/or replace as needed.	C811	5F3; P-1
• Check parking brake operation and indicator light system operation; determine needed action.	C633	5F4; P-1

Time off_____

Time on_____

Total time_____

Materials Required

- Vehicle or brake system simulator
- Vehicle hoist
- Lubricant suitable for parking brake cables (see service information)

Some Safety Issues to Consider

- If you need to start the vehicle, you should ensure that the parking brake is firmly applied; if necessary, use wheel chocks to prevent the vehicle from moving when the vehicle is started to verify the completion of these tasks.
- When running any vehicles in the shop, make sure you use the shop's exhaust ventilation system to discharge all exhaust gas safely outside.
- Only students who have their supervisor's/instructor's direct permission should perform this task due to the safety concerns involved.
- Vehicle hoists are important tools that increase productivity and make the job easier. However, they also can cause severe injury or death if used improperly. Make sure you follow the hoist's and vehicle manufacturers' operation procedures. Also make sure you have your supervisor's/ instructor's permission to use a vehicle hoist.
- **Caution:** Brake dust may contain asbestos, which has been determined to cause cancer when inhaled or ingested. Treat all brake dust as if it contains asbestos and use OSHA-approved asbestos removal equipment. Do not allow brake dust to become airborne by using anything that would disturb the dust. Also, wear protective gloves during this procedure and dispose of or clean them in an approved manner.
- Comply with personal and environmental safety practices associated with clothing; eye protection; hand tools; power equipment; proper ventilation; and the handling, storage, and disposal of chemicals/materials in accordance with local, state, and federal safety and environmental regulations.

Performance Standard

0—No exposure: No information or practice provided during the program; complete training required

1—Exposure only: General information provided with no practice time; close supervision needed; additional training required

2—Limited practice: Has practiced job during training program; additional training required to develop skill

3—Moderately skilled: Has performed job independently during training program; limited additional training may be required

4—Skilled: Can perform job independently with no additional training

Check parking brake system and components for wear, binding, and corrosion; clean, lubricate, adjust, and/or replace as needed.

MAST
5F3

Time off_____

Time on_____

Total time_____

CDX Tasksheet Number: C811

1. **Research the following specifications for this vehicle in the appropriate service information.**

   a. **Specified parking brake cable lubricant:** _____

   b. **Parking brake adjustment:** _____

2. **Safely raise and support the vehicle on the hoist. Trace all parking brake cables to each wheel's brake assembly. Inspect the cables for the following defects and list the location and cause of the defect(s):**

   a. **Wear:** _____

   b. **Rusting:** _____

   c. **Binding:** _____

   d. **Corrosion:** _____

3. **Clean, lubricate, or replace cables as necessary and list the actions performed:**

4. **Check the parking brake adjustment (this could be counting clicks of the ratchet assembly). List your observations:**

5. **If the parking brake needs adjustment, perform that now.**

6. **Have your supervisor/instructor verify satisfactory completion of this procedure, any observations found, and any necessary action(s) recommended.**

Performance Rating

CDX Tasksheet Number: C811

0	1	2	3	4

Supervisor/instructor signature _____ Date _____

Check parking brake operation and indicator light
system operation; determine needed action.

MAST
5F4

CDX Tasksheet Number: C633

1. **Verify that the parking brake is adjusted properly. If necessary, adjust it, being sure to follow the manufacturer's procedure.**

2. **Check the parking brake indicator light by turning the ignition key to the run position (do not start the engine) and observing the brake-warning lamp on the dash. Apply and release the parking brake.**

    a. **List your observations:**

> NOTE If the parking brake light did not go off, check the level of brake fluid in the master cylinder reservoir. If low, top up with the specified brake fluid. If it still is on, research the diagnostic procedure in the service information.

4. **Apply the parking brake. Ensure that no people, tools, or equipment are in front of or behind the vehicle. With instructor permission, start the vehicle and verify that the parking brake properly holds the vehicle when placed in drive and reverse.**

> NOTE Use extreme caution when performing this test. If the vehicle moves, stop.

    a. **Does the parking brake hold the vehicle? Yes: _____ No: _____**

5. **Determine necessary action(s):**

6. **Have your supervisor/instructor verify satisfactory completion of this procedure, any observations found, and any necessary action(s) recommended.**

Performance Rating

CDX Tasksheet Number: C633

0	1	2	3	4

Supervisor/instructor signature _____ Date _____

Power Booster Inspection

Student/Intern information:

Name _____ Date _____ Class _____

Vehicle used for this activity:

Year _____ Make _____ Model _____

Odometer _____ VIN _____

Learning Objective/Task	CDX Tasksheet Number	2017 MAST NATEF Reference Number; Priority Level
• Check brake pedal travel with, and without, engine running to verify proper power booster operation.	C807	5E1; P-2
• Identify components of the brake power assist system (vacuum and hydraulic); check vacuum supply (manifold or auxiliary pump) to vacuum-type power booster.	C808	5E2; P-1
• Inspect vacuum-type power booster unit for leaks; inspect the check valve for proper operation; determine needed action.	C809	5E3; P-1
• Inspect and test the hydraulically assisted power brake system for leaks and proper operation; determine needed action.	C581	5E4; P-3

Time off_____

Time on_____

Total time_____

Some Safety Issues to Consider

- If you need to start the vehicle, you should ensure that the parking brake is firmly applied; if necessary, use wheel chocks to prevent the vehicle from moving when the vehicle is started to verify the completion of these tasks.
- Only students who have a valid driver's license and their supervisor's/instructor's direct permission should perform this task due to the safety concerns involved.
- When running any vehicles in the shop, make sure you use the shop's exhaust ventilation system to discharge all exhaust gas safely outside.
- Comply with personal and environmental safety practices associated with clothing; eye protection; hand tools; power equipment; proper ventilation; and the handling, storage, and disposal of chemicals/materials in accordance with local, state, and federal safety and environmental regulations.

Performance Standard

0–No exposure: No information or practice provided during the program; complete training required

1–Exposure only: General information provided with no practice time; close supervision needed; additional training required

2–Limited practice: Has practiced job during training program; additional training required to develop skill

3–Moderately skilled: Has performed job independently during training program; limited additional training may be required

4–Skilled: Can perform job independently with no additional training

Check brake pedal travel with, and without, engine
running to verify proper power booster operation.

MAST
5E1

CDX Tasksheet Number: C807

1. Research the power booster description, operation, and testing procedure in the appropriate service information.

   a. Type of vacuum supply used: Manifold: _____ Auxiliary
      pump: _____

   b. Minimum vacuum at power booster: _____ in.hg

   c. Minimum time power booster should hold vacuum:
      _____ minutes

2. Test the ability of the power booster to provide assist.

   a. Without starting the vehicle, depress the brake pedal several times. This removes any vacuum from the brake booster. Hold moderate foot pressure on the brake pedal and start the engine.

      i. List the brake pedal action:

      ii. Is the power booster working properly? Yes: _____
          No: _____

   b. If the power booster is not working properly, follow the service manual procedure to determine the cause. List any necessary action(s):

3. Test the ability of the power booster to hold a vacuum.

   a. Without starting the vehicle, depress the brake pedal several times. This removes all vacuum from the brake booster and allows you to feel the brakes without vacuum assist.

      i. Approximately how far down does the brake pedal go with moderate foot pressure w/o assist? _____ in/mm

   b. With your foot off the brake pedal, start the engine, wait a few seconds, and depress the brake pedal once. This allows you to feel the brakes with power assist. This is how the brake pedal should respond if the power booster is holding vacuum properly.

      i. Approximately how far down does the brake pedal travel with moderate foot pressure with assist? _____ in/mm

   c. Remove your foot from the brake pedal, turn off the engine, and wait the specified time the power booster should hold vacuum listed above.

d. After waiting the designated time, and without starting the vehicle, depress the brake pedal once and observe whether the brake pedal travel was the same as in step 3b, indicating the power booster is holding vacuum. List your observations:

e. If the brake pedal responded as in step 3b, no further inspection of the booster is needed.
f. If the brake pedal responded as if it had no vacuum assist (as in 3a), the power booster has a leak, which will need to be diagnosed.

4. Have your supervisor/instructor verify satisfactory completion of this procedure, any observations found, and any necessary action(s) recommended.

Performance Rating

CDX Tasksheet Number: C807

0	1	2	3	4

Supervisor/instructor signature _____ Date _____

Identify components of the brake power assist system
(vacuum and hydraulic); check vacuum supply
(manifold or auxiliary pump) to vacuum-type power booster.

MAST
5E2

Time off_____

Time on_____

Total time_____

CDX Tasksheet Number: C808

1. **Research the components of the brake power assist system in the appropriate service information.**

2. **Identify and list the type of power assist system:**
    _____

3. **If the vehicle is equipped with vacuum-type power assist, complete the following procedure:**

    a. **Following the specified procedure with the engine running, check the vacuum supply at the brake power booster.**

        i. **List the vacuum reading obtained:**
            _____

    b. **Does this meet the specification requirements for this vehicle?**
        Yes: _____ No: _____

        i. **If no, determine the cause(s) of the low vacuum reading and list the condition(s) found.**

    > **NOTE** This could be caused by a leak in the system or an engine mechanical/tune-up problem if manifold vacuum is used. Find the specific cause.

4. **Determine necessary action(s):**

5. **Remove the vacuum gauge and reinstall the check valve in the booster.**

6. **Have your supervisor/instructor verify satisfactory completion of this procedure, any observations found, and any necessary action(s) recommended.**

Performance Rating

CDX Tasksheet Number: C808

0	1	2	3	4

Supervisor/instructor signature _____ Date _____

Inspect vacuum-type power booster unit for leaks; inspect the check valve for proper operation; determine needed action.

CDX Tasksheet Number: C809

1. **Test the ability of the power booster to hold a vacuum.**

   a. **Without starting the vehicle, depress the brake pedal several times with moderate pressure.**

   b. **After the vacuum has bled off, approximately how far down does the brake pedal go? _____ in/mm**

   > **NOTE** This removes any vacuum from the brake booster and allows you to feel the brakes without vacuum assist.

2. **Start the engine, wait a few seconds, and depress the brake pedal once.**

   > **NOTE** This allows you to feel the brakes with vacuum assist. This is how the brake pedal should respond if the vacuum booster is holding a vacuum properly.

   a. **Approximately how far down does the brake pedal go now? _____ in/mm**

3. **Let off the brakes, turn off the engine, and wait the specified time the power booster should hold a vacuum listed previously.**

4. **After waiting the designated time and without starting the vehicle, depress the brake pedal once.**

   a. **Does the brake pedal feel the same as in step 2? Yes: _____ No: _____**

5. **If yes, the power booster and check valve are capable of holding a vacuum, which means the system doesn't have an external vacuum leak (it may still have an internal leak).**

6. **If no, the brake pedal responded as if it had no vacuum assist. Start the vehicle and do the following:**

   a. **Use the electronic stethoscope or the heater hose to listen for vacuum leaks around the outside of the power booster.**

   b. **Listen under the dash at the power booster control valve assembly. List observations found:**

7. Inspect the check valve for proper operation.

   a. Carefully remove the check valve from the power booster, leaving it inserted in the vacuum hose. Start the vehicle and feel whether air is being drawn through the check valve. If it is, this indicates that the valve is not plugged or stuck closed. List observations found:

   b. Reinsert the check valve into the power booster and allow the engine to run for 30 seconds to evacuate the booster. Turn off the engine, wait for the specified minimum time that the power booster should hold a vacuum (listed previously), and then remove the check valve from the booster. There should be a large rush of air into the booster. If there is, the check valve is holding a vacuum and is okay. List observations found:

8. Perform an internal leak test.

   a. Start the engine and let it idle. Apply the brake pedal with moderately firm pressure (20-30 lb) and hold it steady. Without moving your foot, shut off the engine and observe the pedal for approximately one minute. If it stays steady, there are no internal leaks. If the pedal rises, there is an internal leak in either the diaphragm or control valve. List observations found:

9. Based on your observations, determine any necessary actions:

10. Return the vehicle to its beginning condition and return any tools you used to their proper locations.

11. Have your supervisor/instructor verify satisfactory completion of this procedure, any observations found, and any necessary action(s) recommended.

Performance Rating

CDX Tasksheet Number: C809

0	1	2	3	4

Supervisor/instructor signature _____ Date _____

Inspect and test the hydraulically assisted power brake system for leaks and proper operation; determine needed action.

MAST
5E4

Time off_____

Time on_____

Total time_____

CDX Tasksheet Number: C581

Vehicle used for this activity:

Year _____ Make _____ Model _____

Odometer _____ VIN _____

1. **Performance Test: Begin with the vehicle engine off. Apply and release the brake pedal five or six times to discharge the accumulator.**

    a. **Hold the brake pedal down with moderately firm pressure (20–30 lb).**

    b. **Start the engine and observe the brake pedal. If it drops an inch or two, the booster is providing boost. If it does not drop, check the power steering pump belt and power steering pump system. List observations found:**

    > **NOTE** If they are in good condition, consult the service information for further diagnosis.

2. **Accumulator Leak Test: Start the engine, apply the brake pedal, and note the pedal feel and applied height.**

    a. **Release the brake pedal, turn off the engine, and wait at least 10 minutes.**

    b. **Apply the brake pedal with moderately firm pressure (20–30 lb). List observations found:**

    c. **Apply the pedal several more times with the same moderately firm pressure. Each application should result in a higher pedal as the accumulator pressure is released from the booster. If it did, then there are no substantial leaks in the system. If it didn't hold pressure, you will need to perform manufacturer specified tests to determine what is causing the loss in pressure. Determine any necessary action(s):**

3. Have your supervisor/instructor verify satisfactory completion of this procedure, any observations found, and any necessary action(s) recommended.

Hydraulic System Diagnosis and Service

Student/Intern information:

Name _____ Date _____ Class _____

Vehicle used for this activity:

Year _____ Make _____ Model _____

Odometer _____ VIN _____

Learning Objective/Task	CDX Tasksheet Number	2017 MAST NATEF Reference Number; Priority Level
• Diagnose pressure concerns in the brake system using hydraulic principles (Pascal's Law).	C894	5B1; P-1
• Diagnose poor stopping, pulling or dragging concerns caused by malfunctions in the hydraulic system; determine needed action.	C236	5B5; P-1

Time off_____

Time on_____

Total time_____

Materials Required

- Technical service manuals and any other information applicable to the specific activity you are undertaking

Some Safety Issues to Consider

- Diagnosis of this fault may require test-driving the vehicle on the school grounds or on a hoist, both of which carry severe risks. Attempt this task only with full permission from your supervisor/instructor and follow all the guidelines exactly.
- **Caution:** Brake dust may contain asbestos, which has been determined to cause cancer when inhaled or ingested. Treat all brake dust as if it contains asbestos and use OSHA-approved asbestos removal equipment. Do not allow brake dust to become airborne by using anything that would disturb the dust. Also, wear protective gloves during this procedure and dispose of or clean them in an approved manner.
- Lifting equipment such as vehicle jacks and stands, vehicle hoists, and engine hoists are important tools that increase productivity and make the job easier. However, they can also cause severe injury or death if used improperly. Make sure you follow the manufacturer's operation procedures. Also make sure you have your supervisor's/instructor's permission to use any particular type of lifting equipment.
- Although you will not be working on a vehicle, remember that if you had to apply some of the theories contained within this exercise, you should observe all appropriate safety measures when working on a vehicle.
- Comply with personal and environmental safety practices associated with clothing; eye protection; hand tools; power equipment; proper ventilation; and the handling, storage, and disposal of chemicals/materials in accordance with local, state, and federal safety and environmental regulations.

Performance Standard

0–No exposure: No information or practice provided during the program; complete training required

1–Exposure only: General information provided with no practice time; close supervision needed; additional training required

2–Limited practice: Has practiced job during training program; additional training required to develop skill

3–Moderately skilled: Has performed job independently during training program; limited additional training may be required

4–Skilled: Can perform job independently with no additional training

Diagnose pressure concerns in the brake system
using hydraulic principles (Pascal's Law).

MAST
5B1

Time off_____

Time on_____

Total time_____

CDX Tasksheet Number: C894

1. Have your supervisor/instructor assign you a vehicle found in the service
   information (you don't need the actual vehicle for this task). Write the details
   of that vehicle at the top of this page.

2. Write out Pascal's Law here:

3. Research the description and operation of the vehicle assigned in the appropriate
   service manual.

4. Using Pascal's Law and the service manual, answer the following questions:

   a. While braking, how would the vehicle react with a missing left rear wheel
      cylinder piston seal or caliper seal?

   b. While braking, how would the vehicle react with a completely blocked left
      front flexible brake line?

   c. While braking, how would the vehicle react with a torn primary piston
      pressure seal in the master cylinder?

5. Have your supervisor/instructor verify satisfactory completion of this procedure,
   any observations found, and any necessary action(s) recommended.

Performance Rating

CDX Tasksheet Number: C894

0	1	2	3	4

Supervisor/instructor signature _____ Date _____

MAST
5B5

Time off_____

Time on_____

Total time_____

CDX Tasksheet Number: C236

1. List the brake-related (hydraulic system) customer complaint or concern:

2. Research the particular concern in the appropriate service information. List the possible cause(s):

3. With instructor permission, test-drive the vehicle to verify the concern.

   > NOTE Be sure to follow all shop policies regarding test drives.

   a. List your observations:

4. Follow the specified procedure to inspect and diagnose the problem. Document the steps you took to determine the cause, and the results of those steps, in the space below:

5. List the root cause(s) of the concern(s):

6. Determine any necessary action(s):

7. Have your supervisor/instructor verify satisfactory completion of this procedure, any observations found, and any necessary action(s) recommended.

Performance Rating

0	1	2	3	4

Supervisor/instructor signature _____ Date _____

Wheel Bearing Inspection, Maintenance, and Service

Student/Intern information:

Name _____ Date _____ Class _____

Vehicle used for this activity:

Year _____ Make _____ Model _____

Odometer _____ VIN _____

Learning Objective/Task	CDX Tasksheet Number	2017 MAST NATEF Reference Number; Priority Level
• Remove, clean, inspect, repack, and install wheel bearings; replace seals; install hub and adjust bearings.	C810	5F2; P-2
• Replace wheel bearing and race.	C273	5F6; P-3
• Remove, reinstall, and/or replace sealed wheel bearing assembly.	C275	5F7; P-1
• Diagnose wheel bearing noises, wheel shimmy, and vibration concerns; determine needed action.	C267	5F1; P-1

Time off_____

Time on_____

Total time_____

Materials Required

- Vehicle or simulator with serviceable and sealed wheel bearings
- Inch-pound torque wrench
- Ft-lb or Nm torque wrench
- Hammer and brass (or soft) punch
- Specified bearing grease
- Bearing packer (optional)
- New cotter pin/s (if needed)
- Stethoscope

Some Safety Issues to Consider

- Lifting equipment such as vehicle jacks and stands, vehicle hoists, and engine hoists are important tools that increase productivity and make the job easier. However, they can also cause severe injury or death if used improperly. Make sure you follow the manufacturer's operation procedures. Also make sure you have your supervisor's/instructor's permission to use any particular type of lifting equipment.
- **Caution:** Brake dust may contain asbestos, which has been determined to cause cancer when inhaled or ingested. Treat all brake dust as if it contains asbestos and use OSHA-approved asbestos removal equipment. Do not allow brake dust to become airborne by using anything that would disturb the dust. Also, wear protective gloves during this procedure and dispose of or clean them in an approved manner.
- This procedure may require the removal of one or more cotter pin(s). Always replace the removed ones with new ones. Failure to do so could cause a component to come unfastened and cause serious injury or death.

- Comply with personal and environmental safety practices associated with clothing; eye protection; hand tools; power equipment; proper ventilation; and the handling, storage, and disposal of chemicals/materials in accordance with local, state, and federal safety and environmental regulations.

Performance Standard

0—No exposure: No information or practice provided during the program; complete training required

1—Exposure only: General information provided with no practice time; close supervision needed; additional training required

2—Limited practice: Has practiced job during training program; additional training required to develop skill

3—Moderately skilled: Has performed job independently during training program; limited additional training may be required

4—Skilled: Can perform job independently with no additional training

Remove, clean, inspect, repack, and install wheel bearings; replace seals; install hub and adjust bearings.

MAST 5F2

Time off_____

Time on_____

Total time_____

CDX Tasksheet Number: C810

1. Research the wheel bearing disassembly, cleaning, inspection, repacking, and installation procedure in the appropriate service information and list the following specifications:

   a. Specified wheel bearing grease: _____

   b. Steps for adjusting the wheel bearing:

   c. Spindle nut final torque, if specified: _____ in-lb: _____
      ft-lb: _____ N·m: _____

2. Remove the wheel bearings from one wheel assembly, following the specified procedure. Be sure to use the appropriate brake dust removal system to properly remove and dispose of any brake dust. Clean and inspect the wheel bearings and race. Also clean and inspect the spindle. List your observations:

3. Show your supervisor/instructor the wheel bearings and races. Supervisor's/instructor's initials: _____

> NOTE It may make sense to perform the next task, C273 at this time. Ask your instructor.

4. Repack the wheel bearings with the proper grease. Install the inner bearing in the race and replace the old grease seal with a new one (being careful to not damage it).

5. Reinstall the hub and outer bearing onto the spindle.

6. Adjust the wheel bearing preload, or torque spindle nut (depending on application), according to the specified procedure.

> NOTE Most adjustable wheel bearings require a fairly heavy torque to seat the bearings (example: 25 ft-lb) and a lighter torque to preload the bearing (example: 20 in-lb). Failure to loosen the bearing and preload it to the lower torque will result in burned-up bearings.

7. Have your instructor verify the wheel bearing adjustment. Supervisor's/instructor's initials: _____

8. Install a new cotter pin or secure the spindle nut, according to the specified procedure.

9. Have your supervisor/instructor verify satisfactory completion of this procedure, any observations found, and any necessary action(s) recommended.

Performance Rating

0	1	2	3	4

Supervisor/instructor signature _____ Date _____

MAST
5F6

DX Tasksheet Number: C273

1. **Research the wheel bearing and race disassembly and installation procedure in the appropriate service information and list the following specifications:**
   a. **Specified wheel bearing grease:** _____
   b. **Steps for adjusting the wheel bearing:**

   c. **Spindle nut final torque, if specified:** _____ ft-lb/ N·m

2. **Using a hammer and soft punch, carefully drive the race from the hub. Avoid scarring the surface of the hub with the punch and hammer.**

3. **Clean and inspect the wheel bearings and race. List your observations:**

4. **Show your supervisor/instructor the wheel bearing and race. Supervisor's/instructor's initials:** _____

5. **Unless your supervisor/instructor directs you otherwise, replace the wheel bearing and race with new ones, following the specified procedure. Make sure the race is fully seated in the hub.**

6. **Repack the wheel bearings with the proper grease. Install the inner bearing in the race and replace the old grease seal with a new one.**

7. **Reinstall the hub and outer bearing onto the spindle.**

8. **Install the thrust washer and adjustment nut on the spindle. Adjust the wheel bearing preload, or torque spindle nut (depending on application), according to the specified procedure. Supervisor's/instructor's initials:** _____

9. **Install a new cotter pin, or secure the spindle nut, according to the specified procedure.**

10. Have your supervisor/instructor verify satisfactory completion of this procedure, any observations found, and any necessary action(s) recommended.

Performance Rating

0	1	2	3	4

Supervisor/instructor signature _____ Date _____

Remove, reinstall, and/or replace sealed wheel bearing assembly. **MAST** 5F7

Time off_____

Time on_____

Total time_____

CDX Tasksheet Number: C275

1. Research the sealed wheel bearing assembly removal and installation procedure in the appropriate service information.

   a. Hub bolt torque: _____ ft/lbs or N·m
   b. Axle nut torque (if equipped): _____ ft/lbs or N·m

2. Remove the sealed wheel bearing assembly from the vehicle, following the specified procedure.

3. Show your supervisor/instructor the wheel bearing assembly. Supervisor's/instructor's initials: _____

4. Replace or reinstall the wheel bearing assembly, again following the specified procedure. Be sure to properly torque all fasteners and replace any removed cotter pins with new cotter pins.

5. Have your supervisor/instructor verify satisfactory completion of this procedure, any observations found, and any necessary action(s) recommended.

Performance Rating

CDX Tasksheet Number: C275

0	1	2	3	4

Supervisor/instructor signature _____ Date _____

MAST
5F1

Time off_____

Time on_____

Total time_____

CDX Tasksheet Number: C267

Vehicle used for this activity:

Year _____ Make _____ Model _____

Odometer _____ VIN _____

1. List the customer concern/complaint regarding a wheel bearing issue:

2. Research possible causes of the concern in the appropriate service information. List possible causes:

3. Follow the specified procedure for determining the cause of the complaint/ concern. Depending on the actual fault, this could require many steps. List the steps you took to determine the fault:

4. List the cause of the concern/complaint:

5. List the necessary action(s) to correct this fault:

6. Have your supervisor/instructor verify satisfactory completion of this procedure, any observations found, and any necessary action(s) recommended.

Performance Rating

0	1	2	3	4

Supervisor/instructor signature _____ Date _____

Brake Warning Light and Stop Light Inspection and Service

Student/Intern information:

Name _____ Date _____ Class _____

Vehicle used for this activity:

Year _____ Make _____ Model_____

Odometer_____VIN_____

Learning Objective/Task	CDX Tasksheet Number	2017 MAST NATEF Reference Number; Priority Level
• Check operation of brake stop light system.	C272	5F5; P-1
• Identify components of hydraulic brake warning light system.	C947	5B11; P-2
• Inspect, test, and/or replace components of brake warning light system.	C242	5B10; P-3

Time off_____

Time on_____

Total time_____

Materials Required

- Vehicle
- Student assistant
- Test light/multimeter if diagnosis is required

Some Safety Issues to Consider

- Accidental deployment of the airbag system could happen if you inadvertently probe the wrong wire. Most manufacturers use yellow-colored wiring to denote wiring for the airbag system. Always be aware of the system/circuit you are working on.
- **Caution:** Most types of brake fluid are harmful to painted surfaces. Be sure to prevent brake fluid from coming into contact with a vehicle's paint. Use fender covers to minimize this risk and be sure to wipe up any spilled brake fluid immediately with a wet rag.
- Comply with personal and environmental safety practices associated with clothing; eye protection; hand tools; power equipment; proper ventilation; and the handling, storage, and disposal of chemicals/materials in accordance with local, state, and federal safety and environmental regulations.

Performance Standard

0—No exposure: No information or practice provided during the program; complete training required

1—Exposure only: General information provided with no practice time; close supervision needed; additional training required

2—Limited practice: Has practiced job during training program; additional training required to develop skill

3—Moderately skilled: Has performed job independently during training program; limited additional training may be required

4—Skilled: Can perform job independently with no additional training

▶ TASK Check operation of brake stop light system.

Time off_____

Time on_____

Total time_____

CDX Tasksheet Number: C272

1. Research the correct brake light bulb number(s) in the appropriate service information.

   a. Specified brake lamp bulb number: _____
   b. High-mounted stop light bulb number, if equipped with replaceable bulbs:
      _____

2. Have another student step on the brake pedal while you observe the reaction of the brake lights (including the high-mounted stop light, if equipped). List your observation(s):

3. If the brake lights do not work properly, check simple things like individual bulbs to see if individual lights are out. If all of the brake lights are out, check the brake circuit fuse. List your findings:

4. Determine any necessary action(s):

5. Have your supervisor/instructor verify satisfactory completion of this procedure, any observations found, and any necessary action(s) recommended.

Performance Rating

CDX Tasksheet Number: C272

0	1	2	3	4

Supervisor/instructor signature _____ Date _____

MAST
5B11

CDX Tasksheet Number: C947

1. On the appropriate wiring diagram, locate each switch that activates the brake warning light. List those switches here:

2. Locate all of the brake warning light switches on the vehicle/simulator. Be prepared to point them out to your supervisor/instructor.

   a. Point out the location of the switches to your supervisor/instructor.

3. Have your supervisor/instructor verify satisfactory completion of this procedure, any observations found, and any necessary action(s) recommended.

Performance Rating

CDX Tasksheet Number: C947

0	1	2	3	4

Supervisor/instructor signature _____ Date _____

Inspect, test, and/or replace components of brake
warning light system.

MAST
5B10

Time off_____

Time on_____

Total time_____

CDX Tasksheet Number: C242

1. **Locate all of the brake warning light switches on the vehicle/simulator. Be prepared to point them out to your supervisor/instructor. Select one of the switches to demonstrate the proper testing procedure. List which switch you are testing:**

2. **Research the diagnosis procedure for the switch being tested.**

3. **Perform the tests on the designated switch and list the steps you took and the results for each:**

4. **Determine any necessary action(s):**

5. **Have your supervisor/instructor verify satisfactory completion of this procedure, any observations found, and any necessary action(s) recommended.**

Performance Rating

CDX Tasksheet Number: C242

0	1	2	3	4

Supervisor/instructor signature _____ Date _____

Electronic Brake Control Systems

Student/Intern information:

Name _____ Date _____ Class _____

Vehicle used for this activity:

Year _____ Make _____ Model_____

Odometer_____VIN_____

Learning Objective/Task	CDX Tasksheet Number	2017 MAST NATEF Reference Number; Priority Level
• Identify and inspect electronic brake control system components (ABS, TCS, ESC); determine needed action.	C634	5G1; P-1
• Describe the operation of a regenerative braking system.	C950	5G2; P-3

Time off_____

Time on_____

Total time_____

Materials Required

- Vehicle with electronic brake control
- Vehicle with traction control
- Vehicle hoist to see some of the components that are located under the vehicle
- DMM/DVOM
- Lab scope

Some Safety Issues to Consider

- Diagnosis of this fault may require test-driving the vehicle on the school grounds or on a hoist, both of which carry severe risks. Attempt this task only with full permission from your supervisor/instructor and follow all the guidelines exactly.
- Anti-lock brake systems store brake fluid under tremendous pressure that can cause severe injury, even when the engine is not running. Always refer to the service manual to determine how to depressurize the system safely whenever working on it.
- **Caution:** Most types of brake fluid are harmful to painted surfaces. Be sure to prevent brake fluid from coming into contact with a vehicle's paint. Use fender covers to minimize this risk and be sure to wipe up any spilled brake fluid immediately with a wet rag.
- Comply with personal and environmental safety practices associated with clothing; eye protection; hand tools; power equipment; proper ventilation; and the handling, storage, and disposal of chemicals/materials in accordance with local, state, and federal safety and environmental regulations.

Performance Standard

0–No exposure: No information or practice provided during the program; complete training required

1–Exposure only: General information provided with no practice time; close supervision needed; additional training required

2–Limited practice: Has practiced job during training program; additional training required to develop skill

3–Moderately skilled: Has performed job independently during training program; limited additional training may be required

4–Skilled: Can perform job independently with no additional training

► TASK Identify and inspect electronic brake control system
components (ABS, TCS, ESC); determine needed action.

MAST
5G1

CDX Tasksheet Number: C634

1. **Research the electronic brake control system description, theory of operation, and testing procedures for this vehicle in the appropriate service information.**

    a. **List the main components in the electronic brake control system:**

    b. **List the type of wheel speed sensor used:** _____
    c. **Wheel speed sensor resistance (if inductive style):** _____ ohms

2. **Inspect the wheel speed sensors for integrity and condition.**

    a. **Wheel speed sensor resistance: (if inductive style)**
        Left front: _____ ohms
        Right front: _____ ohms
        Left rear: _____ ohms
        Right rear: _____ ohms

    b. **Wheel speed sensor lab scope pattern: Sketch the lab scope pattern of one wheel speed sensor while the wheel is turning.**

3. **Do the wheel speed sensors meet specifications? Yes:** _____ **No:** _____

4. **Have your supervisor/instructor verify satisfactory completion of this procedure, any observations found, and any necessary action(s) recommended.**

Performance Rating

CDX Tasksheet Number: C634

0	1	2	3	4

Supervisor/instructor signature _____ Date _____

Describe the operation of a regenerative braking system.

MAST
5G2

Time off_____

Time on_____

CDX Tasksheet Number: C950

1. **Research the operation of a regenerative braking system on a vehicle equipped with this system in the appropriate service information.**

    a. **In your own words, write out a summary of how the system operates:**

Total time_____

2. **Have your supervisor/instructor verify satisfactory completion of this procedure, any observations found, and any necessary action(s) recommended.**

Performance Rating

CDX Tasksheet Number: C950

0	1	2	3	4

Supervisor/instructor signature _____ Date _____

Electronic Brake Control Hydraulic Service

Student/Intern information:

Name _____ Date _____ Class _____

Vehicle used for this activity:

Year _____ Make _____ Model _____

Odometer _____ VIN _____

Learning Objective/Task	CDX Tasksheet Number	2017 MAST NATEF Reference Number; Priority Level
• Depressurize high-pressure components of an electronic brake control system.	C812	5G5; P-2
• Bleed the electronic brake control system hydraulic circuits.	C637	5G6; P-1

Time off _____

Time on _____

Total time _____

Materials Required

- Vehicle or simulator with ABS
- Depending on the type of concern, special diagnostic tools may be required. See your supervisor/instructor for instructions to identify what tools may be required.

Some Safety Issues to Consider

- Anti-lock brake systems store brake fluid under tremendous pressure that can cause severe injury, even when the engine is not running. Always refer to the service manual to determine how to depressurize the system safely whenever working on it.
- If you need to start the vehicle, you should ensure that the parking brake is firmly applied; if necessary, use wheel chocks to prevent the vehicle from moving when the vehicle is started to verify the completion of these tasks.
- When running any vehicles in the shop, make sure you use the shop's exhaust ventilation system to discharge all exhaust gas safely outside.
- Only students who have their supervisor's/instructor's direct permission should perform this task due to the safety concerns involved.
- Diagnosis of this fault may require test-driving the vehicle on the school grounds. Attempt this task only with full permission from your supervisor/instructor and follow all the guidelines exactly.
- Comply with personal and environmental safety practices associated with clothing; eye protection; hand tools; power equipment; proper ventilation; and the handling, storage, and disposal of chemicals/materials in accordance with local, state, and federal safety and environmental regulations.

Performance Standard

0—No exposure: No information or practice provided during the program; complete training required

1—Exposure only: General information provided with no practice time; close supervision needed; additional training required

2—Limited practice: Has practiced job during training program; additional training required to develop skill

3—Moderately skilled: Has performed job independently during training program; limited additional training may be required

4—Skilled: Can perform job independently with no additional training

Depressurize high-pressure components of an electronic
brake control system.

Time off_____

Time on_____

Total time_____

CDX Tasksheet Number: C812

1. **Research the procedure to depressurize the high-pressure components of the ABS system in the appropriate service information. List the steps to perform this task:**

2. **Perform the steps necessary to depressurize the ABS system, being careful to follow the specified procedure. Determine any necessary action(s):**

3. **Have your supervisor/instructor verify satisfactory completion of this procedure, any observations found, and any necessary action(s) recommended.**

Performance Rating

CDX Tasksheet Number: C812

0	1	2	3	4

Supervisor/instructor signature _____ Date _____

Bleed the electronic brake control system hydraulic circuits.

MAST
5G6

Time off_____

Time on_____

Total time_____

CDX Tasksheet Number: C637

1. **Research the correct procedure to bleed the system in the appropriate service information. List the steps here:**

2. **Using the identified procedure and equipment, bleed the electronic brake control system hydraulic circuits.**

3. **Determine any necessary action(s):**

4. **Have your supervisor/instructor verify satisfactory completion of this procedure, any observations found, and any necessary action(s) recommended.**

Performance Rating

CDX Tasksheet Number: C637

0	1	2	3	4

Supervisor/instructor signature _____ Date _____

Electronic Brake Control Diagnosis

Student/Intern information:

Name _____ Date _____ Class _____

Vehicle used for this activity:

Year _____ Make _____ Model_____

Odometer_____VIN_____

Learning Objective/Task	CDX Tasksheet Number	2017 MAST NATEF Reference Number; Priority Level	
• Diagnose poor stopping, wheel lock-up, abnormal pedal feel, unwanted application, and noise concerns associated with the electronic brake control system; determine needed action.	C635	5G3; P-2	Time off_____
• Diagnose electronic brake control system electronic control(s) and components by retrieving diagnostic trouble codes, and/or using recommended test equipment; determine needed action.	C636	5G4; P-2	Time on_____
• Test, diagnose, and service electronic brake control system speed sensors (digital and analog), toothed ring (tone wheel), and circuits using a graphing multimeter (GMM)/digital storage oscilloscope (DSO) (includes output signal, resistance, shorts to voltage/ground, and frequency data).	C639	5G7; P-2	Total time_____
• Diagnose electronic brake control system braking concerns caused by vehicle modifications (tire size, curb height, final drive ratio, etc.).	C813	5G8; P-1	

Materials Required

- Vehicle or simulator with electronic brake control
- DVOM/DMM
- GMM/DSO
- Scan Tool
- Depending on the type of concern, special diagnostic tools may be required. See your supervisor/instructor for instructions to identify what tools may be required.

Some Safety Issues to Consider

- If you need to start the vehicle, you should ensure that the parking brake is firmly applied; if necessary, use wheel chocks to prevent the vehicle from moving when the vehicle is started to verify the completion of this task.
- When running any vehicles in the shop, make sure you use the shop's exhaust ventilation system to discharge all exhaust gas safely outside.
- Only students who have their supervisor/instructor's direct permission should perform these tasks due to the safety concerns involved.
- Diagnosis of this fault may require test driving the vehicle on the school grounds. Attempt this task only with full permission from your instructor and follow all the guidelines exactly.

- Comply with personal and environmental safety practices associated with clothing; eye protection; hand tools; power equipment; proper ventilation; and the handling, storage, and disposal of chemicals/materials in accordance with local, state, and federal safety and environmental regulations.

Performance Standard

0–No exposure: No information or practice provided during the program; complete training required

1–Exposure only: General information provided with no practice time; close supervision needed; additional training required

2–Limited practice: Has practiced job during training program; additional training required to develop skill

3–Moderately skilled: Has performed job independently during training program; limited additional training may be required

4–Skilled: Can perform job independently with no additional training

Diagnose poor stopping, wheel lock-up, abnormal pedal feel, unwanted application, and noise concerns associated with the electronic brake control system; determine needed action.

MAST
5G3

Time off_____

Time on_____

Total time_____

CDX Tasksheet Number: C635

1. List the ABS brake-related customer complaint/concern:

2. Research the particular concern in the appropriate service information. List the possible causes:

3. Test the vehicle and diagnose poor stopping, wheel lock-up, abnormal pedal feel, unwanted application, and noise concerns associated with the electronic brake control system. List your tests and the results:

4. List the cause of the concern:

5. Determine any necessary action(s) to correct the fault:

6. Have your supervisor/instructor verify satisfactory completion of this procedure, any observations found, and any necessary action(s) recommended.

Performance Rating

CDX Tasksheet Number: C635

0	1	2	3	4

Supervisor/instructor signature _____ Date _____

▶ TASK Diagnose electronic brake control system electronic control(s) and components by retrieving diagnostic trouble codes, and/or using recommended test equipment; determine needed action.

MAST
5G4

CDX Tasksheet Number: C636

1. List the ABS brake-related customer complaint/concern:

2. Research the particular concern in the appropriate service information. List the possible causes:

3. Use a scan tool to retrieve diagnostic trouble codes. List any codes and their descriptions:

4. Diagnose the electronic brake control system electronic control/s and the system components. List your tests and the results:

5. List the cause of the concern:

6. Determine any necessary action(s) to correct the fault:

7. Have your supervisor/instructor verify satisfactory completion of this procedure, any observations found, and any necessary action(s) recommended.

Performance Rating

CDX Tasksheet Number: C636

0	1	2	3	4

Supervisor/instructor signature _____ Date _____

Test, diagnose, and service electronic brake control system speed sensors (digital and analog), toothed ring (tone wheel), and circuits using a graphing multimeter (GMM)/digital storage oscilloscope (DSO) (includes output signal, resistance, shorts to voltage/ground, and frequency data).

MAST
5G7

Time off_____

Time on_____

Total time_____

CDX Tasksheet Number: C639

1. List the ABS brake-related customer complaint/concern:

2. Research the particular concern in the appropriate service information. List the possible causes:

3. Carry out the tests using a graphing multimeter (GMM) or digital storage oscilloscope (DSO) and list your results. The tests should include:

   a. Output signal: _____

   b. Resistance: _____

   c. Shorts to voltage/ground: _____

   d. Frequency data: _____

4. Note your conclusions here:

5. Determine any necessary action(s) to correct the fault:

6. Have your supervisor/instructor verify satisfactory completion of this procedure, any observations found, and any necessary action(s) recommended.

Performance Rating

CDX Tasksheet Number: C639

0	1	2	3	4

Supervisor/instructor signature _____ Date _____

Diagnose electronic brake control system braking concerns caused by vehicle modifications (tire size, curb height, final drive ratio, etc.).

MAST
5G8

Time off_____

Time on_____

Total time_____

CDX Tasksheet Number: C813

1. **List the ABS brake-related customer complaint/concern (caused by vehicle modifications):**

2. **Research the particular concern in the appropriate service information. List the possible cause(s):**

3. **Following the specified procedure, diagnose the electronic brake control concern (caused by vehicle modifications). List your tests and the results:**

4. **List the root cause of the problem:**

5. **Determine any necessary action(s) to correct the fault:**

6. **Have your supervisor/instructor verify satisfactory completion of this procedure, any observations found, and any necessary action(s) recommended.**

Performance Rating

CDX Tasksheet Number: C813

0	1	2	3	4

Supervisor/instructor signature _____ Date _____

Section A6:
Electrical/Electronic Systems

CONTENTS

Vehicle, Customer, and Service Information

Student/Intern information:

Name _____ Date _____ Class _____

Vehicle used for this activity:

Year _____ Make _____ Model _____

Odometer _____ VIN _____

Learning Objective/Task	CDX Tasksheet Number	2017 MAST NATEF Reference Number; Priority Level
• Research vehicle service information including vehicle service history, service precautions, and technical service bulletins.	C286	6A1; P-1
• Demonstrate knowledge of electrical/electronic series, parallel, and series-parallel circuits using principles of electricity (Ohm's Law).	C951	6A2; P-1
• Demonstrate the use of the three Cs (concern, cause, and correction).	N/A	N/A

Time off _____

Time on _____

Total time _____

Materials Required

- Vehicle with available service history records
- Technical Service Bulletins

Some Safety Issues to Consider

- Comply with personal and environmental safety practices associated with clothing; eye protection; hand tools; power equipment; proper ventilation; and the handling, storage, and disposal of chemicals/materials in accordance with local, state, and federal safety and environmental regulations.

Performance Standard

0—No exposure: No information or practice provided during the program; complete training required

1—Exposure only: General information provided with no practice time; close supervision needed; additional training required

2—Limited practice: Has practiced job during training program; additional training required to develop skill

3—Moderately skilled: Has performed job independently during training program; limited additional training may be required

4—Skilled: Can perform job independently with no additional training

Research vehicle service information including vehicle service history, service precautions, and technical service bulletins.

MAST
6A1

CDX Tasksheet Number: C286

1. **Using the VIN for identification, use the appropriate source to access the vehicle's service history in relation to prior electrical system work or customer concerns.**

    a. **List any related repairs/concerns, and their dates:**

2. **Using the VIN for identification, access any relevant technical service bulletins for the particular vehicle you are working on in relation to electrical system updates or other service issues.**

    a. **List any related service bulletins and their titles:**

3. **Research the operation of the headlights.**

    a. **Are they protected by a fuse? Yes: _____ No: _____**
    b. **Are they protected by a circuit breaker? Yes: _____ No: _____**
    c. **Do they use a relay? Yes: _____ No: _____**

4. **Have your supervisor/instructor verify satisfactory completion of this procedure, any observations found, and any necessary action(s) recommended.**

Performance Rating

CDX Tasksheet Number: C286

0	1	2	3	4

Supervisor/instructor signature _____ Date _____

▶ **TASK** Demonstrate knowledge of electrical/electronic series, parallel, and series-parallel circuits using principles of electricity (Ohm's Law).

MAST
6A2

Time off_____

Time on_____

Total time_____

CDX Tasksheet Number: C951

> **NOTE** Use Ohm's Law to solve the circuit information in this task.

1. **Series Circuit: Circuit voltage = 12 volts, R1 = 3 ohms, R2 = 9 ohms**

    a. **Draw this circuit in the space below:**

    b. **Total circuit resistance:** _____ ohms
    c. **Total circuit current flow:** _____ amps
    d. **Voltage drop across R1:** _____ volts
    e. **Voltage drop across R2:** _____ volts
    f. **Current flow through R1:** _____ amps
    g. **Current flow through R2:** _____ amps

2. **Parallel Circuit: Circuit voltage = 12 volts and Branch 1, R1 = 2 ohms and Branch 2, R2 = 4 ohms**

    a. **Draw this circuit in the space below:**

    b. **Total circuit resistance:** _____ ohms
       (Hint: Rt = R1 x R2/R1 + R2)
    c. **Total circuit current flow:** _____ amps
    d. **Voltage drop across R1:** _____ volts
    e. **Voltage drop across R2:** _____ volts
    f. **Current flow through R1:** _____ amps
    g. **Current flow through R2:** _____ amps

3. **Series-Parallel Circuit: Circuit voltage = 12 volts, R1 = 2 ohms is in series with the parallel circuit of R2 = 3 ohms and R3 = 3 ohms**

    a. **Draw this circuit in the space below:**

    b. **Total resistance of the parallel circuit:** _____ ohms
    c. **Total circuit resistance:** _____ ohms
    d. **Total circuit current flow:** _____ amps
    e. **Voltage drop across R1:** _____ volts
    f. **Voltage drop across R2 and R3:** _____ volts

g. Current flow through R2: _____ amps

h. Current flow through R3: _____ amps

4. Have your supervisor/instructor verify satisfactory completion of this procedure, any observations found, and any necessary action(s) recommended.

Performance Rating

0	1	2	3	4

Supervisor/instructor signature _____ Date _____

TASK Demonstrate the use of the three Cs (concern, cause, and correction).

Additional Task

Time off_____

Time on_____

Total time_____

CDX Tasksheet Number: N/A

1. Using the following scenario, write up the three Cs as listed on most repair orders. Assume that the customer authorized the recommended repairs.

   A vehicle is brought to your shop with an electrical concern. The customer tells you that the battery has been going dead for the last few days, but jump starting it would allow him to drive the vehicle. He also said he replaced the battery with a new one, but that didn't solve the problem. You inspect the vehicle and find the following:

   a. The alternator puts out less than half of the current flow at which it is rated. A check of the diodes show shorted diodes, causing a key-off battery drain.
   b. The battery appears to be new and, once charged, passes the capacity test.
   c. The serpentine drive belt appears old, glazed, and excessively cracked.
   d. The starter draw test shows that the starter is drawing the specified amperage; it sounds normal when cranking the engine.
   e. The right front low beam headlamp is burned out.
   f. The battery hold-down is missing.

   > NOTE Ask your instructor whether you should use a copy of the shop repair order or the three Cs below to record this information.

2. Concern/complaint:

3. Cause:

4. Correction:

5. Other recommended service:

6. Have your supervisor/instructor verify satisfactory completion of this procedure, any observations found, and any necessary action(s) recommended.

Performance Rating

0	1	2	3	4

Supervisor/instructor signature _____ Date _____

Battery Diagnosis and Service

Student/Intern information:

Name _____ Date _____ Class _____

Vehicle used for this activity:

Year _____ Make _____ Model_____

Odometer_____VIN_____

Learning Objective/Task	CDX Tasksheet Number	2017 MAST NATEF Reference Number; Priority Level	
• Perform battery state-of-charge test; determine needed action.	C302	6B1; P-1	Time off_____
• Confirm proper battery capacity for vehicle application; perform battery capacity and load test; determine needed action.	C818	6B2; P-1	Time on_____
• Identify electrical/electronic modules, security systems, radios, and other accessories that require reinitialization or code entry after reconnecting the vehicle battery.	C645	6B8; P-1	Total time_____
• Maintain or restore electronic memory functions.	C304	6B3; P-1	
• Inspect and clean battery; fill battery cells; check battery cables, connectors, clamps, and hold-downs.	C644	6B4; P-1	
• Perform slow/fast battery charge according to manufacturer's recommendations.	C819	6B5; P-1	
• Jump-start vehicle using jumper cables and a booster battery or an auxiliary power supply.	C820	6B6; P-1	
• Diagnose the cause(s) of excessive key-off battery drain (parasitic draw); determine needed action.	C817	6A8; P-1	
• Chesney Parasitic Load test	N/A	N/A	

Materials Required

- Battery (assigned by your supervisor)
- Hydrometer and/or DMM
- Protective gloves and apron
- Battery load tester
- Memory minder or jump box with 12V cigarette lighter adapter or DLC connector
- Baking soda and water or commercially available battery cleaner
- Battery terminal cleaner
- Battery brush
- Battery charger
- Auxiliary power supply/jump box or jumper cables

Some Safety Issues to Consider

- Be cautious around electricity. High voltage (enough to injure or kill you) is present on many vehicles. Ignition systems, hybrid vehicles, and 42-volt electrical systems are just a few hazards to be careful of.
- Accidental deployment of the airbag system could happen if you inadvertently probe the wrong wire. Most manufacturers use yellow-colored wiring to denote wiring for the airbag system. Always be aware of the system/circuit you are working on.
- Use extreme caution when working around batteries. Immediately remove any electrolyte that may come into contact with you. Electrolyte is a mixture of sulfuric acid and water. Please consult with the shop safety and emergency procedures when working with or around batteries.
- Batteries give off hydrogen gas during charging and discharging. Never use an open flame, torch or grinder near a battery.
- Comply with personal and environmental safety practices associated with clothing; eye protection; hand tools; power equipment; proper ventilation; and the handling, storage, and disposal of chemicals/materials in accordance with local, state, and federal safety and environmental regulations.

Performance Standard

0—No exposure: No information or practice provided during the program; complete training required

1—Exposure only: General information provided with no practice time; close supervision needed; additional training required

2—Limited practice: Has practiced job during training program; additional training required to develop skill

3—Moderately skilled: Has performed job independently during training program; limited additional training may be required

4—Skilled: Can perform job independently with no additional training

DX Tasksheet Number: C302

1. **Research the following specifications for this vehicle in the appropriate service information.**

    a. **Specified battery capacity: _____ cold cranking amps (CCA)**
    b. **Group size, if specified: _____ BCI group**

    NOTE Check with your supervisor/instructor which of the following tests you are to perform, or whether you should perform all of them.

2. **Perform a Specific Gravity Test. The battery must have removable vent caps.**

    a. **Locate and review the "Specific Gravity State of Charge Test" in the appropriate service information.**
    b. **Clean the top of the battery.**

    NOTE This must be done prior to the removal of the vent caps.

    c. **Remove the vent caps.**
    d. **Verify that the electrolyte level is high enough above the cells to fill the hydrometer.**
    e. **Draw enough electrolyte from a cell so the float is suspended. Determine the specific gravity reading and return the electrolyte into the cell. Repeat this for each cell and record your readings below. Be sure to compensate for temperature if you are using a hydrometer that is not automatically temperature compensated.**

    Cell #1: _____
    Cell #2: _____
    Cell #3: _____
    Cell #4: _____
    Cell #5: _____
    Cell #6: _____

    f. **Calculate the maximum difference between the cell readings: _____**
    g. **What is the maximum allowable difference in cell readings: _____**
    h. **Compare the readings to the information in the service information, and list the state of charge: _____ %**
    i. **Clean the hydrometer and tools.**

3. **Perform an Open Circuit Voltage Test. This test is for maintenance-free or non-vented batteries.**

    a. **Locate and review the "Open Circuit Voltage Test" in the service Information.**
    b. **Make sure the engine is off and the battery is stabilized. If the battery has just been recharged, you must remove the surface charge. Wait at least 5 minutes after removing the surface charge before measuring the open circuit voltage. Please follow the manufacturer's recommendations closely.**

c. Prepare the digital multimeter (DMM) to measure voltage.

d. Place the red lead on the positive post/terminal and the black lead on the negative post/terminal.

e. What is the measured voltage (open-circuit voltage) of the battery? _____ volts

f. The table below represents the open-circuit voltage of the battery. Please select the battery's percent of charge as it relates to the voltage measured.

Voltage	Percent Charge
12.6 or greater	100
12.4–12.6	75–100
12.2–12.4	50–75
12.0–12.2	25–50
11.7–12.0	0–25
0.0–11.7	0; no charge

4. Perform a Conductance Test.

a. Review the process for performing a battery conductance test.

b. Connect the conductance tester to the battery terminals (some testers require the removal of the battery cable for accuracy).

c. Follow the prompts on the conductance tester for the type and CCAs of the battery being tested.

d. Start the conductance test.

e. List the state of charge (usually a % of charge): _____ %

f. Record the available CCAs listed on the conductance tester: _____

5. Determine any necessary action(s):

6. Have your supervisor/instructor verify satisfactory completion of this procedure, any observations found, and any necessary action(s) recommended.

Performance Rating

CDX Tasksheet Number: C302

0	1	2	3	4

Supervisor/instructor signature _____ Date _____

Confirm proper battery capacity for vehicle application;
perform battery capacity and load test; determine needed action.

MAST
6B2

CDX Tasksheet Number: C818

> **NOTE** The battery capacity test is also known as a load test or battery performance test. Follow all directions of the manufacturer whose tool you are using to load test the battery.

1. **Research the specifications and procedures for testing the battery in the appropriate service information.**

    a. **What is the specified battery capacity for the vehicle you are working on?**
    _____ **CCA**

    b. **What type of battery is specified for this battery?**
    Flooded cell: _____ **AGM:** _____ **Other (list):** _____

2. **Inspect the battery and find its listed capacity rating:** _____

3. **Does this battery meet the specified CCA requirements for this vehicle?**
Yes: _____ **No:** _____

4. **Determine the following load test variables for this battery:**

    a. **Required load test amps:** _____ **amps**

    b. **Required load test time (some testers are automatic):**
    _____ **seconds**

5. **Connect the load tester as directed by the equipment manufacturer. Make sure the tester clamps are secure on the battery terminals, and the inductive amps clamp is around the proper cable.**

6. **Load-test the battery. What was the battery minimum voltage (at the end of the load test time)?** _____ **volts**

7. **Did the battery pass the load test? Yes:** _____ **No:** _____

8. **If a battery fails the load test, what should be done next?**

9. **Determine any necessary action(s):**

10. Have your supervisor/instructor verify satisfactory completion of this procedure, any observations found, and any necessary action(s) recommended.

Performance Rating

CDX Tasksheet Number: C818

0	1	2	3	4

Supervisor/instructor signature _____ Date _____

MAST
6B8

Time off_____

Time on_____

Total time_____

CDX Tasksheet Number: C645

1. **Research the components that require reinitialization or code entry on the vehicle you are working on after reconnecting the battery. List those components here:**

2. **List the correct process for reinitialization or code entry for each of the components listed above:**

3. **Have your supervisor/instructor verify satisfactory completion of this procedure, any observations found, and any necessary action(s) recommended.**

Performance Rating

CDX Tasksheet Number: C645

0	1	2	3	4

Supervisor/instructor signature _____ Date _____

▶ TASK   Maintain or restore electronic memory functions.

MAST
6B3

Time off_____

Time on_____

Total time_____

DX Tasksheet Number: C304

1. Research the maintaining or restoring of electronic memory functions for this vehicle in the appropriate service information. Please follow all directions, and note that some vehicle electronic devices REQUIRE specific codes for reinitialization. If you don't have those codes available, do NOT disconnect the battery.

> NOTE Some manufacturers require the use of tools that help maintain memories, such as radios, adaptive strategies, etc. The use of these tools can minimize down time in restoring electronic memories lost when a battery is disconnected. In some cases, the use of a "memory minder," which is basically a battery that plugs into the 12V accessory socket or the data link connector, can be utilized. In all cases, follow the manufacturer's instructions.

2. Restore electronic memory functions.

   a. Change the vehicle's radio pre-set frequencies of the FM (1) stations and list those resets here:

   1. _____ 2. _____ 3. _____ 4. _____

   b. With NO memory minder installed, disconnect the negative battery terminal for at least 15 seconds.

   c. Reconnect the negative battery terminal, and tighten properly.

   d. Check the radio pre-sets. Did they change? Yes: _____ No: _____

   i. Why or why not?

   e. Restore the frequencies, as per manufacturer recommendations, to the stations noted in step 2a.

   f. What would you have to do to restore the vehicle's PCM adaptive learning memory if it is erased?

3. Maintain the electronic memory functions

   a. Reset the radio pre-sets to the same stations you did before.

   b. Install a memory minder to maintain electrical power in the system.

   c. Disconnect the negative battery terminal for at least 1 minute.

   d. Check the radio pre-sets. Did they change? Yes: _____ No: _____

   i. Why or why not?

e. Under this scenario, what happens to the vehicle's PCM adaptive learning memory if the battery is disconnected?

4. What did you learn?

5. Have your supervisor/instructor verify satisfactory completion of this procedure, any observations found, and any necessary action(s) recommended.

Performance Rating

CDX Tasksheet Number: C304

0	1	2	3	4

Supervisor/instructor signature _____ Date _____

Inspect and clean battery; fill battery cells; check battery cables, connectors, clamps, and hold-downs.

MAST
6B4

Time off_____

Time on_____

Total time_____

CDX Tasksheet Number: C644

1. **On the vehicle that was assigned to you by your supervisor/instructor, and following all steps listed in the service information, disconnect the negative battery terminal and move it out of the way so it cannot touch the terminal, or spring back against it. (Consider using a memory minder.)**

2. **Disconnect the positive battery terminal and move it out of the way. Place a glove or other insulating material over the end of the battery cable to prevent shorting out the memory minder.**

3. **Remove the battery hold-down so that the battery is sitting in the battery tray or box.**

4. **Remove the battery from the battery tray.**

5. **Inspect the battery hold-down hardware and the battery tray. List your observations:**

6. **Clean the battery, battery terminals, battery tray, and hold-down hardware with a suitable cleaner or by mixing baking soda and water.**

   NOTE The consistency of the baking soda and water should be like a thin paste. The use of a small brush will help the cleaning process.

7. **Rinse the components with lots of clean water. Wipe the components dry with some paper towels.**

   NOTE DO NOT USE COMPRESSED AIR! It can blow acid around.

8. **Clean the battery terminals and posts with a battery terminal cleaner.**

9. **Check the battery electrolyte level. This can be done only on non-maintenance-free batteries. If the level is low, add only distilled water to the proper level.**

   a. **Have your supervisor/instructor check your work. Supervisor's/ instructor's initials: _____**

10. **Install the battery and hold-down hardware, and reconnect the cables as outlined in the service information.**

11. **Install a battery terminal protective spray onto the battery terminals.**

12. **Determine any necessary action(s):**

13. Have your supervisor/instructor verify satisfactory completion of this procedure, any observations found, and any necessary action(s) recommended.

Performance Rating

CDX Tasksheet Number: C644

0	1	2	3	4

Supervisor/instructor signature _____ Date _____

Perform slow/fast battery charge according to manufacturer's recommendations.

CDX Tasksheet Number: C819

> **NOTE** Recharging a battery differs from manufacturer to manufacturer. It is important that you follow the recharging steps recommended by the manufacturer of the battery that is assigned to you.

1. **Research slow and/or fast battery charging for this vehicle battery in the appropriate service information. Follow all directions. If no directions are given, use the following information:**

   It is best to disconnect the negative battery terminal when charging a battery. Consider using a memory minder to maintain the memories on electronic control modules.

   The ideal rate for charging a battery can be found by dividing the battery's CCA by 70.

   To find the maximum charging rate for fast charging a battery, divide the battery's CCA by 40.

   The faster a battery is charged, the shorter its life.

   Do not exceed: 15.5V on a flooded cell battery; 14.8V on an AGM battery; or 14.3V on a gel cell battery.

2. **List the steps for recharging this battery:**

3. **What method is recommended for recharging the battery?**
   Slow charge: _____ Fast charge: _____

   a. **Have your supervisor/instructor verify the steps above. Supervisor's/instructor's initials:** _____

4. **Charge the battery according to the manufacturer's recommendations.**
   a. **How long did the battery charge?** _____ time
   b. **What was the highest amperage reading during charging?** _____ amps
   c. **What was the lowest amperage reading during charging?** _____ amps
   d. **What was the highest voltage during charging?** _____ volts
   e. **How did you determine the battery was fully charged?**

5. **Determine any necessary action(s):**

6. Have your supervisor/instructor verify satisfactory completion of this procedure, any observations found, and any necessary action(s) recommended.

Jump-start vehicle using jumper cables and a booster battery or an auxiliary power supply.

MAST
6B6

Time off_____

Time on_____

Total time_____

CDX Tasksheet Number: C820

1. **Research "starting a vehicle with a dead battery" or "jump starting procedures" in the appropriate service information for the vehicle you are working on. List the steps as outlined in the service information.**

> **NOTE** Caution: Some vehicle manufacturers prohibit jump-starting of their vehicles. If this is the case, inform your supervisor/instructor.

> **NOTE** Follow these steps exactly!

2. **Why is the last connection away from the battery, preferably on an unpainted solid metal component connected to the engine block?**

3. **Have your supervisor/instructor verify your answers. Supervisor's/instructor's initials: _____**

4. **Connect the jumper cables as outlined in the service information or connect the auxiliary power supply (jump box) as was outlined in the service information.**

5. **Start the engine.**

6. **Remove the cables in the reverse order as they were installed.**

7. **Have your supervisor/instructor verify satisfactory completion of this procedure, any observations found, and any necessary action(s) recommended.**

Performance Rating

CDX Tasksheet Number: C820

0	1	2	3	4

Supervisor/instructor signature _____ Date _____

Diagnose the cause(s) of excessive key-off battery drain (parasitic draw); determine needed action.

MAST
6A8

CDX Tasksheet Number: C817

> **NOTE** Be sure to follow the correct steps for connecting your DMM to check for amperage/current flow. Have your supervisor/instructor check your connections. Improper connection of the DMM may damage your meter.

1. **Research key-off battery drain (parasitic drain) checks in the appropriate service information.**

    a. **List the maximum allowable key-off battery drain (parasitic drain) for the vehicle/simulator that has been assigned to you. What is the maximum allowable drain? _____ mA**

    b. **What is the specified time for the last module to go to sleep? _____ sec/min**

2. **List the appropriate steps to measure the key-off battery drain (parasitic drain):**

3. **Using the steps listed, measure the key off battery drain (parasitic drain):**

    a. **What is the actual drain? _____ mA**

    b. **Is this reading within specifications? Yes: _____ No: _____**

        i. **If no, identify the faulty circuit by pulling and replacing fuses one at a time. Watch the amps reading on the meter to see if it drops. If it drops substantially, you will want to investigate that circuit further, by disconnecting the loads and tracing the wires.**

4. **If pulling the fuses does not identify the faulty circuit, disconnect unfused wires one at a time, such as the alternator output wire and the ignition switch feed wire.**

5. **List the steps you took to diagnose the cause of the parasitic draw and their results:**

6. **Determine any necessary action(s):**

7. **What would the customer concern be that would require you to perform this test?**

8. **Have your supervisor/instructor verify satisfactory completion of this procedure any observations found, and any necessary action(s) recommended.**

CDX Tasksheet Number: N/A

1. Determine what the impedance of the DMM is. List the impedance:
    _____ megohms (meter impedance)

2. Set the DMM to ohms and touch the leads together. This is the delta reading.
    List the reading: _____ ohms (Delta)

    Note: if the meter has a delta adjustment feature, press it so that the meter
    reads 0 ohms when the leads are touching. You won't have to worry about the
    delta reading in this case.

3. With the car off, and all doors closed, wait 30 seconds and then place the
    ohmmeter's black lead on the negative battery terminal and the red lead on the
    alternator case.

4. Read the ohmmeter and subtract the delta reading given previously. List the
    reading: _____ ohms (minus delta reading)

5. Compare this reading to the Chesney Parasitic Load Test graph. Approximately
    how many amps are draining? _____ mA

6. Is the reading within specifications?
    Yes: _____ No: _____

7. Open the driver's door and insure at least one dome light is on.

8. Place the black ohmmeter lead on the battery negative and the red lead on the
    alternator case.

9. Read the ohmmeter and subtract the delta reading given previously. List the reading: _____ ohms (minus delta reading)

10. Compare this reading to the Chesney Parasitic Load Test graph. Approximately how many amps are draining? _____ mA

11. Have your supervisor/instructor verify satisfactory completion of this procedure, any observations found, and any necessary action(s) recommended

Performance Rating

CDX Tasksheet Number: N/A

0	1	2	3	4

Supervisor/instructor signature _____ Date _____

Starting System Diagnosis and Repair

Student/Intern information:

Name _____ Date _____ Class _____

Vehicle used for this activity:

Year _____ Make _____ Model_____

Odometer_____VIN _____

Learning Objective/Task	CDX Tasksheet Number	2017 MAST NATEF Reference Number; Priority Level
• Perform starter current draw tests; determine needed action.	C309	6C1; P-1
• Perform starter circuit voltage drop tests; determine needed action.	C310	6C2; P-1
• Inspect and test switches, connectors, and wires of starter control circuits; determine needed action.	C313	6C5; P-2
• Inspect and test starter relays and solenoids; determine needed action.	C311	6C3; P-2
• Remove and install starter in a vehicle.	C312	6C4; P-1
• Differentiate between electrical and engine mechanical problems that cause a slow-crank or no-crank condition.	C314	6C6; P-2
• Demonstrate knowledge of an automatic idle-stop/start-stop system.	C1002	6C7; P-2

Time off_____

Time on_____

Total time_____

Materials Required

- Vehicle or simulator
- Starting and/or charging system tester
- Digital multimeter (DMM)
- Test light
- Fused jumper wire(s)
- Floor jack and stands or vehicle hoist (preferred)

Some Safety Issues to Consider

- Be cautious around electricity. High voltage (enough to injure or kill you) is present on many vehicles. Ignition systems, hybrid vehicles, and 42-volt electrical systems are just a few hazards to be careful of.
- Accidental deployment of the airbag system could happen if you inadvertently probe the wrong wire. Most manufacturers use yellow-colored wiring to denote wiring for the airbag system. Always be aware of the system/circuit you are working on.
- Use extreme caution when working around batteries. Immediately remove any electrolyte that may come into contact with you. Electrolyte is a mixture of sulfuric acid and water. Please consult with the shop safety and emergency procedures when working with or around batteries.
- Never exceed 16 volts when charging a 12-volt battery. Overheating and explosion hazards are greatly increased.

- Disconnect the battery before using wrenches or sockets to remove wires from the starter or solenoid to prevent short circuits and fires.
- Starter motors are heavy, always use another person to hold the starter while it is being removed and installed.
- Be careful when cranking engines while working under the hood. Keep away from moving belts, pulleys, and other parts.
- Comply with personal and environmental safety practices associated with clothing; eye protection; hand tools; power equipment; proper ventilation; and the handling, storage, and disposal of chemicals/materials in accordance with local, state, and federal safety and environmental regulations.

Performance Standard

0—No exposure: No information or practice provided during the program; complete training required

1—Exposure only: General information provided with no practice time; close supervision needed; additional training required

2—Limited practice: Has practiced job during training program; additional training required to develop skill

3—Moderately skilled: Has performed job independently during training program; limited additional training may be required

4—Skilled: Can perform job independently with no additional training

CDX Tasksheet Number: C309

1. **Research the specifications and procedures for performing starting system tests and repairs.**

    a. **List the starter current draw specs:** _____ **amps at** _____ **volts (if listed)**

2. **Connect the starting system tester as outlined in the appropriate service information.**

3. **This test will require either the fuel system or ignition system to be disabled. Please follow the manufacturer's recommendations for disabling one of these two systems.**

4. **Identify below which system was disabled and the steps you took to do this:**

5. **Have your supervisor/instructor check your connections and how you disabled the fuel or ignition system(s).**

    a. **Supervisor's/instructor's initials:** _____

6. **Conduct the Starter Current Draw Test.**

    a. **What was the current draw during the first second or two?** _____ **amps**

    b. **What was the final current draw (after three or four seconds)?** _____ **amps**

    c. **What was the lowest voltage during the test?** _____ **volts**

7. **Compare your results to the manufacturer's specifications. List your observations:**

8. **Determine any necessary action(s):**

9. Have your supervisor/instructor verify satisfactory completion of this procedure, any observations found, and any necessary action(s) recommended.

Performance Rating

CDX Tasksheet Number: C309

0	1	2	3	4

Supervisor/instructor signature _____ Date _____

Perform starter circuit voltage drop tests; determine
   needed action.

MAST
6C2

CDX Tasksheet Number: C310

1. Research the specifications and procedures for performing the starter circuit voltage drop tests in the appropriate service informaation.

   a. What is the maximum starter circuit (high current cables) voltage drop specification(s) for this test?

      i. Positive side: _____ volts

      ii. Negative (ground) side, if specified: _____ volts

2. Disable the vehicle's fuel or ignition system so it will not start.

3. Conduct the Starter Circuit Voltage Drop Test–Positive/Feed Side (heavy positive battery cable, not the control circuit).

   a. List the voltmeter connection points in the circuit:

      DMM black lead: _____

      DMM red lead: _____

   b. Conduct the Starter Circuit Voltage Drop Test:

      What is the voltage drop on the positive side? _____ volts

      Is this reading within specifications? Yes: _____ No: _____

4. Conduct the Starter Circuit Voltage Drop Test–Ground Side.

   a. List the voltmeter connection points in the circuit:

      DMM black lead: _____

      DMM red lead: _____

   b. Conduct the Starter Circuit Voltage Drop Test:

      What is the voltage drop on the negative side? _____ volts

      Is this reading within specifications? Yes: _____ No: _____

5. Determine any necessary action(s):

6. Have your supervisor/instructor verify satisfactory completion of this procedure, any observations found, and any necessary action(s) recommended.

Performance Rating

CDX Tasksheet Number: C310

0	1	2	3	4

Supervisor/instructor signature _____ Date _____

Inspect and test switches, connectors, and wires of
starter control circuits; determine needed action.

Time off_____

Time on_____

Total time_____

CDX Tasksheet Number: C313

1. **Refering to the appropriate service information, draw a diagram of the starter control circuit (small wires) from battery positive terminal to the starter. On the diagram, list the components the current goes through to get to the starter.**

   a. **List the maximum specified voltage drop across the starter relay/solenoid contacts: _____ volts**

2. **Write a short description of how the starter control circuit operates to enable the starter to crank the engine:**

3. **Disable the vehicle's fuel or ignition system so it will not start.**

4. **Conduct the Starter Control Circuit Voltage Drop Test—Positive Side.**

   a. **List the voltmeter connection points in the circuit:**

   DMM black lead: _____

   DMM red lead: _____

   b. **Conduct the Starter Control Circuit Voltage Drop Test:**

   What is the voltage drop on the positive side? _____ volts

   Is this reading within specifications? Yes: _____ No: _____

   i. **If no, refer to the service information for further tests. List those tests and their results:**

5. **Determine any necessary action(s):**

6. Have your supervisor/instructor verify satisfactory completion of this procedure, any observations found, and any necessary action(s) recommended.

Performance Rating

| 0 | 1 | 2 | 3 | 4 |

Supervisor/instructor signature _____ Date _____

Inspect and test starter relays and solenoids;
determine needed action.

MAST
6C3

Time off_____

Time on_____

Total time_____

CDX Tasksheet Number: C311

1. **Research the procedure and specifications for testing starter relays and solenoids in the appropriate service information.**

    a. **What is this vehicle's starting system equipped with?**
       Starter Solenoid _____ ; Starter Relay _____ ; Both _____
    b. **List the resistance of the starter solenoid windings: Pull in: _____ ohms; hold in: _____ ohms**
    c. **List the specified resistance of the starter relay winding: _____ ohms**

2. **Disable the vehicle's fuel or ignition system so it will not start.**

3. **Following the manufacturer's test procedure, list the voltmeter connection points in the circuit to test the voltage drop across the relay or solenoid contacts.**

    a. **DMM red lead: _____**
    b. **DMM black lead: _____**

4. **Conduct the Starter Relay/Solenoid Voltage Drop Test.**

    a. **List the voltage drop: _____ volts**
    b. **Is this reading within specifications? Yes: _____ No: _____**

5. **Measure the resistance of the starter solenoid windings:**

    a. **Pull in: _____ ohms**
    b. **Hold in: _____ ohms**

6. **Measure the resistance of the starter relay winding: _____ ohms**

7. **Determine any necessary actions:**

8. **Have your supervisor/instructor verify satisfactory completion of this procedure, any observations found, and any necessary action(s) recommended.**

Performance Rating

CDX Tasksheet Number: C311

0	1	2	3	4

Supervisor/instructor signature _____ Date _____

Remove and install starter in a vehicle.

Time off_____

Time on_____

Total time_____

CDX Tasksheet Number: C312

1. **Research the procedure and specifications for removing and installing the starter in the appropriate service information.**

   a. **List the specified starter mounting bolt torque:** _____ **ft-lb/N·m**
   b. **List the first step that should be performed prior to lifting the vehicle to remove the starter:**

2. **Remove the starter following the manufacturer's procedure.**

   a. **Have your supervisor/instructor verify the starter removal. Supervisor's/instructor's initials:** _____

3. **Inspect the gear teeth on the flywheel ring gear all the way around by turning the crankshaft by hand (ignition key "Off"). List your observations:**

4. **Install the starter following the manufacturer's procedures.**

5. **Restore the fuel system/ignition system to its proper operating condition. Start the vehicle and verify proper vehicle operation.**

6. **Have your supervisor/instructor verify satisfactory completion of this procedure, any observations found, and any necessary action(s) recommended.**

Performance Rating

CDX Tasksheet Number: C312

0	1	2	3	4

Supervisor/instructor signature _____ Date _____

Differentiate between electrical and engine mechanical
problems that cause a slow-crank or no-crank condition.

MAST
6C6

CDX Tasksheet Number: C314

Vehicle used for this activity:

Year _____ Make _____ Model_____

Odometer_____ VIN_____

1. **Locate a no-crank or slow-crank starting system symptom chart in the appropriate service information for the vehicle you are working on.**

   a. **Research the repair procedures for the condition of the vehicle, as outlined in the service information, for the vehicle assigned to you.**

2. **Most vehicles can be tested using the following procedure to determine whether the vehicle is experiencing an electrical or mechanical problem: Turn on the headlights and try to start the engine while listening to the starter and watching the headlights. Place a check mark next to the condition below that happened during this test.**

   a. **No starter noises and the headlights stayed at the same intensity:** _____

   > NOTE This fault is likely an electrical fault in the starter itself or the control circuit to the starter.

   b. **Loud single click when the key is turned to "crank" and headlights don't dim, or only dim slightly** _____.

   > NOTE This fault is likely an electrical fault caused by solenoid contacts or starter motor brushes that are excessively worn.

   c. **Loud repeated clicking "machine guns" when the key is turned to "crank":** _____

   > NOTE This fault is likely an electrical fault that may be caused by high resistance in the starter feed cable, a short circuit in the main starter feed cable after the starter relay, or the hold-in windings in the solenoid are open.

   d. **The starter engages and tries to crank, or cranks the engine slowly and the headlights went substantially dim:**

   > NOTE This fault could be an electrical fault or a mechanical fault. It may be caused by a discharged or weak battery, a shorted or dragging starter motor, or an engine that is mechanically bound up, such as from a hydro-locked cylinder, spun main bearing, or seized accessory drive on the engine. Turn the engine over by hand to determine if It is caused by a mechanical condition.

e. The engine cranks substantially faster than normal:

> **NOTE** This fault is likely a mechanical fault caused by low compression due to a broken or slipped timing belt/chain, bent valves, or piston rings that are not sealing.

3. **Diagnose the problem based on these conditions. List the steps you took to diagnose the problem and the results you obtained:**

4. **Determine any necessary actions:**

5. **Have your supervisor/instructor verify satisfactory completion of this procedure, any observations found, and any necessary action(s) recommended.**

Performance Rating

CDX Tasksheet Number: C314

0	1	2	3	4
☐	☐	☐	☐	☐

Supervisor/instructor signature _____ Date _____

Demonstrate knowledge of an automatic
idle-stop/start-stop system.

MAST
6C7

Time off_____

Time on_____

Total time_____

CDX Tasksheet Number: C1002

1. **Research the description and operation of the automatic idle-stop/start-stop system. Describe in your own words how the automatic idle-stop/start-stop system operates:**

2. **Briefly describe the purpose of the automatic idle-stop/start-stop system:**

3. **Write a short description of the different types of idle-stop/start-stop systems used:**

4. **Have your supervisor/instructor verify satisfactory completion of your answers in steps 1-3.**

Performance Rating

CDX Tasksheet Number: C1002

0	1	2	3	4

Supervisor/instructor signature _____ Date _____

Charging System Diagnosis and Repair

Student/Intern information:

Name _____ Date _____ Class _____

Vehicle used for this activity:

Year _____ Make _____ Model _____

Odometer _____ VIN _____

Learning Objective/Task	CDX Tasksheet Number	2017 MAST NATEF Reference Number; Priority Level
• Inspect, adjust, and/or replace generator (alternator) drive belts; check pulleys and tensioners for wear; check pulley and belt alignment.	C317	6D3; P-1
• Perform charging system output test; determine needed action.	C315	6D1; P-1
• Perform charging circuit voltage drop tests; determine needed action.	C319	6D5; P-1
• Remove, inspect, and/or replace generator (alternator).	C318	6D4; P-1
• Diagnose (troubleshoot) charging system for the cause of undercharge, no-charge, and overcharge conditions.	C316	6D2; P-1

Time off _____

Time on _____

Total time _____

Materials Required

- Vehicle/simulator
- Belt tension measuring device
- Charging system tester
- Tachometer, either hand-held or the vehicle's tachometer, if equipped
- Digital voltmeter
- Exhaust hose(s) and wheel chocks

Some Safety Issues to Consider

- If you need to start the vehicle, you should ensure that the parking brake is firmly applied; if necessary, use wheel chocks to prevent the vehicle from moving when the vehicle is started to verify the completion of these tasks.
- When running any vehicles in the shop, make sure you use the shop's exhaust ventilation system to discharge all exhaust gas safely outside.
- Only students who have their supervisor's/instructor's direct permission should perform this task due to the safety concerns involved.
- Diagnosis of this fault may require test-driving the vehicle on the school grounds or on a hoist, both of which carry severe risks. Attempt this task only with full permission from your supervisor/instructor and follow all the guidelines exactly.
- Use extreme caution when working around batteries. Immediately remove any electrolyte that may come into contact with you. Electrolyte is a mixture of sulfuric acid and water. Please consult with the shop safety and emergency procedures when working with or around batteries.

- Never exceed 16 volts when charging a 12-volt battery. Overheating and explosion hazards are greatly increased.
- Be cautious around electricity. High voltage (enough to injure or kill you) is present on many vehicles. Ignition systems, hybrid vehicles, and 42-volt electrical systems are just a few hazards to be careful of.
- Accidental deployment of the airbag system could happen if you inadvertently probe the wrong wire. Most manufacturers use yellow-colored wiring to denote wiring for the airbag system. Always be aware of the system/circuit you are working on.
- Comply with personal and environmental safety practices associated with clothing; eye protection; hand tools; power equipment; proper ventilation; and the handling, storage, and disposal of chemicals/materials in accordance with local, state, and federal safety and environmental regulations.

Performance Standard

0—No exposure: No information or practice provided during the program; complete training required

1—Exposure only: General information provided with no practice time; close supervision needed; additional training required

2—Limited practice: Has practiced job during training program; additional training required to develop skill

3—Moderately skilled: Has performed job independently during training program; limited additional training may be required

4—Skilled: Can perform job independently with no additional training

▶ TASK Inspect, adjust, and/or replace generator (alternator) drive belts; check pulleys and tensioners for wear; check pulley and belt alignment.

MAST
6D3

Time off_____

Time on_____

Total time_____

CDX Tasksheet Number: C317

1. Locate "inspecting, adjusting, and/or replacing generator (alternator) drive belts, pulleys, and tensioners; check pulley and belt alignment" in the appropriate service information for the vehicle you are working on.

    a. List the specified generator (alternator) drive belt tension:
    _____

    b. List the faults to look for when inspecting drive belts, pulleys, and tensioners:

    c. Describe how to check correct pulley and belt alignment:

    d. Locate the belt routing diagram or draw a picture of the current routing arrangement.

2. Install the fender covers.

3. Remove the vehicle drive belt(s).

4. Inspect the vehicle drive belts, pulleys, and tensioners for faults. List your observations for the following:

    a. Vehicle drive belt(s):

    b. Pulleys:

    c. Tensioners:

d. Pulley/belt alignment:

5. Have your instructor verify removal of belt(s) and faults found:

_____

6. Reinstall the vehicle drive belts using the appropriate service information.

7. Re-tension the drive belt(s) using the appropriate service information.

8. Check for correct pulley, tensioner, and drive belt alignment.

9. Have your supervisor/instructor verify satisfactory completion of this procedure, any observations found, and any necessary action(s) recommended.

Performance Rating

CDX Tasksheet Number: C317

0   1   2   3   4

Supervisor/instructor signature _____ Date _____

Perform charging system output test; determine needed action.

MAST
6D1

CDX Tasksheet Number: C315

1. Research "performing a charging system output test" in the appropriate service information for the vehicle you are working on. What is the specified charging system output? _____ amps at _____ volts at _____ rpm

2. Install the fender covers, exhaust hose(s), and wheel chocks, and set the parking brake.

3. Connect the charging system tester as outlined in the appropriate service information.

    a. Heavy red lead to the battery positive terminal
    b. Heavy black lead to the battery negative terminal
    c. Green/Black amps clamp around alternator output wire (facing the correct direction)

4. Have your supervisor/instructor verify your test procedure and connections. Supervisor's/instructor's initials: _____

5. Conduct the charging system output test. List the measured results at the maximum output: _____ amps at _____ volts at _____ engine rpm

6. Compare your results to the manufacturer's specifications. List your observations:

7. Determine any necessary action(s):

8. Have your supervisor/instructor verify satisfactory completion of this procedure, any observations found, and any necessary action(s) recommended.

Performance Rating

CDX Tasksheet Number: C315

0	1	2	3	4

Supervisor/instructor signature _____ Date _____

Perform charging circuit voltage drop tests;
determine needed action.

Time off_____

Time on_____

Total time_____

CDX Tasksheet Number: C319

1. Research the procedure and specifications for performing the charging circuit voltage drop tests in the appropriate service information.

    a. List the maximum allowable voltage drop (generator output terminal to battery positive post): _____ volts

    b. List the maximum allowable voltage drop (generator housing to battery negative post): _____ volts

2. Install the fender covers, exhaust hose(s), and wheel chocks, and set the parking brake.

3. Connect the DMM as outlined in the appropriate service information.

    a. List the points that each voltmeter test lead should be connected to, to test the voltage drop between the output terminal of the alternator and the positive post of the battery:

       i. DMM black lead: _____

       ii. DMM red lead: _____

    b. List the points that each voltmeter test lead should be connected to, to test the voltage drop between the housing of the alternator and the negative post of the battery:

       i. DMM black lead: _____

       ii. DMM red lead: _____

4. Have your supervisor/instructor verify your test procedure and connections. Supervisor's/instructor's initials: _____

5. Conduct the charging system voltage drop test. List the measured results:

    a. Voltage drop between the alternator output terminal and battery positive post is: _____ V at: _____ A

    b. Voltage drop between the alternator housing and battery negative post is: _____ V at: _____ A

6. Compare your results to the manufacturer's specifications. List your observations:

7. Determine any necessary action(s):

8. Have your supervisor/instructor verify satisfactory completion of this procedure, any observations found, and any necessary action(s) recommended.

Performance Rating

CDX Tasksheet Number: C319

0	1	2	3	4

Supervisor/instructor signature _____ Date _____

Remove, inspect, and/or replace generator (alternator).

MAST
6D4

Time off_____

Time on_____

Total time_____

CDX Tasksheet Number: C318

1. **Research the procedure for removing, inspecting and installing a generator (alternator) in the appropriate service information. List any precautions:**

2. **Disconnect battery negative terminal (consider using a memory minder while doing this task).**

3. **Remove the generator (alternator) as per the service information.**

4. **Inspect the generator (alternator) as per the service procedure. List any faults or defects found:**

   a. **Determine any necessary action(s):**

5. **Have your supervisor/instructor verify removal of generator (alternator). Supervisor's/instructor's initials:** _____

6. **Install the generator (alternator) as per the service information and properly tension the belt(s).**

7. **Start the engine to make sure everything is operating correctly. List your observations:**

8. **Have your supervisor/instructor verify satisfactory completion of this procedure, any observations found, and any necessary action(s) recommended.**

Performance Rating

CDX Tasksheet Number: C318

0	1	2	3	4

Supervisor/instructor signature _____ Date _____

Diagnose (troubleshoot) charging system for the cause of undercharge, no-charge, and overcharge conditions.

MAST
6D2

Time off_____

Time on_____

Total time_____

CDX Tasksheet Number: C316

1. **Research the following specifications in the appropriate service information for the vehicle assigned.**

   > **NOTE** Some charging systems use variable charging modes depending on the conditions present, such as battery temperature, driving condition, etc. Make sure you follow the manufacturer's specified testing procedures when testing these systems.

   a. **Rated output for the alternator being tested:** _____ **amps**
   b. **Regulated voltage:** _____ **volts**
   c. **How is the alternator full fielded on this vehicle?**

2. **Install the exhaust hose(s) and wheel chocks, and set the parking brake.**

3. **Connect the charging system tester as outlined in the appropriate service information.**

4. **Test the maximum current output of the alternator. List reading here:** _____ **amps**

5. **Using the diode/stator setting or AC ripple setting, test the integrity of the diodes and stator. List the results:**

6. **Conduct the charging system regulated voltage test. Do this by measuring the maximum voltage that the charging system achieves while the engine runs at approximately 1500 rpm and waiting until the voltage doesn't rise any further. Do NOT allow the voltage to exceed 16 volts. Regulated voltage:** _____ **V**

7. **Compare your results to the manufacturer's specifications. List your observations:**

8. **Determine any necessary action(s):**

9. Have your supervisor/instructor verify satisfactory completion of this procedure, any observations found, and any necessary action(s) recommended.

Performance Rating

0	1	2	3	4

Supervisor/instructor signature _____ Date _____

Lighting System Diagnosis and Repair

Student/Intern information:

Name _____ Date _____ Class _____

Vehicle used for this activity:

Year _____ Make _____ Model _____

Odometer _____ VIN _____

Learning Objective/Task	CDX Tasksheet Number	2017 MAST NATEF Reference Number; Priority Level
• Identify system voltage and safety precautions associated with high-intensity discharge headlights.	C564	6E4; P-2
• Inspect interior and exterior lamps and sockets including headlights and auxiliary lights (fog lights/driving lights); replace as needed.	C956	6E2; P-1
• Aim headlights.	C321	6E3; P-2
• Diagnose (troubleshoot) the cause of brighter-than-normal, intermittent, dim, or no-light operation; determine needed action.	C320	6E1; P-1

Time off_____

Time on_____

Total time_____

Materials Required

- Vehicle or simulator equipped with HID headlights
- DMM/DVOM
- Test light
- Headlight aligner or approved method

Some Safety Issues to Consider

- Be cautious around electricity. High voltage (enough to injure or kill you) is present on many vehicles. Ignition systems, hybrid vehicles, high-intensity discharge headlights, and 42-volt electrical systems are just a few to be careful of.
- Wear lightweight leather-type gloves when removing small light bulbs as they can shatter, severely cutting fingers and tendons.
- Comply with personal and environmental safety practices associated with clothing; eye protection; hand tools; power equipment; proper ventilation; and the handling, storage, and disposal of chemicals/materials in accordance with local, state, and federal safety and environmental regulations.

Performance Standard

0−No exposure: No information or practice provided during the program; complete training required

1−Exposure only: General information provided with no practice time; close supervision needed; additional training required

2−Limited practice: Has practiced job during training program; additional training required to develop skill

3−Moderately skilled: Has performed job independently during training program; limited additional training may be required

4−Skilled: Can perform job independently with no additional training

Identify system voltage and safety precautions
associated with high-intensity discharge headlights.

MAST
6E4

Time off_____

Time on_____

Total time_____

CDX Tasksheet Number: C564

1. **Using appropriate service information, identify system voltage and safety precautions associated with high-intensity discharge (HID) headlights.**

    a. **HID lamp voltage: _____ volts**
    b. **List the safety precautions required when working on HID system:**

2. **Have your supervisor/instructor verify satisfactory completion of this task.**

Performance Rating

CDX Tasksheet Number: C564

0	1	2	3	4

Supervisor/instructor signature _____ Date _____

TASK Inspect interior and exterior lamps and sockets
including headlights and auxiliary lights
(fog lights/driving lights); replace as needed.

MAST
6E2

Time off_____

Time on_____

Total time_____

CDX Tasksheet Number: C956

1. Inspect the operation of the following interior lights (vehicles have different arrangements, so find as many as possible). List your observations for each light listed:

    a. Dome: _____

    b. Map: _____

    c. Dash: _____

    d. Kick panel: _____

    e. Glove box: _____

    f. Vanity mirror: _____

    g. Rear passenger: _____

    h. Other: _____

2. Inspect the operation of the following exterior lights (vehicles have different arrangements, so find as many as possible):

    a. Rear tail: _____

    b. License: _____

    c. Rear-side marker: _____

    d. Brake: _____

    e. Center high-mount stoplight: _____

    f. Back-up: _____

    g. Front park: _____

    h. Front-side marker: _____

    i. Low beam: _____

    j. High beam: _____

    k. Fog: _____

    l. Driving: _____

    m. Cornering: _____

    n. Clearance: _____

    o. Under-hood: _____

    p. Trunk: _____

    q. Other: _____

3. Ask your instructor which bulbs he/she would like you to remove. List them here:

4. List the name of the light and the bulb number for each bulb you removed:

Electrical/Electronic Systems **803**

5. Inspect/clean the sockets for each bulb you removed.

6. Ask your supervisor/instructor if you should apply dielectric grease to the socket of the bulb you have removed.

7. Reinstall the bulb into the socket and reinstall any other pieces that were removed to gain access to the bulb.

8. Have your supervisor/instructor verify satisfactory completion of this procedure.

Performance Rating

CDX Tasksheet Number: C956

0	1	2	3	4

Supervisor/instructor signature _____ Date _____

MAST
6E3

DX Tasksheet Number: C321

1. **Research the headlamp or exterior lighting section in the appropriate service information for the vehicle you are working on.**

    a. **Type of headlights vehicle is equipped with:** _____

    b. **High-beam bulb number:** _____

    c. **Low-beam bulb number:** _____

2. **Research the headlamp aiming process in the appropriate service information for the vehicle you are working on. List (or print off and attach) the steps that are required to aim these headlamps:**

> **NOTE** Do not touch the bulb with your fingers. Some bulbs will fail prematurely due to the oils from your skin.

3. **Aim the headlamps following the specified procedure.**

4. **List any challenges you had performing this task:**

5. **Have your supervisor/instructor verify satisfactory completion of this procedure.**

Performance Rating

CDX Tasksheet Number: C321

0	1	2	3	4

Supervisor/instructor signature _____ Date _____

Diagnose (troubleshoot) the cause of brighter-than-normal, intermittent, dim, or no-light operation; determine needed action.

MAST
6E1

CDX Tasksheet Number: C320

Vehicle used for this activity:

Year _____ Make _____ Model _____

Odometer _____ VIN _____

1. List the customer complaint/concern regarding the lighting system fault:

2. If the lights are dim or do not operate, go to step 3. If the lights are too bright, go to step 9.

3. Research the affected lighting system troubleshooting section and the wiring diagram(s) in the appropriate service information for the vehicle you are working on.

4. Turn on the affected light(s), measure the battery voltage, and list it here: _____ volts

5. Measure the voltage across the power and ground at the light (light illuminated). List the voltage: _____ volts

   a. Calculate the total voltage drop in the circuit and list it here: _____ volt drop
   b. Is the voltage drop excessive? Yes: _____ No: _____
   c. If yes, go to step 7. If no, go to step 6.

6. Inspect the bulb and connections for any faults (wrong bulb, corroded, or loose connection). List your observations:

7. Measure the voltage drop from the battery positive post to the input terminal of the light.

   a. List the voltage drop: _____ volts
   b. Is this within specifications? Yes: _____ No: _____
   c. Determine any necessary action(s):

8. Measure the voltage drop from the bulb ground to the battery negative post.

    a. List the voltage drop: _____ volts

    b. Is this within specifications? Yes: _____ No: _____

    c. Determine any necessary action(s):

9. Install exhaust hose(s) and wheel chocks, and set the parking brake. Start the vehicle.

10. Measure the charging system voltage at the battery, with the engine running at 1500 rpm: _____ volts

    a. Is this within specification? Yes: _____ No: _____

> **NOTE** If the battery voltage is too high, you will need to perform charging system checks to determine the cause of the overcharge.

11. List your observations:

12. Determine any necessary action(s):

13. Have your supervisor/instructor verify satisfactory completion of this procedure, any observations found, and any necessary action(s) recommended.

Performance Rating

CDX Tasksheet Number: C320

0	1	2	3	4

Supervisor/instructor signature _____ Date _____

Fundamentals

Student/Intern information:

Name _____ Date _____ Class _____

Vehicle used for this activity:

Year _____ Make _____ Model_____

Odometer_____VIN_____

Learning Objective/Task	CDX Tasksheet Number	2017 MAST NATEF Reference Number; Priority Level
• Use wiring diagrams during the diagnosis (troubleshooting) of electrical/electronic circuit problems.	C952	6A7; P-1
• Demonstrate proper use of a digital multimeter (DMM) when measuring source voltage, voltage drop (including grounds), current flow, and resistance.	C641	6A3; P-1
• Demonstrate proper use of a test light on an electrical circuit.	C291	6A5; P-1
• Use fused jumper wires to check operation of electrical circuits.	C295	6A6; P-1
• Inspect and test fusible links, circuit breakers, and fuses; determine needed action.	C298	6A9; P-1
• Demonstrate knowledge of the causes and effects from shorts, grounds, opens, and resistance problems in electrical/electronic circuits.	C296	6A4; P-1
• Check electrical/electronic circuit waveforms; interpret readings and determine needed repairs.	C642	6A11; P-2

Time off_____

Time on_____

Total time_____

Materials Required

- Printed copy of wiring diagram
- Crayons, highlighters, or colored pencils
- Calculator
- Vehicle/simulator with an electrical malfunction present
- DMM/DVOM
- Test light
- Fused jumper wires

Some Safety Issues to Consider

- Comply with personal and environmental safety practices associated with clothing; eye protection; hand tools; power equipment; proper ventilation; and the handling, storage, and disposal of chemicals/materials in accordance with local, state, and federal safety and environmental regulations.

Performance Standard

0—No exposure: No information or practice provided during the program; complete training required

1—Exposure only: General information provided with no practice time; close supervision needed; additional training required

2—Limited practice: Has practiced job during training program; additional training required to develop skill

3—Moderately skilled: Has performed job independently during training program; limited additional training may be required

4—Skilled: Can perform job independently with no additional training

Use wiring diagrams during the diagnosis (troubleshooting) of electrical/electronic circuit problems.

MAST
6A7

Time off_____

Time on_____

CDX Tasksheet Number: C952

Total time_____

> NOTE This task requires diagnosis of an electrical problem. Please ask your instructor/supervisor to assign you a vehicle that qualifies for this task and several that follow.

1. List the customer concern/complaint:

2. Which electrical circuit(s) are involved?

3. How many circuit protection devices are there in this circuit? _____

   a. List the circuit protection devices in this circuit:

   b. List the circuit control devices in this circuit:

   c. Which side of the load(s) is controlled?

4. Diagnose the fault and list each test and its result:

5. Determine any necessary actions:

6. Have your supervisor/instructor verify satisfactory completion of this procedure, any observations found, and any necessary action(s) recommended.

Performance Rating

CDX Tasksheet Number: C952

0	1	2	3	4

Supervisor/instructor signature _____ Date _____

Demonstrate proper use of a digital multimeter
(DMM) when measuring source voltage, voltage drop
(including grounds), current flow, and resistance.

MAST
6A3

Time off_____

Time on_____

CDX Tasksheet Number: C641

Total time_____

> **NOTE** This task is best performed on either the CDX DVOM simulator, a physical
> simulator, or a bugged vehicle.

1. **Ask your instructor what lighting circuit he/she would like you to perform the
   following meter readings on. List circuit here:**

2. **Using the appropriate wiring diagram as a reference and a DMM, determine the
   following:**

   a. **Measured source voltage (at battery):** _____ **volts**
   b. **Measured voltage drop (positive side of circuit):** _____ **volts**
   c. **Measured voltage drop (negative side of circuit):** _____ **volts**
   d. **Measured resistance of light:** _____ **ohms**
   e. **Measured current flow through light:** _____ **amps**

3. **Were any of the readings out of specification? Yes:** _____ **No:** _____

   a. **List your observations:**

4. **Have your supervisor/instructor verify satisfactory completion of this procedure
   and any observations found.**

Performance Rating

CDX Tasksheet Number: C641

0	1	2	3	4

Supervisor/instructor signature _____ Date _____

Demonstrate proper use of a test light on an electrical circuit.

CDX Tasksheet Number: C291

1. **Test for proper operation of the test light by connecting it across the vehicle's battery terminals.**

    a. **Connect the clip end (negative) of the test light to the negative battery terminal.**

    b. **Touch the probe end of the test light to the positive battery terminal. The test light should light.**

    c. **Did the test light operate correctly? Yes: _____ No: _____**

    NOTE Please notify your supervisor/instructor if the test light did not operate correctly.

2. **Using the wiring diagram for the left tail lamp/parking light circuit of the assigned vehicle, identify the wire color for both the power (voltage) and ground (negative) wire.**

    i. **Power (positive): _____**

    ii. **Ground (negative): _____**

3. **Using the appropriate tools, remove the taillight assembly and disconnect the tail lamp connector. The headlamp switch should be set to "Off."**

    a. **Visually locate the power and ground wires, as described in step 2.**

    b. **Turn the headlamp switch to the "Park" position.**

    c. **Connect the clip end of the test light to an unpainted metal surface that is a good ground.**

    d. **Touch the test light probe to the positive wire of the vehicle harness tail lamp connector cavity.**

    i. **Did the test light come on? Yes: _____ No: _____**

    ii. **Please explain your results:**

    e. **With the test light probe still connected to the positive wire, test the ground wire by removing the clip end of the test light and touching it to the ground wire of the tail lamp connector cavity, being careful not to cause a short circuit by touching the clip to the probe. The light should come on if there is a good ground.**

    i. **Did the light come on? Yes: _____ No: _____**

3. **Based on your observations, determine any necessary action(s):**

4. Have your supervisor/instructor verify satisfactory completion of this procedure, any observations found, and any necessary action(s) recommended.

Performance Rating

0	1	2	3	4

Supervisor/instructor signature _____ Date _____

▶ TASK   Use fused jumper wires to check operation of electrical circuits.

MAST
6A6

CDX Tasksheet Number: C295

> **NOTE** Using a jumper wire to bypass components can cause damage if performed incorrectly. Never bypass the load in any circuit. Normally it is acceptable to bypass switches and some speed controlling resistors. If in doubt, ask your instructor.

1. **Ask your instructor to assign you a vehicle equipped with an electric cooling fan controlled by a relay.**

2. **Research the wiring diagram for the cooling fan circuit. Draw a diagram of that circuit.**

3. **Locate the cooling fan relay.**

4. **Draw a diagram of the relay socket and label each terminal with where the wire comes from, or goes to.**

5. **Label the diagram with the two points to which you believe the jumper wires should be placed.**

6. **Apply the parking brake and make sure the vehicle is in park or neutral.**

7. **Ask your instructor to verify your answers and where you plan to place the fused jumper wire. Have him/her watch you during the next portion of this task to ensure no damage is done to the vehicle's electrical system.**

    a. **Supervisor's/instructor's initials:** _____

8. **Turn the ignition switch to the run position, but do not start the vehicle (Key On, Engine Off - KOEO).**

9. **Use the fused jumper wire to activate the relay by jumping the terminals that connect to the relay contacts.**

    a. **List your observation(s):**

10. Determine any necessary action(s):

11. Have your supervisor/instructor verify satisfactory completion of this procedure, any observations found, and any necessary action(s) recommended.

► **TASK** Inspect and test fusible links, circuit breakers, and fuses; determine needed action.

MAST
6A9

Time off_____

Time on_____

Total time_____

CDX Tasksheet Number: C298

1. Using the appropriate service information, locate the fuse panel(s) for the vehicle/simulator you are assigned to.

    a. List the locations of the fuse panel(s) and circuit protection devices for this vehicle/simulator:

2. Use a test light to test each fuse and circuit breaker in one of the fuse boxes. List any circuit protection devices that are defective (open).

> **NOTE** Circuit protection devices normally do not wear out. If a circuit protection device is found to be faulty, too much current was/is present. You should determine the reason for the fault.

3. What is the rating (size) of the failed circuit protection device?
   _____ amps

4. Is the correct size fuse installed? Yes: _____ No: _____

5. Determine the cause for the circuit protection device to fail. List your tests and results below.

6. Determine any necessary action(s):

7. Have your supervisor/instructor verify satisfactory completion of this
   procedure, any observations found, and any necessary action(s) recommended.

Performance Rating

CDX Tasksheet Number: C298

0	1	2	3	4

Supervisor/instructor signature _____ Date _____

Demonstrate knowledge of the causes and effects from shorts, grounds, opens, and resistance problems in electrical/electronic circuits.

MAST
6A4

Time off_____

Time on_____

Total time_____

CDX Tasksheet Number: C296

1. Define "short circuit":

2. Define "short to ground":

3. Define "short to power":

4. Define "open circuit":

5. Define "high resistance":

6. List at least two examples of short circuits:

7. List at least two examples of grounded circuits:

8. List at least two examples of open circuits:

9. List at least two examples of high resistance in a circuit:

10. What are the effects of a short circuit in a load?

11. What are the effects on a circuit with an open circuit?

12. What are the effects on a circuit with high resistance?

13. Have your supervisor/instructor verify satisfactory completion of your answers in steps 1–12.

Performance Rating

CDX Tasksheet Number: C296

0	1	2	3	4

Supervisor/instructor signature _____ Date _____

Check electrical/electronic circuit waveforms; interpret readings and determine needed repairs.

MAST
6A11

CDX Tasksheet Number: C642

Vehicle used for this activity:

Year _____ Make _____ Model _____

Odometer _____ VIN _____

1. List the two most common types of electrical waveforms and describe how each of them differ:

2. Research various sensors for the vehicle you have been given.

   a. List at least two sensors that give an analog signal:

   b. List at least two sensors that give a digital signal:

3. Connect a lab scope to at least one analog sensor. Test the sensor, draw a diagram of the waveform, and list the name of the analog sensor:

4. Connect a lab scope to at least one digital sensor. Test the sensor, draw a diagram of the waveform, and list the name of the digital sensor:

5. Do these waveforms meet the manufacturer's specifications?
   Yes: _____ No: _____

6. Determine any necessary action(s):

7. Have your supervisor/instructor verify satisfactory completion of this procedure, any observations found, and any necessary action(s) recommended.

Wire Repair

Learning Objective/Task	CDX Tasksheet Number	2017 MAST NATEF Reference Number; Priority Level
• Inspect, test, repair, and/or replace components, connectors, terminals, harnesses, and wiring in electrical/electronic systems (including solder repairs); determine needed action.	C299	6A10; P-1
• Repair data bus wiring harness.	C955	6A12; P-1

Time off _____

Time on _____

Total time _____

Materials Required

- Wiring harness (on or off the car)
- Terminal removal tool
- Wire stripper/crimper tool
- New replacement terminal
- Soldering iron
- 60/40 rosin core solder
- Heat shrink tube or electrical tape
- Wire strippers
- Heat gun, if using shrink tube

Some Safety Issues to Consider

- Terminal picks can be sharp. Be careful when using them so they don't slip and stab you.
- Always strip wires in a direction pointing away from you so the stripper doesn't slip and hit you in the face.
- Soldering irons get, and stay, extremely hot so always pick them up only by the handle.
- Solder is extremely hot when molten. Prevent it from dripping onto your skin or clothing.
- Comply with personal and environmental safety practices associated with clothing; eye protection; hand tools; power equipment; proper ventilation; and the handling, storage, and disposal of chemicals/materials in accordance with local, state, and federal safety and environmental regulations.

Performance Standard

0—No exposure: No information or practice provided during the program; complete training required

1—Exposure only: General information provided with no practice time; close supervision needed; additional training required

2—Limited practice: Has practiced job during training program; additional training required to develop skill

3—Moderately skilled: Has performed job independently during training program; limited additional training may be required

4—Skilled: Can perform job independently with no additional training

Inspect, test, repair, and/or replace components, connectors, terminals, harnesses, and wiring in electrical/electronic systems (including solder repairs); determine needed action.

MAST
6A10

Time off_____

Time on_____

Total time_____

CDX Tasksheet Number: C299

Vehicle used for this activity:

Year _____ Make _____ Model_____

Odometer _____ VIN_____

1. **Ask your instructor which of the items listed above you should inspect and test. List here:** _____

   If needed locate the wiring diagram for the component that you are testing. Determine the purpose and operation of the suspected component. (Understanding how a component is designed to operate within a circuit will make it easier to diagnose.)

2. **After inspection and testing of the item, list the needed repair:**

3. **Using the appropriate service information, determine the manufacturer's recommended procedure to complete the needed repair.**

4. **Have your instructor verify the repair procedure. Supervisor's/instructor's initials:** _____

5. **Carry out the suggested repair or replacement procedure. List your tests and results:**

6. **Determine any needed action(s):**

7. Have your supervisor/instructor verify satisfactory completion of this procedure, any observations found, and any needed action(s) recommended.

Performance Rating

0	1	2	3	4

Supervisor/instructor signature _____ Date _____

Repair data bus wiring harness.

Time off_____

Time on_____

CDX Tasksheet Number: C955

Total time_____

1. Ask your instructor to assign a data bus wiring harness for you to perform this task on.

2. Research the proper steps to repair the data bus wiring harness in the appropriate service information.

   a. List the steps to properly repair the data bus wiring:

3. With your instructor's permission, cut one wire of the data bus system.

   a. Have your instructor verify the cut wire and repair procedure.
   Supervisor's/instructor's initials: _____

4. Perform the repair; be careful to follow all of the steps of the specified procedure.

5. What did you do to prevent electrical noise from affecting the repaired wires once they are back in service?

6. How did you insulate the soldered joint? _____

7. Have your supervisor/instructor verify satisfactory completion of this procedure, any observations found, and any necessary action(s) recommended.

Performance Rating

CDX Tasksheet Number: C955

0	1	2	3	4

Supervisor/instructor signature _____ Date _____

Horn and Wiper/Washer Diagnosis and Repair

Student/Intern information:

Name _____ Date _____ Class _____

Vehicle used for this activity:

Year _____ Make _____ Model _____

Odometer _____ VIN _____

Learning Objective/Task	CDX Tasksheet Number	2017 MAST NATEF Reference Number; Priority Level
• Diagnose operation of safety systems and related circuits (such as: horn, airbags, seat belt pretensioners, occupancy classification, wipers, washers, speed control/collision avoidance, heads-up display, park assist, and back-up camera); determine needed repairs.	C327	6G4; P-1

Time off_____

Time on_____

Total time_____

Materials Required

- Vehicle/simulator with a safety system fault
- Manufacturer service information
- Depending on the type of concern, special diagnostic tools may be required. See your supervisor/instructor for instructions to identify what tools may be required.
- Digital multimeter (DMM)
- Test light
- Fused jumper wire(s)

Some Safety Issues to Consider

- Windshield wiper motors can be very powerful. Use caution around operating wipers and linkage.
- Accidental deployment of the airbag system could happen if you inadvertently probe the wrong wire. Most manufacturers use yellow-colored wiring to denote wiring for the airbag system. Always be aware of the system/circuit you are working on.
- Only operate the windshield wipers with water or washer solution on the windshield. Otherwise you could burn out the wiper motor.
- Comply with personal and environmental safety practices associated with clothing; eye protection; hand tools; power equipment; proper ventilation; and the handling, storage, and disposal of chemicals/materials in accordance with local, state, and federal safety and environmental regulations.

Performance Standard

0–No exposure: No information or practice provided during the program; complete training required

1–Exposure only: General information provided with no practice time; close supervision needed; additional training required

2–Limited practice: Has practiced job during training program; additional training required to develop skill

3–Moderately skilled: Has performed job independently during training program; limited additional training may be required

4–Skilled: Can perform job independently with no additional training

Diagnose operation of safety systems and related circuits (such as: horn, airbags, seat belt pretensioners, occupancy classification, wipers, washers, speed control/collision avoidance, heads-up display, park assist, and back-up camera); determine needed repairs.

MAST
6G4

CDX Tasksheet Number: C327

1. Ask your instructor to assign a vehicle/simulator with a fault in a safety system. List the system:

2. List the customer concern/complaint:

3. Locate the diagnosis section and the wiring diagram for the safety system fault in the appropriate service information for the vehicle you are working on. Briefly describe the diagnostic procedure for this vehicle's safety system (or attach diagnosis printout):

4. Following the specified procedure, diagnose faults in the safety system. List your tests and their results:

5. List the cause of the customer concern/complaint:

6. Determine any needed repair(s) to correct the fault:

7. Have your supervisor/instructor verify satisfactory completion of this procedure, any observations found, and any needed repair(s) recommended.

Performance Rating

0	1	2	3	4

Supervisor/instructor signature _____ Date _____

Gauges, Warning Devices, and Driver Information Systems Diagnosis and Repair

Student/Intern information:

Name _____ Date _____ Class _____

Vehicle used for this activity:

Year _____ Make _____ Model _____

Odometer _____ VIN _____

Learning Objective/Task	CDX Tasksheet Number	2017 MAST NATEF Reference Number; Priority Level
• Inspect and test gauges and gauge sending units for cause of abnormal gauge readings; determine needed action.	C646	6F1; P-2
• Diagnose (troubleshoot) the cause of incorrect operation of warning devices and other driver information systems; determine needed action.	C325	6F2; P-2
• Reset maintenance indicators as required.	C1003	6F3; P-2

Time off_____

Time on_____

Total time_____

Materials Required

- Vehicle or simulator
- Depending on the type of concern, special diagnostic tools may be required. See your supervisor/instructor for instructions to identify what tools may be required.
- DMM/DVOM

Some Safety Issues to Consider
- If you need to start the vehicle, you should ensure that the parking brake is firmly applied; if necessary, use wheel chocks to prevent the vehicle from moving when the vehicle is started to verify the completion of these tasks.
- When running any vehicles in the shop, make sure you use the shop's exhaust ventilation system to discharge all exhaust gas safely outside.
- Only students who have their supervisor's/instructor's direct permission should perform this task due to the safety concerns involved.
- Diagnosis of this fault may require test-driving the vehicle on the school grounds. Attempt this task only with full permission from your instructor and follow all the guidelines exactly.
- Comply with personal and environmental safety practices associated with clothing; eye protection; hand tools; power equipment; proper ventilation; and the handling, storage, and disposal of chemicals/materials in accordance with local, state, and federal safety and environmental regulations.

Performance Standard

0–No exposure: No information or practice provided during the program; complete training required

1–Exposure only: General information provided with no practice time; close supervision needed; additional training required

2–Limited practice: Has practiced job during training program; additional training required to develop skill

3–Moderately skilled: Has performed job independently during training program; limited additional training may be required

4–Skilled: Can perform job independently with no additional training

Inspect and test gauges and gauge sending units for cause
of abnormal gauge readings; determine needed action.

MAST
6F1

CDX Tasksheet Number: C646

1. List the customer concern/complaint regarding abnormal gauge readings:

2. Research the particular complaint/concern in the appropriate service
    information. List the possible causes:

    a. List any relevant gauge or sending unit specifications:

3. Diagnose the cause of the concern/complaint using the service information and
    wiring diagrams. List your tests and their results:

4. List the cause of the concern/complaint:

5. Determine any needed action(s) to correct the fault:

6. Have your supervisor/instructor verify satisfactory completion of this procedure, any observations found, and any needed action(s) recommended.

TASK Diagnose (troubleshoot) the cause of incorrect operation
of warning devices and other driver information systems;
determine needed action.

MAST
6F2

Time off_____

Time on_____

Total time_____

CDX Tasksheet Number: C325

Vehicle used for this activity:

Year _____ Make _____ Model _____

Odometer _____ VIN _____

1. **List the customer concern/complaint regarding incorrect operation of warning devices and other driver information systems:**

2. **Research the particular complaint/concern in the appropriate service information. List the possible causes:**

   a. **List any relevant specifications:**

3. **Diagnose the cause of the concern/complaint using the service information and wiring diagrams. List your tests and their results:**

4. **List the cause of the concern/complaint:**

5. **Determine any needed action(s) to correct the fault:**

6. Have your supervisor/instructor verify satisfactory completion of this procedure, any observations found, and any needed action(s) recommended.

Performance Rating

CDX Tasksheet Number: C325

0	1	2	3	4

Supervisor/instructor signature _____ Date _____

Time off_____

Time on_____

Total time_____

CDX Tasksheet Number: C1003

1. Research the description and operation of each maintenance indicator and the procedure for resetting the maintenance indicators in the appropriate service information. List each of the maintenance indicators and the reset procedure:

2. Turn the ignition switch to the on/run position (Key On, Engine Off-KOEO). List the status of each maintenance indicator:

3. Start the engine and allow it to run for a few minutes. List the status of each maintenance indicator:

4. List any maintenance indicators that are showing required maintenance:

5. Ask your supervisor/instructor if you should carry out the reset procedure for any maintenance indicators that are showing required maintenance.

6. Have your supervisor/instructor verify satisfactory completion of this procedure, any observations found, and any necessary action(s) recommended.

Performance Rating

0	1	2	3	4

Supervisor/instructor signature _____ Date _____

Accessories Diagnosis and Repair

Student/Intern information:

Name _____ Date _____ Class _____

Vehicle used for this activity:

Year _____ Make _____ Model _____

Odometer _____ VIN _____

Learning Objective/Task	CDX Tasksheet Number	2017 MAST NATEF Reference Number; Priority Level
• Diagnose operation of comfort and convenience accessories and related circuits (such as: power window, power seats, pedal height, power locks, trunk locks, remote start, moon roof, sun roof, sun shade, remote keyless entry, voice activation, steering wheel controls, back-up camera, park assist, cruise control, and auto dimming headlamps); determine needed repairs.	C330	6G1; P-2

Time off_____

Time on_____

Total time_____

Materials Required

- Vehicle/simulator with appropriate fault for each task
- Service information
- DMM/DVOM
- Test light
- Fused jumper wire(s)
- Possible special tools depending on the fault

Some Safety Issues to Consider

- Motor-driven systems contain rotating and moving parts. Be careful to ensure that clothing, your body, and tools are kept clear of moving parts.
- Be cautious around electricity. High voltage (enough to injure or kill you) is present on many vehicles. Ignition systems, hybrid vehicles, and 42-volt electrical systems are just a few hazards to be careful of.
- Accidental deployment of the airbag system could happen if you inadvertently probe the wrong wire. Most manufacturers use yellow-colored wiring to denote wiring for the airbag system. Always be aware of the system/circuit you are working on.
- Only students who have a valid driver's license and their supervisor's/instructor's direct permission should perform these tasks due to the safety concerns involved.
- Comply with personal and environmental safety practices associated with clothing; eye protection; hand tools; power equipment; proper ventilation; and the handling, storage, and disposal of chemicals/materials in accordance with local, state, and federal safety and environmental regulations.

Performance Standard

0-No exposure: No information or practice provided during the program; complete training required

1-Exposure only: General information provided with no practice time; close supervision needed; additional training required

2-Limited practice: Has practiced job during training program; additional training required to develop skill

3-Moderately skilled: Has performed job independently during training program; limited additional training may be required

4-Skilled: Can perform job independently with no additional training

Diagnose operation of comfort and convenience accessories and related circuits (such as: power window, power seats, pedal height, power locks, trunk locks, remote start, moon roof, sun roof, sun shade, remote keyless entry, voice activation, steering wheel controls, back-up camera, park assist, cruise control, and auto dimming headlamps); determine needed repairs.

MAST
6G1

Time off_____

Time on_____

Total time_____

DX Tasksheet Number: C330

1. **Ask your instructor to assign a vehicle with a fault in a comfort and convenience accessory circuit. List the circuit:**

2. **List the customer concern/complaint:**

3. **Locate the diagnosis section and the wiring diagram for the comfort and convenience accessory fault in the appropriate service information for the vehicle you are working on. Briefly describe the diagnostic procedure for this vehicle's comfort and convenience accessory circuit (or attach diagnosis printout):**

4. **Following the specified procedure, diagnose faults in the comfort and convenience accessory circuit. List your tests and their results:**

5. **List the cause of the customer concern/complaint:**

6. **Determine any needed repair(s) to correct the fault:**

7. Have your supervisor/instructor verify satisfactory completion of this procedure, any observations found, and any needed repair(s) recommended.

Performance Rating

CDX Tasksheet Number: C330

0	1	2	3	4

Supervisor/instructor signature _____ Date _____

Accessories Diagnosis and Repair (Entertainment, etc.)

___

Student/Intern information:

Name _____ Date _____ Class _____

Vehicle used for this activity:

Year _____ Make _____ Model_____

Odometer_____VIN _____

Learning Objective/Task	CDX Tasksheet Number	2017 MAST NATEF Reference Number; Priority Level
• Diagnose operation of entertainment and related circuits (such as: radio, DVD, remote CD changer, navigation, amplifiers, speakers, antennas, and voice-activated accessories); determine needed repairs.	C336	6G3; P-3

Time off_____

Time on_____

Total time_____

Materials Required

- Vehicle/simulator with appropriate fault for each task
- Vehicle diagnostic scan tool
- Service information
- DMM/DVOM
- Test light
- Door panel tools
- Manufacturer or job specific tools depending on the fault

Some Safety Issues to Consider

- Be cautious around electricity. High voltage (enough to injure or kill you) is present on many vehicles. Ignition systems, hybrid vehicles, and 42-volt electrical systems are just a few hazards to be careful of.
- Working on the airbag system can be very dangerous. Consult the shop manual for the vehicle you are working on and ensure all safety precautions are followed.
- Accidental deployment of the airbag system could happen if you inadvertently probe the wrong wire. Most manufacturers use yellow-colored wiring to denote wiring for the airbag system. Always be aware of the system/circuit you are working on.
- Only students who have their supervisor's/instructor's direct permission should perform these tasks due to the safety concerns involved.
- Always wear the correct protective eyewear and clothing, and use the appropriate safety equipment, as well as fender covers, seat protectors, and floor mat protectors.
- Make sure you understand and observe all legislative and personal safety procedures when carrying out practical assignments. If you are unsure of what these are, ask your supervisor/instructor.

Performance Standard

0–No exposure: No information or practice provided during the program; complete training required

1–Exposure only: General information provided with no practice time; close supervision needed; additional training required

2–Limited practice: Has practiced job during training program; additional training required to develop skill

3–Moderately skilled: Has performed job independently during training program; limited additional training may be required

4–Skilled: Can perform job independently with no additional training

MAST
6G3

Time off_____

Time on_____

Total time_____

CDX Tasksheet Number: C336

Vehicle used for this activity:

Year _____ Make _____ Model_____

Odometer_____ VIN_____

1. **Ask your instructor to assign a vehicle with a fault in the radio or entertainment system.**

2. **List the customer concern/complaint:**

3. **Locate the diagnostic procedure for the related customer concern/complaint in the appropriate service information for the vehicle you are working on. Briefly describe the diagnostic procedure for the fault (or attach diagnosis printout):**

4. **Following the specified procedure, diagnose the related customer concern/ complaint. List your tests and their results:**

5. **List the cause of the customer concern/complaint:**

6. **Determine any needed repair(s) to correct the customer concern/complaint:**

7. Have your supervisor/instructor verify satisfactory completion of this procedure, any observations found, and any needed repair(s) recommended.

Accessories Diagnosis and Repair (Network, etc.)

Student/Intern information:

Name _____ Date _____ Class _____

Vehicle used for this activity:

Year _____ Make _____ Model_____

Odometer_____VIN_____

Learning Objective/Task	CDX Tasksheet Number	2017 MAST NATEF Reference Number; Priority Level
• Diagnose body electronic system circuits using a scan tool; check for module communication errors (data communication bus systems); determine needed action.	C338	6G5; P-2
• Diagnose operation of security/anti-theft systems and related circuits (such as: theft deterrent, door locks, remote keyless entry, remote start, and starter/fuel disable); determine needed repairs.	C340	6G2; P-2
• Describe the process for software transfers, software updates, or reprogramming of electronic modules.	C649	6G6; P-2

Time off_____

Time on_____

Total time_____

Materials Required

- Vehicle/simulator with appropriate fault for each task
- Vehicle service information
- Vehicle diagnostic scan tool
- DMM/DVOM
- Manufacturer or job specific tools depending on the fault

Some Safety Issues to Consider

- Be cautious around electricity. High voltage (enough to injure or kill you) is present on many vehicles. Ignition systems, hybrid vehicles, and 42-volt electrical systems are just a few hazards to be careful of.
- Accidental deployment of the airbag system could happen if you inadvertently probe the wrong wire. Most manufacturers use yellow-colored wiring to denote wiring for the airbag system. Always be aware of the system/circuit you are working on.
- Only students who have a valid driver's license and their supervisor's/instructor's direct permission should perform these tasks due to the safety concerns involved.
- If you need to start the vehicle you should ensure that the parking brake is firmly applied; if necessary, use wheel chocks to prevent the vehicle from moving when the vehicle is started to verify the completion of this task.
- When running any vehicles in the shop, make sure you use the shop's exhaust ventilation system to discharge all exhaust gas safely outside.
- Always wear the correct protective eyewear and clothing, and use the appropriate safety equipment, as well as fender covers, seat protectors, and floor mat protectors.

- Make sure you understand and observe all legislative and personal safety procedures when carrying out practical assignments. If you are unsure of what these are, ask your supervisor/instructor.

Performance Standard

0–No exposure: No information or practice provided during the program; complete training required

1–Exposure only: General information provided with no practice time; close supervision needed; additional training required

2–Limited practice: Has practiced job during training program; additional training required to develop skill

3–Moderately skilled: Has performed job independently during training program; limited additional training may be required

4–Skilled: Can perform job independently with no additional training

Diagnose body electronic system circuits using a scan tool; check for module communication errors (data communication bus systems); determine needed action.

MAST
6G5

CDX Tasksheet Number: C338

1. **Locate "diagnosis of body electronic systems with a scan tool" in the appropriate service information for the vehicle you are working on.**

   a. **List the safety precautions to be taken when working on the body electronic systems:**

   b. **List the diagnostic procedures for the body electronic systems (or print and attach copy):**

2. **Check for any DTCs (diagnostic trouble codes) in the BCM (body control module) and list them and their descriptions here:**

3. **Following the specified procedure, diagnose faults in the body electronic system. List your tests and observations:**

4. **Determine any needed action(s) to correct the fault:**

5. **Have your supervisor/instructor verify satisfactory completion of this procedure, any observations found, and any needed action(s) recommended.**

Performance Rating

CDX Tasksheet Number: C338

0	1	2	3	4

Supervisor/instructor signature _____ Date _____

Diagnose operation of security/anti-theft systems and related circuits (such as: theft deterrent, door locks, remote keyless entry, remote start, and starter/fuel disable); determine needed repairs.

MAST
6G2

Time off_____

Time on_____

Total time_____

CDX Tasksheet Number: C340

Vehicle used for this activity:

Year _____ Make _____ Model _____

Odometer_____ VIN_____

1. **Locate the diagnostic procedure for the security/anti-theft system in the appropriate service information for the vehicle you are working on.**

   a. **List the safety precautions to be taken when working on the security/anti-theft system:**

   b. **List the diagnostic procedures for the security/anti-theft system (or print and attach copy):**

2. **Check for any DTCs in the security/anti-theft system. List the DTCs and their descriptions here:**

3. **Following the specified procedure, diagnose faults in the security/anti-theft system. List your tests and observations:**

4. **Determine any needed repair(s) to correct the fault:**

5. Have your supervisor/instructor verify satisfactory completion of this procedure, any observations found, and any needed repair(s) recommended.

Performance Rating

0	1	2	3	4

Supervisor/instructor signature _____ Date _____

▶ **TASK** Describe the process for software transfers, software updates, or reprogramming of electronic modules.

MAST
6G6

Time off_____

Time on_____

Total time_____

CDX Tasksheet Number: C649

Vehicle used for this activity:

Year _____ Make _____ Model_____

Odometer_____ VIN_____

1. **List the customer concern(s) related to software updates or the need for reprogramming electronic modules:**

2. **Verify the concern and list your observations including any codes, their descriptions, or any TSBs:**

3. **Research the correct method to perform software transfers, software updates, or reprogramming on electronic modules in appropriate service information.**

   a. **List any precautions here:**

   b. **List the steps needed to reprogram the electronic module (or print and attach):**

   c. **Have your instructor verify your process:** _____

4. Have your supervisor/instructor verify satisfactory completion of this procedure, any observations found, and any necessary action(s) recommended.

Performance Rating

0	1	2	3	4

Supervisor/instructor signature _____ Date _____

Hybrid Electrical Safety

Student/Intern information:

Name _____ Date _____ Class _____

Vehicle used for this activity:

Year _____ Make _____ Model _____

Odometer _____ VIN _____

Learning Objective/Task	CDX Tasksheet Number	2017 MAST NATEF Reference Number; Priority Level
• Identify safety precautions for high voltage systems on electric, hybrid hybrid-electric, and diesel vehicles.	C561	6B7; P-2
• Identify hybrid vehicle auxiliary (12V) battery service, repair, and test procedures.	C874	6B9; P-2

Time off _____

Time on _____

Total time _____

Materials Required

- Hybrid or electric vehicle
- Vehicle service information
- Certified and tested, high voltage electrical gloves.
- Depending on the type of concern, special diagnostic tools may be required. See your supervisor/instructor for instructions to identify what tools may be required.

Some Safety Issues to Consider

- Hybrid and electric vehicles are especially dangerous due to their extremely high DC voltage and current (high enough to kill you). In many dealerships, only fully trained master technicians are allowed to work on hybrid and electric vehicles. Follow all manufacturer procedures exactly, and wear all required personal protective equipment at all times when working around these vehicles.
- Always wear high-voltage personal protective equipment when working around high-voltage sources, components, and wires.
- Only students who have their supervisor's/instructor's direct permission should perform this task due to the safety concerns involved.
- Use extreme caution when working around batteries. Immediately remove any electrolyte that may come into contact with you. Electrolyte is a mixture of sulfuric acid and water. Please consult with the shop safety and emergency procedures when working with or around batteries.
- Comply with personal and environmental safety practices associated with clothing; eye
- protection; hand tools; power equipment; proper ventilation; and the handling, storage, and disposal of chemicals/materials in accordance with local, state, and federal safety and environmental regulations.

Performance Standard

0–No exposure: No information or practice provided during the program; complete training required

1–Exposure only: General information provided with no practice time; close supervision needed; additional training required

2–Limited practice: Has practiced job during training program; additional training required to develop skill

3–Moderately skilled: Has performed job independently during training program; limited additional training may be required

4–Skilled: Can perform job independently with no additional training

▶ TASK Identify safety precautions for high voltage systems on electric, hybrid, hybrid-electric, and diesel vehicles.

MAST
6B7

Time off_____

Time on_____

Total time_____

CDX Tasksheet Number: C561

1. **Research the safety precautions for all high-voltage systems and methods of identifying those systems on the electric, hybrid, hybrid-electric, or diesel vehicle.**

   a. **List the systems that use or create high voltage:**

   b. **List any safety precautions when working on or around these systems and circuits:**

2. **Locate and point out, on the vehicle, the high-voltage circuits and components to your instructor.**

3. **Have your supervisor/instructor verify satisfactory completion of this procedure, any observations found, and any necessary action(s) recommended.**

Performance Rating

CDX Tasksheet Number: C561

| 0 | 1 | 2 | 3 | 4 |

Supervisor/instructor signature _____ Date _____

Time off_____

Time on_____

Total time_____

CDX Tasksheet Number: C874

1. **Research the hybrid vehicle auxiliary (12V) battery service, repair, and test procedures in the appropriate service information.**

   a. **Does this vehicle use a 12V auxiliary battery? Yes: _____**
      No: _____

   b. **List any special testing, service, or repair procedures related to the 12V auxiliary battery:**

2. **If you performed any tests, services, or repairs on the 12V auxiliary battery, list all tests or service performed and any results:**

3. **Determine any necessary action(s):**

4. **Have your supervisor/instructor verify satisfactory completion of this procedure, any observations found, and any necessary action(s) recommended.**

Performance Rating

CDX Tasksheet Number: C874

0	1	2	3	4

Supervisor/instructor signature _____ Date _____

Section A7:
HVAC

CONTENTS

Vehicle, Customer, and Service Information

Student/Intern information:

Name _____ Date _____ Class _____

Vehicle used for this activity:

Year _____ Make _____ Model _____

Odometer _____ VIN _____

Learning Objective/Task	CDX Tasksheet Number	2017 MAST NATEF Reference Number; Priority Level
• Research vehicle service information including refrigerant/oil type, vehicle service history, service precautions, and technical service bulletins.	C342	7A2; P-1
• Identify and interpret heating and air conditioning problems; determine needed action.	C341	7A1; P-1
• Identify hybrid vehicle A/C system electrical circuits and the service/safety precautions.	C827	7B4; P-2
• Demonstrate use of the three Cs (concern, cause, and correction).	N/A	N/A

Time off_____

Time on_____

Total time_____

Materials Required

- Blank work order
- Vehicle with available service history records
- Thermometer or temperature gun
- DMM/DVOM
- Depending on the type of concern, special diagnostic tools may be required. See your supervisor/instructor for instructions to identify what tools may be required.

Some Safety Issues to Consider

- Diagnosis of this fault may require test-driving the vehicle on the school grounds. Attempt this task only with full permission from your instructor and follow all the guidelines exactly.
- When running any vehicles in the shop, make sure you use the shop's exhaust ventilation system to discharge all exhaust gas safely outside.
- Extreme caution must be exercised when working around rotating components.
- Refrigerant can cause serious damage if it comes in contact with a person's unprotected skin and eyes.
- When operating, the air conditioning system is normally subject to very high pressure in the system. Extreme caution must be exercised when working on an operating system.
- Comply with personal and environmental safety practices associated with clothing; eye protection; hand tools; power equipment; proper ventilation; and the handling, storage, and disposal of chemicals/materials in accordance with local, state, and federal safety and environmental regulations.

Performance Standard

0–No exposure: No information or practice provided during the program; complete training required

1–Exposure only: General information provided with no practice time; close supervision needed; additional training required

2–Limited practice: Has practiced job during training program; additional training required to develop skill

3–Moderately skilled: Has performed job independently during training program; limited additional training may be required

4–Skilled: Can perform job independently with no additional training

Research vehicle service information including refrigerant/oil type, vehicle service history, service precautions, and technical service bulletins.

MAST
7A2

CDX Tasksheet Number: C342

1. **Using the VIN for identification, use the appropriate source to access the vehicle's service history in relation to prior related HVAC system work or customer concerns.**

   a. **List any related repairs/concerns and their dates:**

2. **Research the HVAC system description and operation in the appropriate service information.**

   a. **Specified refrigerant:** _____
   b. **Refrigerant capacity:** _____ **lb/kg**
   c. **Specified lubricant:** _____
   d. **Lubricant capacity:** _____ **oz/mL**
   e. **List the specified service precautions when servicing this system:**

3. **Using the VIN for identification, access any relevant technical service bulletins for the particular vehicle on which you are working in relation to any related HVAC issues.**

   a. **List any related service bulletins and their titles:**

4. **Have your supervisor/instructor verify satisfactory completion of this procedure, any observations found, and any necessary action(s) recommended.**

Performance Rating

CDX Tasksheet Number: C342

0	1	2	3	4

Supervisor/instructor signature _____ Date _____

Identify and interpret heating and air conditioning concern; determine needed action.

MAST
7A1

CDX Tasksheet Number: C341

1. **List the customer's heating and air conditioning–related concern(s):**

2. **Research the particular concern in the appropriate service information.**

   a. **List the possible causes:**

3. **Inspect the vehicle to determine the cause of the concern.**

   a. **List the steps you took to determine the fault(s):**

4. **List the cause of the concern(s):**

5. **List the necessary action(s) to correct the fault(s):**

6. **Have your supervisor/instructor verify satisfactory completion of this procedure, any observations found, and any necessary action(s) recommended.**

Performance Rating

CDX Tasksheet Number: C341

0	1	2	3	4

Supervisor/instructor signature _____ Date _____

Identify hybrid vehicle A/C system electrical circuits
and the service/safety precautions.

MAST
7B4

CDX Tasksheet Number: C827

Vehicle used for this activity:

Year _____ Make _____ Model_____

Odometer_____ VIN_____

1. **Research the description and operation of a hybrid vehicle A/C system in the appropriate service information.**

   a. **What powers the A/C compressor (prime mover)?**

   b. **Does the manufacturer use a special designation for the A/C system electrical circuits? Yes: _____ No: _____**

      i. If yes, what is it?

   c. **List the voltage(s) that the A/C system electrical circuits operate on:**

   d. **How is the A/C compressor driven? V belt: _____ Serpentine belt: _____ Direct drive: _____ Other (specify below)**

      i. Specified refrigerant: _____

      ii. Refrigerant capacity: _____ lb/kg

      iii. Specified lubricant: _____

      iv. Lubricant capacity: _____ oz/mL

      v. List the specified safety precautions when servicing this system:

2. Have your supervisor/instructor verify satisfactory completion of this procedure, any observations found, and any necessary action(s) recommended.

Performance Rating

CDX Tasksheet Number: C827

0	1	2	3	4

Supervisor/instructor signature _____ Date _____

Demonstrate use of the three Cs: concern, cause, and correction.

Time off_____

Time on_____

CDX Tasksheet Number: N/A

1. **Using the following scenario, write up the three Cs as listed on most repair orders. Assume that the customer authorized the recommended repairs.**

   Total time_____

   A late model vehicle with 114,000 miles and equipped with an expansion-valve style HVAC system is brought into your shop with an A/C concern. The customer tells you that the A/C has not worked for the past several days. You perform a preliminary check and notice that the compressor clutch does not engage when moving the A/C controls to maximum cold with the A/C fan on high. Further testing shows the following:

   a. Normal static pressure in the system
   b. An open compressor clutch winding
   c. A dirty cabin air filter
   d. An excessively cracked engine serpentine belt
   e. A lightly leaking water pump seal
   f. A coolant freeze point of 20°F (−6°C)

   > NOTE Ask your instructor whether you should use a copy of the shop repair order or the three Cs below to record this information.

2. **Concern:**

3. **Cause:**

4. **Correction:**

5. **Other recommended service:**

6. Have your supervisor/instructor verify satisfactory completion of this procedure, any observations found, and any necessary action(s) recommended

Performance Rating

CDX Tasksheet Number: N/A

0	1	2	3	4

Supervisor/instructor signature _____ Date _____

Preliminary Testing

Student/Intern information:

Name _____ Date _____ Class _____

Vehicle used for this activity:

Year _____ Make _____ Model _____

Odometer _____ VIN _____

Learning Objective/Task	CDX Tasksheet Number	2017 MAST NATEF Reference Number; Priority Level
• Performance test A/C system; identify problems.	C824	7A3; P-1
• Identify abnormal operating noises in the A/C system; determine needed action.	C825	7A4; P-2
• Inspect for proper A/C condenser for airflow; determine needed action.	C356	7B7; P-1
• Inspect evaporator housing water drain; perform needed action.	C830	7B10; P-1
• Identify the source of HVAC system odors.	C655	7D7; P-2

Time off_____

Time on_____

Total time_____

Materials Required

- Appropriate air conditioning manifold gauge set including service hoses
- Air conditioning service station recovery/recycling equipment as necessary
- Auxiliary fan for condenser (if needed)
- Appropriate thermometers
- Infrared temperature gun/thermocouple
- Anemometer
- Stethoscope
- Scan tool

Some Safety Issues to Consider

- Refrigerant can cause serious damage if it comes in contact with a person's unprotected skin and eyes.
- When operating, the air conditioning system is normally subject to very high pressure in the system. Extreme caution must be exercised when working on an operating system.
- Extreme caution must be exercised when working around rotating components.
- When running any vehicles in the shop, make sure you use the shop's exhaust ventilation system to discharge all exhaust gas safely outside.
- Diagnosis of this fault may require test-driving the vehicle on the school grounds. Attempt this task only with full permission from your instructor and follow all the guidelines exactly.
- Comply with personal and environmental safety practices associated with clothing; eye protection; hand tools; power equipment; proper ventilation; and the handling, storage, and disposal of chemicals/materials in accordance with local, state, and federal safety and environmental regulations.

Performance Standard

0–No exposure: No information or practice provided during the program; complete training required

1–Exposure only: General information provided with no practice time; close supervision needed; additional training required

2–Limited practice: Has practiced job during training program; additional training required to develop skill

3–Moderately skilled: Has performed job independently during training program; limited additional training may be required

4–Skilled: Can perform job independently with no additional training

Performance test A/C system; identify problems.

Time off_____

Time on_____

Total time_____

CDX Tasksheet Number: C824

1. Research the procedure and specifications for performance testing the A/C system in the appropriate service information.

    a. List or print off and attach to this sheet the steps to performance test the system:

    b. List or print off and attach to this sheet any specifications that the system should meet:

2. Following the specified procedure, carry out the performance test on the system. List the following readings:

    > NOTE Use an auxiliary fan for additional condenser airflow if conditions warrant.

    a. Engine rpm: _____
    b. Is the compressor clutch cycle time appropriate? Yes: _____
       No: _____
    c. Ambient air temperature: _____ °F/°C
    d. A/C duct air temperature: _____ °F/°C
    e. Difference between ambient temp and A/C duct temp: _____ °F/°C

3. Did the A/C system pass the performance test? Yes: _____ No: _____

4. Determine any necessary action(s):

5. Have your supervisor/instructor verify satisfactory completion of this procedure, any observations found, and any necessary action(s) recommended.

Performance Rating

CDX Tasksheet Number: C824

0	1	2	3	4

Supervisor/instructor signature _____ Date _____

Identify abnormal operating noises in the A/C system; determine needed action.

MAST
7A4

CDX Tasksheet Number: C825

Vehicle used for this activity:

Year _____ Make _____ Model _____

Odometer _____ VIN _____

1. List the A/C noise-related concern:

2. Start the vehicle and operate the A/C system to verify the noise concern. Try to determine the location of the noise. List your observation(s):

3. Research the possible cause(s) and testing procedures in the appropriate service information.

   a. List any possible cause(s):

   b. List or print off and attach to this sheet the steps for identifying the cause of the concern:

4. Following the specified procedure, identify the cause of the concern. List your test(s) and results:

5. List the cause(s) of the concern:

6. Determine any necessary action(s) to correct the fault:

7. Have your supervisor/instructor verify satisfactory completion of this procedure, any observations found, and any necessary action(s) recommended.

Inspect for proper A/C condenser for airflow;
determine needed action.

Time off_____

Time on_____

Total time_____

CDX Tasksheet Number: C356

Vehicle used for this activity:

Year _____ Make _____ Model _____

Odometer _____ VIN _____

1. **Research the procedure and specifications for inspecting the A/C condenser for proper airflow in the appropriate service information.**

    a. **List or print off and attach to this sheet any steps to perform this task:**

    b. **Specified condenser airflow: _____ ft/min**

2. **Following the specified procedure, inspect both sides of the A/C condenser for damage or blockage to the airflow. List your observation(s):**

3. **Following the specified procedure, use the anemometer to measure the condenser airflow: _____ ft/min**

4. **Determine any necessary action(s):**

5. **Have your supervisor/instructor verify your observations and recommendations and initial below. Supervisor's/instructor's initials: _____**

6. **Perform any necessary actions and list your observation(s):**

7. Have your supervisor/instructor verify satisfactory completion of this procedure, any observations found, and any necessary action(s) recommended.

Performance Rating

CDX Tasksheet Number: C356

0	1	2	3	4

Supervisor/instructor signature _____ Date _____

Inspect evaporator housing water drain; perform
        needed action.

MAST
7B10

CDX Tasksheet Number: C830

1. **Research the procedure for inspecting and cleaning the evaporator housing water drain in the appropriate service information.**

    a. **List or print off and attach to this sheet the steps to perform this task:**

2. **Following the specified procedure, inspect the evaporator housing water drain. List your observation(s):**

3. **Have your supervisor/instructor verify your observations. Supervisor's/ instructor's initials: _____**

4. **Perform any necessary action(s) and list your observation(s):**

5. **Have your supervisor/instructor verify satisfactory completion of this procedure, any observations found, and any necessary action(s) recommended.**

Performance Rating

CDX Tasksheet Number: C830

0	1	2	3	4

Supervisor/instructor signature _____ Date _____

Identify the source of HVAC system odors.

MAST
7D7

Time off_____

Time on_____

CDX Tasksheet Number: C655

Vehicle used for this activity:

Year _____ Make _____ Model_____

Odometer_____ VIN_____

Total time_____

1. List the HVAC system odor-related customer concern:

2. Verify the concern by running the HVAC system through all operating conditions. List your observation(s):

3. Research the procedure to identify the odor concern in the appropriate service information.

    a. List the possible cause(s) of the concern:

    b. List, or print off and attach to this sheet, the steps to identify the source of the odor: (If no procedure is given, operate the system in each of the various functions, and see when the smell is the strongest.)

4. Following the specified procedure, inspect the HVAC system to identify the cause of the odor. List your steps and results:

5. List the cause of the concern:

6. Determine any necessary action(s) to correct the fault:

7. Have your supervisor/instructor verify satisfactory completion of this procedure, any observations found, and any necessary action(s) recommended.

Performance Rating

CDX Tasksheet Number: C655

0	1	2	3	4

Supervisor/instructor signature _____ Date _____

Refrigerant Recovery, Recycling, and Handling

Student/Intern information:

Name _____ Date _____ Class _____

Vehicle used for this activity:

Year _____ Make _____ Model _____

Odometer _____VIN _____

Learning Objective/Task	CDX Tasksheet Number	2017 MAST NATEF Reference Number; Priority Level
• Identify refrigerant type; select and connect proper gauge set/test equipment; record temperature and pressure readings.	C650	7A5; P-1
• Leak test A/C system; determine needed action.	C347	7A6; P-1
• Identify A/C system refrigerant; test for sealants; recover, evacuate, and charge A/C system; add refrigerant oil as required.	C836	7E2; P-1
• Recycle, label, and store refrigerant.	C657	7E3; P-1
• Determine recommended oil and oil capacity for system application.	C652	7A8; P-1
• Inspect condition of refrigerant oil removed from the system; determine needed action.	C651	7A7; P-2
• Determine need for an additional A/C system filter; perform needed action.	C863	7B5; P-3

Time off_____

Time on_____

Total time_____

Materials Required

- Refrigerant identifier
- Appropriate air conditioning manifold gauge set including service hoses
- Infrared temp gun or AC thermometer
- Air conditioning service station recovery/recycling equipment as necessary
- Refrigerant detecting equipment
- Specified refrigerant oil

Some Safety Issues to Consider

- Refrigerant can cause serious damage if it comes in contact with a person's unprotected skin and eyes.
- When operating, the air conditioning system is normally subject to very high pressure in the system. Extreme caution must be exercised when working on an operating system.
- Extreme caution must be exercised when working around rotating components.
- When running any vehicles in the shop, make sure you use the shop's exhaust ventilation system to discharge all exhaust gas safely outside.
- Comply with personal and environmental safety practices associated with clothing; eye protection; hand tools; power equipment; proper ventilation; and the handling, storage, and disposal of chemicals/materials in accordance with local, state, and federal safety and environmental regulations.

Performance Standard

0–No exposure: No information or practice provided during the program; complete training required

1–Exposure only: General information provided with no practice time; close supervision needed; additional training required

2–Limited practice: Has practiced job during training program; additional training required to develop skill

3–Moderately skilled: Has performed job independently during training program; limited additional training may be required

4–Skilled: Can perform job independently with no additional training

Identify refrigerant type; select and connect proper gauge set/ test equipment; record temperature and pressure readings.

MAST
7A 5

Time off_____

Time on_____

Total time_____

CDX Tasksheet Number: C650

1. Research the description, operation, and testing procedure for the A/C system in the appropriate service information.

    a. Specified refrigerant type: _____
    b. Specified testing RPM (engine): _____
    c. Does this vehicle require auxiliary condenser airflow for testing?
       Yes: _____ No: _____
    d. Specified high side-pressure range: _____ psi/kPa
    e. Specified low side-pressure range: _____ psi/kPa
    f. Specified air duct temperature range: _____ °F/°C

2. Following the specified procedure, identify the refrigerant type: _____

3. Obtain the proper gauge set/test equipment and connect it to the A/C system service ports.

4. Following the specified procedure, record the operating temperature and pressure readings below.

    NOTE Use an auxiliary fan for additional condenser airflow if conditions warrant.

    a. Engine tested at: _____ rpm
    b. High side-pressure range: _____ psi/kPa
    c. Low side-pressure range: _____ psi/kPa
    d. Ambient air temperature: _____ °F/°C
    e. A/C duct air temperature: _____ °F/°C
    f. Difference between ambient temp and A/C duct temp: _____
       °F/°C

5. Does the A/C system perform according to specifications?
   Yes: _____ No: _____

6. Have your supervisor/instructor verify satisfactory completion of this procedure, any observations found, and any necessary action(s) recommended.

Performance Rating

CDX Tasksheet Number: C650

0	1	2	3	4

Supervisor/instructor signature _____ Date _____

MAST
7A6

CDX Tasksheet Number: C347

1. Research the A/C leak detection procedure in the appropriate service information.

   a. List the leak detection method you will use:

2. Following the specified procedure, leak test the A/C system, including the evaporator, condenser, compressor, and all fittings and hoses.

   a. List your observation(s):

3. Determine any necessary action(s):

4. Have your supervisor/instructor verify satisfactory completion of this procedure, any observations found, and any necessary action(s) recommended.

Performance Rating

CDX Tasksheet Number: C347

0	1	2	3	4

Supervisor/instructor signature _____ Date _____

Identify A/C system refrigerant; test for sealants;
recover, evacuate, and charge A/C system;
add refrigerant oil as required.

MAST
7E2

CDX Tasksheet Number: C836

1. **Research the procedure and specifications to identify A/C system refrigerant; test for sealants; recover the A/C system refrigerant in the appropriate service information.**

    a. **Specified type of refrigerant:** _____

    b. **Specified capacity of refrigerant:** _____ lb/kg

    c. **Specified refrigerant oil:** _____

    d. **Specified refrigerant oil capacity:** _____ oz/mL

    > **NOTE** Refrigerant oil capacity is only applicable in case of a system flush.

2. **List the method you will use to identify any sealant installed in the A/C system:**

3. **Following the specified procedure, test for sealant in the A/C system.**

    a. **Was sealant identified in the A/C system? Yes:** _____
       No: _____

    > **NOTE** If any sealants were identified notify your supervisor/instructor.

4. **List the method you will use to identify the type of refrigerant installed in the A/C system:**

5. **Following the specified procedure, identify the existing refrigerant in the A/C system.**

    a. **Type identified:** _____

    b. **Is this the specified refrigerant? Yes:** _____ **No:** _____

    c. **Determine any necessary action(s):**

6. **Following the specified procedure, recover the refrigerant installed in the A/C system.**

    a. **How much refrigerant was recovered from the system?**
       _____ lb/kg

    b. **How much oil was recovered, if any?** _____ oz/mL

c. Are these the specified amounts? Yes: _____ No: _____

d. Determine any necessary action(s):

7. Research the procedure and specifications for evacuating and charging the A/C system in the appropriate service information.

   a. If you are recharging the system using the high side service port, list the specified time for the low side pressure to reach specifications: _____ seconds

   > NOTE In the absence of a specified time, a good rule of thumb to remember is that the low side pressure should reach 0 psi within 7 seconds if the expansion valve or orifice tube is not restricted.

8. Following the specified procedure, evacuate the A/C system.

   a. Inches of mercury attained: _____

   b. Microns attained: _____

9. Have your supervisor/instructor verify the reading. Supervisor's/instructor's initials: _____

10. Following the specified procedure, add the refrigerant oil to the system, if needed.

    a. List the amount of oil you added to the system: _____ oz/mL

11. Following the specified procedure, charge the A/C system.

    a. List the amount of refrigerant you installed: _____ lb/kg

    b. Did the low side pressure rise within the specified time?
       Yes: _____ No: _____

12. Is equalizing the refrigerant hoses necessary? Yes: _____
    No: _____

13. Start the engine and operate the A/C system.

14. Is the system operating properly? List your observations including pressures and temperatures:

15. **Determine any necessary action(s):**

16. **Have your supervisor/instructor verify satisfactory completion of this procedure, any observations found, and any necessary action(s) recommended.**

Performance Rating

CDX Tasksheet Number: C836

0	1	2	3	4

Supervisor/instructor signature _____ Date _____

CDX Tasksheet Number: C657

1. Research the procedure and specifications for this task in the appropriate service information.

   a. List the type of refrigerant you are working with: _____
   b. List the container color code for the specified refrigerant: _____
   c. What does a bottle with a yellow top and a gray bottom indicate?

   d. List or print off and attach to this sheet the steps to recycle the refrigerant:

   e. What are the labeling requirements for this refrigerant?

   f. What are the requirements for safely storing this refrigerant?

   g. Using the proper refrigerant PT (pressure/temperature) chart, record the specified reading for today's ambient temperature: _____ psi/kPa

2. Following the specified procedure, recycle the refrigerant. List your observations:

3. Following the specified procedure, ensure that the refrigerant is properly labeled. List your observations:

4. Following the specified procedure, properly store the refrigerant. List your observations:

5. Following the specified procedure, check for non-condensable gases. List your observations:

6. Have your supervisor/instructor verify satisfactory completion of this procedure, any observations found, and any necessary action(s) recommended.

Performance Rating

CDX Tasksheet Number: C657

0	1	2	3	4

Supervisor/instructor signature _____ Date _____

MAST
7A8

CDX Tasksheet Number: C652

1. **Research the following specifications in the appropriate service information.**
   a. **Specified refrigerant oil:** _____
   b. **Specified refrigerant oil capacity:** _____ oz/mL

2. **Have your supervisor/instructor verify satisfactory completion of this procedure, any observations found, and any necessary action(s) recommended.**

Performance Rating   CDX Tasksheet Number: C652

0	1	2	3	4

Supervisor/instructor signature _____ Date _____

Inspect condition of refrigerant oil removed from the system; determine needed action.

MAST
7A7

Time off_____

Time on_____

Total time_____

CDX Tasksheet Number: C651

1. **Research the procedure for inspecting the condition of the refrigerant oil in the appropriate service information.**

   a. **List or print off and attach to this sheet the steps to inspect the refrigerant oil:**

2. **Following the specified procedure, inspect the condition of the refrigerant oil. List your observation(s):**

3. **Determine any necessary action(s):**

4. **Have your supervisor/instructor verify satisfactory completion of this procedure, any observations found, and any necessary action(s) recommended.**

Performance Rating

CDX Tasksheet Number: C651

0	1	2	3	4

Supervisor/instructor signature _____ Date _____

Determine need for an additional A/C system filter; perform needed action.

MAST
7B5

Time off_____

Time on_____

Total time_____

CDX Tasksheet Number: C863

1. **Research the conditions that require the need for an additional A/C system filter in the appropriate service information.**

    a. **List the conditions that require an additional filter(s):**

    b. **List the specified location(s) for the filter(s):**

2. **Following the specified procedure, inspect the system to see if an additional filter(s) is (are) needed. List your observation(s):**

3. **Determine any necessary action(s):**

4. **Have your supervisor/instructor verify your observations. Supervisor's/instructor's initials: _____**

5. **Following the specified procedure, install the additional filter(s), if necessary. List your observation(s):**

6. **Have your supervisor/instructor verify satisfactory completion of this procedure, any observations found, and any necessary action(s) recommended.**

Performance Rating

CDX Tasksheet Number: C863

0	1	2	3	4

Supervisor/instructor signature _____ Date _____

Refrigeration System Component Diagnosis and Repair

Student/Intern information:

Name _____ Date _____ Class _____

Vehicle used for this activity:

Year _____ Make _____ Model _____

Odometer _____ VIN _____

Learning Objective/Task	CDX Tasksheet Number	2017 MAST NATEF Reference Number; Priority Level
• Inspect, remove, and/or replace A/C compressor drive belts, pulleys, tensioners, and visually inspect A/C components for signs of leaks; determine needed action.	C653	7B1; P-1
• Inspect, test, service, and/or replace A/C compressor clutch components and/or assembly; check compressor clutch air gap; adjust as needed.	C654	7B2; P-2
• Remove, inspect, reinstall, and/or replace A/C compressor and mountings; determine required oil type and quantity.	C826	7B3; P-2
• Remove and inspect A/C system mufflers, hoses, lines, fittings, O-rings, seals, and service valves; perform needed action.	C355	7B6; P-2
• Remove, inspect, and reinstall receiver/drier or accumulator/drier; determine recommended oil type and quantity.	C829	7B8; P-2
• Remove, inspect, and install expansion valve or orifice (expansion) tube.	C873	7B9; P-1
• Perform correct use and maintenance of refrigerant handling equipment according to equipment manufacturer's standards.	C656	7E1; P-1
• Determine procedure to remove and reinstall evaporator; determine required oil type and quantity.	C831	7B12; P-2
• Remove, inspect, reinstall, and/or replace condenser; determine required oil type and quantity.	C832	7B13; P-2

Time off _____

Time on _____

Total time _____

Materials Required

- Appropriate air conditioning manifold gauge set including service hoses
- Air conditioning service station and recovery/recycling equipment as necessary
- Refrigerant leak detecting equipment
- Refrigerant identifier
- Appropriate thermometers
- Feeler gauge set
- Clutch removal and installer tools
- Belt tension gauge
- Infrared temperature gun/thermocouple
- Anemometer
- DMM/DVOM
- Clean measuring container for refrigerant oil
- Specified refrigerant oil
- Specified vacuum pump oil

Some Safety Issues to Consider

- Refrigerant can cause serious damage if it comes in contact with a person's unprotected skin and eyes.
- When operating, the air conditioning system is normally subject to very high pressure in the system. Extreme caution must be exercised when working on an operating system.
- Extreme caution must be exercised when working around rotating components.
- When running any vehicles in the shop, make sure you use the shop's exhaust ventilation system to discharge all exhaust gas safely outside.
- Diagnosis of this fault may require test-driving the vehicle on the school grounds. Attempt this task only with full permission from your instructor and follow all the guidelines exactly.
- Vehicle hoists are important tools that increase productivity and make the job easier. However, they can also cause severe injury or death if used improperly. Make sure you follow the manufacturer's operation procedures.
- Comply with personal and environmental safety practices associated with clothing; eye protection; hand tools; power equipment; proper ventilation; and the handling, storage, and disposal of chemicals/materials in accordance with local, state, and federal safety and environmental regulations.

Performance Standard

0—No exposure: No information or practice provided during the program; complete training required

1—Exposure only: General information provided with no practice time; close supervision needed; additional training required

2—Limited practice: Has practiced job during training program; additional training required to develop skill

3—Moderately skilled: Has performed job independently during training program; limited additional training may be required

4—Skilled: Can perform job independently with no additional training

Inspect, remove, and/or replace A/C compressor drive belts, pulleys, and tensioners, and visually inspect A/C components for signs of leaks; determine needed action.

MAST
7B1

Time off_____

Time on_____

Total time_____

CDX Tasksheet Number: C653

1. **Research the procedure and specifications to inspect and replace drive belts, pulleys, and tensioners in the appropriate service information.**

    a. **List the specified drive belt tension:** _____ **lb/kg**

    b. **List the faults to look for when inspecting drive belts, pulleys, and tensioners:**

    c. **Describe how to check correct pulley and belt alignment:**

    d. **Locate the belt routing diagram, or draw a picture of the current routing arrangement below:**

2. **Following the specified procedure, remove the A/C drive belt(s).**

3. **Inspect vehicle drive belts, pulleys, and tensioners for faults. List your observations for the following components.**

    a. **Vehicle drive belt(s):**

    b. **Pulleys:**

    c. **Tensioner(s):**

      d. Pulley/belt alignment:

4. **Determine any necessary action(s):**

5. **Have your supervisor/instructor verify belt removal.**
   Supervisor's/instructor's initials: _____

> **NOTE** You may want to continue on to the next task while the belts are removed. If so, return here when you are ready to reinstall the drive belt(s).

6. **Following the specified procedure, reinstall the drive belt(s). Be sure to tension them properly.**

7. **Recheck for correct pulley, tensioner, and belt alignment. List your observation(s):**

8. **Visually inspect all A/C components for signs of leakage. List your observation(s):**

9. **Have your supervisor/instructor verify satisfactory completion of this procedure, any observations found, and any necessary action(s) recommended.**

Performance Rating

CDX Tasksheet Number: C653

0	1	2	3	4

Supervisor/instructor signature _____ Date _____

Inspect, test, service, and/or replace A/C compressor clutch components and /or assembly; check compressor clutch air gap; adjust as needed.

Time off_____

Time on_____

Total time_____

CDX Tasksheet Number: C654

Vehicle used for this activity:

Year _____ Make _____ Model_____

Odometer_____ VIN_____

1. **Research the procedure and specifications to inspect, test, and replace the A/C compressor clutch components in the appropriate service information.**

   a. **Specified compressor clutch coil resistance: _____ ohm**

   b. **Specified compressor clutch air gap: _____ in/mm**

   c. **Specified flat rate time to replace the compressor clutch: _____ hr**

2. **Following the specified procedure, measure the resistance of the compressor clutch coil.**

   a. **Measured clutch coil resistance: _____ ohm**

3. **Following the specified procedure, measure the compressor clutch air gap.**

   a. **Measured clutch air gap: _____ in/mm**

4. **Determine any necessary action(s):**

5. **Have your supervisor/instructor verify your measurements. Supervisor's/instructor's initials: _____**

6. **If approved by your instructor, remove the A/C compressor clutch components following the specified procedure.**

7. **Have your supervisor/instructor verify removal of the clutch components. Supervisor's/instructor's initials: _____**

8. **Following the specified procedure, reinstall the A/C clutch components. Be sure that the air gap is properly adjusted. List your observation(s):**

9. Have your supervisor/instructor verify satisfactory completion of this procedure, any observations found, and any necessary action(s) recommended.

Performance Rating

0	1	2	3	4

Supervisor/instructor signature _____ Date _____

Remove, inspect, reinstall, and/or replace A/C compressor and mountings; determine required oil type and quantity.

MAST
7B3

Time off_____

Time on_____

Total time_____

CDX Tasksheet Number: C826

Vehicle used for this activity:

Year _____ Make _____ Model_____

Odometer_____ VIN_____

1. **Research the procedure and specifications to remove, inspect, and reinstall the A/C compressor in the appropriate service information.**

    a. **Specified refrigerant oil type:** _____
    b. **Specified refrigerant oil quantity to add during replacement of the compressor:** _____ oz/mL
    c. **List or print off and attach to this sheet the steps to remove, inspect, and reinstall the compressor:**

2. **Following the specified procedure, remove the A/C compressor from the vehicle.**

3. **Following the specified procedure, drain the refrigerant oil from the compressor into a clean measuring container.**

    a. **List the quantity of oil drained:** _____ oz/mL

4. **Following the specified procedure, inspect the A/C compressor and mountings. List your observations:**

5. **Determine any necessary action(s):**

6. **Have your supervisor/instructor verify removal and your observations. Supervisor's/instructor's initials:** _____

7. **Following the specified procedure, reinstall the A/C compressor. Be sure to add the proper quantity and type of new refrigerant oil.**

    a. **List the quantity of oil added to the compressor:** _____ oz/mL

8. Have your supervisor/instructor verify satisfactory completion of this procedure, any observations found, and any necessary action(s) recommended.

Performance Rating

CDX Tasksheet Number: C826

0	1	2	3	4

Supervisor/instructor signature _____ Date _____

Remove and inspect A/C system mufflers, hoses, lines, fittings, O-rings, seals, and service valves; perform needed action.

MAST
7B6

CDX Tasksheet Number: C355

Vehicle used for this activity:

Year _____ Make _____ Model_____

Odometer_____ VIN_____

1. **Research the procedures and specifications for removing and inspecting the above A/C components in the appropriate service information.**

   a. **List or print off and attach to this sheet the procedure and specifications for inspecting these components:**

2. **Following the specified procedure, remove the following A/C system components. Inspect each one and list your observations below.**

   a. **Muffler (if equipped):**

   b. **Hoses and lines:**

   c. **Fittings, O-rings, and seals:**

   d. **Service valves:**

3. **Determine any necessary action(s):**

4. Have your supervisor/instructor verify removal and observations. Supervisor's/instructor's initials: _____

5. Perform any necessary actions and list your observation(s):

6. Have your supervisor/instructor verify satisfactory completion of this procedure, any observations found, and any necessary action(s) recommended.

Performance Rating

0	1	2	3	4

Supervisor/instructor signature _____ Date _____

Remove, inspect, and reinstall receiver/drier or accumulator/drier; determine recommended oil type and quantity.

MAST
7B8

Time off_____

Time on_____

Total time_____

CDX Tasksheet Number: C829

Vehicle used for this activity:

Year _____ Make _____ Model_____

Odometer_____ VIN_____

1. **Research the procedure and specifications for removing, inspecting, and reinstalling the receiver/drier or accumulator/drier in the appropriate service information.**

    a. **Specified refrigerant oil type:** _____

    b. **Specified refrigerant oil quantity to add during replacement of the receiver/drier:** _____ oz/mL

    c. **List or print off and attach to this sheet the steps to remove, inspect, and reinstall the receiver/drier:**

2. **Following the specified procedure, remove the receiver/drier or accumulator/drier from the vehicle.**

3. **Following the specified procedure, drain the refrigerant oil from the receiver/drier or accumulator/drier into a clean measuring container.**

    a. **List the quantity of oil drained:** _____ oz/mL

4. **Following the specified procedure, inspect the receiver/drier or accumulator/drier. List your observation(s):**

5. **Determine any necessary action(s):**

6. **Have your supervisor/instructor verify removal and your observations. Supervisor's/instructor's initials:** _____

7. **Following the specified procedure, reinstall the receiver/drier or accumulator/drier. Be sure to add the proper quantity and type of new refrigerant oil.**

    a. **List the quantity of oil added to the receiver/drier or accumulator/drier:** _____ oz/mL

8. Have your supervisor/instructor verify satisfactory completion of this procedure, any observations found, and any necessary action(s) recommended.

Performance Rating

0	1	2	3	4

Supervisor/instructor signature _____ Date _____

▶ TASK Remove, inspect, and install expansion valve or orifice
(expansion) tube.

MAST
7B9

Time off_____

Time on_____

CDX Tasksheet Number: C873

Total time_____

Vehicle used for this activity:

Year _____ Make _____ Model_____

Odometer_____ VIN_____

1. **Research the procedure and specifications for removing, inspecting, and installing the expansion valve or orifice tube in the appropriate service information.**

   a. **List any precautions for this task:**

   b. **List the specified orifice tube color or expansion valve tonnage:** _____

   c. **Does the manufacturer allow interchange of orifice colors or expansion valve tonnage? Yes:** _____ **No:** _____

   d. **List or print off and attach to this sheet the steps to perform this task:**

2. **Following the specified procedure, remove the expansion valve or orifice tube.**

   a. **List the orifice tube color or expansion valve tonnage:** _____

3. **Inspect the expansion valve or orifice tube for proper operation or debris. List your observation(s):**

4. **Determine any necessary action(s):**

5. **Have your supervisor/instructor verify removal and your observations. Supervisor's/instructor's initials:** _____

6. **Reinstall the expansion valve or orifice tube. List your observation(s):**

7. Have your supervisor/instructor verify satisfactory completion of this procedure, any observations found, and any necessary action(s) recommended.

Performance Rating

CDX Tasksheet Number: C873

0	1	2	3	4

Supervisor/instructor signature _____ Date _____

Perform correct use and maintenance of refrigerant handling
equipment according to equipment manufacturer's standards.

MAST
7E1

CDX Tasksheet Number: C656

Vehicle used for this activity:

Year _____ Make _____ Model_____

Odometer_____ VIN_____

1. **Research the operation and maintenance of the refrigerant handling equipment in the appropriate operator's manual.**

    a. **List the manufacturer of the refrigerant handling equipment: _____**

    b. **List the functions this equipment is capable of performing:**

    c. **List any required maintenance tasks and the service intervals for this equipment:**

    d. **List any special precautions when using the refrigerant handling equipment:**

    e. **Review the steps to correctly use the refrigerant handling equipment.**

    f. **List the current EPA machine standards.**

       i. **For recovery-only machines:**

       ii. **For recycling machines:**

2. Following the specified procedure, demonstrate the correct use of the refrigerant handling equipment.

    a. Recovery

       Amount of refrigerant recovered: _____ lb/kg

       Amount of oil recovered, if any: _____ oz/mL

    b. Evacuate

       Inches of mercury attained: _____

       Microns attained: _____

    c. Oil inject

       Amount of oil injected: _____ oz/mL

    d. Recharge

       Amount of refrigerant charged: _____ lb/kg

3. Determine any necessary action(s):

4. Have your supervisor/instructor verify the correct use. Supervisor's/instructor's initials: _____

5. Following the specified procedure, perform the recommended maintenance on the refrigerant handling equipment.

    a. Test the vacuum pump for proper operation.

       Inches of mercury attained: _____

       Microns attained: _____

    b. Change the vacuum oil.

       Type of oil required: _____

       Quantity of oil required: _____ oz/mL

       Condition of oil drained:

    c. Perform a leak test on the machine using specified equipment.

       Equipment used to perform this test:

       Results:

    d. Change the recovery filter.

       List the filter part number: _____

    e. Charge the machine with refrigerant.

       List the quantity charged: _____ lb/kg

6. Determine any necessary action(s):

7. Have your supervisor/instructor verify satisfactory completion of this procedure, any observations found, and any necessary action(s) recommended.

Performance Rating

0	1	2	3	4

Supervisor/instructor signature _____ Date _____

Determine procedure to remove and reinstall evaporator;
determine required oil type and quantity.

MAST
7B12

CDX Tasksheet Number: C831

1. **Research the procedure and specifications for removing, inspecting, and reinstalling the evaporator in the appropriate service information.**

   a. **Specified refrigerant oil type:** _____

   b. **Specified refrigerant oil quantity to add during replacement of the evaporator:** _____ **oz/mL**

   c. **Flat rate time to R&R the evaporator:** _____ **hr**

   d. **List, or print off and attach to this sheet, the steps to remove, inspect, and reinstall the evaporator:**

2. **Have your supervisor/instructor verify satisfactory completion of this procedure, any observations found, and any necessary action(s) recommended.**

Performance Rating

CDX Tasksheet Number: C831

0	1	2	3	4

Supervisor/instructor signature _____ Date _____

Remove, inspect, reinstall, and/or replace condenser; determine required oil type and quantity.

MAST
7B13

CDX Tasksheet Number: C832

1. **Research the procedure and specifications for removing, inspecting, and reinstalling the condenser in the appropriate service information.**

    a. **Specified refrigerant oil type:** _____

    b. **Specified refrigerant oil quantity to add during replacement of the condenser:** _____ **oz/mL**

    c. **Flat rate time to R&R the condenser:** _____ **hr**

    d. **List, or print off and attach to this sheet, the steps to remove, inspect, and reinstall the condenser:**

2. **Before proceeding, have your instructor check your answers and obtain his or her permission to remove the condenser on this vehicle. Supervisor's/instructor's initials:** _____

3. **Following the specified procedure, remove the condenser from the vehicle.**

4. **Following the specified procedure, drain the refrigerant oil from the condenser into a clean measuring container.**

    a. **List the quantity of oil drained:** _____ **oz/mL**

5. **Following the specified procedure, inspect the condenser and mountings. List your observation(s):**

6. **Determine any necessary action(s):**

7. **Have your supervisor/instructor verify removal and your observations and initial below. Supervisor's/instructor's initials:** _____

8. Following the specified procedure, reinstall the condenser. Be sure to add the proper quantity and type of new refrigerant oil.

   a. List the quantity of oil added to the condenser: _____ oz/mL

9. Have your supervisor/instructor verify satisfactory completion of this procedure, any observations found, and any necessary action(s) recommended.

Performance Rating

CDX Tasksheet Number: C832

0	1	2	3	4

Supervisor/instructor signature _____ Date _____

Heating, Ventilation, and Engine Cooling Systems Diagnosis and Repair

Student/Intern information:

Name _____ Date _____ Class _____

Vehicle used for this activity:

Year _____ Make _____ Model_____

Odometer_____VIN_____

Learning Objective/Task	CDX Tasksheet Number	2017 MAST NATEF Reference Number; Priority Level
• Diagnose temperature control problems in the HVAC system; determine needed action.	C362	7C3; P-2
• Inspect engine cooling and heater system hoses and pipes; perform needed action.	C364	7C1; P-1
• Inspect and test heater control valve(s); perform needed action.	C370	7C2; P-2
• Inspect and test HVAC system blower motors, resistors, switches, relays, wiring, and protection devices; determine needed action.	C373	7D1; P-1
• Determine procedure to remove, inspect, reinstall, and/or replace heater core.	C864	7C4; P-2

Time off_____

Time on_____

Total time_____

Materials Required

- Vehicle or simulator
- Cooling system pressure tester
- Infrared temperature gun
- DMM/DVOM
- Drain pan
- Hose slitter

Some Safety Issues to Consider

- Open the radiator cap (or any other part of the cooling system) only with the engine cold. Opening a radiator cap on a warm or hot engine could cause severe burns.
- Electric fans can turn on at any time. Keep hands and fingers away.
- When running any vehicles in the shop, make sure you use the shop's exhaust ventilation system to discharge all exhaust gas safely outside.
- Extreme caution must be exercised when working around rotating components.
- A hose slitter is handy for removing hoses from radiators and heater cores without damaging the metal tubes, but can cut you if not used carefully.
- Refrigerant can cause serious damage if it comes in contact with a person's unprotected skin and eyes.
- When operating, the air conditioning system is normally subject to very high pressure in the system. Extreme caution must be exercised when working on an operating system.

- Comply with personal and environmental safety practices associated with clothing; eye protection; hand tools; power equipment; proper ventilation; and the handling, storage, and disposal of chemicals/materials in accordance with local, state, and federal safety and environmental regulations.

Performance Standard

0–No exposure: No information or practice provided during the program; complete training required

1–Exposure only: General information provided with no practice time; close supervision needed; additional training required

2–Limited practice: Has practiced job during training program; additional training required to develop skill

3–Moderately skilled: Has performed job independently during training program; limited additional training may be required

4–Skilled: Can perform job independently with no additional training

Diagnose temperature control problems in the HVAC
system; determine needed action.

MAST
7C3

Time off_____

Time on_____

Total time_____

CDX Tasksheet Number: C362

1. List the heater/ventilation-related customer concern:

2. Research the customer concern in the appropriate service information. List the possible causes:

3. Following the specified procedure, diagnose the customer concern. List your tests and observations:

4. List the cause of the customer concern:

5. Determine any necessary action(s) to correct the fault:

6. Have your supervisor/instructor verify satisfactory completion of this procedure, any observations found, and any necessary action(s) recommended.

Performance Rating

CDX Tasksheet Number: C362

0	1	2	3	4

Supervisor/instructor signature _____ Date _____

Inspect engine cooling and heater system hoses and pipes; perform needed action.

MAST
7C1

Time off_____

Time on_____

Total time_____

CDX Tasksheet Number: C364

Vehicle used for this activity:

Year _____ Make _____ Model _____

Odometer _____ VIN _____

1. **Research the procedure and specifications for inspecting and replacing cooling system hoses and belts in the appropriate service information.**

   a. **Specified change interval for radiator hoses:** _____ **miles/months**

   b. **Specified change interval for heater hoses:** _____ **miles/months**

   c. **Describe what to look for when inspecting cooling system hoses:**

2. **Inspect the cooling and heater system hoses. List your observations:**

3. **Using a cooling system pressure tester, pressurize the cooling system to the specified radiator cap pressure. Inspect the cooling system for leaks. List your observations:**

4. **Have your supervisor/instructor verify your observations. Supervisor's/instructor's initials:** _____

5. **Perform any necessary actions and list your observation(s):**

6. **Have your supervisor/instructor verify satisfactory completion of this procedure, any observations found, and any necessary action(s) recommended.**

Performance Rating

CDX Tasksheet Number: C364

0	1	2	3	4

Supervisor/instructor signature _____ Date _____

Inspect and test heater control valve(s); perform
needed action.

Time off_____

Time on_____

Total time_____

CDX Tasksheet Number: C370

Vehicle used for this activity:

Year _____ Make _____ Model_____

Odometer_____ VIN_____

1. **Research the procedure and specifications for inspecting and testing the heater control valve(s) in the appropriate service information.**

   a. **Specified type of heater control valve(s): Cable: _____**
      Vacuum: _____ Electric: _____
   b. **What does the temperature adjusting mechanism regulate?**
      Coolant:_____ Air: _____

2. **Following the specified procedure, inspect and test the heater control valve(s). List your tests and observation(s):**

3. **Determine any necessary action(s):**

4. **Have your supervisor/instructor verify satisfactory completion of this procedure, any observations found, and any necessary action(s) recommended.**

Performance Rating

CDX Tasksheet Number: C370

0	1	2	3	4

Supervisor/instructor signature _____ Date _____

Inspect and test HVAC system blower, motors, resistors, switches, relays, wiring, and protection devices; determine needed action.

MAST
7D1

Time off_____

Time on_____

Total time_____

CDX Tasksheet Number: C373

Vehicle used for this activity:

Year _____ Make _____ Model _____

Odometer _____ VIN _____

1. **Research the procedure and specifications to inspect and test the electrical components of the HVAC system in the appropriate service information.**

    a. Specified resistance of the blower motor: _____ ohms

    b. Specified resistance of the blower motor resistors

    Resistance on the highest resisted speed: _____ ohms

    Resistance on medium-high resisted speed: _____ ohms

    Resistance on medium-low resisted speed: _____ ohms

    Resistance on the lowest resisted speed: _____ ohms

    c. List all the protection devices for the blower motor circuit:

2. **Following the specified procedure, inspect and test the following devices. List your observations below.**

    a. **Blower motor:**

    b. **Blower motor resistors:**

    c. **Appropriate switches:**

    d. **Appropriate relays:**

     e. Appropriate circuit protection devices:

     f. Appropriate wiring harness:

3. Determine any necessary action(s):

4. Have your supervisor/instructor verify satisfactory completion of this procedure, any observations found, and any necessary action(s) recommended.

Performance Rating

CDX Tasksheet Number: C373

☐	☐	☐	☐	☐
0	1	2	3	4

Supervisor/instructor signature _____ Date _____

Determine procedure to remove, inspect, reinstall, and/or replace heater core.

MAST
7C4

Time off_____

Time on_____

Total time_____

CDX Tasksheet Number: C864

Vehicle used for this activity:

Year _____ Make _____ Model_____

Odometer_____ VIN_____

1. **Research the procedure and specifications for inspecting and replacing the heater core in the appropriate service information.**

   a. **List the flat rate time for removing and replacing the heater core:**
      _____ hr

   b. **Does this task require evacuation of the A/C refrigerant?**
      Yes _____ No _____

   c. **List, or print off and attach to this sheet, the steps to remove and replace the heater core:**

2. **List, or print off and attach to this sheet, the steps to inspect the heater core:**

3. **Have your supervisor/instructor verify satisfactory completion of this procedure, any observations found, and any necessary action(s) recommended.**

Performance Rating

CDX Tasksheet Number: C864

0	1	2	3	4

Supervisor/instructor signature _____ Date _____

Operating Systems and Related Controls Diagnosis and Repair

Student/Intern information:

Name _____ Date _____ Class _____

Vehicle used for this activity:

Year _____ Make _____ Model _____

Odometer _____ VIN _____

Learning Objective/Task	CDX Tasksheet Number	2017 MAST NATEF Reference Number; Priority Level
• Check operation of automatic or semi- automatic HVAC control systems; determine needed action.	C866	7D8; P-2
• Using a scan tool, observe and record related HVAC data and trouble codes.	C566	7A9; P-3
• Diagnose A/C system conditions that cause the protection devices (pressure, thermal, and/or control module) to interrupt system operation; determine needed action.	C350	7B11; P-2
• Diagnose A/C compressor clutch control systems; determine needed action.	C374	7D2; P-2
• Diagnose malfunctions in the vacuum, mechanical, and electrical components and controls of the heating, ventilation, and A/C (HVAC) system; determine needed action.	C835	7D3; P-2
• Inspect and test HVAC system control panel assembly; determine needed action.	C376	7D4; P-3
• Inspect and test HVAC system control cables, motors, and linkages; perform needed action.	C865	7D5; P-3
• Inspect HVAC system ducts, doors, hoses, cabin filters, and outlets; perform needed action.	C378	7D6; P-1

Time off_____

Time on_____

Total time_____

Materials Required

- Scan tool
- Appropriate air conditioning manifold gauge set including service hoses
- Air conditioning service station and recovery/recycling equipment as necessary
- Refrigerant leak detecting equipment
- Refrigerant identifier
- Appropriate thermometers
- Infrared temperature gun/thermocouple
- DMM/DVOM
- Hand vacuum pump

Some Safety Issues to Consider

- Refrigerant can cause serious damage if it comes in contact with a person's unprotected skin and eyes.
- When operating, the air conditioning system is normally subject to very high pressure in the system. Extreme caution must be exercised when working on an operating system.
- Extreme caution must be exercised when working around rotating components.
- When running any vehicles in the shop, make sure you use the shop's exhaust ventilation system to discharge all exhaust gas safely outside.
- Diagnosis of this fault may require test-driving the vehicle on the school grounds. Attempt this task only with full permission from your instructor and follow all the guidelines exactly.
- Comply with personal and environmental safety practices associated with clothing; eye protection; hand tools; power equipment; proper ventilation; and the handling, storage, and disposal of chemicals/materials in accordance with local, state, and federal safety and environmental regulations.

Performance Standard

0—No exposure: No information or practice provided during the program; complete training required

1—Exposure only: General information provided with no practice time; close supervision needed; additional training required

2—Limited practice: Has practiced job during training program; additional training required to develop skill

3—Moderately skilled: Has performed job independently during training program; limited additional training may be required

4—Skilled: Can perform job independently with no additional training

Check operation of automatic or semi-automatic
HVAC control systems; determine needed action.

MAST
7D8

Time off_____

Time on_____

CDX Tasksheet Number: C866

Vehicle used for this activity:

Year _____ Make _____ Model_____

Total time_____

Odometer_____ VIN_____

1. **Research the description and operation of the HVAC climate control system in the appropriate service information.**

   a. **Is this system a full-authority climate control system? Yes: _____**
      No: _____

   b. **If equipped, how do you test the evaporator thermistors?**

   c. **If equipped, how do you test the three-wire A/C pressure sensors?**

   d. **If equipped, how do you access the trouble codes on this vehicle?**

   e. **How is the heater controlled? Heater control valve: _____ Blend door: _____**

   f. **Research the steps to test the operation of the climate control system:**

2. **Following the specified procedure, test the operation of the climate control system. List your steps and the results:**

3. **Determine any necessary action(s):**

4. **Have your supervisor/instructor verify satisfactory completion of this procedure, any observations found, and any necessary action(s) recommended.**

Performance Rating

CDX Tasksheet Number: C866

0	1	2	3	4

Supervisor/instructor signature _____ Date _____

DX Tasksheet Number: C566

ehicle used for this activity:

ear _____ Make _____ Model_____

dometer_____ VIN_____

1. **List the HVAC-related customer concern:**

2. **Start the vehicle and operate the HVAC system to verify the concern. List your observation(s):**

3. **Following the specified procedure, connect a scan tool to the vehicle. Obtain and record the following information.**

   a. **HVAC-related trouble code(s) and their description(s):**

   b. **HVAC-related data (list at least three readings and their descriptions):**

4. **Have your supervisor/instructor verify satisfactory completion of this procedure, any observations found, and any necessary action(s) recommended.**

erformance Rating

CDX Tasksheet Number: C566

0	1	2	3	4

upervisor/instructor signature _____ Date _____

Diagnose A/C system conditions that cause the protection devices (pressure, thermal, and/or control module) to interrupt system operation; determine needed action.

MAST
7B11

Time off_____

Time on_____

Total time_____

CDX Tasksheet Number: C350

1. List the A/C system protection device-related customer concern:

2. Research the possible cause(s) and testing procedures in the appropriate service information.
   a. List any possible cause(s):

   b. List or print off and attach to this sheet the steps for identifying the cause of the concern:

3. Following the specified procedure, identify the cause of the concern. List your test(s) and results:

4. List the cause of the concern:

5. Determine any necessary action(s) to correct the fault:

6. Have your supervisor/instructor verify satisfactory completion of this procedure, any observations found, and any necessary action(s) recommended.

Performance Rating

CDX Tasksheet Number: C350

0	1	2	3	4

Supervisor/instructor signature _____ Date _____

Diagnose A/C compressor clutch control systems; determine
needed action.

Time off_____

Time on_____

Total time_____

DX Tasksheet Number: C374

Vehicle used for this activity:

Year _____ Make _____ Model _____

Odometer_____ VIN_____

1. **Research the procedure and specifications to inspect and test the electrical components of the A/C compressor clutch control system in the appropriate service information.**

   a. Specified resistance of the clutch winding: _____ ohms
   b. A/C cycling switch specifications (if equipped)
      Off pressure: _____ psi/kPa
      On pressure: _____ psi/kPa
   c. A/C thermoswitch specifications (if equipped)
      Off temperature: _____ °F/°C
      On temperature: _____ °F/°C
   d. A/C duct temperature specifications: _____ °F/°C
   e. A/C high-pressure cut-out switch specifications
      Off pressure: _____ psi/kPa
      On pressure: _____ psi/kPa
   f. A/C low pressure cut-out switch (non-cycling) (if equipped)
      Off pressure: _____ psi/kPa
      On pressure: _____ psi/kPa
   g. A/C compressor clutch relay specifications (if equipped)
      Relay winding resistance: _____ ohms
      Maximum allowable voltage drop across relay contacts:
      _____ volts
   h. List all the fuses and/or fusible links for the A/C compressor clutch circuit:

   i. Does the compressor clutch share a fuse with the blower circuit?
      Yes: _____ No: _____

2. **Following the specified procedure, activate the A/C system.**

   a. Does the compressor clutch engage? Yes: _____ No: _____
   b. If yes, continue on to step 3. If no, skip to step 5.

   _____

3. **List your observations below.**

   a. A/C cycling switch readings (if equipped)
      Off pressure: _____ psi/kPa
      On pressure: _____ psi/kPa
   b. A/C thermoswitch readings (if equipped)
      Off temperature: _____ °F/°C
      On temperature: _____ °F/°C
   c. A/C duct temperature: _____ °F/°C

d. A/C high pressure cut-out switch readings (may require condenser airflow blockage to test). (DUE TO THE SAFETY IMPLICATIONS, ONLY PERFORM THIS TEST IF APPROVED BY YOUR SUPERVISOR/INSTRUCTOR.)
Off pressure: _____ psi/kPa
On pressure: _____ psi/kPa
e. Determine any necessary action(s):

4. Have your supervisor/instructor verify the readings. Supervisor's/instructor's initials: _____

> NOTE If your instructor signed off on this step, skip to the final check off.

5. If the clutch does not engage, install a gauge set and check for minimum refrigerant pressure. If pressure is insufficient, check for refrigerant leaks, then retest after repair. If pressure is sufficient, measure the voltage applied to the compressor clutch winding.

a. Applied voltage to the compressor clutch: _____ volts
b. Compressor clutch winding resistance: _____ ohms
c. A/C compressor clutch relay readings
Relay winding resistance: _____ ohms
Voltage at the relay contact input terminal: _____ volts
Voltage drop across relay contacts (A/C on): _____ volts
d. Describe the circuit protection device(s) condition:

6. Determine any necessary action(s):

> NOTE If repairs are made, return to step 3 and retest.

7. Have your supervisor/instructor verify satisfactory completion of this procedure, any observations found, and any necessary action(s) recommended.

Performance Rating

CDX Tasksheet Number: C374

0	1	2	3	4

Supervisor/instructor signature _____ Date _____

Diagnose malfunctions in the vacuum, mechanical, and electrical
components and controls of the heating, ventilation, and
A/C (HVAC) system; determine needed action.

MAST
7D3

Time off_____

Time on_____

Total time_____

CDX Tasksheet Number: C835

Vehicle used for this activity:

Year _____ Make _____ Model _____

Odometer _____ VIN _____

1. List the vacuum, mechanical, or electrical controls–related HVAC customer
   concern:

2. Verify the concern by operating each of the HVAC vacuum, mechanical, and
   electrical controls through their range and list your observation(s):

3. Research the procedure, specifications, and wiring diagrams for diagnosing the
   concern in the appropriate service information.

   a. List the possible faults:

   b. List or print off and attach to this sheet the steps to diagnose the fault:

4. Following the specified procedure, diagnose the concern. List your tests and the
   results:

5. List the cause of the concern:

6. Determine any necessary action(s) to correct the fault:

7. Have your supervisor/instructor verify satisfactory completion of this procedure,
   any observations found, and any necessary action(s) recommended.

Performance Rating

CDX Tasksheet Number: C835

0	1	2	3	4

Supervisor/instructor signature _____ Date _____

Inspect and test HVAC system control panel assembly; determine needed action.

MAST
7D4

Time off_____

Time on_____

Total time_____

CDX Tasksheet Number: C376

Vehicle used for this activity:

Year _____ Make _____ Model _____

Odometer _____ VIN _____

1. List the A/C-heater control panel–related HVAC customer concern:

2. Verify the concern by operating each of the control panel controls through their range and list your observation(s):

3. Research the procedure and specifications for inspecting and testing the A/C-heater control panel in the appropriate service information.
   a. What kind of controls is this vehicle equipped with? _____
   b. List or print off and attach to this sheet the steps to inspect and test the control panel:

4. Following the specified procedure, inspect and test the control panel. List your tests and results:

5. List the cause of the concern:

6. Determine any necessary action(s) to correct the fault:

7. Have your supervisor/instructor verify satisfactory completion of this procedure, any observations found, and any necessary action(s) recommended.

Performance Rating

CDX Tasksheet Number: C376

0	1	2	3	4

Supervisor/instructor signature _____ Date _____

Inspect and test HVAC system control cables, motors, and linkages; perform needed action.

MAST
7D5

CDX Tasksheet Number: C865

Vehicle used for this activity:

Year _____ Make _____ Model _____

Odometer _____ VIN _____

1. **Research the procedures and specifications to inspect and test the control cables, motors, and linkages in the appropriate service information.**

    a. **List any precautions for this task:**

    b. **List or print off and attach to this sheet any procedures and specifications for this task:**

2. **Verify the operation of all HVAC control cables, motors, and linkages. List your observation(s):**

3. **Following the specified procedure, inspect and test the cables, motors, and linkages. List your tests and results:**

4. **Determine any necessary action(s):**

5. **Have your supervisor/instructor verify satisfactory completion of this procedure, any observations found, and any necessary action(s) recommended.**

Performance Rating

CDX Tasksheet Number: C865

0	1	2	3	4

Supervisor/instructor signature _____ Date _____

Inspect HVAC system ducts, doors, hoses, cabin filters, and outlets; perform needed action.

MAST
7D6

Time off_____

Time on_____

CDX Tasksheet Number: C378

Total time_____

Vehicle used for this activity:

Year _____ Make _____ Model_____

Odometer_____ VIN_____

1. **Research the procedure and specifications for inspecting the above components in the appropriate service information.**

   a. **Is this vehicle equipped with a cabin air filter? Yes:** _____
      No: _____
   b. **What is the recommended replacement interval for the cabin air filter?**
      _____ **mi/km/mo**

2. **Following the specified procedure, inspect the following components. List your observations below.**

   a. **Ducts:**

   b. **Doors:**

   c. **Hoses:**

   d. **Cabin filter(s):**

   e. **Outlets:**

3. **Determine any necessary action(s):**

4. **Have your supervisor/instructor verify satisfactory completion of this procedure, any observations found, and any necessary action(s) recommended.**

Performance Rating

CDX Tasksheet Number: C378

0	1	2	3	4

Supervisor/instructor signature _____ Date _____

Section A8:
Engine Performance

CONTENTS

Vehicle, Customer, and Service Information

Student/Intern information:

Name _____ Date _____ Class _____

Vehicle used for this activity:

Year _____ Make _____ Model _____

Odometer _____ VIN _____

Learning Objective/Task	CDX Tasksheet Number	2017 MAST NATEF Reference Number; Priority Level	
• Research vehicle service information including vehicle service history, service precautions, and technical service bulletins.	C387	8A2; P-1	Time off _____
• Demonstrate the use of the three Cs (concern, cause, and correction).	N/A	N/A	Time on _____
• Identify and interpret engine performance concerns; determine needed action.	C386	8A1; P-1	Total time _____

Materials Required

- Blank work order
- Vehicle with available service history records
- Depending on the type of concern, special diagnostic tools may be required. See your supervisor/instructor for instructions to identify what tools may be required.

Some Safety Issues to Consider

- Diagnosis of this fault may require test-driving the vehicle on the school grounds or on a hoist, both of which carry severe risks. Attempt this task only with full permission from your supervisor/instructor and follow all the guidelines exactly.
- When running any vehicles in the shop, make sure you use the shop's exhaust ventilation system to discharge all exhaust gas safely outside.
- Because the vehicle will be running for an extended amount of time, make sure the vehicle cannot move or roll by applying the parking brake and using wheel chocks.
- You will be working under the hood of a running vehicle. Keep your hands and fingers away from moving belts, fans, and other parts.
- This task may require working with liquid fuel. Prevent serious burns or fires by keeping open flame or any other source of ignition far away.
- Comply with personal and environmental safety practices associated with clothing; eye protection; hand tools; power equipment; proper ventilation; and the handling, storage, and disposal of chemicals/materials in accordance with local, state, and federal safety and environmental regulations.

Performance Standard

0—No exposure: No information or practice provided during the program; complete training required

1—Exposure only: General information provided with no practice time; close supervision needed; additional training required

2—Limited practice: Has practiced job during training program; additional training required to develop skill

3—Moderately skilled: Has performed job independently during training program; limited additional training may be required

4—Skilled: Can perform job independently with no additional training

Research vehicle service information including vehicle service history, service precautions, and technical service bulletins.

MAST
8A2

CDX Tasksheet Number: C387

1. Using the VIN for identification, use the appropriate source to access the vehicle's service history in relation to prior related engine management work or customer concerns.

    a. List any related repairs/concerns, and their dates:

2. Using the VIN for identification, access any relevant technical service bulletins for the particular vehicle you are working on in relation to engine management updates or other service issues.

    a. List any related service bulletins (bulletin number and title):

3. Have your supervisor/instructor verify satisfactory completion of this procedure, any observations found, and any necessary action(s) recommended.

Performance Rating

CDX Tasksheet Number: C387

0	1	2	3	4

Supervisor/instructor signature _____ Date _____

Demonstrate the use of the three Cs
(concern, cause, and correction).

Time off_____

Time on_____

Total time_____

CDX Tasksheet Number: N/A

1. Using the following scenario, write up the three Cs as listed on most repair orders. Assume that the customer authorized the recommended repairs.

   A vehicle has been brought to your shop with an engine performance/driveability concern. The customer tells you that the vehicle used to run rough only when accelerating up a hill but now it is running rough when accelerating even lightly. The MIL light also blinks when the engine is running rough. The customer thought it was bad gas, but after that tank ran out, the customer refilled it with good gas from a very reputable station and it still runs rough even after using half a tank. The customer authorizes your shop to perform a diagnosis and you find the following:

   a. P0305—Engine misfire on cylinder #5.
   b. #5 spark plug boot is leaking high voltage to the cylinder head under light load.
   c. All of the spark plugs are moderately worn.
   d. All of the spark plug wires are original. The vehicle is about 8 years old and has nearly 100,000 miles on it.
   e. Cylinder relative compression is within specifications.
   f. The air filter is dirty.
   g. The oil change is almost 1000 miles and 2 months overdue.
   h. The oil seals and gaskets look to be in good shape with no leaks.
   i. The water pump seal is starting to seep coolant and the coolant is a bit dirty.
   j. The belts look like they have been replaced recently.

   > NOTE Ask your instructor whether you should use a copy of the shop repair order or the three Cs below to record this information.

2. Concern/complaint:

3. Cause:

4. Correction:

5. Other recommended service:

6. Have your supervisor/instructor verify satisfactory completion of this procedure, any observations found, and any necessary action(s) recommended.

Performance Rating

CDX Tasksheet Number: N/A

0	1	2	3	4

Supervisor/instructor signature _____ Date _____

Identify and interpret engine performance concerns;
determine needed action.

MAST
8A1

CDX Tasksheet Number: C386

1. **List the customer concern:**

2. **Research the particular concern in the appropriate service information.**

    a. **List the possible causes:**

3. **Inspect the engine and management system to determine the cause of the concern.**

    a. **List the steps you took to determine the fault and the result for each step:**

4. **List the cause of the concern/complaint:**

5. **List the necessary action(s) to correct this fault:**

6. Have your supervisor/instructor verify satisfactory completion of this procedure, any observations found, and any necessary action(s) recommended.

Performance Rating

0	1	2	3	4

Supervisor/instructor signature _____ Date _____

Mechanical Engine Testing

Student/Intern information:

Name _____ Date _____ Class _____

Vehicle used for this activity:

Year _____ Make _____ Model _____

Odometer _____ VIN _____

Learning Objective/Task	CDX Tasksheet Number	2017 MAST NATEF Reference Number; Priority Level
• Diagnose abnormal engine noises or vibration concerns; determine needed action.	C390	8A3; P-3

Time off _____

Time on _____

Total time _____

Materials Required

- Vehicle or simulator
- Vacuum gauge
- Tachometer (handheld if vehicle is not equipped with an in-dash tachometer)
- Appropriate tool to disable cylinders (scan tool, insulated pliers, etc.)
- Compression tester
- Cylinder leakage tester
- Mechanics stethoscope

Some Safety Issues to Consider

- You will be working under the hood of a running vehicle. Keep your hands and fingers away from moving belts, fans, and other parts.
- Be sure to only disconnect the proper vacuum hose. Many other hoses look alike but could carry gasoline or hot coolant under high pressure.
- During this test, you may be disabling the ignition or fuel systems. Be sure you do so only for the minimum amount of time to get your readings. Operating the engine with cylinders disabled may lead to damage of the catalytic converter or other parts if done for more than a minimum amount of time. If in doubt, ask your supervisor/instructor.
- If you disable the cylinders by disconnecting the spark plug wires, you may expose yourself to extremely high voltage (up to 100,000 volts). Reduce the possibility of electrical shock by using appropriate insulated spark plug wire pliers.
- When running any vehicles in the shop, make sure you use the shop's exhaust ventilation system to discharge all exhaust gas safely outside.
- Always follow your supervisor's/instructor's directions on how to get the piston to top dead center. Failure to do so could cause injury or damage to the vehicle.
- Use caution when turning the engine to top dead center. If you do this by hand, be sure that your fingers, hands, etc. stay clear of belts and pulleys that could cause severe pinching.
- Make sure the ignition switch is in the "off" position and the key is removed from the ignition switch during this job to prevent someone from inadvertently cranking the engine over while you are working on it.

- Comply with personal and environmental safety practices associated with clothing; eye protection; hand tools; power equipment; proper ventilation; and the handling, storage, and disposal of chemicals/materials in accordance with local, state, and federal safety and environmental regulations.

Performance Standard

0–No exposure: No information or practice provided during the program; complete training required

1–Exposure only: General information provided with no practice time; close supervision needed; additional training required

2–Limited practice: Has practiced job during training program; additional training required to develop skill

3–Moderately skilled: Has performed job independently during training program; limited additional training may be required

4–Skilled: Can perform job independently with no additional training

Diagnose abnormal engine noises or vibration concerns; determine needed action.

CDX Tasksheet Number: C390

1. **Ask your instructor to assign you a vehicle with an engine noise or vibration concern. List the customer concern:**

2. **Research possible causes of the concern for this vehicle in the appropriate service information.**

    a. **List any possible causes:**

    b. **List any specified tests to pinpoint the problem:**

3. **With your supervisor's/instructor's permission, operate the vehicle to verify the concern. List your observations:**

4. **Follow the service manual procedure to diagnose the concern. List your tests and results here:**

5. **Determine necessary action(s):**

6. Have your supervisor/instructor verify satisfactory completion of this procedure, any observations found, and any necessary action(s) recommended.

Performance Rating

CDX Tasksheet Number: C390

0	1	2	3	4

Supervisor/instructor signature _____ Date _____

Camshaft Timing

Student/Intern information:

Name _____ Date _____ Class _____

Vehicle used for this activity:

Year _____ Make _____ Model _____

Odometer_____VIN _____

Learning Objective/Task	CDX Tasksheet Number	2017 MAST NATEF Reference Number; Priority Level
• Verify correct camshaft timing including engines equipped with variable valve timing systems (VVT).	C400	8A11; P-1

Materials Required

- Vehicle or simulator
- Possible need of specialized tools such as a scan tool, etc.

Some Safety Issues to Consider

- Because the vehicle will be running for an extended amount of time, make sure the vehicle cannot move or roll by applying the parking brake and using wheel chocks.
- You will be working under the hood of a running vehicle. Keep your hands and fingers away from moving belts, fans, and other parts.
- Do not rotate the crankshaft or camshaft if the timing belt is removed. Moving the cam or the crank could cause valve or piston damage.
- Comply with personal and environmental safety practices associated with clothing; eye protection; hand tools; power equipment; proper ventilation; and the handling, storage, and disposal of chemicals/materials in accordance with local, state, and federal safety and environmental regulations.

Performance Standard

0—No exposure: No information or practice provided during the program; complete training required

1—Exposure only: General information provided with no practice time; close supervision needed; additional training required

2—Limited practice: Has practiced job during training program; additional training required to develop skill

3—Moderately skilled: Has performed job independently during training program; limited additional training may be required

4—Skilled: Can perform job independently with no additional training

Verify correct camshaft timing including engines
equipped with variable valve timing systems (VVT).

MAST
8A11

CDX Tasksheet Number: C400

1. **Research the timing belt inspection procedure for this vehicle in the appropriate service information. List the following specifications:**

   a. **Timing belt replacement interval:** _____ **mi/km**

   b. **Is this engine equipped with variable valve timing (VVT)?**
      Yes: _____ **No:** _____

   c. **Draw a picture or print off a copy of the timing belt alignment diagram:**

2. **Following the specified procedure, verify correct camshaft timing. List your observations here:**

   a. **Is the camshaft timing correct? Yes:** _____ **No:** _____

3. **Have your supervisor/instructor verify satisfactory completion of this procedure, any observations found, and any necessary action(s) recommended.**

Performance Rating

CDX Tasksheet Number: C400

0	1	2	3	4

Supervisor/instructor signature _____ Date _____

Engine Operating Temperature

Student/Intern information:

Name _____ Date _____ Class _____

Vehicle used for this activity:

Year _____ Make _____ Model _____

Odometer _____ VIN _____

Learning Objective/Task	CDX Tasksheet Number	2017 MAST NATEF Reference Number; Priority Level
• Verify engine operating temperature; determine needed action.	C398	8A10; P-1

Time off_____

Time on_____

Total time_____

Materials Required

- Vehicle or simulator
- Infrared temperature gun
- DMM/DVOM
- Drain pan

Some Safety Issues to Consider

- Open the radiator cap (or any other part of the cooling system) only with the engine cold. Opening a radiator cap on a warm or hot engine could cause severe burns.
- Electric fans can turn on at any time. Keep hands and fingers away.
- When running any vehicles in the shop, make sure you use the shop's exhaust ventilation system to discharge all exhaust gas safely outside.
- Comply with personal and environmental safety practices associated with clothing; eye protection; hand tools; power equipment; proper ventilation; and the handling, storage, and disposal of chemicals/materials in accordance with local, state, and federal safety and environmental regulations.

Performance Standard

0—No exposure: No information or practice provided during the program; complete training required

1—Exposure only: General information provided with no practice time; close supervision needed; additional training required

2—Limited practice: Has practiced job during training program; additional training required to develop skill

3—Moderately skilled: Has performed job independently during training program; limited additional training may be required

4—Skilled: Can perform job independently with no additional training

CDX Tasksheet Number: C398

1. Research the following specifications in the service information.

    a. Thermostat opening temperature: _____ °F/°C

    b. Temperature at which the electric fan comes on (if equipped):
       _____ °F/°C

    c. Temperature at which the fan clutch engages (on) (if equipped):
       _____ °F/°C

2. Apply the vehicle's parking brake and secure the vehicle with wheel chocks to prevent the vehicle from rolling.

3. Start the vehicle. Allow the vehicle to warm up while monitoring the engine temperature with the temp gun. Find the spot where the highest temperature reading is found on the engine side of the thermostat housing (on most engines). Monitor the temperature at that spot.

> **NOTE** The temperature should rise to between the thermostat opening temperature and the electric (or clutch) fan "on" temperature (if equipped). If this happens, continue to the next step. If the engine doesn't get that hot, diagnose the problem and go to step 4 below. Do NOT allow the engine to overheat!

    a. If the engine is equipped with an electric fan, the temperature should vary between the electric fan "on" temperature and the electric fan "off" temperature. Record these temperatures:

       i. Electric fan "on" temp: _____ °F/°C

       ii. Electric fan "off" temp: _____ °F/°C

    b. If the engine is equipped with a clutch fan, the temperature should rise above the thermostat opening temperature but not above the clutch fan engagement temperature. Record these two temperatures:

       i. Clutch fan "engaged" temp: _____ °F/°C

       ii. Clutch fan "disengaged" temp: _____ °F/°C

    c. If the engine is equipped with a mechanical fan without a clutch, the temperature should rise to, or slightly above, the thermostat opening temperature and should remain fairly steady. Record this operating temperature:

       i. Engine operating temperature: _____ °F/°C

4. If the engine did not reach the specified thermostat opening temperature, list the max temperature reached: _____ °F/°C

5. Determine any necessary action(s):

6. Have your supervisor/instructor verify satisfactory completion of this procedure, any observations found, and any necessary action(s) recommended.

Performance Rating

0	1	2	3	4

Supervisor/instructor signature _____ Date _____

Ignition System

Student/Intern information:

Name _____ Date _____ Class _____

Vehicle used for this activity:

Year _____ Make _____ Model _____

Odometer _____ VIN _____

Learning Objective/Task	CDX Tasksheet Number	2017 MAST NATEF Reference Number; Priority Level
• Remove and replace spark plugs; inspect secondary ignition components for wear and damage.	C960	8C4; P-1
• Inspect and test crankshaft and camshaft position sensor(s); determine needed action.	C663	8C2; P-1
• Inspect, test, and/or replace ignition control module, powertrain/engine control module; reprogram/initialize as needed.	C664	8C3; P-3
• Diagnose (troubleshoot) ignition system–related problems such as no-starting, hard starting, engine misfire, poor driveability, spark knock, power loss, poor mileage, and emissions concerns; determine needed action.	C712	8C1; P-2
• Access and use service information to perform step-by-step (troubleshooting) diagnosis.	C841	8B2; P-1

Time off _____

Time on _____

Total time _____

Materials Required

- Vehicle(s) with ignition-related concern(s)
- DMM/DVOM
- Spark tester
- Problem-specific tools and equipment such as scan tool, lab scope, etc.

Some Safety Issues to Consider

- Diagnosis of this fault may require test-driving the vehicle on the school grounds or on a hoist, both of which carry severe risks. Attempt this task only with full permission from your supervisor/instructor and follow all the guidelines exactly.
- When running any vehicles in the shop, make sure you use the shop's exhaust ventilation system to discharge all exhaust gas safely outside.
- Because the vehicle will be running for an extended amount of time, make sure the vehicle cannot move or roll by applying the parking brake and using wheel chocks.
- You will be working under the hood of a running vehicle. Keep your hands and fingers away from moving belts, fans, and other parts.
- Modern ignition systems are capable of creating extremely high voltage (many over 80,000 volts). While there is a small risk of death directly from the shock, it can cause substantial pain, leading to injury from jerking away from it and into a sharp object or moving belt.

- Comply with personal and environmental safety practices associated with clothing; eye protection; hand tools; power equipment; proper ventilation; and the handling, storage, and disposal of chemicals/materials in accordance with local, state, and federal safety and environmental regulations.

Performance Standard

0–No exposure: No information or practice provided during the program; complete training required

1–Exposure only: General information provided with no practice time; close supervision needed; additional training required

2–Limited practice: Has practiced job during training program; additional training required to develop skill

3–Moderately skilled: Has performed job independently during training program; limited additional training may be required

4–Skilled: Can perform job independently with no additional training

Remove and replace spark plugs; inspect secondary ignition components for wear and damage.

MAST
8A4

Time off_____

Time on_____

Total time_____

CDX Tasksheet Number: C960

1. Research the following specifications in the appropriate service information:
   a. Spark plug gap: _____ in/mm
   b. Ignition coil–primary winding resistance: _____ ohms
   c. Ignition coil–secondary winding resistance: _____ ohms
   d. Spark plug wire resistance: _____ ohms

2. Using the recommended equipment and following the correct procedure, inspect and test ignition primary and secondary windings of the ignition coil(s). List your observations here:
   a. Ignition coil–primary winding resistance: _____ ohms
   b. Ignition coil–secondary winding resistance: _____ ohms

3. Following the specified procedure, remove the spark plugs (keeping them in the same order) and inspect them. List your observations:

4. Following the specified procedure, inspect the secondary ignition wires. List your observations here:

5. Measure the resistance of each spark plug wire. List your measurements:

6. Have your supervisor/instructor verify removal of the plugs. Supervisor's/instructor's initials: _____

7. Following the specified procedure, gap the spark plugs, apply a small amount of antiseize to the threads if directed, reinstall them by hand, and torque them to the specified torque.

8. Have your supervisor/instructor verify satisfactory completion of this procedure, any observations found, and any necessary action(s) recommended.

Performance Rating

0	1	2	3	4

Supervisor/instructor signature _____ Date _____

Inspect and test crankshaft and camshaft position sensor(s); determine needed action.

Time off_____

Time on_____

Total time_____

CDX Tasksheet Number: C663

Vehicle used for this activity:

Year _____ Make _____ Model_____

Odometer_____ VIN_____

1. List the crankshaft/camshaft sensor-related customer concern/complaint:

2. Research the particular concern in the appropriate service information and list the possible causes:

3. Using the specified equipment and the correct procedure, inspect and test the crankshaft and camshaft position sensor(s). List your test(s) and observations here:

4. What is causing the customer concern?

5. Determine any necessary action(s) to correct the fault(s):

6. Perform any necessary action(s) and note the results here:

7. Have your supervisor/instructor verify satisfactory completion of this procedure, any observations found, and any necessary action(s) recommended.

Performance Rating

CDX Tasksheet Number: C663

0	1	2	3	4

Supervisor/instructor signature _____ Date _____

Inspect, test, and/or replace ignition control module, powertrain/engine control module; reprogram/initialize as needed.

MAST
8C3

CDX Tasksheet Number: C664

Vehicle used for this activity:

Year _____ Make _____ Model _____

Odometer _____ VIN _____

1. **List the ignition control module/powertrain control module-related customer concern/complaint:**

2. **Research the particular concern in the appropriate service information and list the possible causes:**

3. **Using the specified equipment and the correct procedure, inspect, test, and/or replace the ignition control module or powertrain/engine control module. List your test(s) and observations here:**

4. **What is causing the customer concern?**

5. **Determine any necessary action(s) to correct the fault(s):**

6. **Perform any necessary action(s) and list the results here:**

7. Reprogram/initialize the module in accordance with the manufacturer's procedure if necessary. List your results:

8. Have your supervisor/instructor verify satisfactory completion of this procedure, any observations found, and any necessary action(s) recommended.

Performance Rating

0	1	2	3	4

Supervisor/instructor signature _____ Date _____

Diagnose (troubleshoot) ignition system-related problems such as no-starting, hard starting, engine misfire, poor driveability, spark knock, power loss, poor mileage, and emissions concerns; determine needed action.

MAST
8C1

Time off_____

Time on_____

Total time_____

CDX Tasksheet Number: C712

Vehicle used for this activity:

Year _____ Make _____ Model _____

Odometer _____ VIN _____

1. **List the ignition system-related customer concern/complaint:**

2. **Verify the concern and list your observations here:**

3. **Research the particular concern in the appropriate service information and list the possible causes:**

4. **Using the specified equipment and the correct procedure, diagnose the concern. List your tests and results here:**

5. **What is causing the customer concern?**

6. **Determine any necessary action(s) to correct the fault(s):**

7. Have your supervisor/instructor verify satisfactory completion of this procedure, any observations found, and any necessary action(s) recommended.

Performance Rating

0	1	2	3	4

Supervisor/instructor signature _____ Date _____

MAST
8B2

CDX Tasksheet Number: C841

1. **The requirements for this task will be met by any number of Engine Performance diagnostic tasks you satisfactorily complete. Ask your instructor if a particular task you have completed, meets the criteria listed in the description of the task above. If so, list that task number and description:**

2. **List what service information you accessed and how you used it when performing the step-by-step diagnosis:**

3. **Have your supervisor/instructor verify your work. Supervisor's/instructor's initials _____**

Performance Rating

CDX Tasksheet Number: C841

0	1	2	3	4

Supervisor/instructor signature _____ Date _____

Fuel and Induction System Testing

Student/Intern information:

Name _____ Date _____ Class _____

Vehicle used for this activity:

Year _____ Make _____ Model _____

Odometer _____ VIN _____

Learning Objective/Task	CDX Tasksheet Number	2017 MAST NATEF Reference Number; Priority Level
• Inspect and test fuel pump(s) and pump control system for pressure, regulation, and volume; perform needed action.	C868	8D3; P-1
• Check fuel for contaminants; determine needed action.	C420	8D2; P-2
• Inspect, test, and/or replace fuel injectors.	C842	8D7; P-2
• Replace fuel filter(s) where applicable.	C422	8D4; P-2
• Inspect, service, or replace air filters, filter housings, and intake duct work.	C962	8D5; P-1
• Inspect throttle body, air induction system, intake manifold, and gaskets for vacuum leaks and/or unmetered air.	C424	8D6; P-2
• Verify idle control operation.	C665	8D8; P-1
• Diagnose (troubleshoot) hot or cold no starting, hard starting, poor driveability, incorrect idle speed, poor idle, flooding, hesitation, surging, engine misfire, power loss, stalling, poor mileage, dieseling, and emissions problems; determine needed action.	C713	8D1; P-2

Time off_____

Time on_____

Total time_____

Materials Required

- Vehicle/simulator
- Fuel pressure gauge (higher than specified pressure)
- DMM/DVOM
- 1-quart/-liter fuel container
- Graduated test tube (100 mL is optimal)
- Injector pulsing tool
- Shop vacuum
- Leak detection tool (such as a smoke machine or other appropriate device)
- Problem-specific tools and equipment such as: scan tool, lab scope, etc.

Some Safety Issues to Consider

- When performing this task, you will be exposed to gasoline or diesel fuel. Make sure you use the proper gloves to prevent fuel from coming in contact with your skin.
- This task requires working with liquid fuel. Prevent serious burns or fires by keeping open flame or any other source of ignition far away.
- When running any vehicles in the shop, make sure you use the shop's exhaust ventilation system to discharge all exhaust gas safely outside.
- You will be working under the hood of a running vehicle. Keep your hands and fingers away from moving belts, fans, and other parts.
- Comply with personal and environmental safety practices associated with clothing; eye protection; hand tools; power equipment; proper ventilation; and the handling, storage, and disposal of chemicals/materials in accordance with local, state, and federal safety and environmental regulations.

Performance Standard

0–No exposure: No information or practice provided during the program; complete training required

1–Exposure only: General information provided with no practice time; close supervision needed; additional training required

2–Limited practice: Has practiced job during training program; additional training required to develop skill

3–Moderately skilled: Has performed job independently during training program; limited additional training may be required

4–Skilled: Can perform job independently with no additional training

Inspect and test fuel pump(s) and pump control system for pressure, regulation, and volume; perform needed action.

MAST
8D3

DX Tasksheet Number: C868

1. **Research the following specifications/procedures for this vehicle in the appropriate service information.**

   a. **List the type of fuel pump that is used in this vehicle:** _____

   b. **Fuel pump pressure (key on/engine off):** _____ **psi/kPa**

   c. **Fuel pump pressure (key on/engine idling):** _____ **psi/kPa**

   d. **Fuel pump pressure (deadhead):** _____ **psi/kPa**

   e. **Fuel pump volume: pt/L/oz/lb per:** _____ **sec/min/hr**

   f. **List the steps to relieve the pressure in the fuel system:**

2. **Have your supervisor/instructor verify your answers. Supervisor's/instructor's initials:** _____

3. **Test the fuel pump according to the specified procedure and list your observations.**

   a. **Fuel pump pressure (key on/engine off):** _____ **psi/kPa**

   b. **Fuel pump pressure (key on/engine idling):** _____ **psi/kPa**

   c. **Fuel pump pressure (deadhead):** _____ **psi/kPa**

   d. **Fuel pump volume:** _____ **pt/L/oz/lb per:** _____ **sec/min/hr**

   e. **Does the system hold pressure for at least 5 minutes once the key is turned off? Yes:** _____ **No:** _____

   NOTE Keep the fuel in the container for the next task, C420: Check fuel for contaminants; determine needed action.

4. **Determine any necessary action(s):**

5. **Have your supervisor/instructor verify your conclusions. Supervisor's/instructor's initials:** _____

6. **Perform any necessary actions as approved by your supervisor/instructor and list the results here:**

7. Have your supervisor/instructor verify satisfactory completion of this procedure, any observations found, and any necessary action(s) recommended.

MAST
8D2

CDX Tasksheet Number: C420

1. **Obtain a quantity of fuel from the vehicle into the fuel container.**

   NOTE This is best done while performing a fuel pump volume test.

2. **Pour 90 mL of gasoline into the graduated test tube.**

3. **Let this settle for a minute or two. Observe any contaminants in the fuel. List your observations:**

4. **Add 10 mL of water, bringing the total volume to 100 mL.**

5. **Cap the test tube tightly with a cork or other appropriate device.**

   NOTE Be sure you hold the cap firmly in place during this procedure. It will become pressurized, which could force the cap off, spraying fuel a considerable distance.

6. **Slowly and carefully agitate the fuel/water mix for 30 seconds to bring the water into contact with the fuel. If there is any alcohol in the fuel, this will allow the water to be absorbed by the alcohol.**

7. **Allow the mixture to settle for a minute or two. Observe the level of the water in the bottom of the test tube. Anything higher than the initial 10 mL is the amount of alcohol in the fuel. List your observation(s):**

8. **Determine any necessary action(s):**

9. **Have your supervisor/instructor verify your observations. Supervisor's/instructor's initials: _____**

10. **Carefully pour off the fuel in the test tube back to the fuel container. Make sure no water leaves the test tube.**

11. **Properly dispose of the remaining water/fuel mixture.**

12. Have your supervisor/instructor verify satisfactory completion of this procedure, any observations found, and any necessary action(s) recommended.

Performance Rating

CDX Tasksheet Number: C420

☐	☐	☐	☐	☐
0	1	2	3	4

Supervisor/instructor signature _____ Date _____

CDX Tasksheet Number: C842

Vehicle used for this activity:

Year _____ Make _____ Model_____

Odometer_____ VIN_____

1. Research the fuel injector testing procedure for this vehicle in the appropriate service information. List the following:

   a. Specified resistance for the fuel injectors: _____ ohms
   b. Fuel pump pressure (key on/engine off): _____ psi/kPa
   c. List or print off and attach to this sheet the steps to test the fuel injectors.

2. Visually inspect the fuel injectors for leaks, damage, etc. List your observations:

3. Follow the specified procedure to test the fuel injectors. List your observations:

4. If the service information doesn't list a method for testing the injectors, use the following method.

   a. Install the fuel pressure gauge on the fuel rail.
   b. Disconnect the fuel injector electrical connectors.
   c. Connect the injector pulsing tool to one fuel injector, according to the toolmaker's instructions, and set it for the specified amount of time in milliseconds.
   d. Pressurize the fuel rail by turning on the ignition switch for a few seconds. Then turn the ignition switch off.
   e. List the fuel pressure: _____ psi/kPa
   f. Activate the injector pulsing tool for the appropriate amount of time. Watch the pressure gauge and record the pressure after the injector has been cycled on and off (one time). List your readings below. Continue this test on each fuel injector, remembering to pressurize the fuel rail each time before activating the injector pulsing tool.

g. List your readings for each injector.

Injector #1 _____ psi/kPa	Injector #2 _____ psi/kPa
Injector #3 _____ psi/kPa	Injector #4 _____ psi/kPa
Injector #5 _____ psi/kPa	Injector #6 _____ psi/kPa
Injector #7 _____ psi/kPa	Injector #8 _____ psi/kPa

> **NOTE** Uneven pressure drops indicate uneven fuel flow through each injector.

5. Determine any necessary action(s):

6. Measure the resistance of each fuel injector and list your readings.

Injector #1 _____ Ohms	Injector #2 _____ Ohms
Injector #3 _____ Ohms	Injector #4 _____ Ohms
Injector #5 _____ Ohms	Injector #6 _____ Ohms
Injector #7 _____ Ohms	Injector #8 _____ Ohms

7. Determine any necessary action(s):

8. Have your supervisor/instructor verify satisfactory completion of this procedure, any observations found, and any necessary action(s) recommended.

Performance Rating

CDX Tasksheet Number: C842

☐	☐	☐	☐	☐
0	1	2	3	4

Supervisor/instructor signature _____ Date _____

CDX Tasksheet Number: C422

Vehicle used for this activity:

Year _____ Make _____ Model_____

Odometer_____ VIN_____

1. **Research the fuel filter replacement procedure for this vehicle in the appropriate information.**

   a. **List any special procedures and/or tools to perform this task:**

   b. **Look up the flat rate time for this task: _____ hr**

2. **Release any fuel pressure in the system by following the manufacturer's recommended procedure.**

3. **Follow the specified procedure to remove the fuel filter.**

4. **Have your supervisor/instructor verify removal of the fuel filter. Supervisor's/instructor's initials: _____**

5. **Install a new fuel filter (or reinstall the old one if your instructor directed you to do so).**

6. **Once the filter is installed correctly, clean up any spilled fuel and dispose of it properly.**

7. **Apply the vehicle's parking brake and secure the vehicle with wheel chocks to prevent the vehicle from rolling.**

8. **Turn the ignition switch to run and check for any fuel leaks. Immediately shut off the vehicle if a leak is present. Repair any leaks.**

> **NOTE** Ask your supervisor/instructor whether or not to perform the next action before proceeding.

9. **Cut the old filter open with a hacksaw to examine the inside. List what you found inside the filter:**

10. **Have your supervisor/instructor verify satisfactory completion of this procedure, any observations found, and any necessary action(s) recommended.**

Performance Rating

CDX Tasksheet Number: C422

0	1	2	3	4

Supervisor/instructor signature _____ Date _____

Inspect, service, or replace air filters, filter housings, and intake duct work.

MAST
8C5

CDX Tasksheet Number: C962

1. **Research the procedure and specifications for servicing the air filter, housing, and ductwork in the appropriate service information.**

   a. **Specified air filter number:** _____

2. **Following the specified procedure, remove the air filter from the filter housing.**

3. **Inspect the air filter and list the condition:**

4. **Inspect the filter housing and ductwork. List your observations:**

5. **Clean the filter housing following the specified procedure.**

6. **Have your supervisor/instructor verify removal. Supervisor's/instructor's initials:** _____

7. **Following the specified procedure, reinstall the air filter, housing, and ductwork.**

8. **Have your supervisor/instructor verify satisfactory completion of this procedure, any observations found, and any necessary action(s) recommended.**

Performance Rating

CDX Tasksheet Number: C962

0	1	2	3	4

Supervisor/instructor signature _____ Date _____

MAST
8D6

Time off_____

Time on_____

Total time_____

DX Tasksheet Number: C424

Vehicle used for this activity:

Year _____ Make _____ Model _____

Odometer _____ VIN _____

1. Visually inspect the air induction system for any obvious leaks such as cracks, loose fittings, or missing hoses. List your observations:

2. Use an appropriate leak detection tool to test for any non-obvious leaks and/or unmetered air. List your tests and observations:

3. Determine any necessary action(s):

4. Have your supervisor/instructor verify satisfactory completion of this procedure, any observations found, and any necessary action(s) recommended.

Performance Rating

CDX Tasksheet Number: C424

0	1	2	3	4

Supervisor/instructor signature _____ Date _____

MAST
8D8

CDX Tasksheet Number: C665

Vehicle used for this activity:

Year _____ Make _____ Model _____

Odometer _____ VIN _____

1. List the idle speed control-related customer concern:

2. Research and list the desired idle speed: _____ rpm

3. Research the particular concern in the appropriate service information and list the possible causes:

4. Using the specified procedure, verify the vehicle idle speed and list here: _____ rpm

5. Using the specified procedure, test the idle control system operation. List your test(s) observation(s) here:

6. Determine any necessary action(s):

7. Return the vehicle to its beginning condition and return any tools you used to their proper locations.

8. Have your supervisor/instructor verify satisfactory completion of this procedure, any observations found, and any necessary action(s) recommended.

Performance Rating

0	1	2	3	4

Supervisor/instructor signature _____ Date _____

Diagnose hot or cold no starting, hard starting, poor driveability, incorrect idle speed, poor idle, flooding, hesitation, surging, engine misfire, power loss, stalling, poor mileage, dieseling, and emissions problems; determine needed action.

MAST
8D1

Time off_____

Time on_____

Total time_____

DX Tasksheet Number: C713

Vehicle used for this activity:

Year _____ Make _____ Model_____

Odometer_____ VIN_____

1. **List the fuel injection system-related customer concern:**

2. **Verify the concern and list your observations here:**

3. **Research the possible causes for this concern in the appropriate service information.**

   a. **List or print off and attach to this sheet the possible causes:**

   b. **List or print off and attach to this sheet the procedure for diagnosing the concern:**

4. **Follow the specified procedure to diagnose the concern. List your tests and results here:**

5. **List the cause of the concern:**

6. Determine any necessary action(s) to correct the fault:

7. Have your supervisor/instructor verify satisfactory completion of this procedure, any observations found, and any necessary action(s) recommended.

Performance Rating

CDX Tasksheet Number: C713

0	1	2	3	4

Supervisor/instructor signature _____ Date _____

Exhaust Analysis

Learning Objective/Task	CDX Tasksheet Number	2017 MAST NATEF Reference Number; Priority Level
• Diagnose emission and driveability concerns caused by catalytic converter system; determine needed action.	C714	8E6; P-2
• Diagnose the cause of excessive oil consumption, coolant consumption, unusual exhaust color, odor, and sound; determine needed action.	C391	8A4; P-2

Time off _____

Time on _____

Total time _____

Materials Required

- Vehicle or simulator
- Exhaust gas analyzer
- Exhaust hose(s)
- Vehicle with unusual exhaust condition
- Problem-specific tools and equipment, such as stethoscope, compression tester, back pressure gauge, scan tool, etc.

Some Safety Issues to Consider

- When running any vehicles in the shop, make sure you use the shop's exhaust ventilation system to discharge all exhaust gas safely outside.
- Diagnosis of this fault may require test-driving the vehicle on the school grounds or on a hoist, both of which carry severe risks. Attempt this task only with full permission from your supervisor/instructor and follow all the guidelines exactly.
- You will be working under the hood of a running vehicle. Keep your hands and fingers away from moving belts, fans, and other parts.
- This task may require that the engine is loaded while running, which requires the use of wheel chocks to help prevent the vehicle from rolling. Never stand, or allow anyone else to stand, directly in front of or behind the vehicle while performing this procedure.
- Comply with personal and environmental safety practices associated with clothing; eye protection; hand tools; power equipment; proper ventilation; and the handling, storage, and disposal of chemicals/materials in accordance with local, state, and federal safety and environmental regulations.

Performance Standard

0—No exposure: No information or practice provided during the program; complete training required

1—Exposure only: General information provided with no practice time; close supervision needed; additional training required

2—Limited practice: Has practiced job during training program; additional training required to develop skill

3—Moderately skilled: Has performed job independently during training program; limited additional training may be required

4—Skilled: Can perform job independently with no additional training

Diagnose emission and driveability concerns caused by catalytic converter system; determine needed action.

MAST
8E9

CDX Tasksheet Number: C714

1. **Research the catalytic converter testing procedure for this vehicle in the appropriate service information.**

   a. **List or print off and attach to this sheet the procedure to test the converter:**

   b. **If no procedure is available, there are four generally accepted methods of testing a converter:**

      1. **The first is a pre-catalyst/post-catalyst emission test (sometimes called an intrusive or intrusion test).**
      2. **The second is a cylinder ignition-shorting emission test where one cylinder's ignition is disabled and the resulting emissions are measured and compared to the pre-shorted emission readings.**
      3. **On OBDII-equipped vehicles, using the pre-catalyst and post-catalyst O_2 sensor readings to show a difference in exhaust oxygen content will indicate converter efficiency.**
      4. **Using mode 6 data from the vehicle's PCM to indicate the number of failure counts for the catalyst**
      Ask your supervisor/instructor which method to use, and list it here: _____

   NOTE Some local regulatory authorities mandate a loaded cruise test. This test is hard to duplicate in most shops and is best done on a dynamometer. Unless your shop has this piece of equipment available, it would be best not to perform a loaded cruise test. Also, in some states a no-load cruise test is allowed on certain vehicles. Please note that some vehicles can experience transmission failure if this test is performed. Therefore, we do not recommend performing this test on any vehicle unless it is with your supervisor's/instructor's direct authorization and supervision.

2. **Test the catalytic converter following the specified procedure. List your tests and observations:**

3. **Determine any necessary action(s):**

4. Have your supervisor/instructor verify satisfactory completion of this procedure, any observations found, and any necessary action(s) recommended.

Performance Rating

CDX Tasksheet Number: C714

0	1	2	3	4

Supervisor/instructor signature _____ Date _____

Diagnose the cause of excessive oil consumption, coolant consumption, unusual exhaust color, odor, and sound; determine needed action.

MAST
8A4

Time off_____

Time on_____

Total time_____

CDX Tasksheet Number: C391

Vehicle used for this activity:

Year _____ Make _____ Model_____

Odometer_____ VIN_____

1. **List the exhaust-related customer concern:**

2. **Research possible causes of the concern for this vehicle in the appropriate service information.**

   a. **List any possible causes:**

   b. **List any specified tests to pinpoint the problem:**

3. **With your supervisor's/instructor's permission, operate the vehicle to verify the concern. List your observations:**

4. **Follow the specified procedure to diagnose the concern. List your tests and results:**

5. **List the cause of the concern:**

6. Determine any necessary action(s) to correct the fault:

7. Have your supervisor/instructor verify satisfactory completion of this procedure, any observations found, and any necessary action(s) recommended.

Exhaust System Testing

Student/Intern information:

Name _____ Date _____ Class _____

Vehicle used for this activity:

Year _____ Make _____ Model_____

Odometer_____VIN_____

Learning Objective/Task	CDX Tasksheet Number	2017 MAST NATEF Reference Number; Priority Level
• Inspect condition of exhaust system hangers, brackets, clamps, and heat shields; determine needed action.	C963	8D10; P-1
• Inspect the integrity of the exhaust manifold, exhaust pipes, muffler(s), catalytic converter(s), resonator(s), tail pipe(s), and heat shields; perform needed action.	C428	8D9; P-1
• Check and refill diesel exhaust fluid (DEF).	C965	8D12; P-2
• Perform exhaust system back-pressure test; determine needed action.	C429	8D11; P-2
• Test the operation of turbocharger/supercharger systems; determine needed action.	C869	8D13; P-2

Time off_____

Time on_____

Total time_____

Materials Required

- Vehicle
- Large Channellock® (arc joint) pliers
- Exhaust back-pressure gauge
- Tachometer (if the vehicle is not equipped with one)
- Diesel Exhaust Fluid refractometer or hydrometer
- Problem-specific tools and equipment such as: scan tool, lab scope, etc.

Some Safety Issues to Consider

- Vehicle hoists are important tools that increase productivity and make the job easier. However, they can also cause severe injury or death if used improperly. Make sure you follow the hoist and vehicle manufacturer's operation procedures. Also make sure you have your supervisor's/instructor's permission to use a vehicle hoist.
- You will be working under the hood of a running vehicle. Keep your hands and fingers away from moving belts, fans, and other parts.
- When running any vehicles in the shop, make sure you use the shop's exhaust ventilation system to discharge all exhaust gas safely outside.
- Diagnosis of this fault may require test-driving the vehicle on the school grounds or on a hoist, both of which carry severe risks. Attempt this task only with full permission from your supervisor/instructor and follow all the guidelines exactly.

- Comply with personal and environmental safety practices associated with clothing; eye protection; hand tools; power equipment; proper ventilation; and the handling, storage, and disposal of chemicals/materials in accordance with local, state, and federal safety and environmental regulations.

Performance Standard

0–No exposure: No information or practice provided during the program; complete training required

1–Exposure only: General information provided with no practice time; close supervision needed; additional training required

2–Limited practice: Has practiced job during training program; additional training required to develop skill

3–Moderately skilled: Has performed job independently during training program; limited additional training may be required

4–Skilled: Can perform job independently with no additional training

Inspect condition of exhaust system hangers, brackets, clamps, and heat shields; determine needed action.

MAST
8D10

Time off_____

Time on_____

Total time_____

CDX Tasksheet Number: C963

1. Safely raise and secure the vehicle on a hoist.

2. Inspect the following parts for damage, wear, or missing components. Also, check the integrity of the pipes by squeezing them with the large arc joint pliers. List your observations about each.

   a. Exhaust system hangers, brackets, and clamps:

   b. Heat shields:

3. Determine any necessary action(s):

4. Have your supervisor/instructor verify your conclusions. Supervisor's/instructor's initials: time _____

5. Perform any necessary actions as approved by your supervisor/instructor. List them here:

6. Have your supervisor/instructor verify satisfactory completion of this procedure, any observations found, and any necessary action(s) recommended.

Performance Rating

CDX Tasksheet Number: C963

0	1	2	3	4

Supervisor/instructor signature _____ Date _____

Inspect the integrity of the exhaust manifold, exhaust pipes, muffler(s), catalytic converter(s), resonator(s), tail pipe(s), and heat shields; perform needed action.

MAST
8D9

Time off_____

Time on_____

Total time_____

CDX Tasksheet Number: C428

1. **Safely raise and secure the vehicle on a hoist.**

2. **Inspect the following parts for damage, wear, or missing components. Also, check the integrity of the pipes by squeezing them with the large arc joint pliers. List your observations about each.**

    a. **Exhaust manifold(s):**

    b. **Exhaust pipes:**

    c. **Muffler(s):**

    d. **Catalytic converter(s):**

    e. **Resonator(s):**

    f. **Tail pipe(s):**

    g. **Heat shield(s):**

3. Determine any necessary action(s):

4. Have your supervisor/instructor verify your conclusions. Supervisor's/instructor's initials: _____

5. Perform any necessary actions as approved by your supervisor/instructor. List them here:

6. Have your supervisor/instructor verify satisfactory completion of this procedure, any observations found, and any necessary action(s) recommended.

Performance Rating

CDX Tasksheet Number: C428

| 0 | 1 | 2 | 3 | 4 |

Supervisor/instructor signature _____ Date _____

CDX Tasksheet Number: C965

Vehicle used for this activity:

Year _____ Make _____ Model_____

Odometer_____ VIN_____

1. On a diesel vehicle equipped with diesel exhaust fluid, research the following specifications in the appropriate service information.

    a. Specified diesel exhaust fluid: _____
    b. Specified replenishment interval: _____ mi/km/mo
    c. Specified diesel fluid tank capacity: _____
    d. Specified urea content: _____ % or specific gravity
    e. List the purpose of diesel exhaust fluid: _____

2. Following the specified procedure, obtain and measure the urea content or specific gravity of the DEF fluid. List your results:

3. Check the level of diesel exhaust fluid in the reservoir. List your observations:

4. If necessary, refill the diesel exhaust fluid to the proper level.

5. Have your supervisor/instructor verify satisfactory completion of this procedure, any observations found, and any necessary action(s) recommended.

Performance Rating

CDX Tasksheet Number: C965

0	1	2	3	4

Supervisor/instructor signature _____ Date _____

MAST
8D11

Time off_____

Time on_____

Total time_____

CDX Tasksheet Number: C429

1. Research the procedure to test exhaust back-pressure on this vehicle in the appropriate service information.

    a. List the location for installing the back-pressure gauge: _____

    b. List the maximum allowable back-pressure: _____ in/hg or psi/kPa at _____ rpm

2. Install the back-pressure gauge according to the specified procedure.

3. Measure the exhaust back-pressure, being careful to follow the specified procedure.

    a. List your readings obtained: _____ in/hg or psi/kPa at _____ rpm

4. Determine any necessary action(s):

5. Have your supervisor/instructor verify satisfactory completion of this procedure, any observations found, and any necessary action(s) recommended.

Performance Rating

CDX Tasksheet Number: C429

0	1	2	3	4

Supervisor/instructor signature _____ Date _____

MAST
8D13

Time off_____

Time on_____

CDX Tasksheet Number: C869

Vehicle used for this activity:

Year _____ Make _____ Model_____

Total time_____

Odometer_____ VIN_____

> **NOTE** This task is extremely hazardous and should be performed only under close supervisor/instructor supervision. Diagnosis of this fault may require test driving the vehicle on the school grounds or on a hoist, both of which carry severe risks. Attempt this task only with full permission from your supervisor/instructor and follow all the guidelines and laws exactly.

1. **Research the testing and specifications for this vehicle in the appropriate service information.**

   a. **Maximum boost: _____ psi/kPa**

   b. **List, or print off and attach to this sheet, the procedure for testing the turbocharger/supercharger:**

   c. **Have your supervisor/instructor approve the specifications and testing procedure. Supervisor's/instructor's initials: _____**

2. **Following the specified procedure, test the turbocharger/supercharger. List your tests and results:**

3. **Determine any necessary action(s):**

4. **Have your supervisor/instructor verify satisfactory completion of this procedure, any observations found, and any necessary action(s) recommended.**

Performance Rating

CDX Tasksheet Number: C869

0	1	2	3	4

Supervisor/instructor signature _____ Date _____

Powertrain Control System Testing

Student/Intern information:

Name _____ Date _____ Class _____

Vehicle used for this activity:

Year _____ Make _____ Model _____

Odometer _____ VIN _____

Learning Objective/Task	CDX Tasksheet Number	2017 MAST NATEF Reference Number; Priority Level
• Describe the use of OBD monitors for repair verification.	C661	8B4; P-1
• Retrieve and record diagnostic trouble codes (DTC), OBD monitor status, and freeze-frame data; clear codes when applicable.	C659	8B1; P-1
• Perform active tests of actuators using a scan tool; determine needed action.	C867	8B3; P-1
• Inspect and test computerized engine control system sensors, powertrain/engine control module (PCM/ECM), actuators, and circuits using a graphing multimeter (GMM)/digital storage oscilloscope (DSO); perform needed action.	C840	8B7; P-2

Materials Required

- Vehicle or simulator (OBD)
- Scan tool
- DMM/DVOM
- GMM/DSO
- Problem-specific tools and equipment

Some Safety Issues to Consider

- If you need to start the vehicle, you should ensure that the parking brake is firmly applied; if necessary, use wheel chocks to prevent the vehicle from moving when the vehicle is started to verify the completion of this task.
- Only students who have their supervisor's/instructor's direct permission should perform this task due to the safety concerns involved.
- Diagnosis of this fault may require test-driving the vehicle on the school grounds. Attempt this task only with full permission from your instructor and follow all the guidelines exactly.
- When running any vehicles in the shop, make sure you use the shop's exhaust ventilation system to discharge all exhaust gas safely outside.
- Comply with personal and environmental safety practices associated with clothing; eye protection; hand tools; power equipment; proper ventilation; and the handling, storage, and disposal of chemicals/materials in accordance with local, state, and federal safety and environmental regulations.

Performance Standard

0—No exposure: No information or practice provided during the program; complete training required

1—Exposure only: General information provided with no practice time; close supervision needed; additional training required

2—Limited practice: Has practiced job during training program; additional training required to develop skill

3—Moderately skilled: Has performed job independently during training program; limited additional training may be required

4—Skilled: Can perform job independently with no additional training

Describe the use of OBD monitors for repair verification.

Time off_____

Time on_____

Total time_____

CDX Tasksheet Number: C661

1. Research the following details in the appropriate service information:
   a. List which OBD monitors apply to this vehicle:

   b. List the parameters the "Catalyst" monitor must meet before showing a "Ready" status:

   c. List the parameters the "EVAP" monitor must meet before showing a "Ready" status:

2. Describe in your own words the importance of running all OBD monitors for repair verification:

3. Have your supervisor/instructor verify satisfactory completion of this procedure, any observations found, and any necessary action(s) recommended.

Performance Rating

CDX Tasksheet Number: C661

0	1	2	3	4

Supervisor/instructor signature _____ Date _____

Retrieve and record diagnostic trouble codes (DTC), OBD monitor status, and freeze-frame data; clear codes when applicable.

MAST
8B

Time off_____

Time on_____

Total time_____

CDX Tasksheet Number: C659

1. **Connect the scan tool to the vehicle in accordance with the manufacturer's instructions; retrieve and record any diagnostic trouble codes:**

2. **List the monitor status for each OBD monitor:**

3. **List (or print off and attach) the freeze-frame data:**

4. **Clear codes when applicable. This may not necessarily be now.**

> **NOTE** Clearing the codes will also erase the OBD monitor status and freeze-frame data on most vehicles. Clear codes only when the service information directs you to do so.

5. **Have your supervisor/instructor verify satisfactory completion of this procedure, any observations found, and any necessary action(s) recommended.**

Performance Rating

CDX Tasksheet Number: C659

0	1	2	3	4

Supervisor/instructor signature _____ Date _____

Perform active tests of actuators using a scan tool; determine needed action.

Time off_____

Time on_____

Total time_____

DX Tasksheet Number: C867

1. **Connect the scan tool to the vehicle in accordance with the manufacturer's instructions and, while using the scan tool directions, perform active tests on at least two actuators. List the actuators tested and the results of those tests:**

2. **Determine any necessary action(s):**

3. **Have your supervisor/instructor verify satisfactory completion of this procedure, any observations found, and any necessary action(s) recommended.**

Performance Rating

CDX Tasksheet Number: C867

0	1	2	3	4

Supervisor/instructor signature _____ Date _____

Inspect and test computerized engine control system sensors, powertrain/engine control module (PCM/ECM), actuators, and circuits using a graphing multimeter (GMM)/digital storage oscilloscope (DSO); perform needed action.

Time off_____

Time on_____

Total time_____

DX Tasksheet Number: C840

1. **Research the following patterns/test procedures for this vehicle in the appropriate service information.**

   a. **Sketch (or print out) the specified oxygen sensor pattern (front):**

   b. **Sketch (or print out) the specified fuel injector pattern:**

2. **Connect the GMM or DSO to the oxygen sensor circuit, start the vehicle, allow the engine to warm up for the specified amount of time, and observe the pattern on the test equipment.**

   a. **Sketch or print off and attach to this sheet the pattern you obtained here:**

   b. **List your observation(s):**

3. **Connect the GMM or DSO to the fuel injector circuit, start the vehicle, allow the engine to warm up for the specified amount of time, and observe the pattern on the test equipment.**

   a. **Sketch or print off and attach to this sheet the pattern you obtained here:**

   b. **List your observation(s):**

4. Determine any necessary action(s):

5. Have your supervisor/instructor verify satisfactory completion of this procedure, any observations found, and any necessary action(s) recommended.

PCV System Testing

Student/Intern information:

Name _____ Date _____ Class _____

Vehicle used for this activity:

Year _____ Make _____ Model _____

Odometer _____ VIN _____

Learning Objective/Task	CDX Tasksheet Number	2017 MAST NATEF Reference Number; Priority Level
• Inspect, test, service, and/or replace positive crankcase ventilation (PCV) filter/breather, valve, tubes, orifices, and hoses; perform needed action.	C432	8E2; P-2
• Diagnose oil leaks, emissions, and driveability concerns caused by the positive crankcase ventilation (PCV) system; determine needed action.	C666	8E1; P-3

Time off _____

Time on _____

Total time _____

Materials Required

- Vehicle or simulator with related fault
- Problem-specific tools and equipment

Some Safety Issues to Consider

- You will be working under the hood of a running vehicle. Keep your hands and fingers away from moving belts, fans, and other parts.
- When running any vehicles in the shop, make sure you use the shop's exhaust ventilation system to discharge all exhaust gas safely outside.
- Only students who have their supervisor's/instructor's direct permission should perform this task due to the safety concerns involved.
- Diagnosis of this fault may require test-driving the vehicle on the school grounds. Attempt this task only with full permission from your instructor and follow all the guidelines exactly.
- Comply with personal and environmental safety practices associated with clothing; eye protection; hand tools; power equipment; proper ventilation; and the handling, storage, and disposal of chemicals/materials in accordance with local, state, and federal safety and environmental regulations.

Performance Standard

0–No exposure: No information or practice provided during the program; complete training required

1–Exposure only: General information provided with no practice time; close supervision needed; additional training required

2–Limited practice: Has practiced job during training program; additional training required to develop skill

3–Moderately skilled: Has performed job independently during training program; limited additional training may be required

4–Skilled: Can perform job independently with no additional training

Inspect, test, service, and/or replace positive crankcase
ventilation (PCV) filter/breather, valve, tubes,
orifices, and hoses; perform needed action.

MAST
8E2

DX Tasksheet Number: C432

1. **Research the PCV system on this vehicle in the appropriate service information.**
   a. **List the service interval for replacing the PCV valve:** _____ mi/km
   b. **List the service interval for replacing the breather filter:** _____ mi/km

2. **Follow the specified procedure to inspect and test the PCV system. List your observations for each component below:**
   a. **Filter/breather:**

   b. **PCV valve:**

   c. **Tubes, orifices, and hoses:**

3. **Determine any necessary action(s):**

4. **Have your supervisor/instructor verify your conclusions. Supervisor's/instructor's initials:** _____

5. **Perform any necessary action(s) and list them here:**

6. Have your supervisor/instructor verify satisfactory completion of this procedure, any observations found, and any necessary action(s) recommended.

Performance Rating

0	1	2	3	4

Supervisor/instructor signature _____ Date _____

Diagnose oil leaks, emissions, and driveability concerns
caused by the positive crankcase ventilation (PCV) system;
determine needed action.

MAST
8E1

DX Tasksheet Number: C666

Vehicle used for this activity:

Year _____ Make _____ Model_____

Odometer_____ VIN_____

1. **List the customer concern:**

2. **Research the particular concern in the appropriate service information.**

   a. **List the possible causes:**

   b. **List or print off and attach to this sheet the procedure for diagnosing the concern:**

3. **Using the recommended procedure, inspect the vehicle and diagnose any oil leaks, emissions, and driveability concerns caused by the PCV system. List your observations here:**

4. **List the cause of the concern:**

5. **Determine any necessary action(s) to correct the fault:**

6. Have your supervisor/instructor verify satisfactory completion of this procedure, any observations found, and any necessary action(s) recommended.

Performance Rating

0	1	2	3	4

Supervisor/instructor signature _____ Date _____

EGR System Testing

Learning Objective/Task	CDX Tasksheet Number	2017 MAST NATEF Reference Number; Priority Level
• Diagnose emissions and driveability concerns caused by the exhaust gas recirculation (EGR) system; inspect, test, service, and/or replace electrical/electronic sensors, controls, wiring, tubing, exhaust passages, vacuum/pressure controls, filters, and hoses of exhaust gas recirculation (EGR) systems; determine needed action.	C667	8E3; P-2

Time off_____

Time on_____

Total time_____

Materials Required

- Vehicle or simulator with related fault
- Hand vacuum pump (for vacuum-operated EGR components)
- DMM/DVOM (for vehicles equipped with electric/electronic EGR components)
- Problem-specific tools and equipment

Some Safety Issues to Consider

- You will be working under the hood of a running vehicle. Keep your hands and fingers away from moving belts, fans, and other parts.
- When running any vehicles in the shop, make sure you use the shop's exhaust ventilation system to discharge all exhaust gas safely outside.
- Only students who have their supervisor's/instructor's direct permission should perform this task due to the safety concerns involved.
- Diagnosis of this fault may require test-driving the vehicle on the school grounds. Attempt this task only with full permission from your instructor and follow all the guidelines exactly.
- Comply with personal and environmental safety practices associated with clothing; eye protection; hand tools; power equipment; proper ventilation; and the handling, storage, and disposal of chemicals/materials in accordance with local, state, and federal safety and environmental regulations.

Performance Standard

0–No exposure: No information or practice provided during the program; complete training required

1–Exposure only: General information provided with no practice time; close supervision needed; additional training required

2–Limited practice: Has practiced job during training program; additional training required to develop skill

3–Moderately skilled: Has performed job independently during training program; limited additional training may be required

4–Skilled: Can perform job independently with no additional training

Diagnose emissions and driveability concerns caused by the exhaust gas recirculation (EGR) system; inspect, test, service, and/or replace electrical/electronic sensors, controls, wiring, tubing, exhaust passages, vacuum/pressure controls, filters, and hoses of exhaust gas recirculation (EGR) systems; determine needed action.

MAST
8E3

Time off_____

Time on_____

Total time_____

CDX Tasksheet Number: C667

Vehicle used for this activity:

Year _____ Make _____ Model _____

Odometer _____ VIN _____

1. **List the EGR-related customer concern:**

2. **Research the particular concern in the appropriate service information.**

    a. **List the possible causes:**

    b. **List or print off and attach to this sheet the procedure for diagnosing the concern:**

3. **Using the recommended procedure, inspect and diagnose any emissions and driveability concerns caused by the EGR system. List your tests and observations here:**

4. **List the cause of the concern:**

5. Determine any necessary action(s) to correct the fault:

6. Research the procedure for inspecting and testing the electrical/electronic components of the EGR system on this vehicle in the appropriate service information.

   a. List any EGR electrical specifications for this vehicle:

7. Follow the specified procedure to inspect and test the EGR system components. List your observations for each component below:

   a. EGR valve, if electrically operated:

   b. EGR vacuum solenoid, if equipped:

   c. EGR flow sensor, if equipped:

   d. Electrical wiring:

8. Determine any necessary action(s):

9. Have your supervisor/instructor verify your conclusions. Supervisor's/ instructor's initials: _____

10. Perform any necessary action(s) and list them here:

11. Research the procedure for inspecting and testing the EGR system on this vehicle in the appropriate service information.

    a. List the type of EGR valve this vehicle is equipped with: _____
    b. List the service interval for replacing any of the EGR system components:

12. Follow the specified procedure to inspect and test the EGR system. List your observations for each component below:

    a. EGR valve:

    b. EGR tubing and exhaust passages:

    c. Vacuum/pressure controls:

    d. Filters and hoses:

13. Determine any necessary action(s):

14. Have your supervisor/instructor verify your conclusions. Supervisor's/ instructor's initials: _____

15. Perform any necessary action(s) and list them here:

16. **Have your supervisor/instructor verify satisfactory completion of this procedure, any observations found, and any necessary action(s) recommended.**

Performance Rating

CDX Tasksheet Number: C667

0	1	2	3	4

Supervisor/instructor signature _____ Date _____

Evaporative Emissions System Testing

Student/Intern information:

Name _____ Date _____ Class _____

Vehicle used for this activity:

Year _____ Make _____ Model _____

Odometer _____ VIN _____

Learning Objective/Task	CDX Tasksheet Number	2017 MAST NATEF Reference Number; Priority Level
• Diagnose emissions and driveability concerns caused by the evaporative emissions control (EVAP) system; determine needed action.	C844	8E5; P-1

Time off_____

Time on_____

Total time_____

Materials Required

- Vehicle or simulator with related fault
- Hand vacuum pump
- DMM/DVOM
- Infrared temp gun
- Smoke machine
- Problem-specific tools and equipment

Some Safety Issues to Consider

- You will be working under the hood of a running vehicle. Keep your hands and fingers away from moving belts, fans, and other parts.
- When running any vehicles in the shop, make sure you use the shop's exhaust ventilation system to discharge all exhaust gas safely outside.
- Only students who have their supervisor's/instructor's direct permission should perform this task due to the safety concerns involved.
- Diagnosis of this fault may require test-driving the vehicle on the school grounds. Attempt this task only with full permission from your instructor and follow all the guidelines exactly.
- Comply with personal and environmental safety practices associated with clothing; eye protection; hand tools; power equipment; proper ventilation; and the handling, storage, and disposal of chemicals/materials in accordance with local, state, and federal safety and environmental regulations.

Performance Standard

0—No exposure: No information or practice provided during the program; complete training required

1—Exposure only: General information provided with no practice time; close supervision needed; additional training required

2—Limited practice: Has practiced job during training program; additional training required to develop skill

3—Moderately skilled: Has performed job independently during training program; limited additional training may be required

4—Skilled: Can perform job independently with no additional training

Diagnose emissions and driveability concerns caused by the evaporative emissions control (EVAP) system; determine needed action.

MAST
8E5

Time off_____

Time on_____

Total time_____

CDX Tasksheet Number: C844

Vehicle used for this activity:

Year _____ Make _____ Model _____

Odometer _____ VIN _____

1. List the customer concern:

2. Research the particular concern in the appropriate service information.

   a. List the possible causes:

   b. List or print off and attach to this sheet the procedure for diagnosing the concern:

3. Using the recommended procedure, inspect and diagnose any emissions and driveability concerns caused by the evaporative emissions control system. List your tests and observations here:

4. List the cause of the concern:

5. Determine any necessary action(s) to correct the fault:

6. Have your supervisor/instructor verify satisfactory completion of this procedure, any observations found, and any necessary action(s) recommended.

Performance Rating

0	1	2	3	4

Supervisor/instructor signature _____ Date _____

Secondary Air Injection System Testing

Student/Intern information:

Name _____ Date _____ Class _____

Vehicle used for this activity:

Year _____ Make _____ Model _____

Odometer _____ VIN _____

Learning Objective/Task	CDX Tasksheet Number	2017 MAST NATEF Reference Number; Priority Level
• Diagnose emissions and driveability concerns caused by the secondary air injection system; inspect, test, repair, and/or replace electrical/electronically-operated components and circuits of secondary air injection systems; determine needed action.	C843	8E4; P-2

Time off_____

Time on_____

Total time_____

Materials Required

- Vehicle or simulator with related fault
- Hand vacuum pump (for vacuum-operated air injection components)
- DMM/DVOM (for vehicles equipped with electric/electronic air injection components)
- Problem-specific tools and equipment

Some Safety Issues to Consider

- You will be working under the hood of a running vehicle. Keep your hands and fingers away from moving belts, fans, and other parts.
- When running any vehicles in the shop, make sure you use the shop's exhaust ventilation system to discharge all exhaust gas safely outside.
- Only students who have their supervisor's/instructor's direct permission should perform this task due to the safety concerns involved.
- Diagnosis of this fault may require test-driving the vehicle on the school grounds. Attempt this task only with full permission from your instructor and follow all the guidelines exactly.
- Comply with personal and environmental safety practices associated with clothing; eye protection; hand tools; power equipment; proper ventilation; and the handling, storage, and disposal of chemicals/materials in accordance with local, state, and federal safety and environmental regulations.

Performance Standard

0–No exposure: No information or practice provided during the program; complete training required

1–Exposure only: General information provided with no practice time; close supervision needed; additional training required

2–Limited practice: Has practiced job during training program; additional training required to develop skill

3–Moderately skilled: Has performed job independently during training program; limited additional training may be required

4–Skilled: Can perform job independently with no additional training

MAST
8E4

Time off_____

Time on_____

Total time_____

CDX Tasksheet Number: C843

Vehicle used for this activity:

Year _____ Make _____ Model _____

Odometer _____ VIN _____

1. List the customer concern:

2. Research the particular concern in the appropriate service information.

   a. List the possible causes:

3. Using the recommended procedure, inspect and diagnose any emissions and driveability concerns caused by the secondary air injection and catalytic converter systems. List your tests and observations here:

4. Research the procedure for inspecting and testing the electrical/electronic components of the air injection system on this vehicle in the appropriate service information.

   a. List any air injection system electrical specifications for this vehicle:

5. Follow the specified procedure to inspect and test the air injection system components. List your observations for each component below:

   a. Air injection switching valve, if electrically operated:

b. Air injection bypass or diverter valve, if electrically operated:

c. Air pump, if electrically operated:

d. Electrical wiring:

6. Determine any necessary action(s):

7. Have your supervisor/instructor verify your conclusions. Supervisor's/instructor's initials: _____

8. Perform any necessary action(s) and list them here:

9. Have your supervisor/instructor verify satisfactory completion of this procedure, any observations found, and any necessary action(s) recommended.

Performance Rating

CDX Tasksheet Number: C843

0	1	2	3	4

Supervisor/instructor signature _____ Date _____

General Driveability and Emission Diagnosis

Student/Intern information:

Name _____ Date _____ Class _____

Vehicle used for this activity:

Year _____ Make _____ Model _____

Odometer _____ VIN _____

Learning Objective/Task	CDX Tasksheet Number	2017 MAST NATEF Reference Number; Priority Level
• Diagnose engine mechanical, electrical, electronic, fuel, and ignition concerns; determine needed action.	C710	8A9; P-2
• Diagnose the causes of emissions or driveability concerns with stored or active diagnostic trouble codes (DTC); obtain, graph, and interpret scan tool data.	C660	8B5; P-1
• Diagnose emissions or driveability concerns without stored or active diagnostic trouble codes; determine needed action.	C711	8B6; P-1
• Interpret diagnostic trouble codes (DTCs) and scan tool data related to the emissions control systems; determine needed action.	C668	8E7; P-2
• Diagnose driveability and emissions problems resulting from malfunctions of interrelated systems (cruise control, security alarms, suspension controls, traction controls, HVAC, automatic transmissions, non-OEM-installed accessories, or similar systems); determine needed action.	C409	8B8; P-2

Time off_____

Time on_____

Total time_____

Materials Required

• Vehicle or simulator with related fault
• DMM/DVOM
• Problem-specific tools and equipment such as: scan tool, lab scope, etc.

Some Safety Issues to Consider

• You will be working under the hood of a running vehicle. Keep your hands and fingers away from moving belts, fans, and other parts.
• When running any vehicles in the shop, make sure you use the shop's exhaust ventilation system to discharge all exhaust gas safely outside.
• Only students who have their supervisor/instructor's direct permission should perform this task due to the safety concerns involved.
• Diagnosis of this fault may require test driving the vehicle on the school grounds. Attempt this task only with full permission from your instructor and follow all the guidelines exactly.
• Comply with personal and environmental safety practices associated with clothing; eye protection; hand tools; power equipment; proper ventilation; and the handling, storage, and disposal of chemicals/materials in accordance with local, state, and federal safety and environmental regulations.

Performance Standard

0–No exposure: No information or practice provided during the program; complete training required

1–Exposure only: General information provided with no practice time; close supervision needed; additional training required

2–Limited practice: Has practiced job during training program; additional training required to develop skill

3–Moderately skilled: Has performed job independently during training program; limited additional training may be required

4–Skilled: Can perform job independently with no additional training

Diagnose engine mechanical, electrical, electronic, fuel, and ignition concerns; determine needed action.

MAST
8A9

Time off_____

Time on_____

Total time_____

CDX Tasksheet Number: C710

1. List the driveability-related customer concern:

2. Research the particular concern in the appropriate service information.

   a. List the possible causes:

3. Using the specified procedure, inspect and diagnose any engine mechanical, electrical, electronic, fuel, and ignition concerns. List your tests and results here:

4. List the cause of the concern:

5. Determine any necessary action(s) to correct the fault:

6. Have your supervisor/instructor verify satisfactory completion of this procedure, any observations found, and any necessary action(s) recommended.

Performance Rating

CDX Tasksheet Number: C710

0	1	2	3	4

Supervisor/instructor signature _____ Date _____

TASK Diagnose the causes of emissions or driveability concerns with stored or active diagnostic trouble codes (DTC); obtain, graph, and interpret scan tool data.

MAST
8B5

Time off_____

Time on_____

Total time_____

DX Tasksheet Number: C660

Vehicle used for this activity:

Year _____ Make _____ Model_____

Odometer_____ VIN_____

1. **List the emissions- or driveability-related customer concern:**

2. **Research the particular concern in the appropriate service information.**

   a. **List the possible causes:**

3. **Using the correct equipment, retrieve and record diagnostic trouble codes, OBD monitor status, and freeze-frame data, then interpret the scan tool data:**

   a. **List any stored DTCs and their descriptions:**

   b. **List the status of all monitors:**

   c. **List any freeze-frame data:**

4. **With the aid of the stored data or active diagnostic trouble codes, diagnose the cause of emissions or driveability concern. List your tests and results here:**

5. List the cause of the concern:

6. Determine any necessary action(s) to correct the fault:

7. Have your supervisor/instructor verify satisfactory completion of this procedure, any observations found, and any necessary action(s) recommended.

Diagnose emissions or driveability concerns without stored or active diagnostic trouble codes; determine needed action.

MAST
8B6

Time off_____

Time on_____

Total time_____

CDX Tasksheet Number: C711

Vehicle used for this activity:

Year _____ Make _____ Model _____

Odometer _____ VIN _____

1. **List the emissions- or driveability-related customer concern:**

2. **Research the particular concern in the appropriate service information.**

   a. **List the possible causes:**

3. **Follow the service manual procedure to diagnose the cause of the concern. List your tests and results here:**

4. **List the cause of the concern:**

5. **Determine any necessary action(s) to correct the fault:**

6. Have your supervisor/instructor verify satisfactory completion of this procedure, any observations found, and any necessary action(s) recommended.

Performance Rating

0	1	2	3	4

Supervisor/instructor signature _____ Date _____

Interpret diagnostic trouble codes (DTCs) and scan tool data related to the emissions control systems; determine needed action.

MAST
8E7

CDX Tasksheet Number: C668

Vehicle used for this activity:

Year _____ Make _____ Model_____

Odometer_____ VIN_____

1. List the emissions system-related customer concern:

2. Research the particular concern in the appropriate service information.

   a. List the possible causes:

3. Using the correct equipment, retrieve and record diagnostic trouble codes, OBD monitor status, and freeze-frame data:

   a. List any stored DTCs and their descriptions:

   b. List the status of all monitors:

   c. List any freeze-frame data:

4. Using the data listed above, interpret the DTCs and scan tool data results. List your tests and results here:

5. List the cause of the concern:

6. Determine any necessary action(s) to correct the fault:

7. Have your supervisor/instructor verify satisfactory completion of this
    procedure, any observations found, and any necessary action(s) recommended.

Performance Rating

CDX Tasksheet Number: C668

0	1	2	3	4

Supervisor/instructor signature _____ Date _____

Diagnose driveability and emissions problems resulting from malfunctions of interrelated systems (cruise control, security alarms, suspension controls, traction controls, HVAC, automatic transmissions, non-OEM-installed accessories, or similar systems); determine needed action.

MAST
8B8

Time off_____

Time on_____

Total time_____

CDX Tasksheet Number: C409

Vehicle used for this activity:

Year _____ Make _____ Model_____

Odometer_____ VIN_____

1. **List the driveability- or emissions system-related customer concern (interrelated system problem):**

2. **Research the particular concern in the appropriate service information.**

   a. **List the possible causes:**

3. **Using the correct equipment, retrieve and record diagnostic trouble codes, OBD monitor status, and freeze-frame data:**

   a. **List any stored DTCs and their descriptions:**

   b. **List the status of all monitors:**

   c. **List any freeze-frame data:**

4. **Using the data listed above, diagnose the cause of the customer concern. List your tests and results here:**

5. **List the cause of the concern:**

6. **Determine any necessary action(s) to correct the fault:**

7. **Have your supervisor/instructor verify satisfactory completion of this procedure, any observations found, and any necessary action(s) recommended.**

Performance Rating

CDX Tasksheet Number: C409

0	1	2	3	4

Supervisor/instructor signature _____ Date _____

Appendix: CDX/NATEF Correlation Guide

Section A0: General Safety

CDX Tasksheet Number	2017 MAST NATEF Reference and Priority	Corresponding Page(s)
C451	0A1; P-1	5-6
C452	0A2; P-1	37
C453	0A3; P-1	51
C454	0A4; P-1	53-54
C455	0A5; P-1	49
C456	0A6; P-1	7
C458	0A7; P-1	9-10
C459	0A8; P-1	11
C460	0A9; P-1	13
C461	0A10; P-1	21
C462	0A11; P-1	23
C463	0A12; P-1	25
C464	0A13; P-1	71-72
C895	0A14; P-1	73
C465	0A15; P-1	15
C466	0B1; P-1	29-32
C467	0B2; P-1	33-35
C468	0B3; P-1	39
C469	0B4; P-1	41
C896	0B5; P-1	43
C472	0C1; P-1	61
C473	0C2; P-1	47
C474	0C3; P-1	63
C475	0C4; P-1	65
C590	0C5; P-1	67
C476	0D1; P-1	55-56

Section A1: Engine Repair

CDX Tasksheet Number	2017 MAST NATEF Reference number and Priority	Corresponding Page(s)
C885	1A1; P-1	79
C002	1A2; P-1	81-82
C898	1A3; P-1	95
C004	1A4; P-1	93-94
C541	1A5; P-1	185-186
C899	1A6; P-1	171-172
C886	1A7; P-1	89-90
C596	1A8; P-2	187-188
C900	1A9; P-2	83
C671	1A10; P-3	109-111
C673	1B1; P-1	115-116
C674	1B2; P-1	117
C021	1B3; P-2	121
C723	1B4; P-1	139
C676	1B5; P-1	173-174
C677	1B6; P-1	137
C718	1B7; P-3	129-130
C675	1B8; P-3	189-190
C719	1B9; P-3	131
C720	1B10; P-3	133-134
C721	1B11; P-3	135-136
C722	1B12; P-2	123
C724	1B13; P-3	125-126
C027	1B14; P-3	127-128
C679	1C1; P-1	143
C029	1C2; P-1	145-146
C030	1C3; P-2	147-148
C726	1C4; P-2	149
C727	1C5; P-2	153
C034	1C6; P-3	155-156
C728	1C7; P-1	161-162
C036	1C8; P-2	163
C729	1C9; P-3	165
C678	1C10; P-2	151-152
C597	1C11; P-2	175
C040	1C12; P-2	177-178
C730	1C13; P-2	157-158
C731	1C14; P-1	179-180
C578	1D1; P-1	201-202

CDX Tasksheet Number	2017 MAST NATEF Reference number and Priority	Corresponding Page(s)
C598	1D2; P-1	219
C734	1D3; P-1	203-204
C050	1D4; P-1	209-210
C680	1D5; P-2	211-212
C052	1D6; P-2	213-214
C735	1D7; P-1	207-208
C053	1D8; P-1	215-216
C732	1D9; P-1	195-196
C737	1D10; P-1	193-194
C871	1D11; P-3	217
C736	1D12; P-2	197-198
C733	1D13; P-2	167
C392	8A5; P-1	99
C393	8A6; P-2	101-102
C709	8A7; P-1	103-104
C395	8A8; P-1	105

Section A2: Automatic Transmission and Transaxle

CDX Tasksheet Number	2017 MAST NATEF Reference and Priority	Corresponding Page(s)
C599	2A1; P-1	253-254
C681	2A2; P-1	225
C682	2A3; P-1	259
C902	2A4; P-1	255
C903X	2A5; P-1	257
C740	2A6; P-1	235
C743	2A7; P-2	251-252
C741	2A8; P-2	237
C063	2A9; P-3	239-240
C066	2A10; P-1	247-248
C600	2A11; P-1	243-244
C747	2A12; P-2	249-250
C683	2B1; P-1	263-264
C748	2B2; P-2	265
C601	2B3; P-1	245-246
C907	2B4; P-1	269-270
C602	2B5; P-2	267-268
C604	2C1; P-2	309-311
C749	2C2; P-1	313
C605	2C3; P-2	315-316

CDX Tasksheet Number	2017 MAST NATEF Reference and Priority	Corresponding Page(s)
C606	2C4; P-3	227-228
C607	2C5; P-3	229
C684	2C6; P-1	275-276
C685	2C7; P-2	301-302
C686	2C8; P-2	293
C083	2C9; P-1	319-320
C688	2C10; P-2	277-278
C689	2C11; P-1	279
C750	2C12; P-2	285
C690	2C13; P-2	289
C751	2C14; P-2	283
C752	2C15; P-2	281
C753	2C16; P-2	291
C754	2C17; P-2	303-304
C755	2C18; P-2	305-306
C756	2C19; P-2	295-296
C757	2C20; P-1	297
C758	2C21; P-1	299-300
C759	2C22; P-2	287

Section A3: Manual Drive Train and Axles

CDX Tasksheet Number	2017 MAST NATEF Reference and Priority	Corresponding Page(s)
C101	3A1; P-1	327
C102	3A2; P-1	325
C691	3A3; P-1	335
C105	3A4; P-1	337
C106	3B1; P-1	349
C107	3B2; P-1	341-342
C608	3B3; P-1	355-356
C111	3B4; P-1	345-346
C938	3B5; P-1	343
C847	3B6; P-1	353
C848	3B7; P-2	351
C768	3C1; P-2	367-368
C611	3C2; P-2	329
C609	3C3; P-2	359
C693	3C4; P-2	361
C887	3C5; P-3	363
C910	3C6; P-2	369

CDX Tasksheet Number	2017 MAST NATEF Reference and Priority	Corresponding Page(s)
C132	3D1; P-1	373-374
C133	3D2; P-2	379-380
C134	3D3; P-1	377-378
C849	3D4; P-1	375-376
C779	3D5; P-2	381-382
C785	3E1:1; P-1	389-390
C911	3E1:2; P-1	385
C912	3E1:3; P-1	387
C138	3E1:4; P-2	393
C889	3E1:5; P-2	391-392
C780	3E1:6; P-3	395
C890	3E1:7; P-3	397-398
C781	3E1:8; P-3	401
C782	3E1:9; P-3	403
C145	3E1:10; P-3	407
C783	3E1:11; P-3	409
C147	3E1:12; P-3	399-400
C148	3E1:13; P-3	405
C784	3E2:1; P-3	413
C786	3E2:2; P-3	415
C154	3E3:1; P-1	421-422
C155	3E3:2; P-1	425
C156	3E3:3; P-2	427-428
C850	3E3:4; P-2	423
C153	3E3:5; P-2	419-420
C788	3F1; P-3	433-434
C876	3F2; P-3	437-438
C914	3F3; P-3	439-440
C613	3F4; P-2	443
C787	3F5; P-3	431-432
C878	3F6; P-2	441
C875	3F7; P-2	435-436

Section A4: Suspension and Steering Systems

CDX Tasksheet Number	2017 MAST NATEF Reference and Priority	Corresponding Page(s)
C166	4A1; P-1	449-450
C851	4A2; P-1	451
C168	4B1; P-1	523-524
C169	4B2; P-1	525

CDX Tasksheet Number	2017 MAST NATEF Reference and Priority	Corresponding Page(s)
C170	4B3; P-2	529-530
C884	4B4; P-2	517-518
C880	4B5; P-2	519-520
C173	4B6; P-2	527-528
C882	4B7; P-2	505-506
C883	4B8; P-1	503
C177	4B9; P-1	485
C178	4B10; P-2	487
C179	4B11; P-1	491
C180	4B12; P-1	489-490
C181	4B13; P-2	497
C699	4B14; P-2	499
C183	4B15; P-2	493
C184	4B16; P-2	509-511
C185	4B17; P-1	513-514
C186	4B18; P-2	569-570
C551	4B19; P-2	573
C1001	4B20; P-2	495
C852	4C1; P-1	555-556
C853	4C2; P-1	557-558
C790	4C3; P-3	539-540
C791	4C4; P-3	541
C792	4C5; P-2	543-544
C192	4C6; P-3	537
C193	4C7; P-3	535-536
C194	4C8; P-3	551-552
C793	4C9; P-3	533-534
C794	4C10; P-3	547-548
C934	4C11; P-3	549-550
C854	4C12; P-1	563-564
C202	4D1; P-1	561-562
C203	4D2; P-1	565-566
C931	4D3; P-3	571
C206	4E1; P-1	577-578
C617	4E2; P-1	579-580
C618	4E3; P-1	581
C213	4E4; P-2	583
C214	4E5; P-2	585
C216	4E6; P-1	587
C217	4E7; P-2	589-590

CDX Tasksheet Number	2017 MAST NATEF Reference and Priority	Corresponding Page(s)
C795	4E8; P-3	591
C940	4E9; P-2	593
C619	4F1; P-1	457–458
C855	4F2; P-2	479–480
C222	4F3; P-1	459–460
C701	4F4; P-2	475–476
C796	4F5; P-1	481–482
C620	4F6; P-1	461–462
C621	4F7; P-1	465–467
C580	4F8; P-1	471–472
C552	4F9; P-1	473
C937	4F10; P-1	477–478
C936	4F11: P-1	463–464

Section A5: Brakes

CDX Tasksheet Number	2017 MAST NATEF Reference and Priority	Corresponding Page(s)
C229	5A1; P-1	601
C230	5A2; P-1	599
C944	5A3; P-1	603
C251	5A4; P-1	677
C894	5B1; P-1	697
C622	5B2; P-1	617–618
C704	5B3; P-1	619–620
C235	5B4; P-1	621
C236	5B5; P-1	699–700
C237	5B6; P-1	627
C623	5B7; P-2	629
C624	5B8; P-2	631
C239	5B9; P-1	609
C242	5B10; P-3	717
C947	5B11; P-2	715
C705	5B12; P-1	613
C625	5B13; P-1	611
C706	5C1; P-1	665–666
C800	5C2; P-1	667–668
C626	5C3; P-1	669
C248	5C4; P-1	671
C707	5C5; P-2	673–674
C801	5C6; P-1	675–676
C708	5D1; P-1	635–636

CDX Tasksheet Number	2017 MAST NATEF Reference and Priority	Corresponding Page(s)
C802	5D2; P-1	637
C803	5D3; P-1	639
C627	5D4; P-1	643
C805	5D5; P-1	645
C628	5D6; P-1	653
C806	5D7; P-1	655
C629	5D8; P-1	659
C630	5D9; P-1	657
C631	5D10; P-2	647
C632	5D11; P-1	641
C948	5D12; P-1	649
C807	5E1; P-2	687-688
C808	5E2; P-1	689
C809	5E3; P-1	691-692
C581	5E4; P-3	693-694
C556	5E5; P-3	623
C267	5F1; P-1	709-710
C810	5F2; P-2	703-704
C811	5F3; P-1	681
C633	5F4; P-1	683
C272	5F5; P-1	713
C273	5F6; P-3	705-706
C275	5F7; P-1	707
C274	5F8; P-1	661-662
C634	5G1; P-1	721
C950	5G2; P-3	723
C635	5G3; P-2	733
C636	5G4; P-2	735-736
C812	5G5; P-2	727
C637	5G6; P-1	729
C639	5G7; P-2	737
C813	5G8; P-1	739

Section A6: Electrical/Electronic Systems

A. General Electrical System Diagnosis

CDX Tasksheet Number	2017 MAST NATEF Reference and Priority	Corresponding Page(s)
C286	6A1; P-1	745
C951	6A2; P-1	747-748
C641	6A3; P-1	813
C296	6A4; P-1	821-822

CDX Tasksheet Number	2017 MAST NATEF Reference and Priority	Corresponding Page(s)
C291	6A5; P-1	815–816
C295	6A6; P-1	817–818
C952	6A7; P-1	811–812
C817	6A8; P-1	767–768
C298	6A9; P-1	819–820
C299	6A10; P-1	827–828
C642	6A11; P-2	823–824
C955	6A12; P-1	829
C302	6B1; P-1	753–754
C818	6B2; P-1	755–756
C304	6B3; P-1	759–760
C644	6B4; P-1	761–762
C819	6B5; P-1	763–764
C820	6B6; P-1	765
C561	6B7; P-2	861
C645	6B8; P-1	757
C874	6B9; P-2	863
C309	6C1; P-1	773–774
C310	6C2; P-1	775
C311	6C3; P-2	779
C312	6C4; P-1	781
C313	6C5; P-2	777–778
C314	6C6; P-2	783–784
C315	6D1; P-1	791
C316	6D2; P-1	797–798
C317	6D3; P-1	789–790
C318	6D4; P-1	795
C319	6D5; P-1	793–794
C320	6E1; P-1	807–808
C956	6E2; P-1	803–804
C321	6E3; P-2	805
C564	6E4; P-2	801
C646	6F1; P-2	837–838
C325	6F2; P-2	839–840
C330	6G1; P-2	845–846
C340	6G2; P-2	855–856
C336	6G3; P-3	849–850
C327	6G4; P-1	833–834
C338	6G5; P-2	853
C649	6G6; P-2	857–858

CDX Tasksheet Number	2017 MAST NATEF Reference and Priority	Corresponding Page(s)
C341	7A1; P-1	871
C342	7A2; P-1	869
C824	7A3; P-1	879
C825	7A4; P-2	881-882
C650	7A5; P-1	891
C347	7A6; P-1	893
C651	7A7; P-2	903
C652	7A8; P-1	901
C566	7A9; P-3	945
C653	7B1; P-1	909-910
C654	7B2; P-2	911-912
C826	7B3; P-2	913-914
C827	7B4; P-2	873-874
C863	7B5; P-3	905
C355	7B6; P-2	915-916
C356	7B7; P-1	883-884
C829	7B8; P-2	917-918
C873	7B9; P-1	919-920
C830	7B10; P-1	885
C350	7B11; P-2	947
C831	7B12; P-2	925
C832	7B13; P-2	927-928
C364	7C1; P-1	933
C370	7C2; P-2	935
C362	7C3; P-2	931
C864	7C4; P-2	939
C373	7D1; P-1	937-938
C374	7D2; P-2	949-950
C835	7D3; P-2	951
C376	7D4; P-3	953
C865	7D5; P-3	955
C378	7D6; P-1	957
C655	7D7; P-2	887-888
C866	7D8; P-2	943
C656	7E1; P-1	921-923
C836	7E2; P-1	895-897
C657	7E3; P-1	899-900

CDX Tasksheet Number	2017 MAST NATEF Reference and Priority	Corresponding Page(s)
C386	8A1; P-1	967-968
C387	8A2; P-1	963
C390	8A3; P-3	971-972
C391	8A4; P-2	1015-1016
C392	8A5; P-1	
C393	8A6; P-2	
C709	8A7; P-1	
C395	8A8; P-1	
C710	8A9; P-2	1061
C398	8A10; P-1	979-980
C400	8A11; P-1	975
C659	8B1; P-1	1033
C841	8B2; P-1	991
C867	8B3; P-1	1035
C661	8B4; P-1	1031
C660	8B5; P-1	1063
C711	8B6; P-1	1065
C840	8B7; P-2	1037-1038
C409	8B8; P-2	1069-1070
C712	8C1; P-2	989-990
C663	8C2; P-1	985-986
C664	8C3; P-3	987-988
C960	8C4; P-1	983-984
C713	8D1; P-2	1009-1010
C420	8D2; P-2	997-998
C868	8D3; P-1	995-996
C422	8D4; P-2	1001-1002
C962	8D5; P-1	1003
C424	8D6; P-2	1005
C842	8D7; P-2	999-1000
C665	8D8; P-1	1007-1008
C428	8D9; P-1	1021-1022
C963	8D10; P-1	1019
C429	8D11; P-2	1025
C965	8D12; P-2	1023
C869	8D13; P-2	1027
C666	8E1; P-3	1043-1044
C432	8E2; P-2	1041-1042
C667	8E3; P-2	1047-1050

CDX Tasksheet Number	2017 MAST NATEF Reference and Priority	Corresponding Page(s)
C843	8E4; P-2	1057-1058
C844	8E5; P-1	1053-1054
C714	8E6; P-2	1013-1014
C668	8E7; P-2	1067-1068